The Mainstream of
Civilization

1350 to 1815
Fourth Edition

Harcourt Brace Jovanovich, Publishers

San Diego / New York / Chicago / Atlanta / Washington, D.C.
London / Sydney / Toronto

JOSEPH R. STRAYER
Princeton University

HANS W. GATZKE
Yale University

The Mainstream of
Civilization

1350 to 1815
Fourth Edition

The Mainstream of Civilization   *1350 to 1815*
Fourth Edition

Cover: Detail of *A Saxon Courtier* by Lucas Cranach the Elder (ca. 1508), courtesy San Diego Museum of Art. Background design adapted from the *Constance Missal* (1505), Pierpont Morgan Library, New York. Photo from Art Resource.
Maps by Jean Paul Tremblay

Source of Illustrations on pages v–vi constitutes a continuation of the copyright page.

Source of Illustrations

Preface

It requires a certain amount of courage to attempt to write a history of civilization in one volume. Once the task has been accomplished, however, it is easier to do it a second, third, and even a fourth time. As before, we have deliberately omitted certain details so that we could discuss as fully as possible the basic characteristics of each civilization and of different periods in the history of each civilization. We have tried to emphasize connections and interrelations—the ways in which politics, economics, art, scholarship, and religion all influence one another. We have tried to capture the flavor of each age—the unique combination of beliefs, activities, and institutions that distinguishes one society from another. In choosing the illustrations and the inserts in the text we have tried to give some idea of the diverse and ever-changing ways in which people have looked at and lived in their world. Finally, we have tried to consider the most difficult of all historical questions—the nature of and the reasons for change in human communities. Why and how do new institutions, new activities, new ideas rise and flourish? Why do they fade away? There are no easy answers to these problems; all we can do is suggest lines of inquiry that the reader may wish to pursue.

Obviously, it is easier to assess the characteristics and achievements of earlier periods than those of the age in which we live. The English Revolution of the seventeenth century ended long ago; the communist revolutions of the twentieth century continue to develop in unpredictable ways. Obviously also, it is more important to know details about the nature and background of problems that are still with us than details about problems that have been solved (at least partially). For these reasons the book broadens as it reaches the nineteenth century. More information is provided and more events are described in the hope that the reader will better understand the present state of the world.

We trust that no one will passively accept our interpretations or believe that our book is an adequate summary of human history. Our work is only an introduction, an attempt to persuade the reader to think deeply about history and to study it in detail. We are convinced that historical-mindedness is a necessity of human life. Consciously or unconsciously, we all base our estimates of the future on our knowledge of the past. It is important, then, that our knowledge of the past be as accurate and as deep as possible.

We remember with gratitude the contribution of the late Professor E. Harris Harbison to the first edition. He left us a framework that has been useful in subsequent revisions. We have also found the contribution of our former collaborator, Professor Edwin L. Dunbaugh, to be helpful in our work.

We owe special thanks to Conrad Schirokauer, City College of the City University of New York, for his contribution of Chapters 6 and 15.

The authors are greatly indebted to the following historians, who critically read *The Mainstream of Civilization* and made many valuable comments and suggestions: Bernard Bacharch, University of Minnesota; Shiva Bajpai, California State University at Northridge; Stanley Chodorow, University of California at San Diego; Tony Grafton, Princeton University; Frank Kidner, San Francisco State University; Ronald P. Legon, University of Illinois; David Luft, University of California at San Diego; Edward Malefacis, Columbia University; Don McLarney, Highland Community College; M. Gwyn Morgan, University of Texas at Austin; Frederick Murphy, Western Kentucky University; Kenneth Pennington, Syracuse University; and William Sewell, Jr., University of Arizona.

J. R. S.
H. W. G.

Foreword *The Study of History*

Consciously or unconsciously, all of us are historians. We can plan for the future only because we remember the past. We can add to our knowledge only because we do not lose memory of former experiences. Everyone, from the peasant to the scholar, tries to meet new situations by discovering familiar elements that make it possible to evoke analogies with the past. An individual who has lost his memory, who has forgotten his own history, is helpless until he has recovered his past or has slowly built up a new past to which he can refer.

What is true of individuals is also true of societies. No community can survive and no institution can function without constant reference to past experience. We are ruled by precedents fully as much as by formal laws, which is to say that we are ruled by memories of the past. It is the memory of common experiences that unites individuals into communities, and it is the memory of his own experiences that makes a child into an adult. Some of the memories may not be happy ones, but in reacting against them we are still linked to the past that produced them.

If everyone is his own historian, if individuals and societies necessarily draw on their memories of the past in order to deal with the present, then what is the need for formal, scholarly history? Isn't it enough to remember only the history that serves our immediate needs?

It is not enough, for two reasons. Human memory is fallible; individuals and societies forget many things that might be useful in solving their problems. This is why we have written records (which are a kind of formal history); this is why illiterate peoples try to preserve their customs and traditions through repeated oral recitations by the elders of the tribe. Second, the more complicated a society becomes, the narrower the range of individual experience in proportion to the total of possible experiences. A peasant living in a medieval village shared most of the experiences of his neighbors, and village custom gave solutions of a sort even to rare and unusual problems. No one living in an urbanized society shares many of the experiences of his neighbors, let alone the experiences of the millions of people throughout the world with whom he is connected by political and economic ties. No one can sum up the past experiences of his society, and of the societies with which his own interacts, with a few customary formulas; and yet these past experiences place a heavy burden on the present. In facing any problem, we look for familiar elements; if these are lacking, we feel fearful and helpless. Knowledge of history increases the chance of finding something familiar in a new and difficult situation.

Certain card games show how this process works at an elementary level. There is almost no chance that one distribution of cards will be repeated in a subsequent deal in bridge. Yet a person who has played several thousand hands of bridge should be able to make intelligent decisions and predictions even though every deal presents a new situation. He should be able to use his high cards and long suits effectively; he should be able to make some shrewd guesses about the location of cards in other hands. Not every experienced player will develop these skills. Some people are unable to generalize from their past experiences, and others cannot see analogies between the present and the past. But, generally speaking, an experienced player will make better use of his cards than a person who has played only ten hands. There is such a thing as a sense of the realities and possibilities of social activity, which can be developed from a knowledge of history.

At the very least, the past has left us the problems that we are trying to solve and the patterns of living that we are seeking to modify. At the most, we may find in the past suggestions for understanding and coping with the present. It is the historian's task to study the behavior of man in the past, to uncover facts, sort them, mass and link them, and so provide connections between past and present.

At the same time the historian must avoid certain pitfalls along the way. Connections with the past cannot be broken, but they can be misrepresented or misunderstood. Primitive peoples have little sense of chronology; they are apt to stir all their memories into a timeless brew of legend. At a more sophisticated level, the past has been used as a means of justifying present values and power structures. Many writers, from ancient times down to the present, have found historical examples to prove that their people were specially favored by the gods, that their state was founded and strengthened by heroes of superhuman ability, that virtue and wisdom (as defined by the author) have always brought success, while folly and vice have led to disaster. "History is philosophy teaching by example," said an ancient Greek (Dionysius of Halicarnassus), and it was more important for the examples to be edifying than for them to be true.

But it is not difficult to avoid deliberate distortions of the past. What *is* difficult is to avoid distortions caused by the incompleteness of our knowledge of the past. Many human activities have left few traces, especially in written records. For example, for thousands of years agriculture has been the chief occupation of the human race, but there are still serious gaps in our knowledge of the history of agriculture. "The short and simple annals of the poor" are short because information is scanty. If we had better information we would probably find that the life of a poor man in any period was anything but simple; it must have been filled with an unending series of nagging problems. In general, we know more about political history than social history, more about the privileged few than the unprivileged masses, more about the history of art than the history of technology, more about the ideas of philosophers and religious leaders than the beliefs of the common people.

Historians have become more skillful in recent years in finding material that gives a better-balanced picture of the past. Archeology reveals not only the palaces of kings, but the homes of ordinary people with their tools, their toys, their cooking utensils, and even fragments of their food. Gods and heroes may dominate the great works of art, but the common folk going about their ordinary business are there too—on Greek vases, Roman tombs, and portals of Gothic cathedrals. Discoveries of hoards of coins reveal unexpected trade relations. Aerial photography can bring out traces of ancient methods of plowing land and dividing fields. Even the written records, which have been studied for centuries, contain hitherto unused facts about such things as family life, migrations, and changes in economic patterns. There are still many holes in the record, but there is no reason to complain about lack of material.

The historian's greatest difficulty is not in discovering facts, but in deciding what facts can be ignored, or merely sampled, or clumped together in a single generalization. No one could master all the facts in yesterday's issue of the *New York Times,* and there are files of newspapers that run back to the eighteenth century. No one could master all the facts brought out in a single session of the Supreme Court, and the records of American courts and of the English courts from which they were derived go back to the twelfth century. To deal with the overwhelming mass of facts, historians have to arrange them, link them together, establish meaningful sequences of causes and effects.

The massing and linking of facts is not only essential, if history is to rise above the level of a catalogue; it is also inevitable, since it is the way the human mind deals with past experience. We do not recall every word we have exchanged when we decide that a certain person is a good friend. We do not remember every paragraph we have read when we decide that we like a certain book. But, while the process of massing and linking is essential and inevitable, this operation is the point of greatest danger in any kind of historical thinking. Consciously or unconsciously, one can mass facts to produce a misleading impression, even though each individual fact is true. Any governmental system can be made to appear obnoxious by discussing only the cases in which there is clear evidence of corruption or oppresion. Any society can be wreathed in a golden haze by dwelling only on its accomplishments in art, literature, and scholarship. Individuals and communities can become convinced that the whole world is conspiring against them if they remember only the occasions when they were treated unjustly. The nature of the sources themselves may cause distortion. For example, it is very easy to find material on political life in the city of Rome during the first century of the Roman Empire. It is difficult to collect evidence on provincial government or on social and economic development. The natural tendency is to overemphasize court intrigues and to pay little attention to such topics as economic growth or the spread of Latin culture throughout the West.

There is no easy way to overcome these problems, but an understanding of the principle of interconnectedness will help. No one is a purely political or economic or ideological being, and societies are composed of such varied human beings. Historians must look for the ways in which these (and other) forces interact. For example, the kind of food men eat can affect their whole social structure: a society dependent on olive oil for its fats will differ in many ways from one that depends on animal products such as lard, butter, and cheese. Religion can have an influence on trade: medieval churchmen aided the growth of Mediterranean commerce by importing silk for their vestments, incense for their ceremonies, and precious stones for their altar vessels and relic boxes. Trade in turn can influence the development of a religion: often it has been the merchant who prepared the way for the missionary. Ideas, technologies, institutions, social patterns, shifts in consumer preferences interact in complicated and bewildering ways. For example, increased use of easily washable cotton clothing in modern Europe improved personal hygiene and thus may have reduced death rates and contributed to growth of population. At the same time, increased demand for cotton encouraged the extension of slavery in the United States and thus was one of the causes of the Civil War.

Full realization of the connections among all human activities should lead to three conclusions. First, there are multiple causes for every event; single explanations for change are almost always wrong. Second, change in any one part of the social pattern may affect any other part of the pattern. Finally, the connections lead back into the past, and therefore the past influences the present.

The relationship between continuity and change is an interaction that the historian must watch with special care. All societies change, and yet all societies retain some connection with the past. The most "traditional" society is less traditional than it realizes; the most "modern" society is more influenced by tradition than it would like to believe. The Anglo-Saxons, theoretically bound by immemorial custom, invented the office of sheriff about the year 1000 A.D. The Americans, theoretically free to create an entirely new political structure, have preserved the office of sheriff with many of its original powers. Conquests and revolutions do not break all the connections with the past. Even where there has apparently been a complete break, the roots of a society may again grow down into its past. Roman law practically vanished from the West after the fifth century A.D.; it reappeared as a powerful force in the thirteenth century.

If there were no continuity, there would be no use in studying history, since nothing in the past would have any bearing on what is done today. If there were no change, there would be no history; a few years of practical experience would teach anyone all he needed to know about human behavior in society at any time and in any place. But, in the world as it is, the forces that would make for change are modified and even distorted by habit and custom, the forces that make for continuity are weakened and limited by new desires and new ideas. It is of some importance to understand where, why, and to what degree the desire for change prevails.

It is easy to see multiple, interlocking activities and rapid rates of change in the modern world. It is less easy to get a sense of the complexity and capacity for change of premodern and non-European societies, which is why the history of such societies often seems flat and uninteresting. The European Middle Ages are summed up as an "Age of Faith"; the history of much of Asia is dismissed with talk of the "unchanging Orient." Yet the Middle Ages were also a period of state building, economic growth, and technological invention—activities that have influenced the modern world fully as much as the Christian Church. The "unchanging Orient" produced all the great world religions, and each of these religions was a powerful force for change. Moreover, there are advantages in studying societies that are less complex and in which rates of change are less rapid than in our own. It is easier to observe and to draw conclusions about human behavior when the number of variables is small and changes do not come so fast that their effects are blurred.

A good historian, then, will try to give adequate attention to a wide variety of human activities, to discuss the interactions among these activities, and to trace the connections between past and present. But these principles cannot be applied mechanically. A writer who is careful to give an exactly equal amount of space to politics, economics, religion, the arts, and scholarship will probably not produce an adequate description of a society. The importance and even the identity of each of these activities varies with time and place. Religion had more influence on Indian than on Chinese society. Economics and politics merge in primitive societies, such as that of the early Germans. It is probably true that the vast majority of the world's scientists were born in the twentieth century; this could not be said of theologians. Thus the impact of scholarship on early societies is different from its impact on modern societies. To understand such variations and transformations, the historian must be more than a meticulous scholar. He must develop a feel for the period he is writing about, a sense of how people lived and worked and thought. It takes time and experience to acquire this feeling for the past, but once it has been acquired historians can give reasonably accurate, and occasionally penetrating, descriptions of earlier societies.

It is this understanding of the development of human society that gives history its chief value. History, even at its worst, gives us the comforting and necessary feeling that there are some familiar elements in a changing world and that there is some hope of understanding the changes that do occur. History at its best gives us a chance of reacting sensibly to problems as they arise. It does not guarantee the correctness of our responses, but it should improve the quality of our judgment. Good judgment about human behavior in society is badly needed today.

A Note on the Paperbound Editions

This volume is one of a number of variant printings of the Fourth Edition of *The Mainstream of Civilization*. It is not a revised or condensed text. Many users of the Third Edition found the various paperbound versions of that edition useful because the variant printings made it possible for them to fit the text into their own patterns of teaching and scheduling. In the Fourth Edition, the publishers have continued the practice of preparing separate paperbound volumes. Users may choose the volume that best corresponds to the chronological period covered by their courses. The variants are:

1. A two-volume edition

   The first volume (Chapters 1 through 21) starts with the beginnings of western civilization in the ancient Middle East and continues to the eighteenth century. The second volume (Chapters 20 through 35) begins with the seventeenth century and carries the account forward to the present day.

2. A three-volume edition

   The first volume (Chapters 1 through 14) starts with the beginnings of western civilization in the ancient Middle East and continues to the end of the Middle Ages. The second volume (Chapters 13 through 23) begins with the late Middle Ages and ends with Napoleon. The third volume (Chapters 23 through 35) begins with the French Revolution and Napoleon and carries the account forward to the present day.

3. *Since 1500* (one volume)

   Since 1500 (Chapters 16 through 35), after a Prologue that summarizes events to the year 1500, begins with the Renaissance and carries the account forward to the present day.

In all the variant printings, the pagination, index, illustrations, maps (except for the color maps in the three-volume printing), and other related materials from the one-volume version are retained. The difference between the one-volume and the other versions of this book is a difference only in form.

Contents

List of Maps

Introduction

This is a history of civilization, with emphasis on the civilization developed by the peoples of Europe. Like all histories, it must be selective. Incomplete as our record of the past is, it is still too full to permit discussion in a single book of all civilizations or even of all events in the history of one civilization. The principles that have guided our selection of topics may be indicated by a definition of our subject. We must answer two questions: What is civilization, and what has been the role of western civilization in creating the conditions that we find in the world today?

Civilization is derived from the Latin word for city, *civitas.* There is reason to emphasize this derivation, for every great civilization has had great cities, and the basic characteristics of civilization are easiest to observe in cities. Civilization is first of all *cooperation*—men working together to satisfy their material and spiritual needs. It requires *organization*—as soon as several people start working together there must be some sort of social, political, or economic pattern to regulate their activity. It encourages *specialization*—as soon as several people begin to cooperate in an organized way there are obvious advantages in dividing the work so that no one man has to do everything for himself. The character of a particular civilization is determined by the type and degree of the organization and specialization of that civilization. Ten thousand Greeks living in a small city-state could accomplish much more than ten thousand Indians scattered through the forests of North America. A few hundred men specializing in science have done more to change our civilization in the last few centuries than millions of artisans working through past ages. Intensive organization and specialization can produce spectacular results, and they can also create spectacular problems.

Civilization requires faith in certain ideals and values as well as skill in organization and techniques. The immediate and direct advantages of organization and specialization are not very apparent to most people. Organization sets limits on personal freedom, and specialization makes a man dependent on other men who may not be wholly trustworthy. In the long run the advantages are greater than the disadvantages, but farseeing, enlightened self-interest is a very rare human quality, probably rarer than altruism. And if men hesitate to give up present benefits for advantages in their own future, they will be even more hesitant if the advantages are to be gained only by their descendants. There is always resistance to increasing the scale and scope of organization; there is usually resistance to new types of specialization. This resistance can be overcome only by belief that there is something more important than the individual—a religion that emphasizes cooperation, a divinely appointed ruler or ruling class, a nation that has become almost a divinity, a theory of society that has taken on the aspects of a religion. There is a close connection between the dominant beliefs of a people and the kind of civilization it creates.

This history of civilization examines, more than anything else, how and why people have worked together. It is concerned with political history because the political record helps us to understand why people have been more successful at some times than at others in organizing on a large scale, and why some types of organization have proved more effective than others. It is concerned with economic and social history because economic and social organization has a direct effect on both political organization and the type and degree of specialization. It is concerned with the history of ideas and their manifestations in art and literature because organization and specialization are possible only within a framework of accepted beliefs. The interactions among political organizations, economic institutions, and dominant beliefs determine the character and development of a civilization.

Western civilization is only one, and by no means the oldest, of the civilizations that has left a historical record. The earliest civilizations touched Europe and the West only slightly; they centered in the river valleys of Egypt, the Near East, and China. Only with the appearance of the Greek city-states after 1000 B.C. can we see the beginnings of a civilization that belongs to the same family as our own. The Greeks drew heavily on the older civilizations of their neighbors, but they reorganized their borrowed materials and added significant elements to them. Ideas and forms of organization that have remained important in western civilization for over twenty-five hundred years first appear in ancient Greece. The Romans followed the Greeks as the dominant people in the Mediterranean basin. Like the Greeks, they borrowed from their predecessors, rearranged the old materials in new ways, and added ideas of their own, especially in government and law. Roman civilization is the direct ancestor of the civilization of modern European countries. There has never been a time, from the first conquests of the Roman Republic down to the present, when Roman law and Roman political ideas were not being discussed in some parts of the Continent.

Yet, while there is unbroken continuity between the civilization of the Greeks and the Romans and that of the modern West, it is well to remember that continuity is not identity. Much has been added—for example, the ideas brought in by Christianity—and much has been changed. Greco-Roman civilization was neither western nor European; it was Mediterranean. It was most highly developed on the eastern shores of the Mediterranean, and it was greatly influenced by the Orient. France and Spain were colonial outposts that contributed little to Greco-Roman civilization; Germany, Scandinavia, and the Slavic countries were outside the limits of the civilized Mediterranean world.

This Mediterranean civilization ran into trouble in the fourth and fifth centuries A.D. The economic organization proved unsatisfactory, and loyalty to the political organization weakened. As the Roman Empire slowly crumbled, the unity of the Mediterranean basin was destroyed, never to be restored. The southern and eastern shores became part of an Arab empire, part of the non-European Moslem civilization. A remnant of the old Roman Empire, centering around Constantinople, became the Byzantine Empire. This empire developed its own civilization—Christian in belief, Greek in language, but strongly influenced by the East in organization. Byzantine civilization made a great impression on the Slavic peoples of eastern Europe and had some influence on the Latin and Germanic peoples of the West. But it was never fully integrated with the civilization that grew up in western Europe. The western Europeans thought of the Byzantines as remote and somewhat untrustworthy relatives, who might hand out valuable gifts from time to time but who were too eccentric to live with. This attitude, in turn, has made it difficult to integrate eastern and western Europe, since the eastern countries borrowed much more from Byzantium than did those of the West.

With the Arab and Byzantine empires developing separate civilizations, the western European remnant of the old Mediterranean world was thrown back on its own resources. These were at first not very great. Western Europe saved only a fragment of its Roman inheritance, and this Roman inheritance was itself only a fragment of the old Mediterranean civilization. Moreover, the Germanic peoples of northern and central Europe, who had never been included in the Mediterranean world, were for a time dominant in western Europe. They brought in some new ideas and institutions, but they were backward in both political and economic organization. They were slow in assimilating the fragments of Roman civilization that remained, and even slower in developing effective types of organization. In the same way, the Christian religion, which eventually had great influence on European civilization, was only slowly absorbed by the half-barbarized Latins and the half-civilized Germans. For six centuries Europeans struggled with the problems of assimilating the Roman inheritance, integrating Latin and Germanic peoples, and implementing the basic ideas of Christianity. Only when this triple task was done did western Europe at last achieve an independent and consistent civilization. Only then could it profit from its contacts with the more highly developed civilizations of the Arab and Byzantine worlds.

Once it was established as a separate and viable entity, western Europe civilization developed rapidly. Many of our basic institutions and ideas, such as universities and representative assemblies, were worked out in the twelfth and thirteenth centuries. But this western European civilization was confined to a very small area. Its center was in the north, in a triangle bounded by Paris, Cologne, and London. The peripheral countries—Spain, Ireland, Norway, Sweden, Poland, Bohemia, and Italy—did not share in all the manifestations of this civilization, though they accepted its basic ideas. And beyond these countries the influence of western European civilization dropped off sharply. It had little effect on the Moslem world and none whatever on the peoples of Africa and Asia who lived beyond the limits of Moslem influence. It had some impact on Byzantium, but not enough to erase the differences that separated Byzantium from the West. There were some contacts with Russia, but the Russians were probably more influenced by the Byzantines. And the Mongol conquest of the thirteenth century weakened the ties that the Russians had with the West and forced them to face east for two centuries.

Meanwhile, another group of civilizations had developed in the Far East, in India, China, and Japan. Each had its own characteristic values—religious in India, secular and political in China, military in Japan. All three tended to become somewhat self-satisfied and isolated; neither India nor China, for example, was as interested in foreign voyages in the sixteenth century as it had been earlier. In all three the economic system was still based largely on village agriculture. Finally, in spite of promising beginnings, none of the Far Eastern civilizations had developed a strong scientific tradition. These characteristics put the Far Eastern countries at a disadvantage in dealing with Europeans, who were deeply interested in strange lands and peoples, were beginning to develop an economy based on machine production, and were just about to make their first important scientific discoveries.

The great voyages of exploration and the great mechanical inventions, both of which began in the fifteenth century, enabled western European civilization to emerge from its narrow corner and to spread throughout the world. Eastern Europe gradually accepted much of the civilization of the West, though the process was never complete. Three new continents—North America, South America, and Australia—were occupied by Europeans, and a fourth, Africa, was dominated by them. Asia, with its old civilizations and its dense population, was not so easily overrun, but even Asia was profoundly influenced by the European impact. Thus, for the first time, all the peoples of the world were brought into contact with a single civilization. The results of this great experiment are only beginning to be apparent.

There is some justification, then, for the conventional division of history into Ancient, Medieval, and Modern. Ancient history deals with the period in which some of the basic elements of western civilization were developed and passed on to later peoples. But ancient history must be focused on the Near East and the Mediterranean, not on Europe. It must give greater weight to Greece, Asia Minor, Syria, Mesopotamia, and Egypt than to Gaul, Britain, or Germany. Medieval history deals with the period in which a distinct western European civilization appeared. But this civilization was confined to a small part of the European peninsula, and it had little influence outside that area. During the

Middle Ages each great region of the world had its own civilization, and no one civilization was able greatly to modify another. Modern history deals not only with the rapid development of western European civilization in its old homeland but also with relations between that civilization and the rest of the world.

This growth and diffusion of western civilization has gone so far that we have perhaps entered a fourth period in its history. This period is marked by the appearance of distinct types of western civilization in the different areas occupied by Europeans, and, even more, by the revitalization of other civilizations following their contact with the West. Both the appearance of different types of western civilization and the revival of old civilizations are stimulating factors; they should help to prevent ossification and decay. Unfortunately, a stimulus can also be an irritant, and the reactions among competing civilizations may lead to efforts for mutual destruction rather than for mutual instruction.

The history of civilization begins in obscurity and ends with a question mark. Yet past experience is our only guide in solving present and future problems, and knowledge of our history may help us answer the great question with which we are faced today, that of the survival of civilization in any form.

The Mainstream of Civilization

Civilization

1350 to 1815
Fourth Edition

13 The End of the
Middle Ages

The fourteenth and early fifteenth centuries were a time of confusion and chaos in the West. Decade after decade everything seemed to go wrong: economic depression, war, rebellion, and plague harried the people, and neither ecclesiastical nor secular governments seemed capable of easing their distress. At times the whole structure of European society seemed to be crumbling, as it had at the end of the Roman Empire. Yet the Europe that emerged from this time of troubles went on to conquer the world. The science and technology, the navies and the armies, the governments and the business organizations that were to give Europe unquestioned supremacy for four centuries—all were taking shape in the fourteenth and fifteenth centuries. The dire stretch of history marked by the Hundred Years' War, the Black Death, and the Great Schism seems an unlikely seedbed for these great accomplishments. We are struck by the decay of the medieval way of life rather than by the almost imperceptible emergence of new ideas and new forms of organization. But we should not forget that the new ideas were there, that the people of western Europe never quite lost faith in their destiny, never quite gave up striving for a more orderly and prosperous society. There was confusion and uncertainty, but not the complete disintegration that had followed the collapse of the Roman Empire.

ECONOMIC WEAKNESS AND POLITICAL FAILURE

The most obvious cause of the troubles of the last medieval centuries was economic depression. Given the techniques then prevalent, by 1300 western Europe had about reached the limit of its capacity to produce food and manufactured goods, and, consequently, its ability to increase its trade. There were no more reserves of fertile land to bring into cultivation; in fact, a good deal of the land that was already being cultivated was marginal or submarginal in quality. For many years there was no significant increase in industrial output; production might shift from one center to another, but the total output remained about the same. Population ceased to grow, and after the Black Death (see p. 280), declined sharply. Most towns barely held their own, and many, especially in southern France, became smaller. The Italian towns fared better; they increased their share of Mediterranean trade and of the production of luxury textiles. But even Italy had economic difficulties. It, too, was ravaged by plague, and during the middle years of the fourteenth century northern rulers, like Edward III of England, repudiated the debts they owed Italian bankers. In short, until Europe found new sources of wealth and new markets, both governments and individuals were constantly on the verge of bankruptcy.

Economic stagnation created a climate of opinion that made it difficult for people to cooperate for the common welfare. Each individual, each community, each class was eager to preserve the monopolies and privileges that guaranteed it some share of the limited wealth available. It was during these years that the towns and gilds adopted their most restrictive regulations. Ordinary laborers found it difficult to become master workmen; master workmen were discouraged from devising new methods of production. Fortunately the attempt to preserve the status quo was thwarted by the weakness of government and by the ingenuity of enterprising businessmen. Some new techniques were introduced, and some new industries were established. But capital was limited, and it took many years before new techniques or new products had much impact on the economy.

Economic weakness helps explain the weakness of most governments. Rulers were always short of money, for the old taxes brought in less and less revenue and it was very difficult to impose new taxes. Salaries of government officials were insufficient, because of continuing inflation, and were often years in arrears. Most officials supported themselves by taking fees, gifts, and bribes from private citizens; they began to think of their offices as private possessions. Men with this attitude could keep up the routine, which was an important element of stability in a troubled society. But they showed much less zeal in perfecting their

(see p. 280)

Opposite: Manuscript illustration of the crucial point in the meeting of Richard II with the main body of the rebels during the Peasants' Rebellion of 1381. Wat Tyler is being struck down by one of Richard's men.

Black Death

Hundred Years' War

Babylonian Captivity and Great Schism

administrative techniques than had their thirteenth-century predecessors.

Financial difficulties were not the only cause of weakness in government. The assertion of sovereignty by secular rulers at the end of the thirteenth century had been somewhat premature. They had neither the ability to make realistic plans for the welfare of their people nor the authority to impose such remedies as they did devise. Most secular rulers could think only of increasing their revenues by conquering new lands. Such a policy solved no problems; it merely postponed them for the victor and aggravated them for the vanquished. With governments discredited by futile and costly wars, many men lost faith in their political leaders and turned to rebellion and civil war.

The leaders of revolt, however, showed no more ability than the kings and princes against whom they were rebelling. Many of the leaders were members of the landed nobility who still had wealth and influence even though they had lost their old rights of feudal government. But while they found it easy enough to gain power, they did not know how to exercise the power that they gained. Their main purpose was to preserve their own privileges or to direct government revenues to their own pockets—again, policies that solved no basic problems. Impatient with the routine tasks of administration, the aristocracy usually split into quarreling factions. The upper classes sometimes used parliamentary forms to justify their acts, but this only made representative assemblies appear to be vehicles of factionalism and disorder. When the desire for stronger government finally arose again, the kings found it easy to abolish or suspend assemblies; only in England did representative assemblies retain any vitality.

Other classes performed no better than the nobles. The bourgeoisie thought in terms of local or, at most, regional interests, and they were inept in running their own municipal governments. The townsmen split into factions—old families against new families, international traders against local merchants, rich against poor—and the faction in power tried to ruin its opponents by unequal taxation or discriminatory economic legislation. The result was that local self-government collapsed in town after town.

Lawlessness in Fifteenth-Century England

John Paston was the son of a royal judge and well-to-do landowner in Norfolk. His father had bought the manor of Gresham, but in 1448 Lord Molyns claimed it, though he had no right to it. John Paston tried to settle the claim peacefully, but Molyns' men seized the manor house and Paston moved to another "mansion." While he was seeking help from his friends, Paston's wife was left to defend their home. She wrote her husband this letter late in 1448.

Right worshipful husband, I recommend me to you and pray you to get some cross-bows and windlasses to wind them with and arrows, for your house here is so low that no one could shoot out of it with a long-bow, even if we had great need. I suppose you could get these things from Sir John Falstoff [a friend of the Pastons]. And also I would like you to get two or three short pole-axes to guard the doors and as many jacks [padded leather jackets] as you can.

Partridge [leader of Molyns' men] and his fellows are sore afraid that you will attack them again, and they have made great preparations, as I am told. They have made bars to bar the doors cross-wise, and they have made loop-holes on every side of the house to shoot out of both with bows and with hand-guns. The holes made for hand-guns are scarcely knee-high from the floor and no one can shoot out of them with a hand bow.

[Margaret Paston apparently took all this as a matter of course; she then turned to an ordinary shopping list.] I pray you to buy me a pound of almonds and a pound of sugar and some cloth to make clothes for your children and a yard of black broad-cloth for a hood for me.

The Trinity have you in His keeping and send you Godspeed in all your affairs.

Put into modern English from Norman Davis, ed., *Paston Letters* (Oxford: Clarendon Press, 1958), pp. 9–10.

Venice remained powerful and independent under a merchant oligarchy, as did many of the German trading towns. But more often a tyrant seized power, as in the towns of northern and central Italy, or else the officials of a king or a powerful noble took over control of the towns.

As for the peasants, they were far more restive and unhappy than they had been in the thirteenth century. With no new lands to clear and no new jobs to be had in the towns, they had little hope of improving their lot. Some of them managed to ease the burden of taxes and of payments to landlords by renegotiating their leases or by moving from one estate to another, but for most of them this road to advancement was too tedious and uncertain. The peasants rebelled in country after country, killing landlords, burning records, and demanding that payments for their land be lowered or abolished altogether. These rebellions were hopeless; untrained and poorly armed peasants were no match for an aristocracy with a strong military tradition. But the fact that the peasants did rebel reveals the despair and the tendency to violence that marked the end of the Middle Ages.

THE TROUBLES OF THE CHURCH

The failure of secular government would not have been so serious had the Church been able to regain its old leadership. The people of western Europe were still Christians, and they knew that they were not living up to the precepts of their faith. They multiplied religious ceremonies and appeals for the intercession of the saints; they flocked to revival meetings to repent their sins with tears and trembling. But the Church failed to remedy the disorders of western society; in fact, the Church was infected with the same evils that beset secular government. Repentant sinners returned to their careers of violence and fraud because no one could show them any other way to survive.

The Great Schism

The leadership of the Church was further impaired by the Great Schism that followed the Babylonian Captivity. The popes at Avignon, realizing that their exile was impairing their authority, had made several halfhearted efforts to return to Rome. Finally, in 1377, Gregory XI actually moved back to Italy, but he was

Miniature paintings of a fourteenth-century pewterer turning a jug on a lathe (left), and a locksmith (right), from the Guild Book of the Twelve Brothers' Foundation in Nuremberg.

Land giving allegiance to Rome

Land giving allegiance to Avignon

Shifting and divided

appalled by the disorder in Rome and the Papal States. He was about to return to Avignon when he died, in 1378. The Romans, with the papacy once more within their grasp, had no intention of again losing the income from pilgrims and visitors to the papal court. When the cardinals met to elect Gregory's successor, they were besieged by a howling mob demanding that they choose a Roman, or at least an Italian, pope. It is hard to estimate how effective this pressure was; certainly it had some influence. In the end the cardinals elected an Italian archbishop who took the title of Urban VI.

The cardinals may have hoped that Urban would be a pliant and cooperative pope; instead he bullied them, rejected their advice, and denounced their behavior. The majority of the cardinals were French, but even the non-French were outraged by Urban's behavior. The whole group soon fled from Rome and declared that Urban's election was void because it had taken place under duress. They proceeded to choose a new pope, a French-speaking cardinal of the family of the counts of Geneva. He took the title of

Clement VII, set up his court at Avignon, and denounced Urban as a usurper.

Emperors such as Henry IV and Frederick Barbarossa had tried to set up antipopes, but they had never deceived secular and religious leaders. Everyone knew who the true pope was, even if the emperor supported an opponent. But this time there was no such consensus, and most of Europe was honestly bewildered. Both popes had been elected by a majority of duly appointed cardinals; if Urban had the advantage of being the first named, he also had the disadvantage of being repudiated by the very men who had elected him. Rulers could decide which pope to follow only on the basis of political expediency. France, and its ally Scotland, naturally accepted the Avignonese pope; England just as naturally supported Urban at Rome. The Spanish kingdoms backed Clement, while most of Germany and Italy held to the Roman pontiff. Both popes intrigued to gain support in hostile areas, and both created new cardinals. When Urban and Clement died, in 1389 and 1394, respectively, the rival groups of cardinals each elected a new pope, thus prolonging the Great Schism into the next century.

Though the people of western Europe were deeply distressed by the schism, they could see no way out of their troubles. Who could be sure which was the false pope and which the true one? This uncertainty weakened both the organization and the moral influence of the Church. The popes of the Captivity had at least been good administrators, but the schism made effective administration impossible. Reform in the Church's financial system was desperately needed, but a pope who controlled only half the Church could hardly afford to lose revenues or alienate supporters by abolishing profitable abuses. A divided and unreformed Church had little hope of guiding European society.

Reformers and Heretics

The state of the Church during the Captivity and the Great Schism seemed so hopeless that many men began to seek salvation through their own efforts. The mildest, and probably the most numerous, group of reformers did not break openly with the Church; they simply ceased to rely on it. They formed little associations, such as the Brethren of the Common Life, to encourage one another to lead devout Christian lives and to seek direct contact with God through mystical experiences. These groups, which were especially numerous in the Rhineland and the Low Countries, produced some remarkable works of devotion, such as the *Theologia Germanica*, which influenced later reformers. They also founded schools that were to play a great role in the educational revival of the fifteenth and sixteenth centuries; Erasmus (see pp. 376–77) was educated in such a school. These mystical and contemplative reformers were looked on with some suspicion by conservative churchmen, but most of them remained within the bounds of orthodoxy.

A more radical element was not content simply to withdraw into devout groups. These men wanted a thoroughgoing reform of the Church, and many of them felt that only laymen could do the job. An early example of this attitude can be seen in the *Defensor pacis*, written by Marsilius of Padua about 1324. Marsilius, who like many Italians had a completely secular point of view, believed that the state should control the Church just as it controlled other organizations. If the state could regulate the behavior of doctors, it could also regulate the behavior of priests. Marsilius' book was condemned, but his ideas inspired criticism of the Church throughout the fourteenth and fifteenth centuries.

Another dangerous critic of the Church was an Oxford professor, John Wiclif (*ca.* 1320–84). At first concerned mainly with the problem of private property, including the property of the Church, Wiclif decided that the Church was being corrupted by wealth and that it would be better for everyone if church lands were taken over by kings and nobles. This position naturally pleased influential laymen and may explain why Wiclif was never punished for his unorthodox doctrines. Wiclif went on to cast doubt on the Catholic doctrine that the bread and wine in the communion service are transformed into the Body

and Blood of Christ. He wound up by attacking the whole administrative structure of the Church as corrupt and largely unauthorized by the Bible. He taught that the pope could err, that the hierarchy had no absolute authority, and that kings should protect and guide the Church in their own realms.

Though Wiclif had no intention of launching a popular movement, his ideas spread rapidly beyond the scholarly circles for which he had written. By emphasizing scriptural authority, he had encouraged his followers to produce an English translation of the Bible that could be used by wandering preachers. These preachers, taking advantage of social discontent, popularized Wiclif's most radical views and gained a considerable following among the lower and middle classes in England. Some of them became social as well as religious reformers: if the Church had no right to property because it misused it, did the barons and knights

A manuscript illumination showing an antipope receiving his crown from the Devil and in turn crowning an emperor as a pledge of mutual support against the true head of the Church.

have any more right? Such ideas may have helped to touch off the English Peasant's Rebellion of 1381. Fear of economic radicalism may have induced the English upper classes to join with the king in suppressing the religious radicals—or Lollards, as they were called—after 1400. But the suppression was not wholly effective; the Wiclifite translation of the Bible and memories of Lollard doctrines survived until the time of the English Reformation. And the writings of John Wiclif reached as far as Bohemia, where they influenced John Hus, the great fifteenth-century opponent of the Church (see pp. 360–61).

THE BLACK DEATH

The effects of economic depression, political confusion, and religious uncertainty were intensified by terrible outbursts of plague in the middle years of the fourteenth century. The Black Death (probably bubonic plague) first appeared in Italy in the 1340s and swept through Europe during the next two decades. The worst was over by 1360, but repeated, though less severe, outbreaks well into the fifteenth century kept the population from reaching its preplague numbers for many generations. Although no accurate estimate can be made of the mortality, it was especially severe in thickly populated areas. Some towns lost more than two-fifths of their inhabitants, and some monasteries almost ceased to function. Since doctors were helpless, the only way to avoid the plague was to take refuge in isolated country districts.

The panic caused by the Black Death drove the sorely tried peoples of western Europe into emotional instability. It is no accident that the bloodiest peasant rebellions and the most senseless civil wars took place after the plague, and that the witchcraft delusion, almost unknown in the early Middle Ages, then reached its height. This was a double delusion. Innocent men and women were falsely accused of practicing black magic, but there were people, including men of high position, who genuinely believed that they could gain their desires by making a compact with the Devil. More than anything else, the witchcraft delusion demonstrated the state of shock in which western Europe found itself at the end of the fourteenth century. The rationalism and confidence in the future that had been so apparent at the height of medieval civilization had vanished.

ENGLAND IN THE LATER MIDDLE AGES

Even France and England, the two strongest states in the West, were shaken by the events of the fourteenth century. They had enough momentum and solid enough administrative structures to survive as political units, but there were times when neither country had a government capable of preserving law and order. While the bureaucrats were able to keep the machinery of government running, they could not hold back the

---

The Black Death in England

Then that most grievous pestilence penetrated the coastal regions by way of Southampton and came to Bristol, and people died as if the whole strength of the city were seized by sudden death. For there were few who lay in their beds more than three days or two and a half days; then that savage death snatched them about the second day. In Leicester, in the little parish of St. Leonard, more than three hundred and eighty died; in the parish of the Holy Cross, more than four hundred, and in the parish of St. Margaret, more than seven hundred. . . .

And the price of everything was cheap, because of the fear of death, there were very few who took any care for their wealth, or for anything else. For a man could buy a horse for half a mark [about 7 shillings] which before was worth forty shillings, a large fat ox for four shillings, a cow for twelve pence, a heifer for sixpence, a large fat sheep for four pence. . . . And the sheep and cattle wandered about through the fields and among the crops, and there was no one to go after them or collect them. They perished in countless numbers everywhere, for lack of watching . . . since there was such a lack of serfs and servants, that no one knew what he should do. For there is no memory of a mortality so severe and so savage. . . . In the following autumn, one could not hire a reaper for less than eight pence [per day] with food, or a mower at less than twelve pence with food.

From Henry Knighton, *Chronicle*, in *The Portable Medieval Reader*, ed. by J. B. Ross and M. M. McLaughlin (New York: Viking, 1949), pp. 218–19.

rising tide of lawlessness. Under these circumstances, the nobles regained much of the power they had lost in the thirteenth century. They tried to control policy and direct revenues to their own pockets; in England they even deposed their kings.

The expansionist policies of Edward I (see p. 266) had severely strained English resources. A reaction would have taken place in any case; it was made more acute by the character of Edward II (1307–27). So incompetent that no one respected him, Edward turned over the business of government to a series of favorites who were hated by the great lords. The barons tried the old expedient of setting up a committee to control the government, but it worked no better than it had under Henry III. Finally Edward's own wife and her lover, Mortimer, one of the lords of the turbulent lands of the Welsh frontier, led a rebellion against him. Edward was deposed in 1327 and quietly murdered a few weeks later; his young son, Edward III (1327–77), became king.

The Hundred Years' War: The First Phase

Edward III shared his barons' fondness for courtly magnificence and chivalric warfare. More popular with the aristocracy than his father had been, he was also more susceptible to their influence. Never quite willing to risk his popularity by forcing a showdown with the barons, he allowed them to retain a strong position in Parliament and in the Council. This is probably why he drifted into the Hundred Years' War with France. War was a policy on which he and his barons could agree, and so long as the war was successful he could avoid domestic controversies.

There were, of course, other reasons for the war. France was still trying to annex the English holdings in Aquitaine and gain full control of Flanders, which was the best market for English wool. France was aiding Scotland, which had regained its independence in the battle of Bannockburn (1314) and was in a state of almost permanent hostility with England. French and English sailors were intermittently plundering each other's ships. These frictions were enough to cause a war, but they do not quite explain why the war lasted for generations. The king persisted because he gained new and valuable territories; the barons, because they acquired booty and profitable military commands.

After a bad start, caused largely by financial difficulties, Edward came up with an amazing string of victories. He gained control of the Channel in a naval battle at Sluys (1340) and nearly annihilated the French army at Crécy (1346). Then he went on to take Calais, which remained a port of entry for English armies for two centuries. Ten years later, Edward's son, the Black Prince (also

The Later Middle Ages

So violent and motley was life, that it bore the mixed smell of blood and of roses. The men of that time always oscillated between the fear of hell and the most naïve joy, between cruelty and tenderness, between harsh asceticism and insane attachment to the delights of this world . . . always running to extremes. . . .

Bad government, the cupidity and violence of the great, wars and brigandage, scarcity, misery, and pestilence—to this is contemporary history nearly reduced in the eyes of the people. The feeling of general insecurity . . . was further aggravated by the fear of hell, of sorcerers and of devils. Everywhere the flames of hatred arise and injustice reigns. Satan covers a gloomy earth with his sombre wings.

From J. Huizinga, *The Waning of the Middle Ages* (London: Arnold, 1924), pp. 18, 21.

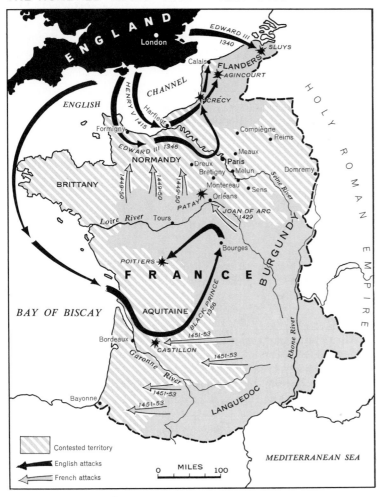

THE HUNDRED YEARS' WAR   1337–1453

(map labels)
ENGLAND · London · EDWARD III 1340 · SLUYS · Calais · FLANDERS · AGINCOURT · ENGLISH · CHANNEL · CRÉCY · HENRY V 1415 · Harfleur · Compiègne · Reims · Formigny · EDWARD III 1346 · NORMANDY · Dreux · Meaux · Paris · Domremy · Bretigny · Melun · 1449-50 · Montereau · Sens · Seine River · BRITTANY · Orléans · 1449-50 · 1449-50 · PATAY · JOAN OF ARC 1429 · Loire River · Tours · Bourges · POITIERS · F R A N C E · BURGUNDY · BAY OF BISCAY · AQUITAINE · BLACK PRINCE 1356 · Bordeaux · 1451-53 · CASTILLON · 1451-53 · Garonne River · Rhone River · Bayonne · 1451-53 · 1451-53 · LANGUEDOC · HOLY ROMAN EMPIRE · MEDITERRANEAN SEA

Contested territory
English attacks
French attacks

MILES   0 _____ 100

---

armor. The only weakness in Edward's formation was that it was essentially defensive; it could not be used for a charge. Only when portable firearms were invented at the end of the fifteenth century was it possible to use missile weapons for an attack.

Like many other generals, Edward found it easier to win victories than to profit from them. The French, with no intention of fulfilling the terms of the treaty they had signed, launched a war of attrition that gradually exhausted their enemies. England simply did not have enough men or enough resources to garrison territories larger than Edward's whole kingdom. The French learned to avoid headlong rushes at large English armies and concentrated instead on picking off isolated garrisons and small detachments. As a result, the English had lost a large part of their conquests by the time of Edward III's death in 1377.

Rebellion and Revolution

Military misfortunes abroad led to bickering at home. There was a complete failure of leadership during Edward's last years. The king was sinking into senility, and the Black Prince, crippled by disease, died a year before his father. One of Edward's younger sons, John of Gaunt, Duke of Lancaster, had more authority than anyone else, but he was disliked and distrusted by many members of the aristocracy. He was accused, with some justice, of associating with a group of corrupt officeholders and, with less justice, of coveting the throne. The duke's taste in art and literature was excellent—he gave a government job and a pension to Geoffrey Chaucer—but interest in the arts has seldom added to the stature of a politician in English public opinion.

The new king, Richard II (1377–99), the son of the Black Prince, was only a child when he inherited the throne. During the first part of his reign England was governed by successive groups of barons. These men did nothing to distinguish themselves; their inefficiency and bad judgment led directly to the Peasants' Rebellion of 1381. The war in France was

named Edward), crushed another French army at Poitiers and took the French king prisoner. In the treaty that followed this victory the French agreed to pay a huge ransom for their king and to cede about two-fifths of their country to the English.

Edward had succeeded because his country was more united than France and gave him more consistent financial support, and also because he had developed new tactics for his army. He mixed companies of archers, armed with the famous English longbow, with companies of dismounted cavalry in heavy armor. A charge, by either mounted or foot soldiers, would be thrown into confusion by showers of arrows. The few men who broke through to the main line could be easily dealt with by the troops in heavy

1066	1154		1399	1461	1485
Norman Kings	House of Plantagenet		House of Lancaster	House of York

1454
Wars of the Roses

still costing large sums of money, even though the English were now almost entirely on the defensive. Casting about for a new source of revenue, the government hit on the idea of a poll tax, a levy of a few pennies on each English subject. This brought to a peak all the smoldering resentment of the peasants and the poorer inhabitants of the towns. They were already suffering from economic stagnation; now they felt that they were being asked to carry an unfair share of the tax burden. All southern England exploded in rebellion. Peasants and artisans burned tax rolls and manorial records, killed unpopular officials and landlords, and finally marched on London. The barons, taken off guard, scurried about trying to raise an army. Meanwhile Richard had to stand by and watch the rebels occupy London, burn the palace of the Duke of Lancaster, and murder the chancellor and the treasurer of England. Forced into humiliating negotiations with the rebel leaders, he was obliged to promise complete forgiveness for all past offenses, the abolition of serfdom, and the remission of almost all manorial dues.

The rebellion was weakened when its leader, Wat Tyler, was killed during a conference with the king. It was suppressed as soon as the barons could get their troops together, for the poorly armed peasants and townsmen were no match for professional soldiers. The king repudiated his promises and apparently all was as before. Actually, the rebellion had two important results. The Black Death had caused a shortage of labor but the revolt had shown that the peasants would not make up for the shortage by accepting increased tax burdens or lower wages. As a result, they were given land for low rents, and serfdom declined steadily after 1381. By 1500 there were almost no serfs left in England. Second, Richard had seen a convincing demonstration of the inefficiency and clumsi-

ness of baronial government. It is not surprising that when he came of age in 1386 he tried to increase royal authority and to concentrate all power in his own hands.

Richard showed considerable skill in his efforts to strengthen the monarchy, but he made two fatal mistakes. The barons might have tolerated the loss of

Richard II, from the portrait by Beauneven of Valenciennes (1398) in Westminster Abbey.

political power, but Richard threatened their economic position as well by confiscating the property of those he distrusted. Moreover, Richard failed to build up a powerful army under his own control. Most of the armed forces in the country were private companies paid by the king but recruited and commanded by barons and knights. This system had developed during the early years of the Hundred Years' War, when it had seemed easier to allow members of the aristocracy to raise troops than for the government to deal with the tedious problem of recruiting. Any lord with a taste for fighting could maintain his own little army at government expense, a situation that encouraged disorder and rebellion. The king's personal bodyguard was no match for the combined forces of several great barons. As a result, Richard was helpless when Henry of Lancaster, son of John of Gaunt and cousin of the king, rebelled in 1399. Henry himself had been driven into exile and stripped of his lands, and he was supported by many members of the aristocracy who feared the same fate. Richard was deposed and died in prison, and Henry of Lancaster

mounted the throne as Henry IV (1399–1413).

The Hundred Years' War: The Second Phase

The Lancastrian kings, who ruled from 1399 to 1461, never quite lived down the violence by which they had come to power. Their title was faulty—there were other descendants of Edward III with a better claim—and they seldom had the unanimous support of the great lords. Henry IV had difficulty suppressing two serious rebellions, and Henry V (1413–22) tried to unite the country by the dangerous expedient of reviving the Hundred Years' War. He was a brilliant general, as he revealed in his victory at Agincourt (1415); he was the first commander of a European army to use siege artillery on a large scale. By securing the alliance of the Duke of Burgundy, a disgruntled French prince, he was able to force the French king, Charles VI, to accept a treaty in which Charles disinherited his son, married his daughter to Henry, and agreed that any son born of this union was to be king of France. The

The battle of Formigny, which was fought at the end of the Hundred Years' War. Notice that the English (right) are on foot and are flanked by bowmen, while the French are delivering a cavalry charge. Usually the English won in such circumstances, but this time they were defeated.

next year both Charles and Henry died, and a one-year-old baby, Henry VI, became king of England and France.

Henry V, with all his ability, would have found it hard to control two kingdoms; Henry VI never had a chance. His long minority was disastrous. In England his uncles and cousins, supported by baronial factions, quarreled bitterly. In France, the disinherited son of Charles VI claimed the throne as Charles VII and carried on the war from the unconquered country south of the Loire. The English pressed him hard, but just as his cause seemed hopeless he was saved by the appearance of Joan of Arc (see p. 288). To the English, Joan was "a limb of the devil." But she stirred the French to drive the English back from the Loire and to win an important victory at Patay (1429). After these successes it hardly mattered that Joan fell into English hands and was burned as a witch, for the courage and enthusiasm with which she had inspired the French survived her. The Burgundians abandoned the English alliance, and the English position in France deteriorated steadily. Forts and provinces fell one by one, until by 1453 only Calais was left. And so after twelve decades of fighting and plundering, the war at last came to an end.

The Wars of the Roses

When the English could no longer blame Joan of Arc for their defeats, they began to blame one another. Commanders were accused of treason and incompetence; some were executed and others exiled. Henry VI, even when he came of age, could do nothing to stop the feuds among the great lords. Humble in spirit and weak in mind, he was dominated by a French wife whom most of the aristocracy disliked. The English barons had acquired the habit of violence, and a decade after the end of the Hundred Years' War they plunged England into the series of civil conflicts known as the Wars of the Roses.* The ostensible reason for these wars was an attempt by

*Long after the wars, the legend arose that the Red Rose was the badge of Lancaster and the White Rose, of York. This error led to the name Wars of the Roses.

some of the barons to replace the Lancastrian king with the Duke of York, who represented the oldest line of descent from Edward III. The attempt succeeded, but the Yorkist kings, who ruled from 1461 to 1485, had almost as much trouble with the barons as their Lancastrian predecessors. In fact, the Wars of the Roses were the last uprising of the barons, the last attempt of a small clique to take over the central government and use it for their own purpose. The wars destroyed everyone who took part in them—the House of Lancaster, the House of York, and many of the great noble families. It was left for the half-alien Tudors, indirect and illegitimate descendants of John of Gaunt, to restore order in England.

England made some economic gains toward the end of this period in spite of the failure of political leadership. The kings of the fourteenth and fifteenth centuries were no economists, but they were able to grasp one simple fact—that so long as England produced only raw materials, she would never grow very rich. From Edward III on, they encouraged the migration of textile workers to England and protected the growing English textile industry. They also encouraged the development of English shipping. The results should not be exaggerated, for even at the end of the fifteenth century England could not rival Flanders in textiles or Italy in shipping. But a good start had been made; England had come a long way from being a country whose chief economic function was to raise raw wool to be carried in foreign ships to Flemish looms.

The Development of Parliament

There were also two important institutional developments: the rise of the justices of the peace and the continuing growth of Parliament. The justices of the peace were created by Edward III in the fourteenth century to take over some of the work of local law enforcement that had formerly been the duty of sheriffs and feudal lords. The justices were men of position and leisure, not great lords but well-to-do local landholders of the class that had long carried heavy respon-

The only known contemporary portrait of Joan of Arc.

sibilities in local government. Like the sheriffs and the tax collectors, they served without pay; their reward was leadership in their own community. By the middle of the fifteenth century their powers had grown to a point where they controlled local government. They arrested criminals and tried minor offenses (major cases were reserved for the circuit judges). They were responsible for en-forcing economic regulations and orders of the central government. They collected information for the Council and were supposed to inform it of plots against the government. In practice, the justices of the peace were often the creatures of the most powerful baron of their region. But when the Tudors reestablished royal authority, the justices of the peace, with their wide local knowledge and influ-

An English court in the later Middle Ages. This miniature is from a law treatise of the reign of Henry IV (early fifteenth century). At the top are the five judges of the Court of King's Bench; below them are the king's coroner and attorney. On the left is the jury, and in front, in the dock, is a prisoner in fetters, flanked by lawyers. In the foreground more prisoners in chains wait their turn. On the center table stand the ushers, one of whom seems to be swearing in the jury.

ence, became the key agents of the crown in the counties.

The century and a half of political instability, stretching from Edward II through Henry VI, gave Parliament a chance to make itself an indispensable part of the government. Weak rulers sought the appearance of public support, and usurpers sought the appearance of legitimacy. Both were eager for parliamentary ratification of important acts, since Parliament represented all the propertied classes of the country. Thus Edward III and Henry IV, after successful revolutions, asked Parliament to accept statements justifying the deposition of their predecessors. Similarly, all taxes and most legislative acts were submitted to Parliament for approval.

Equally important was the union (about 1340) of the county representatives (knights) and the town representatives (burgesses). These groups, which had acted separately under Edward I, now formed the House of Commons and made Parliament a far more effective assembly. Now there were only two houses (Lords and Commons) instead of three, or, as in some countries, even four. And the lower house included an element, the knights, which would have been considered noble in any other country. The knights were landlords, just as the barons were; they could intermarry with baronial families, and some of them became barons themselves. Their presence gave the House of Commons much more influence than a mere assembly of burgesses (such as the French Third Estate) could have. Through the leadership of the knights, cooperation with the lords could be assured. This situation sometimes enabled Parliament to effect significant changes in government, for when both houses attacked a minister of the king they could usually force him out of office.

By the fifteenth century Parliament had become an integral part of the machinery of government, and no important act was valid until it had received parliamentary approval. So well established had Parliament become that it survived even the period of strong kingship that began under the Tudors in 1485. But Parliament only gave legal validity to acts of government; it did not make policy, which was the province of the king or the great lords. For example, Edward II and Richard II were not deposed by the initiative of Parliament; Parliament was merely asked to ratify the results of a revolution engineered by a few great barons. Not until the seventeenth century did Parliament begin to formulate policies of its own.

FRANCE IN THE LATER MIDDLE AGES

The monarchy in France also had its troubles during the fourteenth and fifteenth centuries. The sons of Philip the Fair (see pp. 268–69) died in rapid succession, leaving only daughters to succeed them. The barons, afraid that one of their number might gain excessive power by marrying a reigning queen, invented a rule barring women from the succession. In 1328 they placed Philip of Valois, a cousin of the last king and a nephew of Philip the Fair, on the throne. But since Philip owed his position to the barons, he had to spend most of his reign bestowing favors on his supporters and keeping peace among factions of nobles. The widespread loyalty to the king that had marked the late thirteenth century weakened, and the rebellions and acts of treason plagued the country. These internal disorders help to account for the French defeats in the first few decades of the Hundred Years' War.

Philip's son, John (1350–64), had no better fortune. His capture by the English at Poitiers, with the subsequent loss of territory and the heavy taxes needed to raise his ransom, caused widespread dissatisfaction. In 1358 the peasants rose in a revolt that was no more successful than the English rebellion but much more bloody and destructive. In the same year the Estates General, led by the Paris bourgeoisie, tried to take over the government. The attempt failed, both because the Estates had had little experience in government and because their leaders had no support among the great nobles. John's son, Charles V (1364–80), regained much of the lost ground by suppressing his opponents at home and

987   1328   1589

| House of Capet | House of Valois |

by driving the English from one stronghold after another. If his successor had been a more capable ruler, the French might have escaped another century of troubles.

Unfortunately, most of the brains and determination in the French royal family went to uncles and cousins of the new king rather than to the king himself. Charles VI (1380–1422) was never strong either in mind or in character, and after 1390 he suffered intermittent spells of insanity. The government was conducted largely by princes of the blood royal who quarreled bitterly among themselves over offices, pensions, and gifts of land. When the Duke of Burgundy was assassinated in 1419 by the followers of the Duke of Orléans, the quarrels turned into a civil war and the new Duke of Burgundy allied himself with the English. Since, in addition to Burgundy, he had acquired Flanders and other provinces of the Low Countries, he was the most powerful prince in France and his defection proved disastrous. It was during this period of civil war that Henry V made his rapid conquests and forced Charles VI to recognize Henry's son as heir to the French throne.

The Defeat of England

Charles VII (1422–61) faced an almost hopeless situation when his father died. He had been officially disinherited; the English and their Burgundian allies held the largest and richest part of France. Charles had little military strength, and he was not using what he did have very effectively. It was at this moment that Joan of Arc, a peasant girl from the extreme eastern frontier, appeared at court and announced that heavenly voices had ordered her to drive the English out of the country. Joan, self-confident and persuasive, shook Charles from his lethargy and talked him into the counterof-

fensive that turned the tide of the war. Joan's execution by the English scarcely checked the reconquest, for Charles soon had another stroke of good fortune. England under Henry VI was as torn by factional strife as France had been under Charles VI, and the leader of one faction, an uncle of the English king, mortally offended the Duke of Burgundy. The duke's return to the French cause in 1435 greatly weakened the English and facilitated Charles' recovery of northern France.

Joan of Arc was not unique in having visions, for in those troubled years many men and women were convinced that they had had divine revelations. But in the content of her visions we can see how deep were the roots that the religion of the French monarchy had struck among the people. Joan was convinced that Charles VII was the only rightful king of France and that it was her religious duty to restore him to his throne. She also believed that "to make war on the holy kingdom of France was to make war on the Lord Jesus." Her beliefs were shared by people of all classes. In spite of the misgovernment of the last century there was still a deep reservoir of loyalty to the French monarchy. And in spite of treachery and factionalism there was at least a beginning of national feeling among the French people. Under all the confusion and disorder of the early fifteenth century they clung to two basic beliefs: faith in the French monarchy and faith in the Christian religion. When the two beliefs were united as they were in Joan of Arc, they were irresistible. Joan foreshadowed that union of religion and monarchy on which the absolute states of the early modern period were to be built.

Restoration of Royal Power

France suffered more severely than England during the Hundred Years' War, since all the fighting took place on French soil. Wide areas were devastated by raiding armies and wandering companies of mercenary soldiers who found plundering more profitable than loyal service. But precisely because the French predicament was so much graver than the English, royal power was restored more rapidly and more completely in France. A king who showed any promise of putting an end to disorder could override most limitations on his power to levy taxes. Charles V began the work of freeing the monarchy from these restraints, and Charles VII finished the job. As soon as he had the English on the run he began to levy taxes at will, without asking consent from the Estates. His task was made easier by the fact that provincial feeling was so strong in France that a central parliamentary assembly was seldom called, and when it was called it had little authority. Real influence lay with the provincial and regional assemblies, with the local Estates of Normandy or of Languedoc rather than with the Estates General. And it was relatively easy for Charles to overcome the fragmented opposition of these local assemblies.

The same overwhelming interest in provincial affairs kept the great French nobles from entrenching themselves in the central government, which remained the preserve of the king and his bureaucrats. Thus in the long run the Hundred Years' War reinforced tendencies that had been apparent in France prior to the end of the thirteenth century—tendencies toward a bureaucratic state in which the king was strong and all other political forces were weak and divided. This French pattern became a model for the rest of Europe during the early modern period.

SPAIN IN THE
LATER MIDDLE AGES

Spain, like the rest of western Europe, was wracked by civil wars during the fourteenth and fifteenth centuries. The Spanish kingdoms were especially vulnerable because there was no fixed rule of succession in either Castile or Aragon,

and because, with Moorish power reduced to the little kingdom of Granada, the Spanish tradition of military prowess could be demonstrated only by fighting fellow Spaniards. Far too many kings came to the throne as minors, which meant quarrels over the regency at best, and attempts by other members of the royal family to supplant the legitimate king at worst. There were few peaceful reigns and almost no opportunities to influence European politics. At the lowest point, Castile became a pawn in the Anglo–French conflict. Pedro I was opposed by his illegitimate half-brother, Henry of Trastamara. Pedro was supported by the English, Henry by the French, and it was the victory of the French troops (led by their Constable) over English troops (led by the Black Prince) that gave Henry the throne.

Aragon had a little less trouble, because younger sons could be given small kingdoms such as Majorca (the Balearic islands) or Sicily (and eventually Naples) in Italy. Nevertheless, the disorder continued until John II of Aragon married his son Ferdinand to Isabella, the heiress of Castile. The union of the two crowns (1479) did not mean that the institutions of the two countries were merged, but it did bring a large increase in security for the people of Spain. On the whole, the Catholic Kings (as Ferdinand and Isabella were called) followed the French model; each province was allowed to keep its old customs, but was administered by officials sent out by the central government. Moreover, the Catholic Kings did not bear that name in vain; they made religion a test of loyalty. Jews and Moslems, even if officially converted, were suspected of secretly adhering to their old faiths, and even driven into exile. In the long run, this loss of skilled artisans and capable businessmen weakened Spain, but the loss was not immediately apparent. By 1500 Spain was the strongest kingdom in Europe. It could support both the exploration and the conquest of much of the New World (this was the area that Isabella and the Castilians controlled) and act as the arbiter of European politics (Ferdinand's specialty). Even far-off England found it advisable to ally itself with Ferdinand.

A fifteenth-century Swiss halberd.

GERMANY IN THE LATER MIDDLE AGES

The political history of the rest of western Europe during the later Middle Ages resembled that of France and England. Everywhere there were rebellions, civil wars, and attempts to conquer neighboring territories. But all this furor produced surprisingly little change. A political map of Europe in 1450 looks very like a map of 1300, and the basic characteristics of most of the governments were similarly unchanged.

Certain developments in Germany deserve attention, however. First, during the fifteenth century the dukes of Burgundy gradually gained control over all the provinces of the Low Countries, roughly the equivalent of modern Belgium and the Netherlands. This was one of the richest and most productive regions of Europe. The union of the Low Countries under the House of Burgundy separated their fate from that of the rest of Germany and gradually gave them a distinct national identity. At the same time their wealth made them the object of a long series of European wars that began in the fifteenth century and have continued to our own day.

Second, during the fourteenth century the peasants and townsmen of Switzerland gradually gained their independence from the Habsburg family, which had dominated this part of Germany. In defeating the Habsburgs the Swiss developed well-disciplined infantry formations, armed with long pikes, that could beat off a charge of heavy cavalry. By the fifteenth century companies of Swiss infantry had acquired such a reputation that they were being hired by French kings and Italian princes. The Swiss were also demonstrating the possibility of republican government to a Europe that had had little confidence in this system. The faction-ridden Italian towns were losing their independence to tyrants and the German towns proved unable to form a permanent confederation, although for a while the Hanseatic League (a union of North German towns) controlled trade in the Baltic. But the Swiss Confederation, loosely knit though it was, endured. Each district, or canton, had its own institutions, and no canton was under a feudal lord. The towns were ruled by the wealthier burgesses, but the peasant cantons, where the movement for independence had begun, were almost pure democracies.

The third important development in Germany was the rise of a new power center on the middle Danube as a result of the peculiar electoral habits of the German princes. By the fourteenth century the number of princes taking part in imperial elections had been reduced to seven. These great men feared giving the title to any powerful prince, so for some time they regularly chose as emperors counts with small holdings. Though the title gave no real power, it did confer enough social prestige to enable such counts to marry well-endowed heiresses. Thus the Habsburgs, petty princes in West Germany who had served briefly as emperors around 1300, managed to acquire the duchy of Austria and nearby counties. A little later, the Count of Luxemburg, an equally undistinguished prince, became emperor and arranged a marriage through which his son received the kingdom of Bohemia. Later Luxemburg emperors acquired Silesia and eventually Hungary. When the last male Luxemburg leader died in 1438, his nearest heir was the Habsburg Duke of Austria. The union of the two sets of holdings marked the beginning of the vast Habsburg Empire, for five centuries one of the great powers of Europe.

ART, LITERATURE, AND SCIENCE

The art and literature, the scholarship and the technology of western Europe during this period showed the same uneven development as the politics. There was a considerable amount of sterile imitation, or mere elaboration of familiar themes. On the other hand, no essential skills or ideas were lost, and there were some promising innovations. For example, while many late Gothic churches were cold and uninspired copies of earlier work, in other churches some striking results were achieved by making windows higher and wider, by emphasizing perpendicular lines, and by devising intricate patterns of vaulting. Elaboration could be carried too far; one late Gothic style is rightly known as the Flamboyant, because spikes and gables,

Jan van Eyck, *Giovanni Arnolfini and His Bride* (1434).

traceries and canopies concealed the basic lines of the structure. Better results were achieved in manuscript illumination, because the richly ornamented borders did not hide the text or distract attention from the miniature illustrations, which were becoming more realistic.

In literature there were the same contradictions. Many of the old narrative poems became fantastic romances (such as those Cervantes mocked in *Don Quixote*), and the lyrics became society verse. On the other hand, there were significant gains—deeper psychological insights in describing human behavior, and a notable improvement in the writing of prose. It is much harder to write good prose (especially on technical subjects) than to write acceptable poetry, but a high level of prose writing was reached in all western countries in the later Middle Ages. To take only one example, Nicolas Oresme, a French scholar and bishop, translated Aristotle's *Politics*. He had to invent or redefine many words in accomplishing this task, and in doing so he greatly enriched the French language.

The scholars of the period could also be accused of thrashing old straw without producing much new intellectual grain. Some of their arguments were overrefined—elaborate games that interested only the players. But there were original thinkers, especially, as we shall see, in the fields of science and mathematics.

These contradictory developments in late medieval culture disgusted the Italians of the Renaissance. They damned most medieval work as "gothic," which to them meant barbarous. It took many generations to overcome this prejudice, and even now it has not entirely disappeared.

Literature

The medieval authors who are most widely read today all wrote in the fourteenth and fifteenth centuries. The best-known example is Geoffrey Chaucer (*ca.* 1340–1400), who began as a mere translator and adapter of French works and developed into one of England's greatest poets. His most famous work, the Prologue to the *Canterbury Tales*, reveals his skill in describing individual characters and his wit in depicting human foibles. His people range from the "perfect, gentle Knight" and the poor parson, who taught Christ's lore, "but first he followed it himself," through the earthy Wife of Bath, who had buried five husbands, down to scoundrels like the Miller and the Summoner. Perhaps his knowledge of all levels of English society was due to the fact that Chaucer worked for years in the customs service in the busy port of London. But his subtle portrayal of human behavior, shown also in *Troilus and Criseyde,* came only from his own genius. Chaucer was something of a psychologist as well as a poet, but while he saw through pretense and sham, he never became bitter. He rose fast in English society under the patronage of John of Gaunt; he accepted the world as he found it and rather liked what he found.

François Villon (b. 1431) was less fortunate. A friend of the thieves and prostitutes of Paris, and a convicted criminal himself, he shows how close French society came to breaking down under the strains of the early fifteenth century. He used the old poetic forms to describe with gusto life in taverns and thieves' dens. But his poems also express his bitterness over his wasted life and portray the hopes and fears of the poor and the outcast—the simple piety of an old woman, the last thoughts of men condemned to hang. The tendency toward realism, already evident in Chaucer, became even stronger in Villon.

Devotional works written for laymen were far more numerous after 1300 than they had ever been before. There was a tremendous desire among all classes for more intense and personal religious experience to supplement the conventional observances. Writers of the fourteenth and fifteenth centuries produced innumerable meditations, visions, and moral tracts. Some of the finest religious writings of any period were composed at this time, especially the *Imitation of Christ,* ascribed to Thomas à Kempis. In England there was *The Vision of Piers Plowman* by William Langland, one of the first important works written in English after the long eclipse following the Norman Conquest. We know little of Langland, except that he lived in the middle years of the fourteenth century and that he came of peasant stock. The English of *Piers Plowman* is archaic, but it is recognizably English and not, as Anglo-Saxon was, an early German dialect.

Piers Plowman also illustrates the widespread desire to transform religion into a strong social force. The poet criticizes every class for its worldliness and selfishness; only by a return to the pure principles of the Gospel can the world be saved. There was nothing anti-Catholic in Langland's program, but it did bear testimony to the continuing inability of ecclesiastical authorities to satisfy adequately the aspirations expressed in the poem and in many similar works.

Painting and Sculpture

The same tendency toward realism that we have noted in Chaucer and Villon is also evident in much of the sculpture and painting of the period. This tendency, which had already appeared in some of the details of thirteenth-century works, now began to be expressed in the principal figures. It sometimes took a macabre form: skeletons and corpses were depicted with loving care on funeral monuments and in the Dance of Death, a favorite subject of artists. But we also find at this time the first real portraits painted in western Europe and the first attempts to depict a landscape that is more than a conventional background. There were capable artists everywhere—English, French, and German sculptors, French and German painters. But the most interesting group were those who worked for the dukes of Burgundy. The Flemish school of painting, which developed in the late fourteenth and early fifteenth centuries, was a worthy rival of the Italians of the early Renaissance. In some techniques these painters were ahead of the Italians—the first painting in oils, for example, was done in Flanders. The best-known Flemish painters, such as the van Eycks, van der Weyden, and Memling, combined meticulous attention to detail with genuine religious feeling. And there is nothing in Italy that quite equals the Flemish portraits of this period, such as Jan van Eyck's picture of the Arnolfinis, or his *Léal Souvenir*.

Science

The scholarly work of the period is less well known, and in the nineteenth and early twentieth century it was often dismissed as unoriginal and unimportant. But even when it was unoriginal it was useful to men with ideas of their own. For example, Columbus based most of his ideas about geography on books written in the fourteenth and early fifteenth centuries. And not all the work was unoriginal. In philosophy there was

Death was a favorite subject for illustration in the late Middle Ages. Shown here is the Dance of Death from a manuscript of about 1400. Death, playing a trumpet decked with the papal banner of the keys of St. Peter, summons a pope.

A fifteenth-century representation of Chaucer from the Ellesmere manuscript of the *Canterbury Tales.*

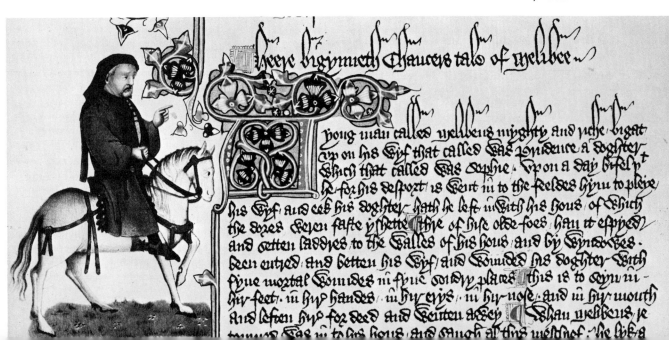

a sharp attack on the system of Thomas Aquinas that freed scholars, to some extent, from their adherence to the Aristotelian ideas that had been incorporated into Thomas' theology. Once Aristotle's ideas had been challenged, there could be wider speculation on scientific questions, especially on explanations of motion. The problems through which Galileo revolutionized the science of physics had already been raised by fourteenth-century scholars. For example, mathematicians at Oxford came very close to a correct solution of the problem of accelerated motion; and the French scholar Oresme, who was interested in physics as well as in political theory and economics, was at least willing to discuss the possibility that the earth rotated.

More important than any specific achievement was the very fact that interest in scientific problems persisted. Up to the end of the Middle Ages, western scholars, relying largely on the work of the Greeks and Moslems, had made no outstanding contributions to scientific knowledge. But they were remarkably persistent and kept working on scientific problems after other peoples had given up. The Greeks and Moslems eventually lost interest in science, as did the Chinese, who had had their own independent scientific tradition. But from the twelfth century on, there were always some scholars in the West who were interested in science, and this long devotion led, in the end, to the great discoveries of the early modern period. Early modern astronomers like Copernicus and Galileo were trained in universities that used the methods and the books of the later Middle Ages.

No one has ever given a completely satisfactory explanation of this continuing interest in science. Certainly westerners were paying more attention to the things of this world during the later Middle Ages and less attention to the aims of the Church. But Chinese society was far more secular, and the Chinese, in the long run, fell behind the Europeans. Perhaps more important was the western tendency to be dissatisfied with the status quo, a tendency that was especially evident in the crucial years between 1300 and 1600. In China, a philosopher like Thomas Aquinas would have become an unchallenged authority; in Europe his system was questioned within a generation after his death. Europeans respected authority, but they always felt that authoritative treatises needed to be reinterpreted. Finally, there was a curious patience with details, a willingness and an enthusiasm to work very hard for very small gains.

Technology

These qualities also explain some of the advances in technology that were made in the last medieval centuries. Perhaps the most important was the development of firearms. Here, as in many other cases, the Europeans capitalized on a technique known to other peoples. The Chinese, for example, were probably the first to discover gunpowder, and they had cannon about as early as the Europeans. But Chinese guns were never very efficient, and the Chinese never developed an army that was primarily dependent on firearms. The Europeans carried their experiments with cannon much further than the Chinese. Although the first European guns were not very good—they were as apt to kill the men who fired them as those at whom they were aimed—they had become fairly reliable by the end of the fifteenth century. The military significance of this development is obvious. It reduced the power of local lords by making their castles untenable; conversely, it increased the

An early gun, lighter and more portable than the first cannon. The gun was placed on a forked stand and was braced against the ground by its long tail (illustration from a German manuscript, ca. 1405).

power of kings and great princes like the Duke of Burgundy, for they were the only ones who could afford the expensive new weapons.

The development of firearms caused a rapid growth in other branches of technology. In order to make gun barrels that would not burst under the shock of an explosion, much had to be learned about metallurgy. And in order to make gun barrels that were truly round and hence could deliver the full effect of the charge, better metalworking tools and more precise measuring instruments had to be developed. Better techniques in using metals led to greater demands for metals, and this in turn stimulated the mining industry. The miners of Germany (including Bohemia and Austria), who were the chief suppliers of metals for Europe, learned to push their shafts deeper and to devise ways of draining off underground water. Increased use of metals and greater skill in mining in the long run transformed European industry. To take the most famous example, pumps operated by a piston traveling in a cylinder were developed in order to remove water from mines; it was this kind of pump that eventually furnished the model for the first steam engine.

The invention of printing in the fifteenth century (see p. 364) also owed much to developments in metallurgy. The essential element in printing was the use of movable type, and good type in turn depended on the availability of a metal that would take the exact shape of the mold into which it was poured. Thanks to their knowledge of metallurgy, the Germans succeeded in developing an alloy that expanded as it cooled, so that it fitted the mold exactly. Type faces molded from this alloy produced sharp, clear impressions.

Another technical advance of western Europe in the later Middle Ages was in ocean shipping. Here there was at first more patient experimentation than striking discoveries. By the end of the thirteenth century the sailors of western countries had ships that could tack against the wind and were seaworthy enough to survive the storms of the Atlantic. The navigators of the period could find their latitude, though not their longitude, by star and sun sights; they knew

that the earth was round, and that the distance to the rich countries of the East was not impossibly great. Very little more was needed for the great voyages of discovery except practice, and during the fourteenth and fifteenth centuries daring men were mastering the art of oceanic navigation. French and Spanish seamen had reached the Canary Islands at least by the early fourteenth century, and the Portuguese by 1400 had pushed down to the bend in the African coast, claiming Madeira and the Cape Verde Islands along the way.

These voyages illustrate the point that was made earlier: Europeans were no more skillful or intelligent than other peoples; they were simply more persistent or more aggressive. During the same years in which the Europeans were making their first sorties into the Atlantic, the Chinese were sending expeditions into the Indian Ocean. There they found rich kingdoms, ancient civilizations, and profitable sources of trade. In contrast, the Europeans discovered only barren islands and the fever-stricken coast of Africa. Yet the Chinese abandoned their explorations because they, or at least their rulers, were satisfied with what they had at home. The Europeans persisted, though it was almost two centuries before they reached the thriving trading centers of the East or the treasures of Mexico and Peru.

Not as striking as the early voyages, but almost as significant, was the invention of the mechanical clock. The first clocks, which appeared in the fourteenth century, were not very accurate, but they were soon improved by the discovery of the principle of escapement—the system by which the train of gears moves only a precise distance before it is checked and then released to move the same distance again. Crude as the first clocks were, they modified, in the long run, the mental outlook of the western peoples. For several centuries one of the sharpest differences between the West and the rest of the world lay in attitudes toward precise measurement, especially the precise measurement of time. Western civilization has come to be dominated by the clock and the timetable, and westerners have had little sympathy with people who have managed to escape this domination.

Mechanical clock made in 1410. The first clocks had only one movable hand.

Suggestions for Further Reading

Note: Asterisk denotes a book available in paperback edition.

Economic Weakness

H. A. Miskimin, *The Economy of Early Renaissance Europe, 1300–1460** (1969), is a good brief survey of the problem. J. W. Thompson's *Economic and Social History of Europe in the Later Middle Ages* (1931), which has excellent material on almost all aspects of European economic life in this period, is a good starting point for further study. There is a very thorough treatment of the methods for the enforcement of early economic legislation in England in B. H. Putnam, *The Enforcement of the Statutes of Labourers* (1908). B. N. Nelson, *The Idea of Usury* (1949), studies the development of a universal morality conducive to systematic capitalist enterprise. The second edition of Vol. I of the *Cambridge Economic History of Europe* is especially good on this period. See also E. E. Power and M. M. Postan, *Studies in English Trade in the Fifteenth Century* (1933), and S. L. Thrupp, *The Merchant Class of Medieval London* (1948).

Attacks on the Church: Marsilius, Wiclif, and Hus

There is a wealth of material available in English on these men, who revolutionized the political and religious thinking of western Europe. A. Gewirth, *Marsilius of Padua*,* Vol. I (1951), is a scholarly and readable treatment of the political philosophy of Marsilius. The great treatise of Marsilius, the *Defensor pacis*, trans. by A. Gewirth (1956), brings out the premises by which Marsilius overthrew the doctrines of the papal plenitude of power and the Gelasian theory of the parallelism between the spiritual and temporal powers.

G. Leff, *Heresy in the Later Middle Ages* (1967), is a good survey of the problem. A good introduction to the political, social, and religious climate on which the thought of Wiclif fell is G. M. Trevelyan, *England in the Age of Wycliff* * (1899). Trevelyan was one of the great social historians of his century and a very good writer. H. B. Workman, *John Wyclif*, 2 vols. (1926), is a study of the impact of Wiclif's thought on his times and on the English Church. See also K. B. McFarlane, *John Wycliffe* (1952). D. S. Schaff, *John Huss* (1915), is an interesting biography of this Czech nationalist and precursor of reformation. The short monograph of M. Spinka, *John Huss and the Czech Reform* (1941), is a study of the influence of Wiclif on the thought of Hus. There is valuable material on the influence of Marsilius and Wiclif on the evolution of political thought in C. H. McIlwain, *Growth of Political Thought in the West* (1932). For an excellent account of the Hussite movement, see F. G. Heymann, *John Ziska and the Hussite Revolution* (1955) and *George of Bohemia* (1965). H. Kaminsky, *A History of the Hussite Revolution* (1967), is also very useful.

The Great Schism

The best background for understanding the Great Schism of the West is W. Ullmann, *Origins of the Great Schism* (1948). W. E. Lunt, *Papal Revenues in the Middle Ages*, 2 vols. (1934), has source material on the finances of the papacy at this time. There is a full account of the Great Schism in M. Creighton, *A History of the Papacy from the Great Schism to the Sack of Rome*, Vols. I and II (1919), and in L. Pastor, *History of the Popes*, Vol. I (trans. 1891), but the interpretation of Creighton is more balanced.

The Black Death

F. A. Gasquet, *The Black Death* (1893), is a good study of this epidemic, with detailed material on the consequences of the plague for the social and economic life of England in the later Middle Ages. The more recent work of A. E. Levett, *The Black Death on the Estates of the See of Winchester* (1916), rejects the older view that the Black Death seriously disrupted the economic development of England. Differing points of view on this problem are presented by W. M. Bowsky, ed., *The Black Death* (1971).

England from 1307 to 1485

A. R. Myers, *England in the Later Middle Ages** (1952), a broad survey of this period, is a good introduction. There is valuable source material on the reign of Edward II in *The Life of Edward II*, trans. by N. Denholm-Young (1957), which goes into considerable detail on the revival of baronial powers and the civil wars under Edward. T. F. Tout, *The Place of the Reign of Edward II in History* (1936), sees this reign as the period of marked transition from court administration to national administration.

J. Froissart, *Chronicles** (many translations), presents a vivid picture of the life and spirit of fourteenth-century England. Froissart is an invaluable source for the reign of Edward III. There is a wealth of primary information on the reigns of Henry VI, Edward IV, and Richard III in *The Paston Letters*, 3 vols., ed. by J. Gairdner (1895). H. L. Gray, *The Influence of the Commons on Early Legislation* (1932), is a scholarly study of the development of the House of Commons in the fourteenth and fifteenth centuries. S. Armitage-Smith, *John of Gaunt* (1904); A. Steel, *Richard II* (1941); and P. M. Kendall, *Richard the Third** (1955), are all interesting reading and based on sound scholarship.

For material on the development of the English constitution, see B. Wilkinson, *Constitutional History of Medieval England,* Vols. II and III (1958).

E. Perroy, *The Hundred Years' War,** trans. by W. B. Wells (1952), is an excellent account of the military history of this period, with a discussion of the implications of the war on the constitutional growth of England. R. B. Mowat, *The Wars of the Roses* (1914), and J. R. Lander, *The Wars of the Roses* (1965), are interesting, if somewhat romantic, treatments of this confusing struggle.

France from 1314 to 1461 H. Pirenne et al., *La fin du moyen age* (1931), is a thorough study of this period by outstanding French historians. The broad scholarly work of E. Lavisse, ed., *Histoire de France,* Vol. IV, Part 2 (1902), is invaluable for the political, economic, military, and cultural history of France in this period.

There is a full documentary account of the trials of Joan of Arc in *Jeanne d'Arc,* ed. by T. D. Murray (1920), a very readable translation. L. Fabre, *Joan of Arc,* trans. by G. Hopkins (1954), is a fine biography of Joan and presents a fascinating picture of France in the period of the Hundred Years' War. Another good biography is S. Stolpe, *The Maid of Orleans* (1956). R. Vaughn in *Philip the Bold* (1962), *John the Fearless* (1966), and *Philip the Good* (1970), gives a good picture of the growth of Burgundian power.

There are two very readable studies of the last Duke of Burgundy: J. F. Kirk, *Charles the Bold, Duke of Burgundy,* 3 vols. (1864–68), is a study of the man in relation to his times; R. Putnam, *Charles the Bold* (1908), concentrates on Charles the man. A good picture of the brilliant life of the Burgundian court is given in O. Cartellieri, *The Court of Burgundy* (1929). The outstanding achievement of J. Huizinga, *The Waning of the Middle Ages** (1924), is a study of the forms of life and thought in France and the Netherlands in the last days of the brilliant court of Burgundy.

Spain in the Later Middle Ages R. Altimira, *A History of Spain* (1949), and H. J. Chaytor, *A History of Aragon* (1933), both provide information on Spain during this period.

Germany in the Later Middle Ages Both J. Bryce, *The Holy Roman Empire* (many editions), and G. Barraclough, *The Origins of Modern Germany** (1947), contain information on Germany in the later Middle Ages. Barraclough presents a fresher historical interpretation. The old study of H. Zimmer, *The Hansa Towns* (1889), is still valuable. C. Bayley, *The Formation of the German College of Electors* (1949), and F. L. Carster, *Princes and Parliaments in Germany* (1959), are also useful.

The origins and development of Switzerland are carefully treated in W. D. McCracken, *Rise of the Swiss Republic* (1901).

The titles by Pirenne, Lavisse, and Vaughn in the section on France above contain information on the rise of the Habsburg dynasty and the Burgundian takeover of the Low Countries.

Art, Literature, Science, and Scholarship in the Later Middle Ages E. Panofsky, *Early Netherlandish Painting* (1953), is a beautiful study of art in northern Europe at this time, and M. Meiss, *Painting in Florence and Siena after the Black Death** (1951), describes the impact the Black Death had on the art of southern Europe. Both volumes are by outstanding art historians and have good reproductions.

Some of the greatest literature of the western world was produced in the later Middle Ages. Chaucer's *Canterbury Tales** (many editions); Villon's *Poems,* trans. by H. D. Stacpoole (1926); and Dante's *Divine Comedy,** trans. by D. L. Sayers (1949–58), are all masterpieces. Each was written in the vernacular, each reflects the changing world view, and each gives a superb picture of the spirit and thought of the times. J. Gardner, *The Life and Times of Chaucer* (1977), is a lively reconstruction of the poet's career. The great English poem of Langland, *Piers the Ploughman,** trans. by J. E. Goodridge (1959), is a fourteenth-century inquiry into the good life as judged by contemporary criteria. G. Lagarde, *Naissance de l'esprit laïque,* 2 vols. (1956–58), a brilliant treatment of late medieval thought and scholarship, traces the development in western Europe of a distinctly secular spirit. There is interesting material on late medieval science in H. Butterfield, *Origins of Modern Science, 1300–1800** (1949), a broad survey. A. C. Crombie, *Medieval and Early Modern Science,** 2 vols. (1959), gives considerable attention to methods in physics in the late Middle Ages and stresses the continuity of the western scientific tradition from Greek times to the present. Crombie includes a good up-to-date bibliography. The thought of the fourteenth century is lucidly presented in G. Leff, *Medieval Thought** (1958), which discusses Occam, science, and political theories. E. Gilson, *History of Christian Philosophy in the Middle Ages* (1954), has information on Occam and the later Schoolmen. There is a wealth of material on the intellectual and spiritual life of the period from 1216 to 1485 in D. Knowles, *Religious Orders in England,* 2 vols. (1954–55).

14 Western Europe's Neighbors During the Middle Ages

At a time when the governments of western Europe were weak, its cities almost nonexistent, and its scholars limited to the study of encyclopedias and digests, both Byzantium and Islam had well-organized bureaucratic states, large commercial cities, and eminent scholars. Understandably, western Europeans felt awkward in dealing with their more fortunate neighbors, and their sense of inferiority often led them into suspicion and hostility. But neighbors they were, and contacts of some sort were inevitable.

THE BYZANTINE EMPIRE

The Byzantine Empire recovered only slowly from the external shock of the Arab conquests and the internal shock of the long religious controversy over the veneration of images. The Moslems remained a constant threat from the south, and the Bulgars, an Asiatic people who gradually mixed with the southern Slavs, menaced Constantinople from the north. But the Empire still had its wealth, its diplomatic skill, and its professional army, and with them it managed to limp through the eighth and early ninth centuries.

With the accession of Basil I (867–886), who founded the Macedonian dynasty, the Byzantine Empire began one of its marvelous recoveries. For a century and a half most of the emperors were first-rate generals. They took advantage of dissensions among their enemies to drive back the Moslems in the south and the Bulgars in the north. They recovered all of Asia Minor and gained control of the eastern Mediterranean, making possible the reconquest of Crete and Cyprus. The Byzantine Empire was never richer or more powerful than it was about the year 1000.

Byzantine Art and Literature

An intellectual and artistic revival accompanied and outlasted the political revival. The schools at Constantinople reached the peak of their activity soon after 1000, when a faculty of philosophy and a school of law were established. This was not quite a university of the western type, since standardized courses and degrees were lacking, but professors

Opposite: Interior of the mosque at Cordoba (*ca.* 785).

299

Byzantine art exhibited Christian influence and a love of ornamentation. Above: a tenth-century clasp bearing the image of a saint. Below: a reliquary cross (probably twelfth century).

were paid regular salaries and often held high positions at the imperial court. Byzantine scholars spent much of their energy copying and commenting on ancient texts, useful though not original work that preserved many books that otherwise would have been lost. Especially important was the Byzantine interest in Plato. The other great group of scholars of this period—those who wrote in Arabic—were much more concerned with Aristotle, and western Europe had inherited only a few fragments of Plato in Latin translation. When the Italians of the fifteenth century became interested in Plato, they had to obtain their texts, and scholars to expound them, from Constantinople and other areas of the collapsing Byzantine Empire.

Not all Byzantine writing, however, was based on ancient materials. The Byzantines produced some notable histories—works that were not impartial, since they were usually written to justify the actions of a ruler or a faction, but that were far superior to contemporary western chronicles. Another interesting genre that flourished during this period was the popular epic. Stories of heroic deeds performed against the enemies of the Empire were written in the language used by the people, and for this reason they were far more widely known than scholarly works written in correct classical Greek. The most famous of these poems, the epic of Digenis Akritas, was still remembered at the time of the Cypriote rebellion of 1957 to 1958.

Under the Macedonian emperors and their immediate successors, Byzantine art entered into its golden age. As in scholarship, so in art there was a revival of classical influence. Byzantine artists were far less imitative, however, than were Byzantine writers. While deriving a certain dignity and sobriety from ancient works, they retained the Byzantine love of color and ornamentation. Unlike the scholars, they had something to say to the people; they portrayed the truths of the Christian faith and the events of recent history. Every church and many private homes had their icons (paintings of sacred personages); every important manuscript was illustrated with miniatures. With hundreds of artists at work, it

is not surprising that many of them were competent and a few great.

Byzantium and the West

Byzantine influence was felt throughout western Europe. Italian merchants came regularly to Constantinople and after 1100 took over most of the carrying trade of the Empire. Byzantine influence remained strong in southern Italy, even after the Norman conquest in the eleventh century of Byzantine holdings there, and in Venice, which had once been a Byzantine protectorate. Popes and German kings exchanged embassies with the emperor at Constantinople, and thousands of western pilgrims passed through the city on their way to the Holy Land. Easy access to the markets of Constantinople speeded up the growth of Italian cities, and the Italian cities in turn led the economic revival of the West. The use of Byzantine artists by Italians—as in the designing of the Venetian Cathedral of St. Mark's—left its mark on Italian art. The first native Italian painters were clearly influenced by Byzantine models.

Western scholars were not greatly interested in the theology or philosophy of the Byzantines. But after 1100 a few westerners journeyed to Constantinople to discover and translate ancient manuscripts. Their work was less appreciated than that of their contemporaries who were working on translations from the Arabic, and sometimes books that had passed from Greek to Syriac to Arabic to Latin were preferred to direct translations from the Greek. Because western translators were primarily interested in Aristotle, they overlooked the opportunity to increase the stock of Platonic works available in Latin. Nevertheless, some important texts, such as the advanced works of Euclid, would have been unknown to western medieval scholars had it not been for the efforts of the translators at Constantinople.

During the eleventh century the Latin and Greek Churches gradually drifted apart. There had long been friction between them, since the patriarch at Constantinople rejected the pope's claims to universal authority and the pope resented the patriarch's claim to independence. There were theological disputes, such as the one over sacred images, and the question raised by Charlemagne about the relationship between the Holy Ghost and the other two Persons of the Trinity. But the basic reason for the split was that the West and Byzantium were becoming so different in institutions and culture that each was suspicious of the other's motives. Finally, in 1054, pope and patriarch excommunicated each other, and the two Churches broke off relations. The break was not taken too seriously at first; such splits had happened before and had always been repaired. But this time, in spite of repeated efforts, the breach could not be healed. Each Church went its own way, and cooperation between them became more and more difficult.

Byzantium and the Slavs

Byzantium's greatest influence was on the peoples of the Balkans and Russia. In spite of frequent wars and rebellions, there were long periods in which the Serbs and the Bulgars were either subject to, or allied with, the Eastern Empire. Byzantine princesses were frequently married to Slavic rulers in order to gain influence in neighboring courts. These ladies brought with them missionaries and teachers, artists and scholars, thus helping to spread the Greek Orthodox religion and Byzantine culture throughout the regions inhabited by the eastern Slavs. The conversion of the Bulgars began in the ninth century and that of the Russians in the tenth; both peoples were soon thoroughly Christianized. For a long time the leading clergymen in Bulgaria and Russia were appointed by the patriarch of Constantinople. Even with a growing tendency toward autonomy in the Slavic churches, Byzantine influence remained strong. Down to the fifteenth century all but two or three of the metropolitans (heads) of the Russian Church were Greeks.

The fact that the eastern Slavs received their religion and culture from Constantinople had lasting consequences for the history of modern Europe. Byzantine civilization and western European civilization had a common origin, but, as we have seen, they drifted apart during the Middle Ages. Byzantium remembered much that the West forgot, and it was always more strongly influenced by eastern ideas and customs. The West went through experiences, such as the Investiture Conflict, and developed institutions, such as feudalism, that scarcely touched Constantinople. Misunderstandings were inevitable, and they were especially bitter because each region expected better things of a related Christian civilization and because each felt that the other was betraying a common heritage. The eastern Slavs, especially the Russians, shared these tensions. The West both attracted and repulsed them, and the current Russian attitude toward the West is a new and intensified form of an old suspicion.

THE MOSLEM CALIPHATE

The Abbasid Caliphate, established in 750, achieved its golden age before the tenth-century revival set in at Constantinople. It reached its peak of power and wealth under Harun-al-Rashid (786–809). Harun, who exchanged letters and gifts with Charlemagne, ruled a far larger empire than his western contemporary. The lands of the caliph stretched from Morocco to the Indus River, from the steppes of central Asia to the Sudan. After 900, although the Caliphate began to break up into separate states, the Moslem world remained an economic and cultural unit. In this vast territory, which was traversed by all the important East–West trade routes, there were dozens of populous and prosperous cities, but Baghdad was the largest and richest.

Byzantine masons at work (miniature from a psalter, 1066).

Arabic Scholarship

The city of Baghdad attracted books and scholars just as it did merchandise and traders. The Abbasids did even more than the Ommiads to transform their empire into a center of scholarship. Hundreds of Greek works, especially on philosophy, science, and mathematics, were translated into Arabic, and much was learned from Persian and Jewish sources. Chinese scholarship had little influence, but the Abbasids borrowed many ideas from the Indians, notably the system of arithmetic notation that we call Arabic figures. By the ninth century Moslem scholars had assimilated the work of their predecessors and were beginning to make original contributions of their own. From 900 to 1200 the most important work done anywhere in the world in mathematics, astronomy, physics, medicine, and geography was done in Moslem countries.

Much Arabic scholarship merely added details to support established scientific theories—for example, accurate observations of star positions or clinical descriptions of certain diseases. More was done in geography because the Arabs knew more about the world than had the ancient writers. But their most remarkable contribution was in physics and mathematics. In physics they performed interesting experiments in reflection and refraction. In mathematics, besides greatly simplifying arithmetical operations through the use of the new Arabic figures, they carried trigonometry far beyond the Greek accomplishment. And their work in algebra was even more impressive, for they fashioned a whole mathematical discipline out of the few hints provided by their predecessors. Their contribution is recorded in the very word *algebra*, which is Arabic.

Two notable Moslem mathematicians were al-Khwarizmi (d. *ca.* 840) and the poet Omar Khayyám (d. *ca.* 1120). Al-Khwarizmi recognized, more clearly than many of his contemporaries, the value of the new Hindu-Arabic figures, especially the zero. Use of the zero made it possible to reckon by position and simplified all work in arithmetic. Al-Khwarizmi did much to popularize this new arithmetic; he also wrote a text on algebra that was used in both Moslem and Christian countries for centuries. Omar Khayyám calculated the length of a solar year with great accuracy and devised methods of solving algebraic equations that had been too complicated for his predecessors.

Arabic Influence on the West

Moslem interest in mathematics and the natural sciences had a decisive influence on the course of western civilization. The Byzantines tended to neglect these subjects, and little was known about them in western Europe. The Chinese had great technical skill—for example, they discovered the principle of the compass very early—but they developed few general theories. And the Indians, after a promising start, lost their interest in scientific problems. Thus the Moslem world was the only region that was both actively interested in science and close enough to western Europe to touch off a revival of scientific interest there. Western European scholars made their first attempts to recover ancient scientific texts by going to the Moslems of Spain and Sicily; only after the revival was well under way did they begin to seek manuscripts in Constantinople. Certainly the West would not have developed a scientific tradition of its own as rapidly as it did without the assistance of Moslem scholarship, and quite possibly it never would have developed the tradition at all.

It is somewhat anachronistic, however, to separate science so sharply from other studies. For Moslem scholars, as for medieval Christians, science was merely one aspect of philosophy. Aristotle, the great authority on science for both peoples, was thought of primarily as a philosopher, and one of the chief intellectual problems of the Middle Ages was to reconcile his philosophy with the revealed truths of religion. Here again, Moslem scholars led the way. Avicenna (ibn-Sina, 980–1037), who wrote a famous book in Arabic on medicine, also prepared commentaries on Aristotle that influenced western scholars during the twelfth and thirteenth centuries. Even more important was the Spanish Moslem Averroës (ibn-Rushd, 1126–98), some of whose assertions shocked both Islam and Christendom—for example, that the world is eternal, and that there is no personal immortality. But Averroës was no freethinker; one of his strongest convictions was that there can be no real conflict between the truths of philosophy and the truths of revealed religion. This doctrine, which was taken over by Christian scholars in the thirteenth century, made it easier for them to justify the assimilation of Greco-Arabic philosophy into the Christian tradition. Maimonides (Moses ben Maimon, 1135–1204), a Spanish Jew living under Moslem rule, was thoroughly familiar with the Arabic versions of Aristotelian philosophy and tried to reconcile them with the Jewish faith. His proofs of the existence of God are very like those advanced a half-century later by Thomas Aquinas.

Until the Moslems broke away from the Koran's strict ban on representing living beings, they could do nothing with sculpture and painting. They were, however, great builders and created a distinctive style out of such old forms as the dome, the arcade, and the tower. Moslem architectural styles made a deep impression on every country in which they appeared; their influence may still be seen in Spain and India. Moslem buildings were lavishly decorated with colored tiles and intricate geometric carvings—ideas that were imitated by neighboring countries.

THE DECLINE OF BYZANTIUM AND THE CALIPHATE

The Byzantine Empire and the countries controlled by the Abbasid Caliphate remained important centers of commerce and intellectual and artistic activity throughout the European Middle Ages. But after the tenth century they began to decline as political units. Some problems were common to both states—for example, the lack of a fixed rule of succession to the throne. Neither the emperor nor the caliph was necessarily the eldest son of his predecessor; he might be anyone connected with the ruling family who had been able to win the support of the bureaucracy and the army. Theoretically

this practice might have assured the selection of the ablest man; actually it encouraged palace intrigues and civil wars. The western European tendency to insist on the rule of primogeniture was not an ideal way of picking a ruler, but in practice it gave greater stability and continuity to political institutions. Another problem common to both the Byzantine Empire and the Arab Caliphate was that of raising an army. It was easier to hire soldiers from among the neighboring barbarians than to disrupt civilian life by forcing city workers and peasant farmers into the army. But mercenaries were never entirely reliable, and the better they were as fighting men, the greater the danger that they might try to take over the government.

Each state also had problems of its own. In Byzantium there was a growing hostility between the bureaucracy of the capital city and the great landlords of the

A Moslem pharmacist concocting a medicinal wine (from a thirteenth-century manuscript of Dioscorides' *Materia Medica*). The text reads: "The making of a drink (*shirab*) for catarrhs, coughs, swelling of the belly, and loosening of the stomach." The recipe calls for wine mixed with myrrh, roots of licorice, and white pepper.

rural districts. The bureaucrats, quite rightly, felt that the landlords were trying to reduce the peasants to a state of serfdom and to make themselves independent rulers in the outlying provinces. The landlords felt, quite rightly in turn, that the bureaucracy was a nest of intrigue and corruption. Attempts to weaken the landlords or reform the bureaucrats merely intensified the bad feelings between the two groups. These disruptive tendencies were held in check during the tenth century, but after the death of the last great Macedonian emperor, Basil II, in 1025, they grew more virulent.

The problems peculiar to the Caliphate sprang from its size and from the peculiar nature of Moslem law, which emphasized ethical and religious duties, but left enforcement to the whims of the ruler. It was almost impossible to establish a centralized administrative system for such widely separated regions, each with its own traditions. Regional viceroys had to be given extensive powers, and there was always the danger that one of them would set himself up as an independent ruler. Moreover, though the caliphs had built up a bureaucracy on Roman and Persian models, and though they had developed a comprehensive legal system, Moslem government was always rather arbitrary and unpredictable. No one wanted to be bound by rules, least of all the caliph and his officials. Since everything depended on the whim of the man in power, it was better to catch his ear than it was to try to win a case at law. This lack of respect for legal principles encouraged intrigue and disobedience. Instability was increased by religious divisions among the Moslems. Minority groups that questioned the Abbasid ruler's claim to be the orthodox successor of Mohammed naturally felt very little respect for his government.

The first crack in the Caliphate showed itself in 756, when a member of the deposed Ommiad dynasty established an independent state in Spain. The loss of this outlying territory did little damage, but the next secessions were more serious, for they cost the Caliphate all of North Africa. In the tenth century much of this area was seized by the new Fatimid dynasty. This family claimed descent from Fatima, the daughter of Mohammed, a claim that gave it the support of the Shi-ites, the largest group of dissenters in Islam. The Shi-ites believed that Islam must always be led by a lineal descendant of Mohammed; they had rejected the Ommiad caliphs and were now ready to turn against the Abbasids. By taking the title of caliph in 909, the founder of the new dynasty directly challenged the claim of the Abbasid ruler to be leader of all the Moslems. In 969 the Fatimids conquered Egypt, thereby gaining one of the wealthiest Moslem provinces; they established their capital in the newly built city of Cairo in 973. The Fatimid domains now stretched from Morocco to the Red Sea and even included Jerusalem. At the height of their power the Fatimid caliphs of Cairo were far stronger than the Abbasid caliphs of Baghdad.

The Coming of the Turks

By the end of the eleventh century the Fatimid Caliphate was beginning to weaken. The Abbasids, however, profited little from the decline of their rivals. In an effort to hold on to their remaining provinces, they had come to rely more and more on mercenary soldiers, especially the Seljuk Turks. A branch of the nomadic stock of central Asia, the Turks had all the toughness, bravery, and love of conquest of their eastern relatives. They became devout Moslems and fought well for their new religion, but they also fought for themselves. Having become the dominant military power in the lands of the Abbasid Caliphate, they soon began to seek political power as well. By the eleventh century the Turkish sultans (kings) had become the real rulers of most of Syria and Mesopotamia. They preserved the caliph as a religious leader, but they did not allow him any real power in government.

The rise of the Turks had serious consequences for the Byzantine emperors as well. Disputes over the succession to the imperial throne and quarrels between the bureaucrats of Constantinople and the great landlords had seriously weakened the Eastern Empire. Suspecting that they would meet with little resistance, the Turks began to push into Asia Minor; when the emperor Romanus IV tried to drive them out he was defeated and captured at the battle of Manzikert in 1071.

The Byzantine Empire never fully recovered from this defeat. After Manzikert the Turks overran almost all of Asia Minor; they even took Nicaea, only fifty miles from Constantinople. Through heroic efforts a new Byzantine dynasty, the Comneni, regained some of the lost territory, but it could never eject the Turks from central and eastern Asia Minor. This was a serious loss to the Empire, for the provinces seized by the Turks had furnished large numbers of fighting men and had protected the wealthy coastal regions. Skillful diplomacy and the wise use of limited resources enabled Byzantium to survive, but the Eastern Empire under the Comneni never had the vigor it had displayed under the Macedonians.

Fortunately for the Byzantines, the first Turkish Empire began to disintegrate almost as soon as it was established. As might have been expected in this part of the world, the lack of a fixed rule of succession did most of the damage. Each sultan established little principalities for junior members of the family, and military commanders began to turn their governorships into independent states. Each ruler fought and intrigued with his neighbors in order to gain more land. In the end the old Abbasid Caliphate dissolved into a welter of petty states, only loosely associated by their theoretical allegiance to caliph and sultan.

The Early Crusades

It was this confusion in the Middle East that made possible the success of the first Crusade and the establishment of the crusader Kingdom of Jerusalem in 1099. The Moslems were too divided to cooperate against the common enemy, and some of them even encouraged the Christians to attack their rivals. Only a part of the Turkish forces could be assembled to fight the crusaders at Antioch; once Antioch had been lost to the Christians, few of the Syrian Moslems cared about the fate of Jerusalem. Jerusalem, after all, was held by the Fatimid heretics, who were little better than the Christian infidels. The Fatimids, on their part, regarded Jerusalem as an outlying possession of little military or political value and made no great effort to regain the Holy City. A dynasty of Christian kings, descended from the crusader Baldwin of Lorraine, held Jerusalem and most of Palestine from 1099 to 1187.

The emperor Alexius Comnenus (1081–1118) must have looked on the First Crusade as a very successful piece of Byzantine diplomacy. He had shown remarkable skill in whisking unruly western armies through his lands with a minimum of friction and looting, and he had used the crusading forces to screen his reoccupation of much of western Asia Minor. The establishment in 1099 of the Kingdom of Jerusalem and the northern

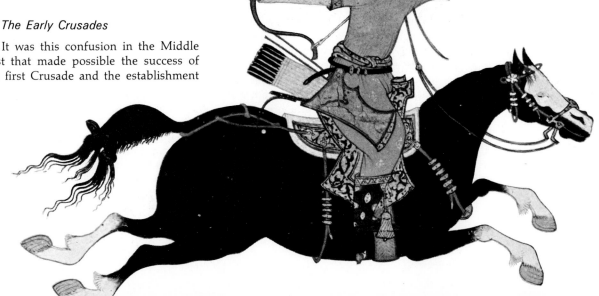

Turkish miniature depicting an Asiatic bowman. Unencumbered by armor, he could move swiftly on his small, strong horse.

crusading states of Tripoli, Antioch, and Edessa drove a wedge into the Moslem states of the Middle East and made co-operation among them more difficult than before. Moreover, by posing a threat to Islam, the crusading states also distracted Moslem attention from Byzantine expansion in Asia Minor.

The crusade was not all profit for the Byzantines, however, for it reinforced western suspicions of Byzantine morals and motives. The leaders of the crusade were sure that Alexius' failure to aid them in the siege of Antioch showed that he was more interested in recovering his lost provinces than in freeing the holy places from the Moslems. Western hostility to Byzantium was strengthened by the events of the Second and Third Crusades. The Byzantines were not really interested in fostering these movements; in fact, they twice withdrew into neutrality in return for advantageous treaties with the Turks. The westerners, dismayed by this subtle diplomacy, soon began to think that the Byzantines were almost as great a threat to Christendom as the Moslems. The sack of Constantinople by a crusading army in 1204 was the price Byzantium paid for arousing these suspicions.

The Moslems recovered only slowly from the shock of the Christian conquest of Jerusalem. Gradually a series of able army commanders began to reunite the scattered Moslem states. The first of these generals, Zangi, took the outlying Christian county of Edessa in 1144 and held it against the badly mismanaged Second Crusade. Even more decisive was the work of Zangi's son, Nureddin (Nūr-al-Dīn), who put an end to the decaying Fatimid Caliphate of Egypt in 1171. Nureddin was already master of most of Syria; by adding Egypt to his domain he became far stronger than the Christian kings of Jerusalem. He was succeeded by his ablest general, Saladin (Salāh-al-Dīn), who overran the Kingdom of Jerusalem and seized the Holy City itself in 1187. The Christians were left with only a few seacoast towns.

The loss of Jerusalem sent a shock of horror throughout Latin Christendom. The three greatest kings of the West—Frederick Barbarossa of Germany, Philip Augustus of France, and Richard Lionheart of England—agreed to unite their forces in an attack on Saladin. But this Third Crusade was only partially successful. Frederick was drowned while crossing Asia Minor with his army, and Philip Augustus, after helping to recapture Acre, rushed back to France to look after the affairs of his kingdom. Richard hung on, fighting so bravely that he became a legend among the Moslems, but he never had a large enough army to risk an attack on Jerusalem. He did reconquer a long strip of coastal territory, thus prolonging the life of the Kingdom of Jerusalem for a century. But the revived kingdom was never strong; it played a far less important role in the thirteenth century than it had in the twelfth.

The Later Crusades

Saladin's empire began to dissolve soon after his death in 1193. As so often happened in the Moslem world, his states were divided among members of his family, who promptly began intriguing against one another. The Christians could once more hope to regain Jerusalem, and they staged three major and several minor expeditions to the Middle East in the first half of the thirteenth century. None of these crusades was successful; when Frederick II briefly regained Jerusalem he did it through a treaty with the sultan of Egypt. On the other hand, the thirteenth-century crusades, by weakening both Saladin's dynasty and the Byzantine Empire, aided the rise of new powers in the Middle East.

The Byzantine Empire in 1200 was neither as rich nor as powerful as it once had been. Most of its commerce was in the hands of Italian merchants; the Byzantine navy had almost ceased to exist; and the army, composed largely of mercenaries, was too weak to guard all the frontiers. The Turks were threatening Asia Minor, and a revived Bulgarian kingdom was attacking Thrace. Internal dissension had reached a dangerous point, with many of the great families lined up against the emperor. More or less by accident, the first people to take advantage of this inviting situation were a group of crusaders.

The Fourth Crusade started in 1202 as a routine expedition against the Moslems of the East. But the army was heavily in debt to the Venetians, who had supplied ships to carry it to the East. The Venetians, who cared little about crusades but a great deal about profit, made the army work off part of its debt by capturing Zara, a rival trading town across the Adriatic. Then a pretender to the Byzantine throne turned up with a very tempting proposition: he would pay all the army's debts and augment its forces if the crusaders would make him emperor. The Venetians saw a chance to acquire a monopoly of trade with Byzantium, and under their urging, most, though not all, of the crusaders agreed to attack Constantinople. Aided by Byzantine weakness and disunity, the small western force—probably not more than twenty thousand fighting men—managed to seize one of the most strongly fortified positions in the world (1203).

They soon quarreled with their puppet emperor and took over the city for themselves (1204), sacking churches and stealing relics. Then they elected one of

A Byzantine View of the Crusaders

Anna Comnena, the author of this piece, was the daughter of the Emperor Alexius I.

Now he [the emperor] dreaded the arrival of the Crusaders, for he knew their irresistible manner of attack, their unstable and mobile character, and all the peculiar . . . characteristics which the Frank retains throughout; and he also knew that they were always agape for money, and seemed to disregard their truces readily for any reason that cropped up. . . . The simpler-minded Franks were urged on by the real desire of worshipping at our Lord's Sepulchre, but the more astute, especially men like Bohemund . . . had another secret reason, namely the hope that . . . they might by some means be able to seize the capital itself. . . . For the Frankish race . . . is always very hot-headed and eager, but when it has once espoused a cause, it is uncontrollable.

From Anna Comnena, *The Alexiad,* trans. by E. A. S. Dawes (London: Kegan Paul, 1928), pp. 248, 250.

A Crusader's View of Byzantium

Odo of Deuil, the author of this piece, was a historian of the Second Crusade.

And then the Greeks degenerated entirely into women; putting aside all manly vigor, both of words and of spirit, they lightly swore whatever they thought would please us, but they neither kept faith with us nor maintained respect for themselves. In general they really have the opinion that anything which is done for the holy empire cannot be considered perjury. . . . When the Greeks are afraid they become despicable in their excessive abasement, and when they have the upper hand they are arrogant. . . .

Constantinople itself is squalid and fetid. . . . People live lawlessly in this city, which has as many lords as rich men and almost as many thieves as poor men. . . . In every respect she exceeds moderation, for just as she surpasses other cities in wealth, so too does she surpass them in vice. . . .

[The bishop of Langres] added that Constantinople is Christian only in name and not in fact . . . and that her emperor had ventured a few years ago to attack the [Crusader] prince of Antioch. . . . "Though it was his [the emperor's] duty to ward off the near-by infidels by uniting the Christian forces, with the aid of the infidels he strove to destroy the Christians."

From Odo of Deuil, *De profectione Ludovici VII in orientem*, trans. by V. G. Berry (New York: Columbia University Press, 1948), pp. 57, 65, 69.

their own leaders, Baldwin, Count of Flanders, as emperor, and divided most of Greece and Thrace among the Venetians and western feudal lords. This Latin Empire of Constantinople lasted only a half-century (1204–61), but feudal principalities held by western lords survived in Greece to the end of the fourteenth century, and Venice held some of the Greek islands and ports in the Peloponnesus until the seventeenth century.

Innocent III, who was pope at this time, at first severely condemned the diversion of the Fourth Crusade. After 1204, however, he was seduced by the prospect of ending the schism with the Greek Church and gave full support to the Latin Empire. His first reaction was the sounder one; the capture of Constantinople was a disaster for western Christendom. Instead of healing the breach between the two Churches, it intensified Byzantine hatred of the Latins and convinced the Greeks that the independence of their Church was synonymous with national survival. Even when they were about to be conquered by the Turks, the Greeks refused to consider union with Rome. As one of them said: "Better the turban of the sultan than the tiara of the pope." Nor did the capture of Constantinople help the Kingdom of Jerusalem; instead, it meant that western money and fighting men had to be diverted to support the Latin Empire and the feudal principalities of Greece. By ruining the Byzantine Empire the crusaders exposed all southeastern Europe to Turkish conquest. Even though the Latins were driven out of Constantinople in 1261, the revived Byzantine Empire was only a shadow of what it had been. It held only a fragment of the Balkans and a small strip of Asia Minor; it could not check the Turkish advance into Europe in the fourteenth century.

Saladin's dynasty would have lost power in any case, but the thirteenth-century crusades speeded up the process. Louis IX of France precipitated a crisis by leading an army against Egypt in 1248. The sultan of Egypt by this time was almost entirely dependent on his household slaves, who formed the core of his army and held many high administrative posts. There were many able men among these slaves, or Mamelukes, as they were called, and they were weary of fighting to keep a decaying dynasty in power. The early successes of the crusading army led them to assassinate the sultan and to replace him with one of their own commanders. For centuries Egypt was to be ruled by Mameluke generals who rose from the ranks of a slave army. Only tough and brutal men could reach the top, and when one of them showed signs of softening, he was apt to be replaced by a younger and more vigorous fighter. But in spite of their internal quarrels, the Mamelukes were a first-rate military power. They were determined to drive the westerners out of the Middle East, and they rapidly accomplished their purpose. By 1271 they had occupied the entire area except for a few coastal towns, and in 1291 Acre, the last stronghold of the crusaders, was taken by the Mameluke sultan.

The fall of Acre did not end the crusades; there were some large-scale expeditions against the Turks in the fourteenth century, and popes talked of crusades as late as 1464. But none of the later crusades gained a permanent foothold in the East or did much to halt the Turkish advance. Whatever influence the crusades had on western civilization had been exerted by the end of the thirteenth century. And that influence was considerable: the crusades had helped to stimulate the growth of the Italian naval power that was to make the Mediterranean a Christian lake for three centuries. The fact that thousands of westerners lived in, or visited, Syria and Palestine encouraged the demand for eastern luxuries and thus changed western standards of living, although there would have been some increase in demand in any case.

On the other hand, the crusaders showed little evidence of intellectual or cultural interests. Armies of occupation are more likely to bring home material objects than ideas. Western scholars learned more from peaceful contacts with the Moors of Spain and the Greeks of Constantinople than they did from the inhabitants of the Kingdom of Jerusalem. In short, the significance of the crusades in East–West relationships was primarily political and economic. The crusades marked the first attempt of western Europe to expand into non-European areas, and they added to the difficulties of both the Byzantine Empire and the Moslem Caliphates. They did little to promote understanding or intellectual contacts among the three civilizations that bordered the shores of the Mediterranean Sea.

THE MONGOL EMPIRE

Far more important than the later crusades was the advance of the Mongols into Russia and the Middle East. The Mongols were another of those nomadic peoples of central Asia who from time to time developed great military power and burst into the lands of their civilized neighbors. The pattern was a familiar one: an able leader would organize his own tribe into an effective striking force and then subjugate other tribes belonging to the same racial stock. Once he had established himself as the predominant power in the vast steppes of central Asia, other nomadic peoples would join him either out of fear or in the hope of sharing in the loot. Finally, the united forces would become strong enough to strike out at China, India, or Europe. This had been the story of the Huns, and it was to be the story of the Mongols.

A small group originally, the Mongols became the dominant element in a great federation of nomadic tribes. But while the Mongols followed the old pattern, they expanded more widely and held their conquests longer than any of their predecessors. The leader who began the expansion of Mongol power, Genghis Khan (*ca.* 1160–1227), was the ablest of all the nomad rulers, and his immediate descendants were almost as competent. The Mongol khans were not only first-rate generals; they also knew how to organize and administer an empire. As a result, the Mongols became the dominant power in Asia and eastern Europe for a century and a half, and they remained a formidable force well into the fifteenth century.

The Mongols first concentrated their forces against China; they took Peking in 1215 and had occupied most of northern China by the death of Genghis in 1227. The Sung dynasty in the South held out longer, and the Mongols were not able to gain control of the whole country until the 1270s. Meanwhile they found easier conquests to the west. A strong army, under one of the ablest Mongol generals, set out against Persia and Mesopotamia. The Mongols overran Persia quickly, and in 1258 they took Baghdad, plundered the city, and put the caliph to death. This attack ended the Abbasid Caliphate, the last symbol of Moslem unity.

For a time it looked as if the Mongols were going to conquer all the Middle East. But when they attempted to take Syria, they were completely defeated by the Mameluke sultan of Egypt (1260). Since no one else from the Mediterranean to the Yellow Sea could claim to

Genghis Khan (detail from a manuscript illustration, *ca.* 1310).

Iron and silver helmet found at the site of a battle between the sons of a Russian prince (1216). The helmet bears the figure of the archangel Michael.

have defeated a Mongol army, this victory gave the Mamelukes great prestige. The Mongols made little effort to advance further, and the Mamelukes in Egypt and the Turks in Asia Minor remained independent.

Russia and the Mongols

Meanwhile another Mongol horde had attacked Russia, the chief outpost of Byzantine culture. The viking leaders, who had invaded Russia in the ninth century, had built a strong state around Kiev. This state controlled the trade route between the Black Sea and the Baltic, a route that in the early Middle Ages probably carried as many Oriental wares as the route across the Mediterranean. The princes of Kiev grew rich from their trade and were powerful enough to attack Constantinople itself on several occasions. But after the conversion of the Russians to Greek Orthodox Christianity

at the end of the tenth century, relations between Kiev and Byzantium were generally friendly. The Russians accepted the civilization of the Eastern Empire along with its religion; they built their churches in the Byzantine style, and their scholars translated Byzantine texts into Russian. Although the Russians added ideas of their own, Kiev at the height of its power in the early eleventh century must have resembled Constantinople in many ways. It was certainly larger, wealthier, and more of an intellectual center than either the Paris of the first Capetian kings or the London of William the Conqueror.

In the twelfth century Kiev began to decline. It lost some of its trade to the Italians, who exploited the Mediterranean route and sent their ships into the Black Sea. It suffered even more from the Pechenegs, a nomadic people who pushed through the gap between the Urals and the Caspian and cut the trade

THE MONGOL EMPIRE AND ITS SUCCESSOR STATES Thirteenth century

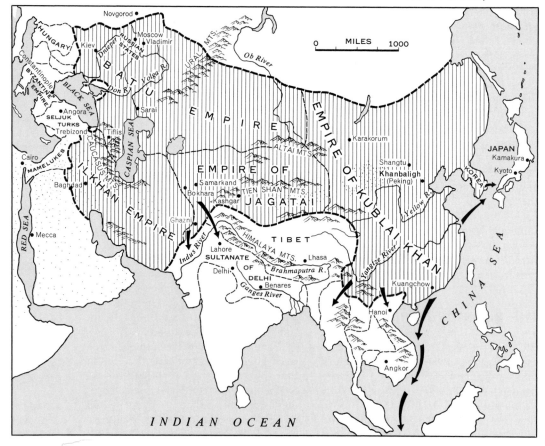

route between Constantinople and Kiev. Meanwhile other centers of power were developing in the upper Volga basin. The princes of Kiev had given outlying towns to younger members of their family to be ruled as dependent principalities. This practice worked well enough at first, but as Kiev declined and family ties weakened, the junior princes became greedy for power. They sacked Kiev itself in 1168, and this disaster, combined with commercial difficulties, put an end to the unity and prosperity of early Russia. The strongest ruler was now the prince of Suzdal, a region that included the newly founded town of Moscow, but his territories were poor and backward compared with Kiev in its great days. Once a land of cities and merchants, Russia was now becoming a land of peasants scratching out a bare living from the thin soils of the north. Declining prosperity, however, did not put an end to feuding among the princes, who found it almost impossible to take combined action against a common enemy such as the Mongols.

It is not surprising, then, that the Mongols conquered Russia so easily. Their first serious attack came in 1237; by 1241 they had overcome all resistance and were pushing across the Carpathians into Hungary. Hungarians resisted no more successfully than Russians—their armies were slaughtered near Budapest—but the death of the Great Khan ended the Mongol threat to central Europe. The commander of the Mongol army rushed home to influence the choice of a new ruler, and he never resumed his attack. The Mongols were at last satiated. They had every right to be, for they had created one of the largest empires the world has ever known.

The Mongols used terror as a means of conquest, wrecking cities and executing entire populations in order to convince their foes of the dangers of resistance. But once they had established their empire, they were willing to profit from the knowledge and skills of their subjects. In China and Persia, where they came in contact with relatively advanced civilizations, they soon became assimilated and carried on the old administrative and cultural traditions. In Russia, where they had less to learn, they held

RUSSIA ABOUT 1200

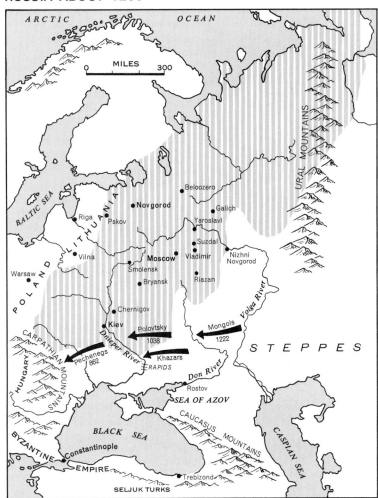

themselves apart and retained more of their own characteristics. They occupied only the steppes north of the Caspian, a region in which there never had been very many Slavs.

Western Europe and the Mongols

The coming of the Mongols might have changed the history of all Europe if western Europeans had been more alert. For several decades the most dangerous opponents of the Mongols were Mamelukes and Turks, and the Mongols repeatedly suggested to Christian rulers that they form an alliance against the common Moslem enemy. None of these suggestions was ever followed up very seriously, however, and an alliance may well have been impossible. Nevertheless, an alliance between Mongols and Christians might have checked the rising power of the Turks.

Europe also missed the opportunity to convert the Mongols. They were not greatly attached to their own primitive beliefs, and at times they seemed attracted to Christianity. The first Mongol viceroy of Persia had a Christian wife and favored her coreligionists, and the Mongol khan of China, Kublai, asked the pope several times to send him missionaries. Unfortunately, the thirteenth-century popes were occupied with matters nearer at hand, such as their feud with the Hohenstaufens and their efforts to preserve the crusading states. They sent a few envoys, but no solid corps of permanent missionaries. The popes of the early fourteenth century made a greater effort, but by that time it was too late. The western Mongols had already been converted to Islam, one more example of the advantage the simpler Moslem faith enjoyed in missionary competition. The Mongols of China were becoming submerged in the sea of Chinese culture and were soon to lose their power. The few missionaries who were sent from the West made thousands of converts, and a Catholic archbishop sat in Peking for a few years. But the whole effort was swept away when the Mongols were overthrown in 1368 and the strongly antiforeign Ming dynasty came to power.

Some Italian merchants took advantage of the opening of the overland route to China. The most famous of them was Marco Polo, who went to China in 1275 and spent many years in the country, part of the time as an official of the Mongol government. After he returned to Italy, Marco wrote a long and fairly accurate account of his travels, and his description of the wealth and splendor of the Far East did much to encourage the great explorations of the fifteenth century. But Marco had less influence on the people of his own time. He was accused of wild exaggeration and nicknamed "Marco Millions"; few other merchants followed in his footsteps. Here was another lost opportunity. At the end of the thirteenth century the European economy was grinding toward stagnation; it

Kublai Khan (1259–94), a descendant of Genghis Khan and ruler of China at the time of Marco Polo's visit.

desperately needed the stimulus of new markets. But fourteenth-century Europe lacked the capital, the energy, and the technical skill needed to open direct trade with the Far East. It was not until the late fifteenth century that western merchants could again dream of reaching China.

RUSSIA: ISOLATION AND AUTOCRACY

During the Mongol occupation, the Russians were allowed to live under their own princes and had little direct contact with the Mongols. So long as the princes paid tribute and sought confirmation of their authority from the khan, they could have whatever laws and religion they pleased.

Loss of Contact with the West

Nevertheless, the period of Mongol domination was a difficult one for Russia. Contacts with the West were sharply reduced, for both in commerce and in diplomacy the Russians had to deal primarily with the Mongols. The Russians were also blocked off from the West by the growing power of Poland and Lithuania.

Poland had received its religion and much of its civilization from the West. It had been converted at the end of the tenth century by Roman Catholic missionaries, and for a long time it was a vassal state of the German Empire. Often weak and divided, the Poles gradually began to grow stronger in the fourteenth century, as the German Empire fell apart. Their trade was largely with the West; their official language, for government as well as for religious affairs, was Latin; and they were rather inclined to look down on the Russians as a backward people.

The Lithuanians were a very ancient people, of the Indo-European language group, who had struggled for centuries to maintain their independence in their home on the south Baltic coast. Both Russians and Germans had tried to convert them, but the bulk of the population remained pagan until well into the fourteenth century. Just as the Poles profited from German weakness, so the Lithuanians gained by the collapse of Kievan Russia. They expanded south and east, acquiring some of the most fertile Russian lands.

In 1386 the Poles and the Lithuanians united. The Poles accepted the Lithuanian grand duke as their king; in return the Lithuanians were supposed to become Latin Christians. Poland-Lithuania was oriented to the West and was usually hostile to the Russians. Down to the sixteenth century, Poland-Lithuania was larger and stronger than all the Russian principalities put together. It intervened again and again in Russian politics, and it acquired so much Russian land that Moscow, at times, was almost a frontier city. Except for the Russian republic of Novgorod, which in the fourteenth century held much of northern Russia and traded directly with merchants coming up the Baltic, Russia was cut off from the sea and had few dealings with any western states.

Russia's loss of contact with the West was at first compensated for by increased contacts with the East. As long as the Mongols remained relatively united, the long land route across the Eurasian plain to China was heavily traveled—more heavily than it was to be again until the nineteenth century. But the subordinate khans who governed outlying regions of the Mongol Empire gradually became independent of the Great Khan, who had his headquarters in Mongolia. Thus the Russians had little to do with the relatively civilized Mongols of China and Persia. They dealt primarily with the so-called Golden Horde, the Mongols of the lower Volga region, who were the least advanced of all the Mongol groups.

Thrown back on themselves, the Russians took refuge in their religion. Their faith differentiated them from the Mongols, but it separated them almost as sharply from the West. They became fiercely orthodox and even less willing than the Greeks to compromise with the Roman Church. This stubbornness, added to their fear of the Catholic Poles, made them suspicious of westerners and western influences that might change their way of life and endanger their faith.

The Rise of the Autocratic Russian State

Isolation, poverty, and constant wars were not ideal conditions for the growth of Russian society. Opportunities diminished for all classes, especially for the peasants. The most the peasants could hope for was to keep their freedom and a little piece of land, and often they found even these modest desires thwarted. Almost the only productive group in the country, the peasants had to support the Mongols, the princes, the nobles, and the Church. The easiest way for their overlords to make sure that they would meet all these obligations was to bind them to the soil; thus serfdom grew in Russia at

The Church of the Savior at Novgorod (twelfth century). This is an early example of what became a typical style of ecclesiastical architecture in Russia.

the very time it was declining in the West. In order to escape serfdom, some peasants moved off into the desolate forest regions of the northeast, but even there the princes caught up with them and assigned them as serfs to monasteries and nobles.

The government of the princes became increasingly arbitrary, though its arbitrariness was always tempered by administrative inefficiency. Economic pressure forced the princes into absolutism; their states were small, and the burdens of Mongol tribute and war expenses were great. The princes had inherited a tradition of autocracy from Byzantium,

and Mongol demands encouraged the growth of absolutism. A prince who could not collect his tribute was sure to be in trouble; it did him no good to explain that he could not raise the money without violating the rights of his nobles and peasants.

During the fourteenth century the principality of Moscow became the strongest state in Russia. Its rise was due partly to chance; for several generations only one heir to the principality survived, and thus it was not weakened by constant divisions. Moreover, the metropolitan of Russia moved his seat to Moscow, thus bestowing on the Muscovite princes

THE GROWTH OF THE GRAND PRINCIPALITY OF MOSCOW   1300–1584

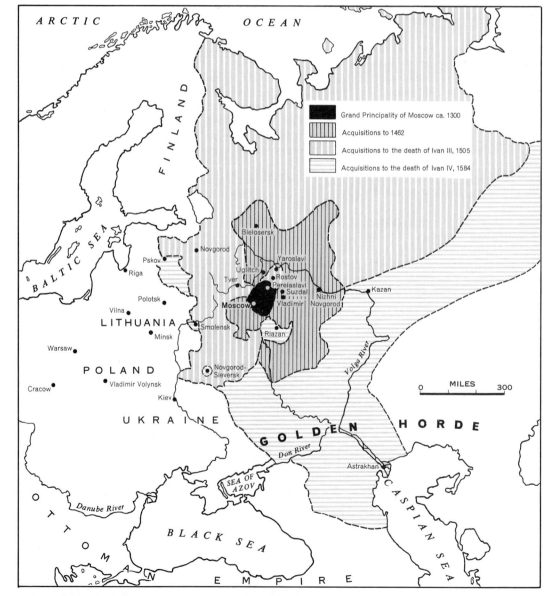

ARCTIC OCEAN

Grand Principality of Moscow ca. 1300
Acquisitions to 1462
Acquisitions to the death of Ivan III, 1505
Acquisitions to the death of Ivan IV, 1584

FINLAND

BALTIC SEA

Bielosersk
Novgorod
Pskov
Riga
Uglitch
Yaroslavl
Tver
Rostov
Pereiaslavl
Suzdal
Moscow
Vladimir
Nizhni Novgorod
Kazan
Polotsk
Vilna
LITHUANIA
Smolensk
Riazan
Minsk
Warsaw
Novgorod-Sieversk
POLAND
Vladimir Volynsk
Cracow
Kiev
UKRAINE
Volga River
MILES 0 300
GOLDEN HORDE
Don River
Astrakhan
SEA OF AZOV
CASPIAN SEA
OTTOMAN
Danube River
BLACK SEA
EMPIRE

the support of the highest religious authority in the country. Many of the Muscovite princes were men of superior ability, both in diplomacy and in war. They managed to keep on relatively good terms with the Mongols and were given the title of Grand Prince, which meant that they were the chief tribute collectors for the entire country. This position gave them an excuse to intervene in the incessant quarrels of other principalities and an opportunity to annex surrounding territory. As the Mongols weakened, the Grand Princes of Moscow became bolder; one of them actually defeated a Mongol army in 1378. Their assertion of independence was premature, however, for the Mongols still had a strong enough army to defeat the Grand Prince and burn Moscow a few years later. Mongol suzerainty was reestablished and continued into the fifteenth century. Nevertheless, the Grand Prince had established himself as leader of the Russians, and his victory over the Mongols was better remembered than his subsequent submission.

During the fifteenth century a civil war broke out in Moscow, but it served to strengthen the principality. The legitimate heir won the final victory and established the principle that Moscow was not to be divided as other Russian states had been. From this point on, the growth of the Muscovite state was phenomenal. It quickly absorbed neighboring principalities and, under Ivan the Great (Ivan III, 1462–1505), annexed the Republic of Novgorod, which held all northern Russia to the White Sea and the Arctic. Ivan also rejected, once and for all, Mongol suzerainty, and the Russians soon began to annex Mongol lands along the lower Volga. By the end of the sixteenth century the Muscovite state had expanded into a Russian Empire, with territories stretching from the White Sea to the Caspian and from the Lithuanian frontier well into western Siberia. The original principality of Moscow had covered only about five hundred square miles; the Russian Empire of the sixteenth century was the largest state in Europe.

Absolutism grew with the growth of the Muscovite state. The peasants had lost their rights long before; now it was

Russia, the Heir of the Byzantine Empire

Letter of Abbot Philotheus of Pskov to Tsar Vasily III in 1511.

The Church of ancient Rome fell because of the Apollinarian heresy; as for the second Rome, the Church of Constantinople, it has been cut down by the axes of the Hagarenes [Turks]. But in the third, new Rome, the Universal Apostolic Church under thy [Tsar Vasily III] mighty rule sends out the Orthodox Christian faith to the ends of the earth and shines more brightly than the sun. And may thy lordship realize, pious Tsar, that all Christian kingdoms have come together under thy sole empire; thou alone in all the earth art Tsar to the Christians. . . . Two Romes have fallen, but the third stands, and there will be no fourth.

Adapted from Thornton Anderson, *Russian Political Thought* (Ithaca, N.Y.: Cornell University Press, 1967), p. 72.

the turn of the nobles. They were not as independent as the nobles of the West. Most of them had become servants of the princes and held their estates only so long as they performed services for the ruler. They had no permanent power base, such as a duke of Lancaster or a duke of Burgundy had in the West. Soon their very life and property depended on the whim of the prince. By the sixteenth century the greatest men in the land could be put to death on the mere suspicion of disloyalty, and bishops and metropolitans who contradicted the wishes of the sovereign were sent into exile. The old title of Grand Prince no longer seemed sufficient to express this concentration of power. Ivan the Great, who married a niece of the last Byzantine emperor, soon began to think of himself as successor to the Caesars. Moscow was to be the "Third Rome" that would endure forever, and Ivan began to call himself Autocrat and Sovereign of All Russia. He also occasionally used the title of tsar (a Russian form of Caesar), but this did not become official until the reign of Ivan the Dread (Ivan IV, 1533–84). Ivan the Dread was a great conqueror and one of the bloodiest tyrants in history. He massacred nobles and townsmen with little reason and killed his own son in a fit of rage.

Part of the dowry of the marriage of Byzantine Princess Zoe to Ivan the Great (1462–1505) was the right to adopt the Byzantine two-headed eagle as the tsar's royal coat of arms.

Roman Empire
Divided in Half
395 A.D.

Turks Take
Constantinople
1453

Byzantine Empire

In spite of its size and the authority of its ruler, sixteenth-century Muscovy was not yet a powerful state. Still cut off from the main trade routes, its only outlet to the ocean was in the far north, on the White Sea. It was thinly settled; probably there were more people in France than in all the territories of the tsar. It was poor; it had almost no industry, and agriculture was backward. It was still militarily weak, open to attack by Poles from the west and Turks and Tatars from the southeast. The bulk of the peasants were still farming the poor soils of the north by primitive methods, and there were few settlers in the rich black-earth districts of the south. It was far behind its neighbors in all intellectual activities, in science and technology as well as in scholarship and literature. Only after 1600 did the Russians begin to overcome these great handicaps.

THE ADVANCE OF THE TURKS

The problem for much of Europe was not the Mongols but the Turks. As we have seen, the Mongol advance left the Turks of Asia Minor relatively unharmed, and the Byzantine Empire had been fragmented by the Fourth Crusade. The Serbs and Bulgars dominated the back country, western feudal lords ruled most of Greece, and Venice held the islands. The Byzantine Empire, as revived in 1261, possessed only Constantinople and a narrow strip of land on each side of the Straits. The new Turkish dynasty of the Ottomans, founded in 1299, rapidly exploited the weakness of the Christians. As good at war as their predecessors, the Seljuks, the Ottomans showed far more ability in building a permanent state with a strong administrative system. After conquering most of western Asia Minor, they began, in the 1350s, to make permanent settlements on the European side

of the Straits. The Christians offered no concerted resistance, and by 1365 the Turks had established their capital in Adrianople, not far from Constantinople. In 1389 they broke the power of the Serbs, who had the strongest state in the Balkans, at the battle of Kossovo. This victory brought the Turks to the borders of Hungary, and the West at last began to take alarm. The pope proclaimed a crusade, and a large army—mostly German and Hungarian with some French knights—advanced against the Turks. But bad generalship and poor discipline ruined whatever chance of success it had, and the crusaders were thoroughly defeated at the battle of Nicopolis in 1396.

The battle almost destroyed Christian power in the Balkans, but before the Turks could fully exploit their victory they were attacked from the east. Timur the Lame (Tamerlane), who claimed to be a descendant of Genghis Khan, had created a nomad army worthy of his supposed ancestor. The Mongols were once more on the march, and this time the Ottoman Turks were one of their chief enemies. In 1402 the two armies met at Ankara, where Timur won a complete victory. The Mongols captured the Turkish sultan and occupied most of his lands in Asia Minor.

Timur died soon after his victory, and his successors made little effort to hold the remote regions he had taken from the Turks. Nevertheless, the defeat at Ankara, followed by a generation of civil war, was a severe test of the Ottoman political system. The fact that the state was pulled together once again showed that the early sultans had done their work well. They had created a corps of disciplined and capable administrators, and it was with their assistance that one of the Ottoman princes was able to reestablish himself as sole ruler. By the 1440s the Turks were once more advancing in the Balkans. Their chief opponents this time were the Hungarians, commanded by John Hunyadi. Though a first-rate general, Hunyadi lost two major battles to the Turks.

The End of the Byzantine Empire

Now the road lay open to Constantinople. The last Byzantine emperor, Constantine XI, made a desperate appeal to the West for aid. Over the strong opposition of his subjects, he agreed to reunite the Greek and Latin Churches in return for western aid. But the union was never effective, and the popes of the fifteenth century lacked the prestige needed to rouse the West. Constantine received no real help and was left to fight the final battles alone. In 1453 the Turks made an all-out attack on the imperial city. The emperor was killed defending a breach in the walls, and the Turks poured into Constantinople. This was the end of the Byzantine Empire and of the emperors who claimed to be heirs of Caesar and Augustus. For many years there had been nothing Roman about them except their titles, but they were not unworthy of those titles in their last struggle.

Turkish advances in Europe continued after the fall of Constantinople, largely at the expense of Hungary. The Hungarians fought valiantly but were pushed back little by little until the Turks reached their high-water mark of conquest at the unsuccessful siege of Vienna in 1529.

As the Turkish advance slowed down in Europe, it speeded up in Asia and Africa. During the sixteenth century Syria, Mesopotamia, and Arabia were added to the Turkish Empire in Asia, and Egypt, Tunisia, and Algeria in North Africa. With this Turkish conquest of the southern and eastern coasts of the Mediterranean, Moslem naval power began to revive. The Turks never closed the Mediterranean to Christian shipping, but they and the semipiratical fleets of their subjects did interfere seriously with commerce from time to time. It was not until the 1800s that the Mediterranean became as safe for western merchants as it had been in the thirteenth century.

The Decline of Moslem Civilization

The rise of the Turks coincided with a decline in Moslem intellectual activity. Both the Turks and the Mongols have often been blamed for this decline, but neither people seems to have been entirely responsible. It is true that both Turks and Mongols were originally rough warriors from the steppes with little interest in intellectual matters, but both of them absorbed Moslem civilization with great rapidity. Art and literature flourished under the Mongol rulers of Persia. In fact, Persia was the leading cultural center of Islam in the fifteenth century, but its influence was felt more in the East, especially in India, than in the West. The Turks did some remarkable work in architecture and developed a highly literate corps of administrators. Moreover, one of the most eloquent laments over the decline of Moslem learning came from the historian ibn-Khaldun (1332–1406), who spent most of his life in North Africa, a region that was never touched by the Mongols and that fell under Turkish control only in the sixteenth century. There must have been more deep-seated causes, prevalent throughout the Moslem world, of the decline of Moslem civilization.

Ibn-Khaldun, probably the greatest of all Moslem historians, tried to work out a historical theory to explain the decline.

Mohammed II, ruler of the Turks when they took Constantinople in 1453.

His idea was that there had always been antagonism between the educated, open-minded, prosperous city dwellers and the ignorant, narrow-minded, poverty-stricken inhabitants of the desert and the steppes. When the city people became soft and decadent, as they had in his time, power passed to the crude but warlike tribes of the open country. This political shift in turn caused a shift in the climate of opinion. Rigid orthodoxy was favored, and science and philosophy were looked on with contempt and suspicion.

There is some truth in ibn-Khaldun's explanation. The dominant dynasties of the Moslem world in the fourteenth century were all nomad in origin, and some of them did emphasize strict Moslem orthodoxy. But this is only part of the story. Earlier nomadic conquerors, beginning with the Arabs themselves, had absorbed the intellectual heritage of the ancient world without difficulty, and fourteenth-century orthodoxy did not prevent the rise of mysticism in the Moslem world. Some leaders of the mystical movement, who had large followings, advanced ideas that went far beyond the early teachings of Islam, so that we cannot say that a sort of Islamic fundamentalism blocked all forms of speculation. It seems rather that Moslem science and philosophy had reached a dead end, and that the educated classes had become uninterested in them.

Perhaps Moslem learning had reached its peak too early and too rapidly. Few new ideas entered the world of Islam after the tenth century, and all the changes on the old themes had been rung by the thirteenth century. With nothing new to be done, there was naturally a loss of interest in academic subjects. In comparison, western scholarship, which was far inferior to that of the Moslem world in the tenth century, received a fresh stimulus every time it was about to reach a dead end. There were the translations from the Arabic in the twelfth century, the revival of Greek studies in the fifteenth, and the great scientific discoveries of the early modern period. Moreover, theology, philosophy, and science were so closely associated in Christian thought that activity in one field prompted activity in the others. Extraordinary interest in theology in the fourteenth century stimulated activity in philosophy and science. The theology of Islam, on the other hand, was much less complicated. Some Moslems took it for granted; others simply memorized the Koran, paying no attention to philosophy. Thus religious education in Moslem countries did not require corresponding activity in philosophy or science. Finally, as we have seen, western scholars were not quite so bound to authoritative, scholarly interpretations; more innovation was possible in fourteenth-century Paris than in fourteenth-century Cairo.

Whatever the value of these explanations, one basic fact is clear: for the first time in history, western Europe was to take the lead in certain types of scholarly investigation. Byzantine scholarship, never very original, was blighted by the Turkish conquest. Moslem scholarship was rapidly decaying in the fourteenth and fifteenth centuries. Of all the peoples who had inherited the great Greek tradition of philosophical and scientific inquiry, only the scholars of western Europe were still active. And their activity was to give the West an incalculable advantage in the next four centuries.

Suggestions for Further Reading

Note: Asterisk denotes a book available in paperback edition.

Byzantium 750–1453

S. Runciman, *Byzantine Civilization* * (1933), gives a good general picture of Byzantine institutions and culture and is the best introduction. The most thorough and scholarly study is G. Ostrogorsky, *History of the Byzantine State,* trans. by J. M. Hussey (1956). The older work of A. A. Vasiliev, *History of the Byzantine Empire,* 2 vols. (1928), is more readable than Ostrogorsky but not as thorough nor as fresh in historical interpretation. There is valuable material on the commercial activities of the Italian city-states within the Byzantine Empire in E. H. Byrne, *Genoese Shipping in* *the Twelfth and Thirteenth Centuries* (1930). G. Every, *The Byzantine Patriarchate* (1947), compares the liturgical and doctrinal differences between the eastern and western Churches, and J. M. Hussey, *Church and Learning in the Byzantine Empire* (1937), is useful for understanding Byzantine intellectual activity. See also the titles by Baynes, Diehl, Grabar, and Talbot-Rice mentioned after Chapter 8. An interesting survey of Byzantine civilization and its influence on the West is S. Vryonis, *Byzantium and Europe** (1967). The best account of the Latin conquest of Constantinople is *Latin Conquest of Constantinople,* ed. by D. E. Queller (1971).

The Caliphate
750–1258

B. Lewis, *The Arabs in History** (1966), a broad, quick survey, is a good starting point for study. B. Spuler, *The Muslim World,* Vol. I, trans. by F. R. C. Bagley (1960), is an authoritative survey of the entire period and a useful handbook. The old account of T. W. Arnold, *The Caliphate* (1963), is still valuable for the theory and development of the Caliphate. There is considerable material in P. K. Hitti, *A History of the Arabs** (1956), the standard treatment of the subject, invaluable for the facts of the period but quite controversial in historical interpretation. For the Caliphate as an institution, see E. Tyan, *Le Califut* (1954), and E. I. J. Rosenthal, *Political Thought in Medieval Islam* (1958). The growth of Turkish power is well treated by P. Wittek, *The Rise of the Ottoman Empire* (1958).

The Crusades

There are several accounts of the later crusades that give us real insight into the spirit and motivation of the crusaders. Both Geoffrey de Villhardouin, *The Conquest of Constantinople** (Everyman's Library), and Robert of Clari, *The Conquest of Constantinople,* trans. by E. H. McNeal (1936), are fascinating eyewitness accounts of the Fourth Crusade. Philippe of Novara, *The Wars of Frederick II Against the Ibelins,* trans. by J. L. La Monte (1936), contributes a great deal to our knowledge of Frederick II and his crusades. The counselor Joinville's *Life of St. Louis** (Everyman's Library) has exciting material on St. Louis' expeditions to Egypt and Tunis on the Sixth and Seventh Crusades.

E. Barker, *The Crusades* (1923), is old but still valuable. The best recent study is the beautifully written and highly urbane account by S. Runciman, *A History of the Crusades,** 3 vols. (1951–54). Runciman includes a thorough bibliography. There is good material on the crusades in the books by Setton, Hitti, and La Monte listed after Chapter 10, in the fourth section. For crusading efforts after 1300, see A. S. Atiya, *The Crusades in the Later Middle Ages* (1938).

East–West
Relations

See Deno J. Geankoplos, *Byzantine East and Latin West: Two Worlds of Christendom in Middle Ages and Renaissance* (1976) and *Medieval Western Civilization and the Byzantine and Islamic Worlds* (1979).

The Mongols
in the Arab World
and Russia

B. Spuler, *The Muslim World,* Vol. II: *The Mongol Period,* trans. by F. R. C. Bagley (1960), is excellent. G. Le Strange, *The Lands of the Eastern Caliphate* (1905), a study of the historical geography of the Near East and central Asia in the Middle Ages, is an old treatment but very good reading. Juvaynī 'Alā' al-Din 'utā Malik, *The History of the World Conqueror,* trans. by J. A. Bayle (1952), is an important study, while V. V. Barthold, *Four Studies on the History of Central Asia* (1955), contains the authoritative history of central Asia and the Mongols. Probably the best treatment of the Mongol rule of Russia is G. Vernadsky, *The Monguls and Russia* (1953), a scholarly and readable work by a leading authority on Russian history.

Russia
1100–1600

There are several very good studies of this period of Russian history. M. T. Florinsky, *Russia: A History and Interpretation,* Vol. I (1955), has valuable material on this formative period of the Russian state. The old work of V. O. Kliuchevsky, *A History of Russia,* 2 vols. (1912), is very interesting reading and still important. Undoubtedly the best treatment of Russia from 1100 to 1600 is G. Vernadsky, *Russia at the Dawn of the Modern Age* (1959). Vernadsky includes excellent maps and genealogical tables and up-to-date bibliographic material. *A History of the U.S.S.R.,* ed. by A. M. Pankratova (1947), is a modern Marxist interpretation of the evolution of the Russian state. See also F. Nowak, *Medieval Slavdom and the Rise of Russia* (1930).

The Decline
of Arabic Learning

Most of the titles mentioned in the second section above contain information on Arabic learning. R. Landau, *Islam and the Arabs* (1958), devotes considerable attention to Moslem culture. T. W. Arnold and A. Guillaume, *The Legacy of Islam* (2nd ed. by J. Schacht and C. E. Bosworth, 1972), provide a good summary that traces those elements in European culture that have roots in the Islamic world.

15 South and East Asia, *ca.* 600–1600 A.D.

During the millenium considered in this chapter, the civilizations of South and East Asia continued to develop in their own distinctive ways. Even the two momentous events that transformed much of Eurasia during this period, the spread of Islam and the creation of the world's largest empire by the Mongols, affected India and China very differently. Meanwhile, the history of Southeast Asia continued to reflect—but not to mirror—that of India while in Northeast Asia Japan fashioned its own culture and institutions under the stimulus of Chinese civilization.

INDIA

After the Guptas, India was divided into a number of states of varying duration and geographical extent. In studying this complex period, it is useful to distinguish North India from South India, even though some states for a time bridged this gap and even though major differences existed *within* each area.

In South India power tended to be focused in two major centers. One was the Western Deccan where the rugged terrain of Maharashtra produced tough fighters. There the Chalyukas of Badani (their capital), beginning with Pulakeshin I (r. 535–66), developed an empire which reached its largest extent under Pulakeshin II (610–42). After this emperor was killed in battle, the Chalyukas were overthrown by the Rashatrakutas who seized Badani in 752. Their empire was even larger than that of the Chalyukas, but their most permanent monument is to be found at their capital of Ellora where they sponsored one of the world's greatest temples.

The second southern power center was in the Tamil-speaking area of the Coromandal Coast region. Here first the Pallavas (roughly 250–910, with their highpoint around 600) and then their Chola successors (844–1279, highpoint eleventh century) built their states. One reason for taking special note of these two states is their influential role in Southeast Asian history. The Tamil area over which they ruled was a major source for the diffusion of Indian culture to the region. The Cholas, moreover, were able to launch several naval expeditions to Ceylon (Sri Lanka), and in 1020 they even concluded a successful maritime campaign against the Sumatran-Malay state of Shrivijaya.

The southern states, particularly that of the Cholas, were among the most extensive and long lasting of the Indian states during this period. Although they differed in structure, they were similar in being centered on the sacral authority of

Shiva as Lord of the Dance (Chola period, twelfth or thirteenth century).

Temple pavillion at Ellora, hewn from natural rock (eighth century).

the king who was identified with Indra and other deities. Consecrated in most solemn enthronement ceremonies, the king commanded the reverent submission due to the protector of the world. One Cholas institution that provided an important ritual and ideological link between the center and outlying regions was special villages on the plains governed by *brahman* assemblies but also including residents of other castes. The *brahman* priests were linked to the center of authority by their religion while at the same time they provided religious services to the peasant castes with whom they formed close ties.

This relationship between the *brahman* and the peasantry was facilitated by the growth of devotionalism that had already appeared earlier in Hinduism. This movement, particularly in the South but by no means limited to that region, incorporated local deities into the Hindu pantheon and formed a religion basically congenial to settled cultivators. This faith inspired fervent hymns dedicated to Shiva and Vishnu performed in song and dance in Tamil temples. Their main themes were love for God and the personal inadequacy of the devotee. These hymns helped to fire the vitality of Hinduism and to undermine the appeal of Buddhism and other rival faiths.

Hinduism was also strengthened on the philosophical level, most notably by Shankara (*ca.* 788–820), India's most famous philosopher whose basic teaching was an absolute monism. Although a Southerner, Shankara wrote in Sanskrit and traveled widely in India, including the North, debating challengers, founding schools and generally spreading his ideas.

Political fragmentation was characteristic of the North as well as the South. Here too, particularly from the eleventh century, a king exercized only a general overlordship over local warriors outside

the area controlled directly by the throne. In a system somewhat similar to Western feudalism, the obligations of these warriors included financial payments, the use of the king's currency, military service, and attendance at the king's court as well as recognition of the king's sacral authority. A local warrior might also be obliged to offer his daughter to the king in marriage. Among the most notable northern rulers were the Rajputs ("Sons of Kings") probably at least partly of central Asian descent but fiercely dedicated to the values associated with India's warrior (*kshatriya*) tradition. The Rajputs were able to stem the tide of Arab Islamic expansion in the eighth century. They and other Hindu rulers in North India maintained their independence until the establishment of the Delhi Sultanate.

The Moslem Invasions and the Delhi Sultanate

The first substantial and lasting Moslem presence in India came early in the eighth century when Arabs annexed Sind, the Indus delta region separated from the rest of India by desert. They incorporated their conquests into the Umayyad Empire and soon recognized Hindus as *dhimmis* (protected people, second-class subjects liable for special taxes, see pp. 327–28). The Arabs were prevented from further expansion primarily by the Gujara-Pariharas (*ca.* 750–1027) who created an empire rivalling that of the Rashatrakutas in the south. However, Arab expansionism was only a minor episode in the broad sweep of Indian history. As ever the main threat came from the northwest.

As we have seen, tough Hunna invaders from central Asia put an end to the Gupta Empire. Such incursions of warlike people from the northwest remained a major theme in Indian history, but with the coming of Islam a new element was added. Now the warrior peoples were imbued with a fierce sense of holy mission; they brought into India a world view which in many essential respects clashed with the native Hindu tradition. The Moslem faith in one God, one prophet, and one book contrasted with the complexity and tolerance of

THE MOSLEM CONQUEST OF INDIA
1192–1320

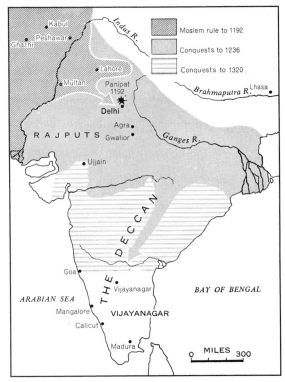

Tree of Life and Knowledge
(southern India, seventeenth
century).

quarter of the twelfth century a new group of Turko-Afghans appeared and in 1206 founded the Delhi Sultanate, which was to last for 320 years. The victory of Islam was accompanied by the wholesale destruction of Buddhist temples and centers of learning. Moslems had long resented Buddhism, which, like Islam, was a proseletyzing religion. Buddhism had already suffered a severe blow in 751 when Islamic forces inflicted a severe defeat on a Chinese army on the Talas River near Samarkand, thereby hastening the end of the period when Buddhism flourished along the central Asia trade routes. Now the Turko-Afghans effectively destroyed a Buddhism already weakened by Hindu opposition and competition. The result was that the faith virtually disappeared in India until 1956 when a substantial number of Untouchables converted to Buddhism.

The Delhi Sultanate was founded by a Turkish slave-general, a Mamluk of the type prominent also in Egypt during this same period. The Mamluk Dynasty (1206–90) was the first of five dynasties to rule in Delhi during the Sultanate. At this time, Turks, many of them slaves, and other foreigners filled key positions in the military and political establishments. In 1221, Chengis Khan, the great conqueror, led a Mongol expedition to the banks of the Indus but then withdrew from India. However, the Sultanate maintained a large army ready in case the Mongols returned. Military leaders were compensated for their service by grants of income from tax-exempt lands.

The Sultanate's decision to maintain a large army was only one of the ways the Mongols influenced the history of the subcontinent. Another was that, being cut off from central Asia, the rulers in Delhi necessarily concentrated their energies on India. A different effect of the Mongol conquests was that the destruction of urban centers in central Asia and Iran brought to India numerous refugee scholars, artists, and religious teachers who carried with them much of the high culture of their homelands. Notably, this included Persian as the prime literary language, which became the language of India's Moslem elite. But Persian influence was not confined to literature; it was apparent in architecture, textile design,

Hinduism, and there was a wide gulf between the hierarchical Hindu view of society and the Islamic belief that the ideal social order consisted of an essentially egalitarian community of believers. The interaction between Islam and Hinduism, often marred by misunderstandings, tension, and conflict, was to become a major theme in the history of the subcontinent.

By the eleventh century the region to India's northwest was under the control of warlike Turkic peoples who penetrated deeply into India on their raids from their base in modern Afghanistan. The most bloody and destructive of the raiding expeditions were those repeatedly conducted by Mahmud of Ghazni (971–1030) who used the wealth looted from India to turn his own capital in eastern Afghanistan into a major center of Islamic culture.

For several centuries Turko-Afghan invaders were content to return to their home territory beyond the passes carrying their loot with them. But in the last

and generally in court life and ceremonial.

After the Mongol threat receded, the Sultanate's armies were occupied first in plundering expeditions and then in subduing much of the rest of India. The regime reached the height of its power under the second and third dynasties, the Khajli (1290–1320) and the Tughluq (1320–1414) achieving its greatest territorial extent under the second Tughluq sultan, Muhammad (r. 1325–51) when most of India (except for Kashmir, the lower Indus Valley, and parts of the Rajput area) temporarily accepted Delhi's overlordship. However, the Sultanate had overextended itself and lacked the means to consolidate its conquests into a functioning empire. Nor did it have the power to compel the allegiance of distant tribute-paying vassals. Thus in 1336 the Hindu kingdom of Vijyanagar was founded, a state which remained the major southern power for two centuries. Elsewhere, Moslem leaders also declared their independence. One of these proclaimed himself Sultan of the Deccan (South India) in 1347 and founded the Bahmini Dynasty, Vijyanagar's rival. It should be noted, however, that even though Vijyanagar appealed to Hinduism for its ideology, it regularly employed Moslems in its armies just as Moslem states did not hesitate to employ Hindus.

A low point in the Sultanate's fortunes came in 1398 when Tamerlane invaded India and sacked Delhi—the same Tamerlane who checked the advance of the Ottoman Turks in the West. Under the fourth dynasty, the Sayyid (1414–51), Delhi remained weak, unable to prevent various regional rulers from establishing their own sultanates even in North India. The Sayyid dynasty was replaced by the Afghan Lodi (1451–1526), but it remained for a new group of foreign conquerors to match and surpass the earlier achievements of the Sultanate.

During the Sultanate period, Islam was firmly established in the Indian sub-continent although the majority of Indians remained Hindus. The main agency for the spread of Islam was not the sultanate and its military and civilian organs; nor was it the *ulama*, that is, "the class of state-supported judges, theologians, and preachers who were collectively responsible for upholding Islamic orthodoxy" in India as elsewhere in the Moslem world. Instead, the prime spreaders of Islam were Sufis, mystics not employed by the state. These men of religion belonged to various orders and varied widely in their methods and personalities: "Some of them wielded swords, others the pen, others a royal land grant, and still others a begging bowl. Some were introverted to the point of reclusive withdrawal, others extroverted to the point of militancy. Some were orthodox to the point of zealous puritanism, others unorthodox to the point of heresy."* This quotation, taken from a recent study of the Sufis in a single Indian state, suggests the adaptability and variety of Islam's holy men but also the dangers of over-generalization.

*Richard M. Eaton, *Sufis of Bijapur 1300–1700* (Princeton: Princeton Univ. Press, 1978), p. 283.

Moslem and Hindu in the Fourteenth Century

Ala-ud-Din [sultan of Delhi, 1296–1316] was a king who had no acquaintance with learning and never associated with the learned. He considered that policy and government were one thing and law another. "I am an unlettered man," he said, "but I have seen a great deal. Be assured that the Hindus will never become submissive and obedient until they are reduced to poverty. I have therefore given orders that just enough shall be left them of grain, milk, and curds from year to year, but that they must not accumulate hoards and property."

From the Moslem historian Barani, as quoted in H. G. Rawlinson, *India: A Short Cultural History* (New York: Appleton-Century, 1938), p. 228.

THE MUGHAL EMPIRE 1605

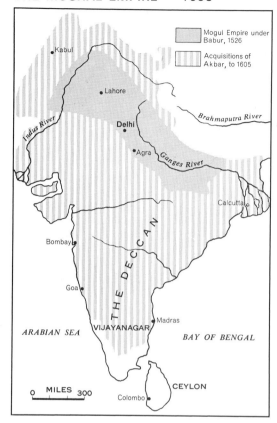

| Mogul Empire under Babur, 1526 |
| Acquisitions of Akbar, to 1605 |

Kabul

Lahore

Delhi

Agra

Ganges River

Indus River

Brahmaputra River

Calcutta

Bombay

THE DECCAN

Goa

Madras

ARABIAN SEA

VIJAYANAGAR

BAY OF BENGAL

CEYLON

Colombo

0 MILES 300

Many people came to Islam through peaceful conversion, not holy war; naturally many of the converts came from among those lowest in the Hindu social hierarchy. There was also a trend for Hindu devotionalism and Islamic mysticism to converge, as in the teachings of Kabir (1440–1518), a Moslem weaver, who asked, "If God be within the mosque, then to whom does this world belong?" He won many followers; his verses, written in the vernacular, drew on both Persian and Sanskrit vocabulary to express themes derived from both traditions. Another syncrecist was Nanak (1469–1538), the founder of Sikhism, who was born a Hindu but rejected caste and taught devotion to God. Under a succession of gurus (teachers) the Sikhs, spurred on by Mughal intolerance, later developed into a militant community in Nanak's home area, the Punjab (in the northern Indus Valley).

The Mughals

The Mughal empire was founded by Babur (1483–1530), but it was his grandson Akbar (1657–1707) who secured its future and constructed its institutional foundations. Babur and Akbar were Iranicized Turko-Mongols and as such continued certain policies of the Delhi Sultanate including the furtherance of Persian culture. Akbar was unusual in marrying Rajput princesses—most of the Mughal emperors had Iranian consorts, including the lady buried in the world's most beautiful and perhaps most lavish mausoleum, the Taj Mahal. (Although designed by two Persian architects, this mid-seventeenth century building represents a blend of Persian and Indian elements.) Akbar's marriage policy was just one example of his general inclination toward religious tolerance and toward seeking to reconcile those he could not subdue by military force. His good will toward Hindus was expressed not only in his own religious attitude but more concretely in his abolition of the tax levied on non-Moslems, and he further placated Hindus by forbidding the slaughter of cows.

Akbar divided the empire into provinces, and his government was conducted by *mansabdars*. These officials were holders of a *mansab*, a military rank defined in terms of the number of troops its holder was obliged to supply. The *mansabdars* were supported by *jagirs*, assignments to collect revenue for the government as well as their salaries and expenses from designated lands. These lands were fre-

---

Akbar's Religious Beliefs

O God, in every temple I see those who seek thee.
And in every tongue that is spoken Thou art praised.
Polytheism and Islam grope after Thee.
Each religion says, "Thou art One, without equal."
Be it mosque, men murmur holy prayers; or church,
The bells ring for the love of Thee.
Awhile I frequent the Christian cloister, anon the mosque,
But Thee only I seek from fane to fane.
Thine elect know naught of heresy or orthodoxy, whereof
Neither stands behind the screen of Thy truth.

From a poem by Akbar's secretary, Abul Fazl, as quoted in H. G. Rawlinson, *India: A Short Cultural History* (New York: Appleton-Century, 1938), p. 310.

quently scattered, subject to reassignment, and not hereditary. One reason for the Mughal success was that the emperors granted *jagirs* to and thereby made allies of a diverse elite including Rajputs and Afghans, Turkish and Iranian immigrants, South Indian Moslems, and prominent Hindus as well as Moslems from conquered regional states. The system was designed to prevent *mansabdars* from turning into local power-holders, but it was hard on the people who actually worked the land because the holder of a *jagir* had no incentive to further develop land he would soon loose. His interest was not in the well-being of the peasantry but in garnering the maximum revenue in the shortest possible time.

A substantial minority of townspeople were Moslem, but the great majority of peasants were Hindus as were the revenue collectors. Aside from paying their taxes, the villagers had little contact with the state; kinship and village groups remained dominant in their lives. Even in the cities the state rarely interfered directly in people's lives, and various communities and groups enjoyed a substantial degree of autonomy. For example, when the Portuguese became the dominant seapower along India's western coast, the merchants of Gujarat in northwest India dealt with the Europeans quite independently of their sultan who remained unconcerned as long as his own prerogatives were not involved.

The Mughal empire reached its greatest geographical extent under Aurangzeb (1657–1707), a controversial ruler known for his strict adherence to Islam. His reimposition of the tax on nonbelievers was just one of the meas-

The Taj Mahal (seventeenth century).

Akbar inspecting building operations at a royal city in the Ganges Valley (illumination from the Akbar-nama manuscript, *ca.* 1590).

Mughal military power at a time when it was increasingly challenged by Marathas from India's west and by Afghans and Iranians from beyond the passes. In 1739 Nadir Shah (r. 1736–47), who ruled Iran, became the last foreign conquerer to enter India, devastate the North, and sack Delhi. Although after that, a titular emperor remained in Delhi, actual power was in the hands of local potentates.

In 1765 one of these local rulers granted the British East Indian Company the right to collect revenue in his domains, and eventually the British became the heirs to the Mughal empire. Up to this time, Europeans accepted and worked within the Mughal system. Although they had earlier gained control of the seas and thereby influenced India's trade and economy and although individual Europeans helped to introduce new methods of warfare into India, they had remained largely peripheral to the mainstream of the subcontinent's history.

SOUTHEAST ASIA

Much of the diffusion of Indian culture described earlier (see Chapter 6) took place during the period we are concerned with in this chapter. Other major events, such as the decline of Kampuchea and changes affecting the states of interior Java, were largely determined by internal developments. But Southeast Asia was also affected by Mongol expansionism and by the spread of Islam.

Although Mongol ambitions extended to Southeast Asia and Khublai Khan attempted to force Southeast Asian states into submission, the Mongols did not establish themselves in the area. The giant armada which Khublai sent against Java where his troops landed in 1293 and the armies which he dispatched into what is modern Vietnam, where Hanoi was occupied three times, affected the local balance of power but do not appear to have drastically altered the course of history. More lasting was the Mongol impact on Burma where, mastering the techniques of elephant warfare, they defeated the Burmese and conquered Pagan (1287). Yet their efforts to control

ures resented by Hindus. However, more serious than religious resentments was the developing crisis in the state's political economy. Most damaging was a growth in the number of *mansabdars* far in excess of the availability of *jagirs* with which to reward them. Pressures on the peasantry increased and there was rural unrest, but the discontent of the elite proved most dangerous to the regime. The succession after Aurangzeb of weak, uninspiring men to the throne and a general decline in administrative efficiency also placed strains on the loyalty of the empire's servants, undermining

Burma through a client regime failed and the end result was to leave Burma divided for two centuries. However, the destruction of Burmese power at a time when Kampuchea was in decline facilitated the emergence of the Thais as a major power in the region.

In contrast to the fleeting impact of the Mongols, Islam became a permanent force in the Malay Peninsula and maritime Southeast Asia. The first Moslems in the area were doubtlessly traders, and the religion generally spread along the trade routes. Its fortunes were greatly increased by the growth of Malacca whose ruler is said to have been converted to Islam in 1414. Malacca, which commands the straits of the same name, became a great center of trade linking Sumatra, Java, and most of the other islands of modern Indonesia to far off China, India, and ports on the Red Sea. The city participated in a giant international commercial network whose other major center was Gujarat, birthplace of many of the Moslem missionaries who came to Southeast Asia. Islam served as a common link between Malacca and small states along the coasts of Sumatra and Java as well as ports in India and points west. It is worth noting that legends from Java, unlike those from Malaya, suggest a gradual process of conversion to Islam. Generally the diffusion of Islam was a gradual, uneven process which continued for many centuries and still continues today.

In this connection it is well to bear in mind the great vitality and powers of expansion exhibited by Islam during the fifteenth century which saw the fall of Constantinople, at the other end of Asia, in 1453. The rise of Europe to global supremacy came later. But the vanguard of European expansionism, the Portuguese, did arrive in Southeast Asia at the beginning of the sixteenth century. They seized Malacca in 1511 but were unable to maintain its commercial prominence. Instead the trade was dispersed to the benefit of, among others, the sultanates of Johor at the tip of the Malay Peninsula and of Aceh on Sumatra. The first Dutch expedition reached the East Indies in 1596; a precursor to a much more ambitious effort than that mounted by the

Europeans Arrive in Malacca

After a while there came a ship of the Franks from Goa trading to Malaka; and the Franks perceived how prosperous and well populated the port was. The people of Malaka for their part came crowding to see what the Franks looked like; and they were all astonished and said, "These are white Bengalis!" Around each Frank there would be a crowd of Malays, some of them twisting his beard, some of them fingering his head, some taking off his hat, some grasping his hand. . . .

From *Sejarah Melayu or Malay Annals* trans. by C. C. Brown (New York: Oxford Univ. Press, 1970), p. 151.

Portuguese, it initiated a new age in the history of the islands which became modern Indonesia.

THE COSMOPOLITAN CIVILIZATION OF T'ANG CHINA

China was reunified in 589 by the Sui Dynasty which laid the foundations on which the T'ang (Tang, 618–907) built one of China's most illustrious dynasties. Under the T'ang, Chinese power once again extended to the Pamirs, and the influence of Chinese culture profoundly affected distant Japan. Within China, the South was more fully integrated into the society because the rich ricelands of the lower Yangzte River were now linked to the capital in the North by the Grand Canal built by the Sui.

The central government was organized into six ministries: the Ministries of Personnel, Revenue, Rites, War, Justice, and Public Works. These ministries reflected the range of government concerns and were to be retained by subsequent regimes into the twentieth century. Staffing the government were officials of aristocratic background, for most officials entered the civil service through family connections even though a government examination system was initiated by the Sui and continued by the T'ang. Indeed, the T'ang was the last great age for the hereditary high aristocracy.

Seated court lady, sculpture of the T'ang period (618–906).

Stone relief of a horse and groom from the tomb of a T'ang emperor.

Marble guardian lion (T'ang period).

The magnificence of the T'ang was well expressed in its capital, Ch'ang-an (Changan modern Xian or Sian). Encompassing about thirty square miles, it was the largest planned city ever built anywhere. Its roughly one million inhabitants also made it the most populous city in the world in its day; another million people lived in the area outside its walls. In accord with tradition, Ch'ang-an was oriented so that both the city and the imperial palace faced south. Leading up to the palace and the government complex was an avenue five hundred feet wide, well designed to impress envoys from lesser lands with the might and grandeur of the Chinese empire. The people of the city lived in rectangular wards, each a self-contained unit surrounded by walls, with entry provided through a gate that was closed each night.

T'ang culture was doubly cosmopolitan: first, in the sense that China was open to cultural influences from India and the distant west; second, in the sense that China itself was the cultural model for the other settled societies of East Asia. Both aspects were reflected in the numerous foreigners to be found in Ch'ang-an. Some were students, including some eight thousand Koreans said to have been in Ch'ang-an in 640. Other foreigners were engaged in commerce, coming from such distant lands as India, Iran, Syria, and Arabia. At Ch'ang-an's West Market exotic foods and beverages were on sale, and one could watch performances of foreign acrobats, magicians, and actors. Stylish T'ang ladies sported foreign coiffures, while painters and potters had a good time rendering the outlandish features of the "barbarians" from distant lands. It was characteristic of the robust and cosmopolitan spirit of the age that one of the favorite pastimes of its aristocratic ladies and gentlemen was polo, a game that originated in Persia.

The participation of women in such athletic activities is worth emphasis in light of the very different ethos that was to prevail later.

Ch'ang-an was a religious as well as political center. Manichean, Nestorian, and Zoroastrian temples testified to T'ang tolerance, but their congregations were largely foreign. The opposite was true of the many Taoist and even more numerous Buddhist establishments. This was the golden age of Buddhism in China. Just as its pagodas dominated the capital's skyline, the Buddhist faith predominated on the intellectual and spiritual horizon.

In the countryside Buddhist temples performed important economic functions by operating mills and oil presses, maintaining vaults for safe-deposits, and performing other banking services including pawnbroking. The temples also held much land, and they profited from their connections with wealthy patrons who sought to evade taxation by registering land under a temple name. Some temples provided medical care; others entertainment. Architecture flourished, and Chinese Buddhist sculpture reached a classical highpoint. At their very best, T'ang sculptures blend Indian delight in the corporality of mass with a Chinese sense of essentially linear rhythm.

The T'ang was also the classic age of Chinese poetry producing a number of excellent poets including the two who came to be admired as China's very best, Li Po (Li Bo, 701–63) and Tu Fu (Du Fu, 712–70). Li Po was a free spirit who preferred to compose verse in a free style of his own rhythmic and verbal patterns. One of his favorite themes was wine, and there is even a story, most likely spurious, that on a nocturnal drinking expedition on a lake he fell into the water while trying to fish out the moon and died by drowning. Tu Fu, in contrast, was particularly effective in a style of verse governed by elaborate rules of tone and rhythm as well as verbal parallelism. He wrote on many themes but is most admired for his social conscience and compassion. Some of his most moving poems describe the suffering and hardships of ordinary people. He could be biting in his political and social commentary:

楽 涼 體 安
佳 徐 有 風
動 凄 金 無
氣 蒸 鬵
侍 景 蒸 爨
流 尤 至 之 炎

Inside the red gates wine and meat go bad;
On the roads are bones of men who died of cold.*

These lines are from a long poem Tu Fu wrote shortly before the dynasty was shaken and almost destroyed by the rebellion of An Lu-shan (An Lushan), a general stationed in the Northeast. The rebellion began in 755, only four years after the defeat of a T'ang army on the banks of the Talas River opened central

An example of Chinese calligraphy. This stone rubbing was made from an inscription in the Regular Style by Ou-Yang Hsün, a scholar and calligrapher of the T'ang period.

*Quoted in A. R. Davis, *Tu Fu* (New York: Twain, 1971), p. 46.

581	618		906		1126	1234	1368		164
Sui Dynasty	T'ang Dynasty		Disunity	Sung Dynasty	Chin Empire		Mongol Empire	Ming Dynasty	

960   1279

Asia to Islam, and it lasted until 763. Although the dynasty rallied after the defeat of An Lu-shan and made some important reforms, the general tendency was for regional military governors to assert their independence. Secular culture continued to flourish, but Emperor Wu-tsung (Wuzong, 840–46), beset by financial problems, was unable to resist the temptation posed by the wealth of the Buddhist establishment. In the resulting persecution, monastic lands and wealth were confiscated, monks and nuns returned to lay life, and Buddhist economic power was broken. The government did not concern itself with questions of belief, and the anti-Buddhist policy was promptly reversed by Wu-tsung's successor, but great damage had been done.

During its last fifty years the dynasty was beset by factionalism and the growth of eunuch power at court, mistrust between officials in the capital and those in the field, mismanagement, corruption, and incompetence. Bandit gangs, refuges of the desperately poor and dislocated, increased in number, size, and ambition. Forming themselves into confederations, they progressed from raiding to rebel-

lion. Power, whether bandit or "legitimate," went to the strong and ruthless. Even though the dynasty made occasional gains, each rally was followed by further decline. In the end, Ch'ang-an was ruined. The city which the first Han emperor had made his capital over a thousand years earlier, was never again to be China's seat of power.

The Sung Dynasty (960–1279)

China was reunited by the Sung (Song), but this dynasty never matched the T'ang in military power or geographical extent. Indeed, in the twelfth century North China was lost to the alien Juchen people, although the dynasty continued in the South for another century and a half (1127–1279). What makes this period of crucial importance is that it established some of the basic patterns of China's future. Major developments included the emergence of elite scholar-officials in place of the old hereditary aristocracy, dramatic economic growth, and the creation of a new intellectual synthesis.

The turbulence that marked the decline and fall of the T'ang destroyed many of the old aristocratic families and opened the way for a new elite which scholars have termed the "gentry." Ideally, this elite gained its prestige from literary learning, its status and power from office holding, and its wealth from land ownership. Although these attributes often did not overlap, when all three were present they reinforced each other: wealth enabled a family to educate one or more sons; education was the key to an official career; and office provided opportunities for the acquisition and retention of wealth. A local gentry also gradually developed of usually well educated families with local prominence, even though generations might pass without a member attaining office. Such families served as intermediaries be-

THE SUNG AND CHIN EMPIRES
Twelfth century

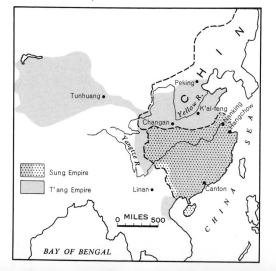

332

First portion of the oldest printed book, *The Diamond Sutra* (868). It was printed on a scroll from wooden blocks. This page gives discourses of Buddha and shows him teaching.

tween their own communities and the state.

The civil service examination system now came into its own. The examinations were open to all men, excluding only a small minority such as the sons of criminals and the like, but we may assume that most candidates came from families of some means or status. Structurally the system provided for an orderly progression through a series of written tests (three in the Sung, more later). These began at the local level, included an examination in the capital, and culminated in a palace examination held under the emperor's personal auspices. The government went to great lengths to secure impartiality; papers were identified by number and copied by clerks before being submitted to the readers who were thereby prevented from recognizing the author of a paper through his calligraphy. For centuries the battle of wits between would-be cheaters and the authorities was pursued with great ingenuity on both sides. Despite occasional scandals, the system enjoyed a deserved reputation for honesty.

In the absence of the old aristocratic counterweight, the throne gained in power, but Sung officials were by no means faceless bureaucrats. They had their own moral code and political views. Bureaucratic politics, however, tended toward factionalism. Factions could consist of men who agreed on policy matters, but they were likely to be formed around personal relationships and temporary alliances. The ultimate power of decision rested with the emperors who usually ruled by manipulating rather than intimidating their officials. The most outstanding statesman of the Sung was not an emperor but China's foremost reformer, Wang An-shih (Wang Anshi, 1021–86). Many of his measures dealt with fiscal and economic matters. He intended to help the small farmer, for instance, by establishing a program of state farm loans. Other reforms dealt with military and personnel problems. Some of his measures involved an increased use of money and thus represented a response to broader economic trends. However, his program ran into strong opposition, and Wang lost office

seven years after he had initiated the reforms.

The increased use of money, including the first appearance of paper money, was but one aspect of impressive economic growth. This included progress in paper making, book production, ceramics, tea processing, shipbuilding, and a spectacular advance in the production of coal and iron. Coal and iron were mined in North China in an arc from southern Hopei (Hebei) to northern Kiangsu (Jiangsu). Iron was also carbonized to make steel for weapons, drilling bits for digging wells, and chains used to support suspension bridges.

Because coal and iron were found in the north, production declined drastically when North China was lost to the Juchen, but advances in agriculture benefited the South. Yields were increased by the use of improved tools, advances in water control, wider application of fertilizers, and the introduction of new strains of rice, most notably an early ripening variety native to central Vietnam. In the

Detail of a handscroll showing scenes of daily life in the Southern Sung Dynasty (thirteenth century).

southeast it became common for a rice paddy to produce two crops a year, either two harvests of rice or one of rice followed by a crop of wheat or beans.

With increased production commerce flourished. Large ocean-going ships were built to carry several hundred passengers. They navigated with the aid of the compass, were steered by an axial rudder, protected by watertight bulkheads, and armed with small rockets. After the loss of the North, the government derived considerable revenue from foreign trade encouraged by maintaining harbors and canals, building breakwaters, erecting beacons, operating warehouses, and even setting up hotels. One item of export encouraged by the government was ceramics, and the discovery of Sung shards not only throughout South and Southeast Asia but also in the Middle East and along the east coast of Africa attests to the wide popularity of the Sung product.

Cities flourished; foremost among them was Hangchow (Hangzhou), the capital after the fall of the North. Its merchants, organized in guilds, offered their customers all kinds of products ranging from the staples of life to exotic perfumes and fine jewelry. Like the earlier Sung capital in the North and unlike Ch'ang-an of the T'ang, Hangchow grew haphazardly and featured all the attractions of a lively and thriving center of culture and entertainment, as well as the grimmer aspects of urban life—fire and

crime. Hangchow seems to have merited the praise it received from the cosmopolitan Venetian Marco Polo. Even though he saw the city late in the thirteenth century when it was no longer the capital, he described it as, "without doubt the finest and most splendid city in the world."

Sung intellectual and artistic life was varied and lively. This was, for instance, the classic age of landscape painting. Most influential was a revival of Confucianism that took many forms. It inspired reformers like Wang An-shih, led to a revival of classical scholarship, and stimulated new achievements in historical studies and philosophical thought. The new Confucianism was at once a creed

Detail from *Clearing Autumn Skies over Mountains and Valleys,* Sung landscape scroll attributed to Kuo Hsi (*ca.* 1020–90).

The Neo-Confucian Creed

Heaven is my father and Earth is my mother, and even such a small creature as I find an intimate place in their midst.

Therefore that which fills the universe I regard as my body and that which directs the universe I consider as my nature.

All people are my brothers and sisters, and all things are my companions.

Opening lines of "The Western Inscription" by Chang Tsai (1020–77) from *A Source Book in Chinese Philosophy,* trans. and compiled by Wing-tsit Chan (Princeton, N.J.: Princeton Univ. Press, 1963), p. 497.

581	618		906		1126	1234	1368	164
Sui Dynasty	T'ang Dynasty	Disunity	Sung Dynasty	Chin Empire	Mongol Empire		Ming Dynasty	

960   1279

that gave meaning to the life of the individual, an ideology supporting state and society, and a philosophy that provided a convincing framework for understanding the world. This constellation of values and ideas, called Neo-Confucianism in the West, was an organic system in which each aspect reinforced the others. It is called Neo-Confucianism to distinguish it from earlier forms of Confucianism, but its formulators and practitioners thought of themselves simply as Confucians. More than that, they believed that they had retrieved the true meaning of the tradition, lost since Mencius. The most influencial neo-Confucian was Chu Hsi (Zhu Xi, 1130–1200) and his most influential writings were his commentaries on the *Four Books: The Analects, The Mencius* plus *The Great Learning* and *The Doctrine of the Mean*, two chapters of the *Record of Rites* singled out by Chu Hsi.

Although influenced by Taoism and Buddhism, the Neo-Confucians rejected

Porcelain winepot of the Sung Dynasty.

the two rival doctrines as fundamentally anti-social and immoral in advocating withdrawal from society and seeking purely personal (and therefore selfish) salvation. To Confucians social values were real and compelling. Associated with Sung Neo-Confucians was an emphasis on moral seriousness and a moralism that made heavy demands on men and women. At the same time, the old concept of *jen* (*ren,* humaneness) received new emphasis.

The tone of Sung civilization was profoundly civilian, but for many years it sustained itself against external threats by maintaining a large well-equipped, if not always effective army. The Sung also entered into treaties with neighboring states that sometimes entailed payments and furthered its own interests by playing these states off against each other. After it lost the North, it survived in the South protected in part by its naval supremacy and the difficulty northern cavalry had in operating in the south with its paddies and waterways. Even after the Mongols conquered North China in 1234, the Sung held out another forty-five years before succumbing to the formidable world conquerors.

The Mongol Yuan Dynasty (1279–1368)

Even before Khublai Khan (r. 1260–94) completed the conquest of China, he transferred his capital from Mongolia to Peking (Beijing), adopted the Chinese name "Yuan" for his state, and also instituted Chinese court ceremonial. Thus he was careful to give at least an appearance of ruling in the Chinese manner. But his ambitions were not limited to China; we already noted his expeditions to Southeast Asia and to these must be added naval expeditions to Japan. To the west, he maintained control of Mongolia but was forced to give up any ambition to control central Asia. As a result, the

336

Yuan was essentially a Mongol regime in China, not the Chinese part of a wider Mongol empire.

To prevent dependence on Chinese officials, the Mongols made a point of employing foreigners, mostly central Asians although the most famous is Marco Polo. The Mongols accorded highest status to Mongols. Next came Mongol allies including central Asians and men from the Near East, such as Turks, Persians, and Syrians. The third status group included inhabitants of North China, the native Chinese or descendants of other groups such as the Juchen. At the bottom were the southerners who had resisted the Mongols longest and continued to be regarded with suspicion. This fourfold division of society was expressed in the recruitment and appointment of officials, in the conduct of legal cases, and in taxation.

The Yuan generally accorded military officials preference over civilians, and the provinces had a great deal of autonomy. Since the Mongols were slow to reinstitute the examination system and to patronize scholarly learning, men who in other periods would have become scholars turned to other occupations such as medicine, fortune-telling, and the theater. It is no accident that this was the classic age of Chinese drama. Painting also flourished; the idea that a painting reveals the character of the man who created it was already found in the Sung, but it was prevalent under the Yuan and inspired work in a great variety of styles. It is worth noting that even though China was once again open to foreign influences and hospitable to travelers from afar, this had no appreciable impact on the world of the scholar-painter nor was there any awareness, let alone appreciation, of the art of the Chinese literati to be found in the writings of Marco Polo and his successors. Although there was a Catholic archbiship in Peking and relations across the great Eurasian land mass were often cordial, these relations had a low priority on both sides of the world, for the distances were enormous and both Europe and China faced more immediate challenges and opportunities closer to home.

The Ming Dynasty (1368–1644)

The declining years of the Yuan saw the emergence of regional power centers and popular rebellion. One leader of rebellion, Chu Yuan-chang (Zhu Yuanzhang, r. 1368–98), emerged victorious and founded the Ming Dynasty. He was a harsh and vigorous autocrat who personally decided all significant matters and even some not so significant. During the later days of the Ming too the effectiveness as well as tone of government was to a large degree determined by the character of the emperors and their devotion to the work of government. Ming government thus ranged from the energetic efficiency of the first two emperors to the laxity of some of the Late Ming rulers, one of whom did not hold an audience for over twenty-five years.

Meanwhile the local gentry presided over local society that continued to move to its own rhythms. Prominent gentry lineages maintained cohesion by compiling lineage geneologies, maintaining

Marco Polo Describes Chinese Paper Money

ca. 1275

When ready for use, it [a specially prepared paper] is cut into pieces of money of different sizes, nearly square, but somewhat longer than they are wide. . . . The coinage of this paper money is authenticated with as much form and ceremony as if it were actually of pure gold or silver, for to each note a number of officers, specially appointed, not only subscribe their names, but affix their signets also; and when this has been done . . . the principal officer, deputed by his majesty, having dipped into vermilion the royal seal committed to his custody, stamps with it the piece of paper, so that the form of the seal remains impressed upon it, by which it receives full authenticity as current money, and the act of counterfeiting it is punished with death. When thus coined in large quantities, this paper currency is circulated in every part of the grand khan's domains, nor dares any person, at the peril of his life, refuse to accept it in payment. All his subjects receive it without hesitation, because, wherever their business may call them, they can dispose of it again in the purchase of merchandise they may have occasion for, such as pearls, jewels, gold, or silver.

From *The Travels of Marco Polo* (New York and London: Everyman's Library, 1950), p. 203.

THE MING EMPIRE
Fourteenth to seventeenth centuries

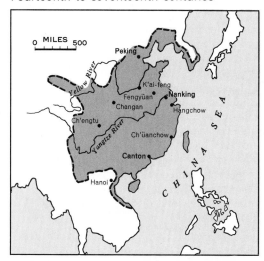

ancestral halls and graveyards, conducting ceremonial sacrifices to lineage ancestors, and maintaining general guides for the conduct of lineage members as well as formal lineage rules. A penalty for severe infractions of these rules was expulsion from the family.

The Ming was generally a period of economic growth and considerable prosperity. It was also capable of strong military assertiveness; from 1405 to 1433 seven great maritime expeditions, commanded by a Muslim eunuch, were launched to Southeast Asia but also reached the Indian Ocean, Arabia, and the east coast of Africa. These expeditions illustrate Chinese strength in the fifteenth century, but, an economic drain, they were discontinued leaving it to the Europeans to take the lead in world navigation and discovery.

Printing, which had been invented in the Late T'ang and spread during the Sung, continued to expand in the Ming and with it there was an increase in literacy. Bookshops did a brisk business; among their best sellers were collections of model examination papers used by candidates to cram for their tests. But they also sold encyclopedias, colored prints, novels, and collections of short stories. There were also guides explaining the classics in simple language and books of moral instruction. Most prized by those who love Chinese literature are the Ming novels. Despite their literary excellence, they did not win respectability until the twentieth century. In traditional China reading a novel was a surreptitious pleasure, something students did when their teacher was not looking—or vice versa.

This period also made notable contributions to drama, painting, and ceramics, and Neo-Confucian thought also flourished. Wang Yang-ming (1472–1529) stands second only to Chu Hsi in influence and importance. He insisted on the importance of inwardness and is also famed for his doctrine of the unity of knowledge and action. For Wang, knowing and acting are not only inseparable, they are two dimensions of a single process.

The Late Ming was an exciting time intellectually and artistically, but it was also a period of political decay that took a heavy toll in government efficiency and finally led to its collapse. It was brought down by popular uprisings, but the real heirs of the dynasty were not Chinese rebels but Manchu leaders in the area Northeast of China who were in the process of constructing a state in the Chinese manner. They established China's last dynasty, the Ch'ing (Qing, 1644–1911) which sought and won legitimization by ruling in a Chinese manner and continuing many Ming institutions while preserving special privileges for the Manchu elite.

Both the Ming and the Ch'ing were much more concerned with China's Inner Asian frontiers, home of the Mongol and other nomadic invaders, than they were with European maritime expansionism. Indeed, it was under the Ch'ing that China reached its greatest territorial extent. As elsewhere, the first Europeans to arrive in Chinese waters were the Portuguese whom the Chinese kept at arms length since they could not drive them off. In 1557 they were allowed to use Macao in return for an annual payment. Of more interest to the Chinese court and officials were Jesuit missionaries who brought with them European science and technology as well as religion. By demonstrating the superiority of their astronomical predictions, they managed to displace Moslem and Chinese experts and established themselves in the Bureau of Astronomy, an important and prestigious office. The Jesuits even made some notable converts and were not seriously affected by the change of dynasties.

However, they were there on Chinese terms, and the mission petered out in the middle of the eighteenth century when an impasse developed between the Ch'ing emperor and the pope.

Porcelain jar of the Ming period showing ladies playing a game of *go*.

The Silver Pavillion at Kyoto combining both Japanese and Chinese elements.

JAPAN

A major theme in Japanese history is the interplay between native and imported elements. In Japan's early history, culminating in the Nara Period (710–84) Chinese influence was enormous. Nara itself, Japan's first capital, was a miniature Ch'ang-an; the court and political structure were modeled on those of China; writing, Buddhism, and Confucian moral values were among the Chinese imports. Yet Japan never became just a smaller China. Here geography helped, for, while close enough to the continent to receive its influences, Japan was far enough away not to be dominated by it. Other factors too made for the integrity of Japanese culture including a language completely different from and unrelated to Chinese, a strong native animistic religion (Shinto), and a very special aesthetic tradition. Furthermore, even during the Nara period, the Japanese state and society had their own character.

One difference between Japan and China was the role of the emperor. The Japanese emperor, unlike his Chinese counterpart, had an irrevocable sacred mandate based on divine descent. Thus, the Mencian idea that the mandate could be lost was disregarded. Political change in Japan took the form, not of deposing the emperor, but of controlling him; after the Nara period the emperor retained his religious aura and his powers of legitimization without any real political authority. In somewhat similar fashion, descent remained a major source of status in Japan which never adopted the Chinese examination system.

The Nara period was followed by the Heian period (794–1185) when the capital was established in Kyoto and many Chinese imports were modified or discarded. Now, although Chinese remained the official written language, Japanese was written without depending solely on Chinese characters to render Japanese sounds. Instead, linguistic elements without Chinese equivalents were written in a syllabary (*kana*) with Chinese characters retained for nouns and the stems of words and adjectives to avoid confusion between homonyms. Art and architecture also departed from the international T'ang style of the Nara period and became more Japanese in their concern with the texture of natural materials, especially wood, and a general penchant for asymmetry.

This period was famed for its aristocratic culture when noble gentlemen and ladies devoted their lives to beauty and love. One product of this culture was the world's first major psychological novel, *The Tale of Genji*, written by Lady Murasaki. Prince Genji had perfect taste, wrote a beautiful hand, was exquisitely graceful, and ever sensitive to the beauty and sadness of nature's changing moods as he was responsive to the delicate emotions of his many ladies. What he lacked were the martial virtues of the warrior.

The Kamakura (1185–1333) and Ashikaga (1336–1573) Shogunates

During the Kamakura period the warrior class emerged and gradually occupied center stage. While there had earlier been a provincial warrior aristocracy, these men had been willing to serve civilian masters until the Heian system broke down and warriors were called in to the capital to help settle a political

dispute. After some years of turmoil, there emerged a peculiarly Japanese institution: the shogunate. The shogun derived his military power from the loyalty of vassals in an essentially feudal system but received his title and legitimacy from the emperor. In theory he was the emperor's supreme military commander, but in practice he controlled the emperor.

The first shogunate got its name from Kamakura, a village in eastern Japan far away from the imperial court in Kyoto. The choice to keep warriors away from the charms of the imperial capital was a deliberate attempt to preserve the values of the warrior: valor, manly pride, vigor, and undying loyalty. Yet such loyalty had to be rewarded. This was easily accomplished when the shogunate was fighting recalcitrant Japanese, but there were no spoils when Mongol attacks were defeated in 1271 and 1284 and this was followed by the need to maintain a force for many years in anticipation of a third Mongol attack which never came.

The Kamakura shogunate was followed by that of the Ashikaga family who established themselves in Kyoto. In many respects but particularly in culture the ensuing period represented a fusion of aristocratic and samurai traditions. There was a great cultural flowering, for this was the age of the Nō drama, of tea masters and Zen aesthetics, of excellent pottery, of the classic Japanese garden, and of fine architecture drawing on Sung as well as on native Japanese forms. However, politically the Ashikaga period degenerated into a century of warfare (1467–1573) followed by a shorter period (1573–1600) of unification and ended with the establishment of the last and strongest shogunate.

The Tokugawa Shogunate (1600–1868)

Under the Tokugawa the shogunate was once more separated from the imperial court in Kyoto. The shogun's capital was Edo, the old name for Tokyo. There the shogunate's officials kept a close watch over regional lords who were burdened with new obligations—including an obligation to spend alternate years in Edo and leave wives and children behind as hostages when they did go back to their domains. Yet within these domains the local lords were free to pursue their own administrative and economic policies.

A number of Tokugawa policies were meant to ensure a stable future. Thus there was a freezing of class lines with a clear line drawn between samurai and commoners. The most visible sign of samurai privilege was the exclusive right to wear a sword, yet in a time of peace his duties were largely civilian. Accordingly, the samurai were sent to school to attain at least a degree of Chinese learning, and the shogunate patronized Neo-Confucianism as a philosophy appropriate for the new age.

Intent on stability, the Tokugawa shogunate was not about to tolerate interference from abroad. Originally Portuguese ships and Jesuit missionaries had been warmly received in Japan, but this changed as Japanese leaders became aware not only of the dangers of European expansionism as exemplified by the Spanish seizure of the Philippines but also of the subversive potential of foreign influence. In 1606 Christianity was declared illegal, and in 1614 there was a serious campaign to expel missionaries. Many of the 300,000 Japanese Christians suffered grievously under Tokugawa persecution. In 1637–38 a rebellion in Shimabara, near Nagasaki, was fought under Christian slogans against a lord who combined merciless taxation with cruel religious suppression. Furthermore, trade as well as Christianity was seen as potentially subversive since it would benefit the maritime lords. Consequently, the Tokugawa prohibited not only the foreign religion but expelled all foreigners from the country and only allowed the Dutch to send an annual vessel to a tiny artificial island in Nagasaki harbor. Moreover, Japanese were prohibited from traveling abroad.

In the long run, of course, the Tokugawa shogunate did not achieve the stability envisioned by its architects. They, no more than anyone else, could stop change. Indeed, their very success in ensuring peace and tranquility led to unprecedented economic growth. Cities such as Edo and Osaka grew and developed their own distinct urban culture. An increased use of money and a new economy baffled the samurai and undermined the social and political order. By the middle of the nineteenth century, many felt that Japan was ripe for a change.

However, in the seventeenth century it would have taken superhuman clairvoyance for a statesman in Japan, China, or India to realize that European civilization represented anything but a minor problem. In all three countries, leaders could look back on traditions that had withstood the test of time and contemplate the future with confidence. Little could they know that the future was to bring radically new challenges.

Interior of a house in Yoshiwara during the Tokugawa period (eighteenth century woodcut print).

Suggestions for Further Reading

Note: Asterisk denotes a book available in paperback edition.

General For a comparative perspective on the developments discussed in this chapter see Edward L. Farmer, et al, *Comparative History of Civilizations in Asia*, 2 vols. (1977), also William H. McNeill, *The Rise of the West** (1963).

India For general works see the suggestions in Chapter 6. A major advanced analytical study is Burton Stein, *Peasant, State, and Society in Medieval South India* (1980). Two highly regarded books deal with Islam in India: Aziz Ahmad, *Studies in Islamic Culture in the Indian Environment* (1964) and Sheikh Mohamad Ikram, *Muslim Civilization in India* (1964). A more specialized study is Richard M. Eaton, *Sufis of Bijapur 1300–1700: Social Roles of Sufis in Medieval India* (1978). Percival Spear, "The Mughul Mansabdari System," in Edmund Leach and S. N. Mukherjee, *Elites in South Asia* (1970) is a concise account of that complicated system. M. N. Pearson, *Merchants and Rulers in Gujarat: The Response to the Portuguese in the Sixteenth Century* (1976) offers important insights into India under the Mughuls.

Southeast Asia D. G. E. Hall, *A History of South-East Asia* (4th ed. 1981) is authoritative. Clifford Geertz, *Negara: The Theatre State in Nineteenth Century Bali** (1980) is helpful in thinking about earlier Indianized states of Southeast Asia. Richard Winstedt, *The Malays: A Cultural History* (1950) is a standard treatment. *Sejarah Melayu 'Malay Annals'** (1970) trans. by C. C. Brown is sometimes tedious but also includes passages of great charm. M. C. Ricklefs, *A History of Modern Indonesia c. 1300 to the Present* (1981) is a solid account.

China *The Cambridge History of China*, Vol. 3, *Sui and T'ang China, 589–906* (1979) edited by Denis Twitchett is a major work. Also recommended are Arthur F. Wright, *The Sui Dynasty** (1978), Wright and Twitchett, *Perspectives on the T'ang** (1973), Edwin O. Reischauer, *Ennin's Travels in T'ang China* (1955), and Arthur Cooper *Li Po and Tu Fu** (1973). Good books on the Sung include James T. C. Liu, *Reform in Sung China: Wang An-shih (1021–1086) and His New Policies* (1959); Jaques Gernet, *Daily Life in China on the Eve of the Mongol Invasion** (1962); Shiba (Yoshinobu) *Commerce and Society in Sung China** (1970) trans. by Mark Elvin; and Brian McKnight, *Village and Bureaucracy in Southern Sung China* (1971). For the Yuan see John W. Dardess, *Conquerors and Confucians: Aspects of Political Change in Late Yüan China* (1973) and John D. Langlois ed., *China under Mongol Rule** (1981). Also see R. E. Latham, trans. *The Travels of Marco Polo** (1958). A succinct and definite account is Charles O. Hucker, *The Traditional Chinese State in Ming Times* (1961). Hucker is also the editor of *Chinese Government in Ming Times: Seven Studies* (1969). For a fascinating account of a major Ch'ing emperor see Jonathan Spence, *Emperor of China: Self-Portrait of K'ang-Hsi** (1974). There is a growing literature in English on Neo-Confucianism. A good place to begin is Wm. Theodore de Bary, *Neo-Confucian Orthodoxy and the Learning of the Mind-and-Heart* (1981). An important institution is treated in *China's Examination Hell: The Civil Service Examinations of Imperial China** (1976) by I. Miyazaki, trans. by Conrad Schirokauer.

Japan For a general history of Japan particularly good on institutional history see John W. Hall, *Japan from Prehistory to Modern Times** (1970). This can be used in conjunction with H. Paul Varley, *Japanese Culture: A Short History** (1973). A fascinating evocation of the life of the Heian aristocracy is provided by Ivan Morris, *The World of the Shining Prince** (1964). For the Ashikaga period see John W. Hall and Toyoda Takeshi, eds. *Japan in the Muromachi Age** (1977). Ryusaku Tsunoda et al, *Sources of Japanese Tradition** (1958) is a valuable anthology for Japanese intellectual history in general. For Tokugawa politics see Harold Bolitho, *Treasures Among Men: The Fudai Daimyo in Tokugawa Japan* (1974) and Conrad Totman, *Politics in the Tokugawa Bakufu, 1600–1843* (1967). An important study of social history is *Education in Tokugawa Japan* (1965) by Ronald P. Dore.

Contacts with Europe C. R. Boxer, *The Christian Century in Japan* (1951) is well-written and informative. Also see George Elison, *Deus Destroyed: the Image of Christianity in Early Modern Japan* (1973). Recommended for China is L. J. Gallagher, trans. *China in the Sixteenth Century: the Journals of Matteo Ricci* (1953).

16 The Revival of Europe

During the course of the fourteenth century economic depression, plague, and war had weakened western Europe. Secular rulers, who in 1300 had seemed close to establishing absolute monarchies, had lost much of their power over the privileged classes and thus much of their ability to maintain law and order. The prestige of the Church had declined during the Babylonian Captivity and the Great Schism. Most men believed in monarchy as the best form of government; almost all believed in the Church as the only source of salvation. But with both these traditional authorities functioning badly, there seemed to be little hope for religious reform or a revival of security and prosperity. Everyone desired peace, a healing of the schism in the Church, better government, and increased production and trade. But there was little agreement on where to begin, and none of the many projects for reform was very successful.

By the end of the fifteenth century, a startling change had taken place. The economic depression had ended; new industries at home and new trade routes overseas had opened up new opportunities and created new wealth. Kings and princes had clearly gained the upper hand over the privileged classes, especially in France, Spain, and England. The papal schism was ended, and Rome was once more the capital of Western Christendom. New forms of learning based on an intensive study of the classics were competing with or modifying older stud-

ies. New forms of art were challenging the late Gothic style. Most important, there was a note of optimism and confidence, of excitement and enjoyment. There was talk of a "new age" dawning, a "dark age" past, a rebirth of the best qualities of classical civilization. By 1500 the basic characteristics of our "modern" world were becoming visible: its dynamic economy and fluid society, its sovereign nation-states and international anarchy, its secular ideals, and its intellectual and moral values.

We can now see that the political and economic revival of Europe was led by the north, while intellectual, literary, and artistic innovations were largely the work of Italy. But this sharing of responsibilities was less obvious in the fifteenth century than it was later, and in the transition from the medieval to the modern world the Italians had the great advantage of being the first to realize that a transition was taking place. They were the ones who talked of a new age, of a break with the barbarous past; they were the ones who believed that a new civilization could be created that would be a worthy heir of Greece and Rome. As a result, in the two centuries between the death of Dante (1321) and the sack of Rome by mutinous imperial troops (1527), Italy exerted increasing influence over the rest of Europe. Italians set the style in architecture, sculpture, and painting; they dictated the literary taste that Europe was to follow for generations. By combining the old ideal of the

Opposite: Donatello, equestrian statue of the Venetian *condottiere* Erasmo di Nardi, who was called Gattamelata (*ca.* 1445–50), in the Piazza del Santo, Padua.

chivalric, courtly knight with their own interest in learning, they developed a genuinely new social ideal, that of "the gentleman," and the educational ideal of a "liberal education." Italy was the school of Europe. Northerners flocked there by the thousands, and Italians, in turn, appeared in every northern court, even in remote Muscovy.

There were several reasons for Italy's leadership in the change from medieval to early modern ways of life. Italy had always been somewhat different from the rest of Europe during the Middle Ages. It was never completely feudalized, and it early rejected most feudal institutions. It rejected a unified monarchy under the German emperor even more decisively.

Scholasticism never dominated Italian thinking, nor did the Gothic style ever dominate Italian art. Since the medieval tradition in Italy was weak, it could easily be rejected. Moreover the Italian cities had great wealth, large populations, and complete independence. When they tried new experiments in art, literature, and politics, they became powerful instruments of social change.

THE CITY-STATES OF NORTHERN ITALY

The northern Italian cities were dominated by international trade. A third of the population of Florence lived by im-

A Renaissance prince and his wife: Giovanni Bentivoglio, lord of Bologna, and Ginevra Bentivoglio (details from paintings by Ercole Roberti, *ca.* 1480).

porting wool from agricultural countries and selling finished cloth all over Europe and the Levant. Almost all the population of Venice depended directly or indirectly on trade in Oriental goods such as silk and spices. In such communities, capitalists—the banker, the export merchant, the large-scale manufacturer—were the most important figures.

The Italian towns controlled the countryside around them as most northern European towns did not. They had broken the power of the landed nobility and had absorbed the defeated class into their own communities. Peasant villages and small market towns had been annexed by large urban centers. Thus city-states were created—that is, a strong city government controlled not only its own immediate area but hundreds of square miles of rural territory.

There were sharp differences among the people of these city-states. Obviously there were differences in wealth, from the international merchants and bankers—the *popolo grasso*, or "fat people"—through the craftsmen, shopkeepers, and all the lesser bourgeoisie—the *popolo minuto*, or "little people"—down to the growing proletariat of wage workers, and the peasants living outside the city walls. But Italian urban politics cannot be explained in terms of a class struggle. The wealthy men did not stick together. By and large the old rich disliked the new rich, but one old family might dislike another old family even more than it did an upstart neighbor. Men with common interests and ambitions formed political groups that cut across all class lines. The basic rules of the game were to build up the group through alliances among influential families, to gain support among middle and lower income groups through granting protection and political favors, to find a plausible slogan (usually no more complicated than "throw the rascals out!"), and then to stage a *coup d'état* or a revolution. Sometimes there was merely a change in the holders of the principal offices; sometimes there was a fairly drastic revision of the town constitution to ensure the perpetuation of the new dominant oligarchical group; very rarely, as in Florence in 1378, the lower classes demanded, and got, some social and economic reforms. Such reforms

were not only infrequent, they were also short lived.

During the fourteenth century few Italian towns went as long as thirty years without a *coup d'état*. This instability caused material damage and forced many useful citizens into exile (the most eminent example was Dante). Thus when an able man, backed by a strong coalition, gained power (often by perfectly constitutional means) and tried to put an end to political turbulence, his advent was usually accepted with some relief. Some of these leaders were at first not much more than military dictators (for example, the Sforza in Milan). Some of them were primarily very capable political bosses (for example, the Medici in Florence). They allowed no opposition; those who turned against them were eliminated by exile, imprisonment, or execution. On the other hand, these "despots," as they were eventually called, were usually careful to improve the city's public works, strengthen its defenses, devise efficient systems of taxation, and tighten internal security. By and large these programs were helpful to business, but one can hardly say that the despots were principally concerned with the welfare of the business community. They were wise enough to see that their power depended on attention to the common welfare. In return, they could spend much of the money derived from the fruits of restored political stability on "glory" (wars with their neighbors) and "splendor" (buildings and works of art). One should note, however, that Venice, the most prosperous Italian town, had no despot, and yet was just as warlike and just as lavish in expenditures on art as its neighbor, Milan, which is often taken as the typical example of despotism.

War and Diplomacy

Oligarchs and despots realized that the merchants and shopkeepers disliked military service and that armed subjects might easily turn against their rulers. Therefore they replaced citizen militias, which had never been very effective, with mercenary troops called *condottieri*. These soldiers were well trained and fairly reliable—as long as they were paid. In a pinch, however, their first loyalty was to their generals rather than to their employers. Moreover, as time went on, the generals sought to preserve their military assets by winning wars through clever maneuvers and negotiations rather than by pitched battles. But while they did not fight very much, they did have a monopoly of military power, and some generals displaced weak despots or divided city governments and became despots themselves.

What distinguished northern Italy most sharply from the rest of Europe was the total independence of its city-states from any central government. From Venice, oldest and proudest of the city-states, on down to towns of a few thousand inhabitants, city governments acted as if they were subject to no superior power. Motivated by economic and political self-interest, each city-state engaged in endless wars, making and breaking alliances, and jealously watching the most powerful state of the moment to make sure that it did not become strong enough to conquer the peninsula. Early in the fifteenth century the Italian city-states began to maintain resident ambassadors at the courts of foreign states to keep rulers in constant touch with governments that might one day become either useful allies or dangerous enemies.

In the second half of the century, a kind of "balance of power" began to operate among the five leading states in Italy—Venice, Milan, Florence, the Papal States, and the Kingdom of Naples—in response to an unwritten (and perhaps instinctive) understanding that no one of the five must be allowed to gain enough power to threaten the others. When France and Spain intervened in Italy at the close of the fifteenth century, both these practices—the basic machinery of modern diplomacy and the balancing of power among a group of sovereign states—spread to the larger stage of Europe. By the mid-sixteenth century, resident ambassadors were common throughout central and western Europe, and a rough balance of power had been established between the ruling dynasties of the two most powerful states, France and Spain.

Milan, Venice, and Florence

Behind these generalizations lie the striking variety and individuality of the Italian cities of this era. Milan, the largest city of the Po Valley, was perhaps the most typical. It submitted early to a despot, and about 1400 a Milanese ruler, Gian Galeazzo Visconti, came as close as any strong man of the time to eliminating

THE ITALIAN CITY-STATES   1454

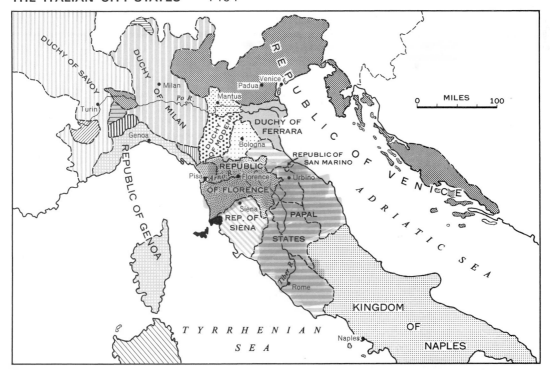

The rise of the Medici: Cosimo de' Medici has the look of the wily businessman, while his grandson Lorenzo appears every inch the prince. Above: Cosimo, detail from a fresco by Gozzoli. Below: Lorenzo, by an unknown artist.

his rivals and uniting northern Italy. He failed, but the fear he inspired persisted, and no other despot managed to come so close to dominating northern Italy. On the other hand, he did make Milan one of the leading manufacturing and trading towns of the peninsula, and he encouraged improvements in agriculture, which is more than some of his rivals did.

Venice, the greatest commercial power of the peninsula, was absorbed in its widespread Mediterranean interests and was relatively isolated from Italian politics until it began to acquire territory on the mainland in the fifteenth century. Its republican constitution was the oldest and its government the most stable in Italy. There was no despot in Venice—the doge, or duke, was a figurehead—but a tight-knit commercial aristocracy ran the city through a small and tough-minded executive committee, the Council of Ten. Perhaps because the energies of the whole population were so absorbed in commerce, there were no real revolutions and few conspiracies in Venetian history. The constitution of the "most serene republic" (the official title of Venice) stood as a model of republican stability to other Italians.

Florence, like Venice, was proud of being a republic among the welter of despotisms and was especially proud of having helped to frustrate Gian Galeazzo Visconti's attempt to snuff out republican liberties in Italy. But in every other respect Florence and Venice were unalike. Venice lived primarily by commerce; Florence primarily by banking and industry. The most astute bankers and the finest textiles in Europe were both to be found in Florence. The energies of Venetians were directed outward toward the sea; the energies of Florentines were focused on industry and politics within Tuscany. Venetian society and Venetian government exhibited a high degree of stability, whereas nothing seemed stable in Florence. Political intrigues were a constant problem, and changes in the constitution were frequent.

During the fourteenth and early fifteenth centuries the Florentines tried to solve their political problems by riots, by changes in electoral procedures and in governmental structure, and even by calling in outside mediators (who usually did more harm than good). In the end, the Florentines settled for boss rule. In 1434 a new-rich party within the oligarchy, led by one of the city's wealthiest and shrewdest bankers, Cosimo dé Medici, gained power. For almost sixty years Cosimo, his son Piero, and his grandson Lorenzo the Magnificent (d. 1492), ran the city by seeing that their candidates won elections, and by tinkering with the republican constitution. Cosimo was a banker who had been forced to play politics in order to save his financial interests. Lorenzo was more of a politician, little concerned with the family banking business. But each devoted his energy, his money, and his taste to the job of protecting, expanding, and beautifying the city. The most glittering example of Italy's golden age was Florence under the Medici.

ITALIAN URBAN CIVILIZATION

In these busy, crowded cities of northern Italy the structure of society and the ideals of the upper classes had to be modified. There had been a good deal of upward mobility during the fourteenth and early fifteenth centuries, and a new aristocracy was being formed—an aristocracy that included both descendants of old landed families who had prospered in the cities and wealthy merchants and bankers. The Medici, for example, had not been feudal lords, yet they eventually became dukes and married their daughters to kings of France. In the smaller towns, on the other hand, the despot was often a member of the old nobility who had learned how to deal successfully with urban problems. The situation was complicated by the growing prominence and wealth of writers, artists, and scholars. Most of these men did not, and never would, belong to the aristocracy, but their services and talents were necessary for the adornment of aristocratic life and their ideas of beauty, good taste, right behavior, and sound learning were accepted by the aristocracy. Finally, the aristocracy had to pay some attention to economic problems—problems far more complicated than those of managing landed estates. Communities dependent on continental markets and faced with sharp competition from their neighbors produced revenues that varied sharply from year to year. Frequent wars could bring even prosperous towns to the edge of bankruptucy. Loans had to be floated and new taxes devised. The oldest and most stable of the Italian aristocracies, that of Venice, was very skillful in managing its economic affairs; others were less successful.

The new ideal of the Italian aristocracies was a combination of old feudal-chivalric values and new urban-cultural values. It might be expressed as the ideal of the cultivated gentleman. A famous sixteenth-century book by Baldassare Castiglione, *The Courtier*, summed up this ideal. The courtier has all the chivalric virtures—physical dexterity, courage, skill in combat, courtesy—and all the new virtues—knowledge of the classics, appreciation of art and literature, eloquence, and good taste. Above all, he has grace; he excels in each activity without visible effort.

But besides the aristocrats there were the self-made men—not many, it is true, but just for that reason conspicuous. There was the *condottieri* general Sforza, who made himself ruler of Milan; the low-born artists, such as Leonardo da Vinci; the famous scholars, such as Lorenzo Valla; even a pope (Pius II) who may have had noble ancestors but who made his reputation as a scholar. How could these people be fitted into a common scheme? The answer was that they were men of *virtù*. This was the quality that made a man a free man (Latin, *vir*). It meant more than "virtue" in the modern sense; it also meant "virtuosity," that combination of genius and determination that made for greatness in statesmanship, artistic creation, or literature. In fact, by the time of Machiavelli, the word *virtù* was losing its moral connotation, and simply meant the qualities that led to success.

Individualism

At the upper levels of this society, there was growing individualism. Few of the old authorities carried the weight they had once carried for the aristocrat or highly talented city dweller. If his local government oppressed him, he could always move to another city. Many painters and sculptors were members of gilds, but gild regulations could not control their work. Scholars did not need university appointments in order to concentrate on their work, nor were they dependent on a single patron; a well-known writer could draw subsidies from many sources. And although the Italians considered themselves good Christians, they had little respect for the pronouncements of the clergy and accepted clerical rulings only when they were backed by strong ecclesiastical sanctions.

Thus for the upper classes and the cultural leaders there was a new emphasis on man as a private person, mainly concerned with himself, his own immediate family, his friends, and his own self-development. Such individualism sometimes went to extremes, as it did in the case of Benvenuto Cellini (1500–71), a sculptor and goldsmith who described his violent and colorful career in a famous *Autobiography*. Cellini assumed

A Man of Virtù

Benvenuto Cellini, a Florentine goldsmith and sculptor, had struck medals and coins for Pope Clement VII (1523–34). He claimed that he had been insulted by a jeweler named Pompeo (who also worked for the pope), and after several quarrels, Cellini stabbed Pompeo to death in a street brawl. Clement VII had just died; Cardinal Farnese was elected pope on October 13, 1534, and took the name of Paul III.

After he had put affairs of greater consequence in order, the new Pope sent for me, saying that he did not wish any one else to strike his coins. To these words of his Holiness one of his gentlemen named Latino Juvinale [a Humanist] answered that I [Cellini] was in hiding for the murder of Pompeo of Milan, and set forth what could be argued for my justification in the most favorable terms. The Pope replied: "I know nothing of Pompeo's death but plenty of Benvenuto's provocation, so let a safe-conduct be at once made out for him." A great friend of Pompeo's was there; he was a Milanese called Ambrogio [Ambrogio Recalcati, a papal secretary]. This man said: "In the first days of your papacy it is not well to grant pardons of this kind." The Pope answered: "You know less about such matters than I do. Know then that men like Benvenuto, unique in their profession, stand above the law."

From Benvenuto Cellini, *The Life of Benvenuto Cellini*, trans. by John Addington Symonds (New York: Scribner's, 1926), p. 144.

Minters making silver thalers (from which comes our word *dollar*). A heated metal disk has been placed on top of the die, another die has been placed on top of the disk, and the minter is striking the top die with an iron mallet (detail from the Miners' Altar by Hans Hesse, Church of St. Anne, Annaberg, Saxony).

that the ordinary laws of morality were made for ordinary people and that they neither could nor should be enforced in the case of geniuses like himself. He also assumed that autobiography, a literary form that had been very rare in the Middle Ages, was a natural form of expression and one that would find eager readers. He begins his book: "All men of whatsoever quality they be, who have done anything of excellence, . . . ought to describe their life with their own hand." Later he remarks, "I make no profession of writing history. It is enough for me to occupy myself with my own affairs." Cellini was obviously interesting to himself, and he was sure he was interesting to others.

Secularism

The second mark of this new society was its predominantly secular tone. This does not mean that it was pagan or anti-Christian. It means that the things of this world increasingly occupied the time and attention of the Italian townspeople—the balance of profit and loss, well-built

houses and fine clothes, rich food and drink, and enjoyment of leisure—and that the ascetic and otherworldly ideals of the medieval Church seemed more and more remote to them. Their tastes and attitudes are already evident in the ribald stories of Boccaccio's popular *Decameron* (*ca.* 1350). The heroes and heroines are not exactly irreligious or critical of Christian ideals, but they despise the hypocrisy of priests and monks, and they rejoice in the triumph of clever people of the world over clerical busybodies.

The secularism of Italian society can thus be broken down into two components: preoccupation with worldly pursuits, and contempt for those who professed the ascetic ideal but did not live up to it. There were a few pagans or atheists. But most men simply thought more constantly of this world than of the next, without denying the ultimate importance of the next. There was a latent conflict between the older and the new ideals. This conflict troubled many writers and artists even in the most worldly cities, such as Florence. In fact, tension between worldly and otherworldly ideals was more typical of the period than was the frank and untroubled enjoyment of temporal pleasures.

Humanism

The third mark of Italian urban society was its enthusiasm for classical antiquity. The men most deeply concerned with the classics were called Humanists— from the Latin *humanitas*, as used by Cicero to describe the literary culture proper to a well-bred man. The Middle Ages had always lived in the shadow of Rome, and interest in classical literature was nothing new. John of Salisbury in the twelfth century had a first-rate knowledge of Latin literature, and the greatest medieval poet, Dante, made it his conscious concern to blend the best of both classical and Christian ideals throughout the *Divine Comedy*. However, Francesco Petrarca, or Petrarch (1304–74), is rightly called the father of a new Humanism. His enthusiasm for Cicero, his admiration for Rome (he said he wished he had been born in the ancient world instead of his own), and his feel for the style of classical Latin were contagious. He loved the classics for their own sake, not only because they could be used to explain the language of the early Church Fathers but also because he believed that they taught the central ethical values later embodied in Christianity. Within a generation or two after his death Petrarch's followers were busily discovering classical manuscripts in monastic libraries, writing letters to one another in impeccable Ciceronian Latin, pouring contempt on the Latin style of medieval scholastic philosophers, and, most important, getting jobs as secretaries at the papal Curia and the courts of the despots, or as teachers of the children of the ruling classes in the cities.

These professional Humanists were something new in European society. Generally they were laymen who made a living by their learning, not clerics or monks devoting spare time to classical study. They were self-made men who were peddling a new type of scholarship to their contemporaries—and who found the market very good. Enthusiasm for the classics was heightened after 1395, when refugee scholars from the Byzantine Empire began to teach Greek to eager students in Florence and elsewhere. And by the end of the fifteenth century a few Italians were even beginning to learn Hebrew and Arabic. Humanism was both a scholarly movement and a social fad. The Humanists revived the study of classical Latin, Greek, and Hebrew, and they got the ruling classes of the Italian cities excited about what they were doing.

The Humanists initiated a revolution in educational theory and practice. Formal education in the Middle Ages had been dominated by the clergy and directed mainly to the production of clerics. Even the students of law were technically members of the clergy, and many of them ended their careers as cathedral canons, as bishops, or even as popes. The nobility had its own program of training knights to hunt and fight and behave properly at court. But neither of these systems of education offered much to the sons of business and professional town dwellers, and by the thirteenth century, if not earlier, there were town schools, primarily for laymen, that taught arithmetic and Latin grammar. The Human-

ists of the fifteenth century rediscovered what Greco-Roman writers had meant by the "liberal arts": the liberating effect on mind and imagination of the study of great literature and philosophy. To this they added courteous behavior and athletic skill and so formed a new pattern of education. The result was a program designed to produce well-read laymen, able to write classical Latin and perhaps Greek, well mannered and at home in polite society, physically strong, and skillful in the art of war. "We call those studies liberal," wrote one Humanist educator, "which are worthy of a free man . . . that education which calls forth, trains, and develops those highest gifts of body and of mind which ennoble men." In practice this education too often degenerated into a narrowly literary training, floundering in the grammatical details of dead languages. It was available only to a few, and it was consciously aristocratic in its ideals. But at its best it passed on to later generations, including our own, the goal of turning out well-balanced human beings, devoted to both classical and Christian ideals, and able to become better businessmen or lawyers or statesmen because of their liberal education.

Young student reading Cicero (detail from a painting by Vincenzo Foppa).

Petrarch on the Classics and Christianity

You are well aware that from early boyhood of all the writers of all ages and races the one whom I most admire and love is Cicero. You agree with me in this respect as well as in so many others. I am not afraid of being considered a poor Christian by declaring myself so much a Ciceronian. [This is an allusion to a famous vision of St. Jerome in which God told him: "You are a Ciceronian and therefore not a Christian."] To my knowledge, Cicero never wrote one word that would conflict with the principles proclaimed by Christ. If, perchance, his works contained anything contrary to Christ's doctrine, that one fact would be sufficient to destroy my belief in Cicero and in Aristotle and in Plato. . . .

Christ is my God; Cicero is the prince of the language I use. I grant you that these ideas are widely separated, but I deny that they are in conflict with each other. Christ is the Word, and the Virtue and the Wisdom of God the Father. Cicero has written much on the speech of men, on the virtues of men, and on the wisdom of men—statements that are true and therefore surely acceptable to the God of Truth.

From a letter to Neri Morando, 1358, in *Petrarch's Letters to Classical Authors*, trans. by M. E. Cosenza (Chicago: University of Chicago Press, 1910), pp. 18–19.

Historical Self-Consciousness

The fourth and final mark of this urban society was its historical self-consciousness. The historical sense of the Middle Ages was not highly developed. The crucial events of the Christian drama had already happened, and time now had only to run on and out to its conclusion in the Last Judgment. Caesar and Charlemagne wore the same costume in medieval drawings. Frederick Barbarossa thought it perfectly reasonable to insert his own edicts in the *Corpus Juris* of Justinian. There had been no essential change since the triumph of Christianity. There was no significant difference between Constantine and Otto III, or between St. Peter and Innocent III. The passage of time brought only minor variations in a persisting pattern.

Petrarch and his Humanist successors in the fifteenth century revolutionized this conception of the past. They became more interested in this world and its history. Their enthusiasm for classical antiquity enabled them for the first time to see the ancient world as a civilization that had run its course. It had been born, it had flourished, and it had died. They talked of the "Fall of Rome" and of a "Dark Age" that had followed. Above all, they talked of a "rebirth," or "revival," that was beginning in their age. Rome had had its golden age and had fallen; darkness had succeeded, but now the light was beginning to dawn again. The Humanists and their followers were highly conscious of their position in history and of their historical mission.

THE "RENAISSANCE"

While the Italian Humanists were sure that they lived in an age of rebirth, they were not nearly so sure of the profound implications of their work as were later historians. Chief of these was the Swiss Jacob Burckhardt, who wrote a brilliant book called *The Civilization of the Renaissance in Italy* (1860). Thanks to Burckhardt, western historians accepted the idea that there was a "Renaissance," or rebirth, after the Middle Ages, that it marked a sharp break with medieval ideals and practices, and that it was centered in Italy. There was much truth in Burckhardt's thesis, but he exaggerated

both the sharpness of the breach with the medieval past and the uniqueness of Italy compared with the rest of Europe.

The term *Renaissance* is most useful when it is applied to the revolutionary change in the arts, in literature, and in the concept of man that took place in Italy in the fourteenth, fifteenth, and early sixteenth centuries. It is less useful when applied to political and ecclesiastical history because it is hard to say what "rebirth" means in these areas. And it is quite useless when applied to economic and social history, in which changes are always slow and in which the important developments began as far back as the eleventh century. Historians of art and literature are relatively sure of what *Renaissance* means; other historians are unsure in varying degrees to the point of total doubt. This does not mean that artistic and literary develpments had no connection with economic and social change. They created new opportunities for able young men and they modified the behavior of the upper classes. It means simply that the word *Renaissance* is best used to describe the changes in artistic and literary taste and skill that occurred at the close of the Middle Ages.

Literature, Philosophy, and Scholarship

Wherever there were classical models to fall back on, the tendency at first was for both writers and artists to lose themselves in simple imitation, in the first flush of excited rediscovery. It was easy, for instance, for Humanists to imitate the

letter writing, the orations, the moral essays, and even the poetry of the Romans—and they did, relentlessly, in the early fifteenth century. When it became possible for educated Florentines to read Plato in the original Greek, the Medici fostered an informal group of scholars who became known as the Platonic Academy. Their leading members, Marsilio Ficino (1433–99) and Pico della Mirandola (1463–94), tried to reconcile Platonism and Christianity, as Thomas Aquinas had tried to reconcile Aristotelianism and Christianity. It was the one serious attempt at philosophical synthesis during the Renaissance, and it was a failure. But enthusiasm for Plato and Platonism was infectious and had widespread influence on poets and painters throughout Europe in the next century. In fact, Plato dominated the imagination of the Renaissance as Aristotle had earlier dominated the thought of medieval scholars.

All was not mere imitation in Italian thought and writing, however. Modern critical scholarship, in the sense of careful linguistic and historical analysis of the literary remains of the past, dates from the Renaissance, and particularly from one of the keenest minds of the age, Lorenzo Valla (ca. 1405–57). Valla analyzed the language and the historical background of the so-called Donation of Constantine, one of the main bulwarks of the popes' claims to temporal power, and proved beyond a shadow of a doubt that the document was a clumsy forgery of the early Middle Ages. He further compared several Greek manuscripts of the New Testament with the accepted Latin translation, the Vulgate, and showed that the translation was full of errors and distortions. The critical spirit and scholarly technique that he inaugurated influenced Erasmus, Pierre Bayle, and Voltaire and resulted in the "scientific" scholarship of the nineteenth century.

Social and Political Thought

Much of Renaissance thought about the relation of man to man simply paraphrased the ethics and political theories of the Greeks and Romans. But sometimes a man wrote freshly from his own experience and spoke directly to the members of his own society. For example, Leon Battista Alberti (1404–72) in his book *On the Family*, described the interests and ideals of the Florentine families he knew: prudence and thrift, strong family feeling and little concern for larger causes outside, appreciation of comfort, planning and foresight, and pride in owning a house in the city and an estate in the country to produce all the family's food. It is one of the earliest idealized portraits of what will later be called the bourgeois virtues.

A social stratum just above that described by Alberti is sketched in the earlier mentioned work of Baldassare Castiglione (1478–1529), *The Courtier*. This book, based on Castiglione's memories of the court of the Duke of Urbino, describes the gentleman—graceful, attractive, courteous, liberally educated, noble in spirit if not necessarily in birth, at home either on the field of battle or

The Adimari Wedding, by an anonymous painter (*ca.* 1450). The painting shows the parade of guests at the wedding reception, held under a canopy outside a church in Florence. Such paintings often adorned the bride's *cassone,* a wedding chest designed to hold her trousseau.

Machiavelli on Cruelty and Clemency

Is it better to be loved than feared or feared than loved? It may be answered that one should wish to be both, but it is much safer to be feared than loved when one of the two must be chosen. Men on the whole are ungrateful, fickle, false, cowards, covetous. As long as you succeed, they are yours entirely. They will offer you their blood, property, life, and children when the need is distant, but when it approaches they turn against you. And a prince who, relying entirely on their promises, has neglected other precautions, is ruined. . . . Men have fewer scruples in offending one who is beloved than one who is feared, for love is preserved by the link of obligation which, owing to the baseness of men, is broken at every opportunity for their advantage, but fear preserves you by a dread of punishment which never fails.

Nevertheless, a prince should inspire fear in such a way that if he does not win love, he avoids hatred; because he can endure very well being feared while he is not hated, and this will be true as long as he abstains from taking the property of his subjects or their women. But when it is necessary for him to take the life of someone, he must do it with proper justification and for manifest cause, and above everything he must keep his hands off the property of others, because men more quickly forget the death of their father than the loss of their heritage.

From Niccolò Machiavelli, *The Prince,* trans. by W. K. Marriott (London: Dent, n.d.), pp. 134–35.

Machiavelli on the Policy of Princes

You must know, then, that there are two methods of fighting, the one by law, the other by force: the first method is that of men, the second of beasts; but as the first method is often insufficient, one must have recourse to the second. It is therefore necessary for a prince to know well how to use both the beast and the man.

A prince being thus obliged to know well how to act as a beast must imitate the fox and the lion, for the lion cannot protect himself from traps, and the fox cannot defend himself from wolves. One must therefore be a fox to recognise traps, and a lion to frighten wolves. Those that wish to be only lions do not understand this. Therefore, a prudent ruler ought not to keep faith when by so doing it would be against his interest, and when the reasons which made him bind himself no longer exist. If men were all good, this precept would not be a good one; but as they are bad, and would not observe their faith with you, so you are not bound to keep faith with them.

From Niccolò Machiavelli, *The Prince,* in *The Prince and the Discourses,* ed. by Max Lerner (New York: Modern Library, 1940), Ch. 18, p. 64.

among cultivated ladies. The concept of "the gentleman" owed much to chivalry and other traditional sources, but Castiglione presented it as a genuinely fresh ideal in the history of European civilization.

In the case of Niccolò Machiavelli (1469–1527), wide reading in the classics illuminated years of practical political experience. Machiavelli's career as ambassador and secretary of the Florentine government during a period when the Medici were out of power helped him to understand the political history of Rome as described by Livy, and Livy helped him to understand the power politics of his own age. Exiled by the restored Medici to his country home in 1512, he began to read widely and to reflect on what makes states expand and grow, what are the causes of political breakdown, how political leaders get and hold power, what can be learned from the past.

Machiavelli set down his reflections in a long, rambling book, *Discourses on Livy,* and in a briefer and more famous essay, *The Prince.* He made it clear that he was describing things as they were, not as they ought to be. Ideal states he left to others; in the world as it is, power is what counts. The Roman Republic, he thought, was the best example in history of successful state building. Its constitution was a masterly blend of monarchy, aristocracy, and democracy; it had good laws and a good citizen army; its religion supported the civic virtues of justice, prudence, and courage, not those of patience and humility; its rulers knew that the good of the state came before the dictates of individual morality. And so Rome, unlike any Italian city-state of Machiavelli's day, had been able to unite the whole of Italy and to endure for centuries.

But Machiavelli realized that this ideal, real though it once had been, might be too difficult for a corrupt and divided group of Italian city-states to revive. Perhaps a prince of real *virtù,* with the courage of a lion and the cunning of a fox, might be able to learn the laws of politics from history and experience and use them to build a strong state in Italy. He would know that men in their collective relations with one another are bad, and therefore he would not be held back by any moral scruples. If others broke faith with him, as they certainly would, the prince must be prepared to break faith with them for the good of his state. Fortune might frustrate his work, but a man of *virtù* had at least an even chance of overcoming bad luck. If his generation had both the intelligence and the will, Machiavelli believed, something could be done about the helpless state of Italy, which was falling under the heels of France and Spain.

Machiavelli's *Prince* was to become a grammar of political and diplomatic practice to heads of state as remote as Mussolini and Hitler. In its origin it was a perfect example of the fruitful combination in Renaissance thought of classical "rebirth" and contemporary "new birth," of historical example and practical experience. Both Machiavelli's disillusioned analysis of things as they were and his passionate plea for reform were entirely characteristic of the age.

The Arts

The influence of classical examples was strong also in the visual arts, but here original elements were even more noticeable than in social and political thought. Roman buildings survived, of course, all over Italy. Brunelleschi (1377?-1446), the greatest architect of his generation, absorbed their spirit and designed new churches in semiclassical style after 1420, thus inaugurating a return to the classical from the Gothic style in architecture. The late Roman sculpture that was dug up (hardly any of the Greek works of the classical age were yet known) inspired sculptors to imitation. But there were no ancient paintings to look at (Pompeii was not unearthed until the eighteenth century), and so Italian painters had to depend on the inspiration of their medieval predecessors and their own genius in elaborating their art.

Italian Renaissance painting, like that of France and Flanders, tended more and more toward realism. Giotto (1266?-1337), the first Italian to develop the new style, was little influenced by northern art; later on some ideas were borrowed from the Low Countries (notably the use

A late–sixteenth-century portrait of Niccolò Machiavelli by Santi di Tito. The artist has tried to suggest both the intellectual brilliance and the shrewdness of the man.

of oil paint). But north or south, the dominant interest of fourteenth-century writers, artists, and philosophers was in the concrete, individual thing as it actually existed, not in the general idea or eternal truth behind and in all things, which had been the typical concern of earlier medieval thinkers. Late medieval artists and writers tried to represent nature and man more and more realistically—to model a leaf as it actually appeared in nature, to chisel the features of a real man or woman, to sketch the character of a person in concrete detail, as both Boccaccio and Chaucer did with such success in their collections of tales. In fifteenth-century painting, particularly in the Netherlands, this effort resulted in the most astonishing skill in representing the smallest details of visual reality.

It was an Italian painter, however, who first realized that surface realism is not enough, that the artist must conceive the human figure as a whole, place it in three-dimensional perspective, and arrive at a more sophisticated realism that sacrifices minute details to organic unity. This painter was Masaccio (1401-28?), the founder of Renaissance painting and

Donatello's *David* (*ca.* 1430–32). Compare this statue with the *David* by Michelangelo on the opposite page.

one of the great innovators in the history of the art.

Italian painting of the fifteenth and sixteenth centuries is far too rich in content and varied in technique for us to describe in detail. Some of its general characteristics may be suggested, however. The first thing that strikes the historical observer is the separation of painting and sculpture from architecture. It was as if the sculptured prophets and many-colored saints had stepped down from their niches and stained-glass windows in the great medieval cathedrals to be reincarnated in bronze statues in Italian public squares or painted portraits in Italian palaces. Painting and sculpture were no longer arts subordinate to architecture. Painters began to adorn the walls of monasteries and houses with frescoes. After they had learned from Flemish artists the technique of painting with oils, the Italians went on to develop the easel painting, meant to be hung in a palace or house and to be enjoyed for its own sake. Donatello (1368–1466), in his *David*, was the first sculptor since the ancients to model a free-standing nude figure, and from then on to the great works of Michelangelo (1475–1564) sculptors developed their art with no thought but of its own perfection.

The zest for solving fresh problems infected architects as well as painters and sculptors. Brunelleschi went far beyond classical or medieval models in designing and building his famous dome over the transept of the cathedral in Florence (1420–36). Architecture, sculpture, and painting each went its own way. An individual artist might turn his hand to all three, and a painter might borrow ideas from sculpture. But in each case the artist could create as he pleased without subjecting one art to another.

The second characteristic worth noting was the heightened individuality and social prestige of the artist. A famous passage in Cellini's *Autobiography* describes the unveiling of his bronze statue of Perseus in the central square of Florence in 1554. "Now it pleased God," he wrote, "that on the instant of its exposure to view, a shout of boundless enthusiasm went up in commendation of my work, which consoled me not a little." Such a shout might have greeted the proclamation of a crusade in the eleventh century or the triumphant conclusion of a world war in the twentieth. But the public appreciation of a work of art, the assumption that great art is the product of individual "genius," which is something to be nurtured—these were as characteristic of the Renaissance as they were atypical of ages before and after. Artists and writers felt that they should be to the age of the Renaissance what the saint had been to the Middle Ages. Reality did not always correspond to their expectations; some patrons treated their painters and architects like any other employees. On the other hand, some mediocre men received excessive adulation and high rewards. By and large, Italy's Golden Age was the golden age of the artist and the writer.

In seeking a higher realism, Italian painters studied the laws of spatial perspective about the same time that Humanists were restudying the temporal or historical perspective of their day. As a result, the artists pictured real persons whom they knew, in recognizable space. Some of them spent their lives probing the psychological depths of human beings and trying to put on canvas what they found. The chief of these was the lonely scientific and artistic genius Leonardo da Vinci (1452–1519), whose curiosity about the secrets of nature was as insatiable as his curiosity about the nature of man. In painting *The Last Supper*, he chose not the moment when Christ breaks the bread and remarks, "This is my body . . .," as a medieval artist might have done, but the more humanly dramatic and startling moment when he announces, "One of you will betray me." The resulting psychological crisis experienced by each disciple is carefully portrayed. The climactic episode of the Creation, as Michelangelo painted it on the ceiling of the Sistine Chapel in St. Peter's, was the creation of Adam—an almost superhuman man at the threshold of self-consciousness, languid, wondering, awakening—almost as if he were a symbol of the man of the Renaissance. In one of his most famous sculptures, Michelangelo chose to portray Moses at the moment when he has caught sight of his people's idolatrous Golden Calf and is struggling to control himself.

These few examples typify the Renaissance point of view. The central concern is man here in this world, troubled, striving, with unknown possibilities. Thus Renaissance art is humanistic in the broader, more philosophical meaning of the word. Not that the artists rejected God or ignored nature. God is still there, and Renaissance landscapes are charming. But God is seen through man, through man's heroism and his tragedy; and generally nature is of interest only as background or setting to the human drama. The most important question is what is to become of man. Pico della Mirandola, in a famous *Oration* on man's dignity (1486), pictured God as giving man something he had given to no other creature, the unique gift of freedom:

> Thou, constrained by no limits, in accordance with thine own free will, in whose hands We have placed thee, shalt ordain for thyself the limits of thy nature. . . . We have made thee neither of heaven nor of earth, neither mortal nor immortal, so that with freedom of choice and with honor, as though the maker and molder of thyself, thou mayest fashion thyself in whatever shape thou shalt prefer.

Every other creature had its pattern and its limits, but to Pico man's nature and destiny were in his own hands. The men of the Renaissance had not lost belief in God, but they were convinced, in a way their medieval ancestors would not have understood, that man was on his own.

The greatness of Italian art lay in the fact that it reflected all the tensions and contradictions in the prevailing attitudes toward man. There was no party line in Renaissance art; there were no premature solutions of sharp differences, no accepted syntheses. Some artists were realists, others idealists. Donatello modeled despots as he saw them, with hard and observant realism, while Raphael (1483–1520) a generation later idealized the peasant girls he knew as calm and self-possessed Madonnas of ethereal beauty. Some artists were scientists and psychologists like Leonardo, who tried to peer into the souls of men and women, while others were like the Venetian Titian

(1477–1576), who was more interested in the external marks of character and the glorious play of color on the objects about him. Michelangelo, perhaps the most typical as well as the greatest artist of them all, gave his life to attempting the impossible: to reconciling the classical ideal of harmony, balance, and "nothing in excess," with the limitless goals and boundless love of Christian piety. This attempt to reconcile the Greco-Roman and Hebraic-Christian worlds was the central striving of the Renaissance. It failed, but the failure left an imperishable record in the arts.

Michelangelo's *David* (1501–04). Instead of representing David after his victory over Goliath, as Donatello had done, Michelangelo chose to represent him as watchful of the approaching foe, with muscles tensed in gathering strength.

Raphael, detail from *Madonna with the Goldfinch* (1505–06).

Michelangelo, *Creation of Adam* (fresco from the ceiling of the Sistine Chapel of the Vatican, 1508–12).

Leonardo da Vinci, *Ginevra de' Benci* (*ca.* 1481).

Natural Science

The Renaissance contributed relatively less to the progress of natural science than to the arts, but the contribution was still important. The Humanists in general were more interested in man than in nature and more absorbed in literature than in mathematics and physics. Nevertheless, even at the height of the Renaissance, the Humanists never had full control of higher education. The old medieval curriculum, which included mathematics and physics, drew as many students as the new curriculum based on the classics. And on the practical side, the desire of the upper classes for greater comfort, and the striving of artists for greater realism, led to significant advances.

Moreover, the interest in Greek meant that new Greek scientific texts became available, and the interest in Latin led to criticism of works such as Pliny's *Natural History*. Above all, the emphasis on man on this earth gave confidence that man could understand and shape his environment.

Some of this confidence was based on a mistaken reliance on ancient texts on magic, but some of it derived from actual experience. As craftsmen, mechanics, and engineers, the Italians were the best in Europe. In the science of perspective, their painters worked out the mathematical principles of representing figures in space. Their artists and doctors together advanced the knowledge of human anatomy beyond where it had been left by the Greeks. The *Notebooks* of Leonardo da Vinci, a landmark in the history of both art and science, show how closely the two interests were related in the fifteenth-century mind. His studies of anatomical detail, for instance, are of equal interest to painters and doctors. Furthermore, the medieval interest in science survived in the northern Italian universities, particularly Padua. There the study of mathematics flourished, and the arguments over Aristotelian laws of motion, which had been begun at Paris and Oxford, continued. Padua eventually passed on to Galileo a theory of scientific method in something like its modern form.

THE COUNCILS AND THE PAPACY

Italian energy and enthusiasm did something to dissipate the pessimism of the late fourteenth century. But Europe was still profoundly Christian and could not be entirely satisfied until its religious problems were solved. Of the three difficulties that faced the Church in 1400—the schism, heresy, and administrative reform—only one was completely overcome. By the mid-fifteenth century there was only one pope in Rome, even if the prestige of his office had not regained its thirteenth-century height. The most dangerous heresies had been walled off or driven underground, but the religious atmosphere was still heavy with discontent and revolt. And the more men talked of religious and administrative reforms in the Church, the more impossible it seemed to effect them.

The Great Schism had imposed an almost intolerable psychological burden on Europe. In theory there could not possibly be two true Vicars of Christ, yet there was no way of being sure which of the two claimants was the real successor. Men felt as if they were in a sinking ship: "If we remain in it," a contemporary wrote, "we must perish with it, and if we stray outside, salvation escapes us, since outside the ship there is no salvation." Many Lollards and other heretics had strayed outside. Those who remained on board tried desperately to find some solution.

The stubborn behavior of the two lines of popes at Rome and Avignon, in refusing to resign or to submit to arbitration, had increased antipapal feeling among both clergy and laity throughout Europe. In 1395 the French became so exasperated with their own pope that the French clergy, under pressure from the government, withdrew their obedience from him for five years. This was the first appearance of a policy that was to have an ominous future: secession from papal jurisdiction by the clergy of a large nation under the pressure of the secular government. Even in the fifteenth century there were signs that Christendom might dissolve into independent national churches.

Mobile bakers, one of the various groups who provided for the delegates to the Council of Constance (1414–18). Notice the "pretzels" in the upper right corner (detail from a manuscript version of Ulrich Richental's *Chronicle*, 1465).

The Conciliar Movement

As early as 1379, the year after the schism developed, scholars at the University of Paris had suggested a more conservative and practical scheme than the withdrawal of obedience. They urged that a general council of the Church be called. The leading advocates of the idea at the university picked up and amplified a concept of the Church that had been advanced in the thirteenth and fourteenth centuries to support their proposal. The Church, they argued, was not centered in the papacy but was made up of the whole body of believers. Thus the final authority in the Church was a council representing all the faithful, and the pope was only a limited monarch responsible to this representative assembly. The so-called fullness of power, which canon lawyers claimed for the pope, was a usurpation. Authority in the Church came from the bottom up, not from the top down. This conciliar theory of the constitution of the Church was to have strong appeal to secular rulers who were looking for a club to hold over the papacy. It was also to have a strong attraction for reformers during the next century.

In 1408 most of the cardinals of both sides deserted their popes and summoned a general council to meet at Pisa the next year. For a moment, a group of cardinals without a pope confronted two popes without any cardinals, but the result was simply the election of a third pope by the council. Unfortunately, neither the Roman nor the Avignonese pope resigned, as had been hoped. After five more years of confused negotiations, the German emperor Sigismund compelled the Pisan pope, John XXIII, to summon a genuinely representative assembly.

This great council, which met at Constance in Switzerland from 1414 to 1418, made a strong impression on the imagination of the age. It healed the schism by bullying John XXIII into resigning, persuading the Roman pope to resign after he had gone through the formality of resummoning and approving the council himself, and deposing the Avignonese pope, who by now had fled to Spain and was supported only by Aragon. In 1417 the council elected a new pope, Martin V, who soon commanded the allegiance of all western Christendom. The council was less successful in instituting reform. The English and German delegates worked in vain to have reform considered before the election of a new pope; the Latin nations were more anxious to heal the schism first and let reform come later. Once Martin V was elected, interest flagged in even the mild report of a committee to study abuses, and the council dispersed without ever really facing the complicated malpractices in the hierarchy. On the other hand, the council dealt energetically, though shortsightedly, with the problem of heresy.

John Hus

The danger spot in 1414 was Bohemia. Here during the preceding century the emperor Charles IV (who was also king of Bohemia) had helped to foster a national and cultural awakening among the Czechs. But Czech scholars ran into two obstacles: a corrupt and leaderless Church, and a steady influx of

Germans into the cities and into the newly founded University of Prague. Since the Czechs tended to be reformers, while the Germans generally supported the status quo, the gifted group of Czech preachers and teachers who attacked ecclesiastical abuses soon found themselves leading a movement that was as much patriotic as it was religious. In 1402 a brilliant young leader appeared in John Hus (*ca.* 1369–1415). The burden of his preaching was that faith must be based on the Bible as the only source of authority, that Christ, not the pope, was the true Head of the Church, and that a man is saved by God through Christ, not by trusting in ceremonies and in a mediating priesthood that was thoroughly corrupt. Hus knew and used the ideas of Wiclif, whose books had been brought to Bohemia by Czech students returning from England, but he had developed his basic theories independently. By 1414 Hus had been excommunicated by the Roman pope, but he was at liberty and his ideas were accepted by a majority of the Czech people.

Hus eagerly seized the opportunity to journey to Constance to present his case before the council. He was almost immediately imprisoned for heresy. The emperor, who had granted him a safe-conduct, withdrew his protection the moment the dreaded charge of heresy was made. The conciliar leaders would have preferred a public recantation that could have been publicized throughout Bohemia, but Hus stood firm. In the dramatic trial that followed, the essential issue was whether the Bible and a man's conscience are the ultimate religious authority, as Hus argued, or whether the Catholic Church represented by the clerical hierarchy is the sole authority, as the council declared. Hus was condemned and burned at the stake outside the walls of Constance in May 1415. His follower, Jerome of Prague, was burned on the same spot the following spring.

Before the council disbanded, civil and religious warfare had broken out in Bohemia. It lasted for almost twenty years. The upshot was an agreement in 1436 between the more conservative Hussites and the Church. This agreement recognized a national church in Bohemia with local control over ecclesiastical ap-pointments and with its own liturgical practices, notably the right to offer the cup as well as the bread to the laity when giving communion. For the first time the Church had made an agreement on equal terms with condemned heretics after excommunicating them and solemnly preaching a crusade against them. Wiclif's Lollards had been driven underground in England, but the Hussite heresy had simply been walled off in Bohemia.

The Papacy's Triumph over the Conciliar Movement

The restored papacy, which owed its existence to the Council of Constance, was more successful in defeating the conciliar movement than it was in extirpating heresy. The fathers had decreed at Constance that general councils must be summoned every ten years. But the superior diplomacy and the more efficient administrative machinery of the Roman papacy soon made this provision a dead letter. The temper of the times was changing; the idea that a ruler should be controlled by an assembly now seemed to lead only to confusion. Just as most European kings weakened their parliaments and humbled their nobles, so the popes weakened the conciliar ideal, stopped holding councils at regular intervals, and humbled the princes of the Church, the cardinals. By the time Nicholas V became pope (1447–55) the threat

John Hus being burned at the stake in 1415. He wears a fool's cap with pictures of the Devil and the word *heresiarch* (leader of heretics).

that the Church might be transformed into a limited monarchy was over. Never again was there a general council of the Church that the pope could not control.

The popes' triumph over the councils left the papacy stronger in some respects but weaker in others. No one within the Church itself could challenge the papal "fullness of power," but the victory had been bought by making wide concessions to secular rulers. In opposing the reforming element in the councils, the popes had isolated themselves from clerical and lay leaders of opinion, particularly in the north of Europe. As a result, the popes depended on the support of lay rulers and could not resist their efforts to control the clergy within their own realms. In 1438 the king of France summoned an assembly of the French clergy and issued a solemn decree known as the Pragmatic Sanction of Bourges. This decree strictly limited the pope's power of appointment and taxation in France and in effect set up a national, or "Gallican," Church, as it was called. In later years the popes were able to persuade the French monarchs to modify this one-sided action by "concordats," or agreements, between the papacy and the French crown. But in these agreements the monarchy always retained its control over appointments to the higher clergy. With some differences, the kings of England and Spain established similar limitations on papal power during the fourteenth and fifteenth centuries. In Germany, where there was no central government strong enough to stand up to the pope, papal rights of appointment, taxation, and jurisdiction were not limited as they were in the stronger monarchies. The popes had eliminated all their clerical rivals for power, only to be faced by much more greedy and formidable lay rivals—the monarchs.

The Renaissance Papacy

The eighty years between the accession of Nicholas V to the papacy (1447) and the sack of Rome (1527) are often called the period of the Renaissance papacy. It was a brilliant but tragic era in the history of the Church. Some of the popes of the period were patrons of Humanism and the arts, notably Nicholas V, founder of the Vatican Library, and Julius II (1503–13), builder of St. Peter's. Pius II (1458–64) had been Aeneas Sylvius, a celebrated Humanist, before his election. Two were particularly noted for their wars: Sixtus IV (1471–84), who was rumored to have died of rage at the conclusion of a peace settlement; and Julius II, who was known to his generation as "the Warrior Pope." More than one was notorious for his nepotism, as favoritism to relatives, including bastard children, was

Aerial view of St. Peter's in Rome. In 1505 Pope Julius II commissioned Bramante to construct a church that would mirror the classical-Christian aspirations of the sixteenth century. The plans were changed several times, and the building was not completed until 1626. Michelangelo designed the dome; the colonnades were designed by Bernini in the 1600s.

called. Roderigo Borgia, Alexander VI (1492–1503), was by far the worst of the lot. His mistresses lived openly with him; his voracious Spanish relatives got whatever they asked for; and his illegitimate son, Cesare Borgia, made a bloody attempt to become the ruler of all central Italy with his father's help.

All the accumulated evils of many years seemed to become intensified in the papal court: simony, nepotism, immorality, involvement in secular politics and warfare. Two centuries before, Innocent III had been immersed in secular diplomacy, but it had been on a Europe-wide scale, and the excuse had always been the advancement of the Church's cause. Now the scale of involvement was limited to the Italian peninsula, and the popes were generally motivated by selfish family interests. As time went on, the papacy became thoroughly Italianized, perhaps out of fear of another schism. (Since the end of the schism in 1417, only two non-Italian popes have been elected, in 1522 and 1979.) Most secular rulers came to assume that as ruler of the Papal States the pope would act like any Italian despot, at the dictates of his own personal and family interests—with the unfair competitive advantage, of course, that he was considered to be the Vicar of Christ. But even when the papacy seemed to be simply another Italian principality it was sustained by the basic belief that the office was greater than the man, that the moral character of the pope did not lessen his authority in spiritual matters.

The open corruption of the papal Curia during the fifteenth century had much to do with the Protestant revolt that began in 1517. As one historian has put it, the popes of the Renaissance tried to substitute splendor for reform. In the hands of an intelligent and devoted Humanist like Nicholas V this was not an unworthy idea. To him it meant reconciling Christianity with the best in ancient civilization and rebuilding Rome as the capital of a revived Christendom. But this ideal did not satisfy the mystical and moral strivings of thousands of the faithful, particularly those outside Italy. Significantly, it was under a cultivated son of Lorenzo de' Medici, Pope Leo X (1513–21), that much of Germany rebelled against the papacy, and under an illegitimate son of Lorenzo's brother, Pope Clement VII (1523–34), that England set up a national Church.

ECONOMIC GROWTH IN THE NORTH

While Italy was building city-states on the wealth derived from its monopoly of Mediterranean trade, northern and western Europe was building nation-states based on new industries and new trade routes. The cumulative effects of technological change began to stimulate the transalpine economy during the fifteenth century. Thus gradual improvements in building and rigging sailing ships made possible the great voyages of Vasco da Gama to India and of Columbus to America. Da Gama's voyages gave the Atlantic countries an increasing share of the lucrative trade in Oriental goods. Columbus gave the same countries a monopoly of the wealth of a New World. Even though Italian trade remained close to its old level, it was dwarfed by the much greater trade of Portugal and Spain, of France, England, and the Netherlands.

In Europe, new and profitable industries began to appear. For example, improved techniques in metallurgy made it possible to take full advantage of the discovery of gunpowder and to make cannon for sieges and naval warfare. Since more metal was needed, mining methods had to be improved and blast furnaces had to be enlarged to enable metal workers to acquire an increased supply of iron. The Atlantic states were able to gain control of world sea lanes not only because their ships were slightly better than those of their rivals but because they were more powerfully armed with naval cannon. On land the use of siege cannon weakened the noblemen and strengthened the monarchs, and so increased security. The noble's castle was no longer a secure retreat, and no ordinary noble could afford the vast cost of heavy guns. If they were to maintain their military tradition, the nobles had to become officers in the armies of kings

Cesare Borgia, anonymous copy of an authentic portrait.

and princes who could afford to buy the new weapons. They were not always well-disciplined officers, but they were no longer independent war-lords.

As we have seen, the invention of printing from movable type also depended on advances in metallurgy. And that invention, in the middle of the fifteenth century, had even more revolutionary effects than the invention of the cannon. So long as books had to be laboriously copied by hand, only a few men could aspire to higher learning. But as printing presses spread rapidly from the Rhine Valley to Italy, the Netherlands, France, Spain, and England, Europeans had a flood of books available at prices that would have been unbelievable a century earlier. There were "standard editions" of the Bible, the Church Fathers, and the classical writers in both Greek and Latin, scientific works, devotional treatises, and popular manuals in the vernacular languages. Like all mechanical inventions, printing brought both good and evil in its train. The "standard editions" could multiply errors as well as corrections, and the pamphlets that were now so easy to print and circulate in large numbers could mislead as well as inform. But one thing was clear: learning would never again be the monopoly of a small upper class in European society. Anything human beings had written could now be multiplied and placed quickly and cheaply in the hands of anyone who could read.

Industry and Agriculture

New industries such as cannon founding and printing required large initial investments in plant and machinery. They were organized from the start as capitalistic enterprises—that is, enterprises in which accumulated wealth was deliberately used to produce more wealth. In addition to capital, these industries needed and attracted free laborers from town or country who could be employed for a wage and dismissed when business slacked off.

Even in rural areas capitalistic methods calculated to produce a profit were occasionally being applied to the land. Landlords had long realized that raising sheep for wool might be more profitable than accepting a customary rent. Legally or illegally, many of them, particularly in England, managed to fence off, or "enclose," lands formerly reserved for the common use of villagers, or to convert ploughed land to pasture. Since tending sheep required far fewer man-hours than raising food on the same amount of land, many families were displaced from the soil. Occasionally "improving landlords" turned to more intensive cultivation of the soil in order to produce a larger cash crop of food for the growing urban markets, often riding roughshod over the preference of villagers for timeworn methods.

In short, capitalism was being applied to industry and agriculture wherever individual entrepreneurs saw profit to be made in producing books, weapons, clothing, or food for sale in the open market. For some peasants and workers this meant new opportunity. Many an ambitious peasant was able to better his position, as Martin Luther's father did by

An early printing press, as shown in an early–sixteenth-century French print.

becoming a miner. But a great deal of misery and unemployment also resulted from the breaking down of customary economic relationships, the eviction of peasants from their holdings, and the movement of population to the new industrial centers. "Sturdy beggars" and "vagabonds" were a constant problem for sixteen-century town governments; eventually prisons and workhouses had to be built to contain them.

Wealth derived from the new industries and commerce tended to concentrate in a few hands in a few places. For a brief period the most powerful banking house was that of the Fuggers of Augsburg in south Germany. Jakob Fugger (1459–1525), as banker for the Habsburgs and the pope, could invest in Austrian mines and Spanish colonies and carry on dealings with every part of the Continent. On the whole, however, from about 1476 to 1576 Antwerp was the Wall Street of northern Europe, with Lyons not far behind. Then, for a century after 1576, it was Amsterdam. The wealth that poured in from the Orient and the New World had a way of gravitating to the commercial centers of the Netherlands. Where the investment market was freest, where the largest and most aggressive firms transacted most of their business, here were the nerve centers of European finance. Italy was losing its old place as the banking center of Europe. Financial power was clearly shifting to the north.

POLITICAL CONSOLIDATION AND CENTRALIZATION

The most highly developed monarchies of western Europe—England and France—had undergone a severe crisis in the fourteenth century (see Chapter 13). The successors of Edward I and Philip the Fair allowed their political ambitions to outstrip their financial resources. The Hundred Years' War (1337–1453) exhausted both France and England, and plague and social revolt added their toll of misery to war. The monarchs were not equal to the strain. As the fifteenth century opened, France was ruled by a king who had periods of insanity (Charles VI), and England was ruled by a usurper who owed his throne to his fellow barons and

THE FINANCIAL EMPIRE OF JAKOB FUGGER
ca. 1485–1525

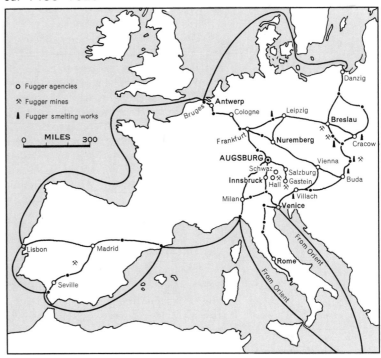

Jakob Fugger with his bookkeeper. The cabinet in the rear lists the names of cities where Fugger had branch offices—Innsbruck, Nuremberg, and Lisbon, among others (detail from a painting by Matthaus Schwartz, 1516).

to Parliament (Henry IV). The future did not seem very bright for the monarchies that had been so painfully built up in the twelfth and thirteenth centuries.

The later fifteenth century, however, saw a remarkable recovery of monarchical institutions in western Europe. As people grew more and more weary of war, violence, and anarchy, the forces striving to restore some semblance of law and order rallied to the support of the monarchs in France, the Spanish kingdoms, and England. Even weak rulers profited from the demand for peace and strong government. And economic growth made it easier to support stronger armies and more effective bureaucracies.

France

At times during the Hundred Years' War the authority of the French king had almost disappeared, but there had been considerable recovery before the war ended in 1453. Charles VII was not a great king, but he was clever enough to find able men to work for him (he was known in his time as Charles the Well-served). He began his reign by using the widespread enthusiasm aroused by Joan of Arc to expel the English and to restore law and order to the French countryside. In 1438, by the Pragmatic Sanction of Bourges, he asserted his authority over the French clergy at the expense of papal power. In the 1440s he solved the financial problem of the crown by obtaining consent from the Estates to a broad-based tax on land called the *taille;* he then continued to levy the tax on his own authority. He organized a small standing army (at most, 25,000 men) under direct royal control, gained the support of wealthy merchants who supplied him with a siege train of heavy artillery, and methodically ousted the English from all their strongholds on the Continent except Calais.

Louis XI (1461–83) carried on his father's work and left the monarchy stronger than it had been since Philip IV. Louis, a slovenly and superstitious man with a morbid fear of death, had none of the majesty of kingship. He was called "the Spider" because he preferred to trap his enemies in diplomatic webs than to fight them. Machiavelli admired him, with reason. The greatest threat to the French monarchy was the powerful state that the dukes of Burgundy had built up on France's eastern frontier, including the wealthy provinces of the Netherlands as well as Burgundy proper. Louis never actually defeated his rival, Charles the Bold, Duke of Burgundy (1467–77), but he shrewdly helped Charles defeat himself. Louis encouraged quarrels between Charles and his eastern neighbors, and in the end the duke was killed in battle against the Swiss. The richest portion of his inheritance, the Netherlands, fell to the Emperor Maximilian (1493–1519) through his marriage with Mary, daughter of Charles the Bold; but the strategically located Duchy of Burgundy went to the king of France. At home, Louis encouraged trade and kept a firm rein on the nobles and higher clergy. His successor Charles VIII (1483–98) married the heiress of Brittany and so brought the last remaining feudal duchy under direct royal control.

With France fully under control, Charles felt strong enough to invade Italy (1494) in order to assert his claims to Naples as the remote heir of Charles of Anjou (see Chapter 12). Spain, which also had claims in Italy, quickly reacted, and foreign armies fought over the peninsula for half a century. The Italian city-states were helpless; even if they had been united they probably could not have resisted such powers as France and Spain. As it was, Spain gradually gained a dominant position in Italy, and with the loss of independence Italian life lost much of its vigor and excitement. On the other hand, while France suffered financially because of its losses in the Italian wars, the position of the king was not weakened and France remained one of the most influential states in Europe.

Spain

As we have seen, the Iberian Peninsula had suffered almost as severely as France from war and anarchy in the fourteenth and early fifteenth centuries. In 1469, however, a momentous marriage took place between Ferdinand of Aragon (1479–1516) and Isabella of Castile

Joint Reign of Ferdinand and Isabella

750		1085		1252		1479 1504

Reconquista in the North

Amalgamation of Kingdoms into Portugal, Aragon, and Castile

Moslem Rule in Spain

Moslem Rule in Granada

1481 1492

Reconquest of Granada

(1474–1504). The marriage brought no organic fusion of the political institutions of the two states, but husband and wife followed a common foreign policy and their heir could properly be called king of "Spain." A new national monarchy had been born from a dynastic union.

Isabella reestablished the authority of the crown in Castile and with her husband led a successful eleven-year "crusade" (1481–92) to expel the Moors (as the Moslems in Spain were called) from their last holding in Spain, the kingdom of Granada. The victory touched off a wave of national patriotism and religious intolerance, which had been slowly gathering force during the later fifteenth century. In 1492 all Jews in both kingdoms were ordered either to become Christians or leave the land, and ten years later, in spite of promises of toleration when Granada fell, all Moors in Castile were offered the same choice. In 1478 some Dominicans had persuaded the pope to authorize Ferdinand and Isabella to set up the Spanish Inquisition. This dreaded instrument became a powerful force toward royal absolutism when the monarchs directed it against "converted" Jews and Moors who were suspected of secretly adhering to their old beliefs. There was thus a note of religious fervor and racial hatred, which was lacking elsewhere, in the birth of Spain as a great power.

A second marriage was greatly to affect Spain's European destiny in the sixteenth century. The Emperor Maximilian and his wife, Mary of Burgundy, had a son, Philip, who was heir to Austria through his Habsburg father and to the Netherlands through his mother. Philip married Joanna, the daughter of Ferdinand and Isabella. Their son Charles, born in 1500, eventually became king of Spain (1516–56) and ruler of the Netherlands, Austria, Milan, Naples, and the Spanish possessions in America. In 1519 the German princes elected him

emperor as Charles V. Thus Spain was thrust out into the full stream of European politics and world empire by coming under the Habsburg dynasty in 1516.

Spain was not a wealthy country, nor were its two halves, Castile and Aragon, ever thoroughly amalgamated. Even today Catalonia is markedly different from Castile. But the Spanish armies soon proved themselves the best in Europe during campaigns in Italy and

Illumination of Ferdinand and Isabella of Spain— known as the "Catholic Kings"—with their daughter Joanna.

the Netherlands, and Columbus' discoveries brought in a stream of gold and silver from the New World that surpassed all European dreams of wealth. As a result, Spain was to become the leading power in Europe in the sixteenth century.

England

The Hundred Years' War had been a heavy burden on England. But the most severe trial followed the end of the war, when a restless nobility and professional soldiery returned from France to plunge into thirty more years of intermittent civil strife in the Wars of the Roses (1454–85). The excuse for the wars was the rivalry between the House of Lancaster and the House of York (both descended from Edward III) for the throne. Actually the

Effigies on the tombs of Ferdinand of Aragon and Isabella of Castile, who created a united Spain.

wars were contests between shifting factions of nobles for control of the government. When it was all over, the first of the Tudors was on the throne as Henry VII (1485–1509), by right of conquest and a dubious hereditary claim. The bloodshed and violence of the wars had sickened the people, and plots and counterplots had killed off most of the leaders of the nobility. Taking advantage of the opportunity to restore the monarchy, Henry proved himself one of the ablest rulers in English history. He kept England out of foreign wars, encouraged trade, restored the sources of royal revenue, and eliminated all pretenders to the throne. His son, Henry VIII (1509–47), inherited a full treasury, a united nation, and (for its day) an efficient administration. Henry VIII soon wasted the treasury surplus in war with France, but he and his overbearing minister, Cardinal Wolsey, did manage to concentrate power in their own hands. Henry VIII's England could compare well with either France or Spain in governmental efficiency and potential military strength, even though it had only about half Spain's population and a fourth that of France.

The Monarchs and the Nobility

Louis XI, Ferdinand and Isabella, and Henry VII all had common problems, which they met in strikingly similar ways. The chief obstacle in the path of rebuilding royal authority in the later fifteenth century was the military, political, and economic strength of the great nobles in each country (the kings were wise enough never to attack the social prestige of the nobility). The monarchs used various expedients in their cold war with overmighty subjects. The key to success was to make the royal Council an effective agency of central government. Councillors were selected from among nobles who were loyal to the king and from members of the upper middle class (especially lawyers) who sought power and promotion. Key councillors, often at their own expense, developed groups of agents who kept them informed about internal and external threats to the security of the state. At the same time the Council, or one of its committees, was given supreme judicial power so that it could act quickly in any emergency. Thus in England the Secretaries of State, who were the most influential members of the Council, were well aware of plots against the throne through their close contacts with local authorities, with English ambassadors abroad, and with a network of spies. The Star Chamber, the judicial arm of the Council, could be used to suppress any manifestations of aristocratic independence, and the ordinary courts almost never failed to convict men accused by the Council. In France and Spain the Council was equally well informed and had even greater judicial power.

The Monarchs and the Representative Assemblies

A second possible obstacle to royal absolutism was the representative assembly: the Estates General in France, the Cortes in the Spanish kingdoms, and Parliament in England. These assemblies had reached the peak of their influence in the fourteenth century. In the fifteenth century, they declined everywhere but in England. This was due more to the ineffectiveness of assemblies than to the hostility of monarchs. Except in England, provincial feeling was so strong that it was difficult to reach agreement on any issue. Assemblies were more ready to grumble than to act. In France, for example, the Estates General, in spite of repeated requests, neither supported, nor proposed clear-cut alternatives to, royal policies. It is also true that the kings had weakened the Estates by depriving them of their financial powers; old taxes were continued and new ones imposed by royal authority alone. Thus the Estates General of France were weak and useless and gradually ceased to meet. In Spain, the monarchs played off class against class by summoning only the representatives of the cities when they needed money, thus depriving the townsmen of the possible aid of the great nobles. Anxious to support royal authority, the town representatives usually consented readily to whatever taxes the king demanded. Deprived of any real power, the Cortes of Castile, like the Estates General of France, met less and less frequently after the end of the fifteenth century.

In England Henry VII apparently had little respect for Parliament and, after the first years of his reign, seldom summoned it. But since the English Parliament could speak for all the privileged classes and all parts of the country, it was more difficult to ignore than the weak and divided assemblies of other countries. In England provincial rivalries scarcely existed; landowners and the bourgeoisie usually cooperated, and no general tax could be levied without Parliamentary consent. When Henry VIII got into trouble with the pope, he summoned Parliament to give him support. This use of Parliament as an accomplice had unanticipated results. By 1600, thanks to the frequent use Henry VIII and his successors made of it, Parliament had become a more powerful force in English government than ever before. By that time the representative assemblies on the Continent, in states governed by absolute monarchs, had become hollow forms.

The Monarchs and the Church

The final obstacle to the development of monarchical power was the Church. Against this obstacle the kings moved cautiously. Louis XI was proud to be called "Most Christian King" of France; Ferdinand and Isabella were proud to be known as the "Catholic Kings"; and Henry VIII was especially proud of his title "Defender of the Faith," which the pope granted him in 1521. But on the three crucial questions of appointment of the higher clergy, taxation of the clergy, and the appeal of ecclesiastical cases to Rome, not one of the monarchs admitted the full papal claims. The kings of England and France had established their right to tax their own clergy by 1300. The French kings had asserted their right to control clerical appointments in the Pragmatic Sanction of Bourges (1438), and the pope had granted Francis I the right to nominate the higher clergy and to settle the bulk of ecclesiastical disputes in France in the Concordat of Bologna in 1516. Even the "Catholic Kings" of Spain asserted and maintained their right to appoint, to tax, and to reform the clergy within their kingdoms, despite papal objections. Thus long before the Protestant Reformation, kings were trying to build "national churches"— churches that looked to the authority of the secular ruler in matters of appointment, taxation, and even jurisdiction, although not in doctrine.

Consolidation and Centralization Elsewhere in Europe

These tendencies in western Europe toward the consolidation of territory and the centralization of political power also appeared in the kingdoms of Norway and Sweden. They appeared too in Russia, where Ivan the Dread (1533–84) ruthlessly broke the power of the aristocracy. In Italy, however, there was no central government to be strengthened (much to the despair of observers like Machiavelli). In the German Empire the central government was a sham. There was no imperial army and no effective system of imperial taxation. There was an imperial supreme court, but it was so inefficient that it had little authority. An attempt at the close of the fifteenth century to strengthen the imperial govern-

ment was almost a total failure. When Charles V became emperor in 1519, his real strength lay in the fact that he was duke of Austria, lord of the wealthy towns of the Netherlands, and king of Spain, with its well-equipped armies and overseas treasure. Becoming emperor added something to his prestige, much to his responsibilities, but little to his power. Many German princes expanded their territories at the expense of weaker neighbors and increased their authority within their principalities by methods very similar to those of the kings of western Europe. But in 1500 there was no central authority in Germany strong enough to resist papal exactions, foreign intervention, or the spread of heresy.

This lack of central authority was to be of crucial importance for the future. On the one hand, it meant that the Protestant Reformation, once it started, could not be brought under control. On the other, it meant that the emperor could rely only on his own hereditary domains in meeting a new threat that came from the East. The Turks had advanced steadily after the fall of Constantinople in 1453. The greatest of their sultans, Suleiman the Magnificent (1520–66), captured Belgrade, won most of Hungary in the battle of Mohacs (1526), and almost took Vienna in 1529. With a divided Germany behind him and a dangerous enemy facing him in the Danube Valley, the emperor could not play his old role of defender of Christendom until he had built a new state out of the old Habsburg territories.

Suggestions for Further Reading

Note: Asterisk denotes a book available in paperback edition.

General   J. Burckhardt's great "essay," *The Civilization of the Renaissance in Italy** (1860), is still the starting point for study. W. K. Ferguson, *The Renaissance in Historical Thought* (1948), traces the development of the idea of "rebirth" from the Humanists themselves through Burckhardt to the present. His *Europe in Transition: 1300–1520* (1963) is a good survey of the period. So is L. W. Spitz, *The Renaissance and Reformation Movements*,* 2 vols. (1971). M. P. Gilmore, *The World of Humanism: 1453–1517** (1952), makes excellent use of recent monographic material and offers a critical bibliography. D. Hay, *The Italian Renaissance** (1977), is a newer work of considerable value. See also his *Europe in the Fourteenth and Fifteenth Centuries* (1971).

Italian Society and Politics
There is interesting material on Renaissance businessmen and bankers in M. Beard, *A History of the Business Man* (1938), and R. de Roover, *The Rise and Decline of the Medici Bank* * (1963). I. Origo, *The Merchant of Prato* (1957), is an enjoyable study of a small-town businessman. G. Mattingly, *Renaissance Diplomacy* * (1955), traces the origins of modern diplomacy in Italy in a fascinating way. There are histories of all the major Italian states, but the most important for an understanding of the Renaissance are those on Florence. G. Brucker, *Renaissance Florence* (1969), is the best brief treatment in English. D. Herlihy, *Pisa in the Early Renaissance* (1958), and W. M. Bowsky, *The Finances of the Commune of Siena* (1970), provide the histories of two other leading cities. H. Baron, *The Crisis of the Early Italian Renaissance,* * 2 vols. (1966), is an important study of Florentine politics and culture in the early fifteenth century. Perhaps the best single volume on Machiavelli is F. Chabod, *Machiavelli and the Renaissance* * (1958). Felix Gilbert, *Machiavelli and Guiccardini* (1965) is also very good. D. Merejkowski's novel, *The Romance of Leonardo da Vinci* * (1902), gives a vivid and unforgettable picture of Italian society based on sound historical scholarship. D. S. Chambers, *The Imperial Age of Venice: 1380–1580* * (1970), examines Venice's power as a commercial enterprise. On another kind of enterprise, see M. Mallet, *Mercenaries and Their Masters* (1974), an excellent study of the *condottieri*.

Literature and Art
Most of the general works listed above contain discussions of the literary and artistic achievements of the age. The classic literary history, still well worth reading, is F. de Sanctis, *History of Italian Literature* (1870; trans. 1931), R. R. Bolgar, *The Classical Heritage* (1954), traces Greek and Roman influences on western literature. P. O. Kristeller, *Renaissance Thought,* * 2 vols. (1961, 1965), is a brief but penetrating analysis. The best introduction to the educational theories of the Humanists is W. H. Woodward, *Vittorino da Feltre and Other Humanist Educators* * (1905). Of the many works on Italian Renaissance art, three by masters of their subjects may be mentioned: B. Berenson, *The Italian Painters of the Renaissance,* * rev. ed. (1930), E. Panofsky, *Renaissance and Renascences in Western Art,* 2 vols. (1965) and M. Baxendall, *Painting and Experience in Fifteenth Century Italy* (1972). An older handbook, still useful, is H. Wölffin, *The Art of the Italian Renaissance* * (1903; edited as *Classic Art,* 1952). A. C. Krey, *A City That Art Built* (1936), is an interesting brief attempt to relate cultural flowering to economic and political circumstances in Florence. See also A. Smart, *The Renaissance and Mannerism in Italy* (1971), and A. Blunt, *Artistic Theory in Italy, 1450–1600* * (1962).

Contemporary Writings
It is easy to become acquainted with the thought of Renaissance writers because of the number of readily available translations. Two source collections are particularly good: *The Renaissance Philosophy of Man,* * ed. by E. Cassirer (1948), which includes Pico's *Oration,* and *The Portable Renaissance Reader,* * ed. by J. B. Ross and M. M. McLaughlin (1953), which includes a selection from Alberti's *On the Family.* See also W. L. Gundersheimer, *The Italian Renaissance* * (1965). There are many editions of Boccaccio's *Decameron,* Cellini's *Autobiography,* and Castiglione's *The Courtier.* N. Machiavelli, *The Prince and the Discourses* * (trans. 1940; Modern Library), is the most convenient edition. C. B. Coleman has edited *The Treatise of Lorenzo Valla on the Donation of Constantine* (1922), and E. A. McCurdy has edited *The Notebooks of Leonardo da Vinci,* 2 vols. (1938). *The Vespasiano Memoirs* * (trans. 1926) offer contemporary thumbnail sketches of Humanists, artists, and princes. G. Bull has translated Vasari's *Lives of the Artists* * (1965).

The Church
There is a full account of the councils of Constance and Basel and of the Renaissance popes in the five-volume work by an Anglican bishop, M. Creighton, *A History of the Papacy from the Great Schism to the Sack of Rome* (1919). The best account, however, based on the Vatican archives, is the still larger work of the Swiss Catholic L. Pastor, *History of the Popes,* 40 vols. (trans. 1891–1953). On conciliar ideas, see B. Tierney, *Foundations of the Conciliar Theory* (1955), and E. F. Jacob, *Essays in the Conciliar Epoch* (1953). H. Jedin, *A History of the Council of Trent,* Vol. I (trans. 1957), gives a good account of the events leading up to the council.

Technological and Economic Growth in the North
On printing, see P. Butler, *The Origin of Printing in Europe* (1940); D. C. McMurtrie, *The Book: The Story of Printing and Bookmaking,* 3rd rev. ed. (1943); E. P. Goldschmidt, *The Printed Book of the Renaissance* (1950); and V. Scholderer, *Johann Gutenberg* (1963). R. Ehrenberg, *Capital and Finance in the Age of the Renaissance* (trans. 1928), is a study of the Fuggers. The Fugger Newsletters of the later sixteenth century are available in *News and Rumor in Renaissance Europe.* * E. Eisenstein, *The Printing Press as an Agent of Change* (1979) is a good account of this great innovation. On science, see M. Boas, *The Scientific Renaissance, 1450–1630* * (1962), W. Wightman, *Science and the Renaissance,* 2 vols. (1962), and F. A. Yates, *Giordano Bruno and the Hermetic Tradition* (1964).

17 Reform and Revolution in Western Christendom

At the opening of the sixteenth century, the Roman Church was in greater danger than it had been at any time since the Great Schism. Suspicion of Church policy and contempt for the leadership of the Church were widespread. Even the peasants were annoyed by the financial demands of the clergy and bored by routine services. Laymen would flock to their churches for the great feasts or to Rome for a papal jubilee, but many of them were also ready to respond to radical evangelical preachers. There had always been some tension between the Church and the bourgeoisie. The Church had never been able to incorporate business ethics into its system of values, and the bourgeoisie had never been happy about the Church's special financial privileges. The better educated the townsmen became, the more clearly they saw the weaknesses of the Church. The nobility either denounced the corruption of the Church or profited from it.

Most dangerous of all were the secular rulers who were limiting the papacy's powers of taxation, jurisdiction, and appointment. Caught in the maelstrom of Italian power politics, the popes of the fifteenth century found themselves threatened by leagues of Italian princes and thus forced to seek help from and make concessions to more distant and more powerful rulers. The popes had no military power of their own. Moreover, by 1500 they were regularly in debt, with little prospect of finding any easy way out of their financial straits.

THE NEED FOR REFORM IN THE WESTERN CHURCH

Even able and devoted Vicars of Christ might have had difficulty defending the independence of the papacy and raising its moral prestige. But this was the era of the Renaissance popes—at best, good administrators and patrons of artists and scholars; at worst, corrupt and immoral men with secular tastes and interests. Some, like Alexander VI, used the contributions of the faithful to carve out principalities for their illegitimate sons. Most of them, under financial pressure, sold justice in their courts and appointments to office in their councils.

Bishops and archbishops throughout Europe were generally of noble blood, and many of them had been nominated by monarchs or by the pope for loyal service rather than for their piety or administrative ability. Some held more than one bishopric, although this was contrary to canon law, and some rarely visited their sees (one bishop visited his only once, when he was buried there). Even conscientious bishops found that their power to appoint the clergy and to reform abuses within their dioceses had diminished. Many powers that properly belonged to the bishop had either fallen into the hands of local laymen or had been "reserved" by the pope. The ignorance and immorality of the parish clergy were bywords among contemporary writers. The parish priest in fact was no better or worse than he had been for centuries, but moral sensitivity to clerical misconduct had been rising. Furthermore, the tithes that the priest levied and the fees that he charged for baptisms, marriages, and burials were burdensome to peasants and small craftsmen. In earlier centuries monks and friars had made up for many of the deficiencies of the parish clergy, but by 1500 the religious orders had little influence on laymen. Monastic life no longer attracted the pious, as it had several centuries earlier, and monasteries now had to search out recruits to keep their numbers up.

The most widespread complaints were caused by practices that could be interpreted as the selling of spiritual benefits. The Church was rich in land but poor in the newer forms of wealth. It cost money to maintain such a large institution, and the clergy had a right to ask for a fair share of the growing wealth of Europe. But the methods used to raise money and the purposes for which the money was spent (such as waging war to regain territory claimed for the Papal States) outraged many believers. Papal demands for money were passed from the bishops to the parish clergy to the people. Thus some priests demanded the best garment of a deceased parishioner as a "mortuary fee" and had regular tables of charges for other religious rites. Even worse were the abuses that the pope allowed to creep into the sale of indulgences.

Lucas Cranach the Younger, *Martin Luther and the Wittenberg Reformers* (*ca.* 1543).

Indulgences

Indulgences, in fact, were the raw nerve of the Church's whole financial system. An indulgence was a remission of the temporal penalty for sin (penances in this life and the pains of Purgatory after death) imposed by a priest in the sacrament of penance. It was granted on condition of true contrition for the sin and in consideration of some pious deed performed, such as going on a crusade or

373

A pair of woodcuts by Lucas Cranach the Elder contrasting Jesus and the pope. On the left, Jesus is driving the moneychangers from the temple; on the right, the pope is taking money for indulgences.

a pilgrimage. During the Middle Ages a money "contribution" became the normal consideration, and the necessity for contrition was often forgotten by the believer. In the fourteenth century the popes developed the doctrine that Christ and the saints had accumulated a "treasury of merits" from which Christ's Vicars could dispense benefits to the faithful through indulgences. In the fifteenth century Sixtus IV, on the strength of this doctrine, claimed the power to release the souls of the dead from the penance they were undergoing in Purgatory as the temporal penalty for their sins. This claim helped make the indulgence trade even more lucrative. It was hard to withhold a contribution that would release the soul of a dead parent from years of suffering in the next world. In theory, the money was a "contribution" for pious purposes. But many laymen concluded that the Church was selling salvation at a price—and was then wasting the money on petty wars and luxurious living.

The Dangers of Criticism

Criticism of the Church was not new. Though the Church was divinely instituted, everyone knew that it was administered by fallible human beings—that is,

by sinners. The moral level of the clergy was probably better in 1500 than in the year 1000. But the world of 1500 was far different from that of 1000, and it is well to review some of the main differences in order to understand why criticism now constituted a real danger to the Church.

The European world of 1500 was more secular in its interests and ideals, as we have seen. The artist, the despot, the sea captain, and the businessman were pursuing careers that seemed more exciting than sainthood, and the medieval interpretation of life in this world as a pilgrimage to life after death seemed unsatisfying, even though it was not yet openly rejected. Granted that salvation was the goal of mankind, some men began to ask: Was renunciation of the world the only, or even the surest, way to gain that goal?

While the fifteenth century was an age of increasing secular interests for some, it was an age of heightened religious sensitivity and piety for others. Both the worldly minded and the devout were becoming critical of the growing complexity of the Church's sacraments and ceremonies. Popular piety of the late Middle Ages had nurtured a luxuriant growth of religious practices that seemed to verge on superstition and idolatry. The cult of the saints and the veneration of

In the first of this pair of woodcuts, Cranach shows Jesus kissing the feet of his disciples as he washes them. The other woodcut shows the pope offering his foot to be kissed by kings and nobles.

relics became a kind of obsession. For almost every human ill there was a saint, who, if properly approached, could prevent or heal the affliction. And as the number of sacred symbols and ceremonies multiplied, their religious significance almost disappeared. A fifteenth-century French artist painted a sensual, photographic portrait of the French king's mistress as the Virgin Mary, apparently without being conscious of any blasphemy. As a modern historian has put it, the religious atmosphere of the later Middle Ages was "supersaturated," and the most observant church leaders of the fifteenth century grew worried. They saw that the Church was becoming dangerously vulnerable to radicals who might ask: What is the core of Christianity? Is it to venerate an image of St. Anthony, to avoid meat on Fridays, and to go on a pilgrimage? Or, rather, is it to love one's neighbor and to live a Christlike life?

A final reason why ecclesiastical abuses were so dangerous to the Church in 1500 was that there were now secular rulers strong enough to use the cry for reform for their own purposes. The monarchs of western Europe were already appointing and taxing the clergy. The upper classes all over Europe coveted the wealth of the Church. Many

secular rulers, should they so decide, now had the power to confiscate the Church's lands, buildings, and revenues in the name of reform. Reform by royal command sometimes had good results. In Spain, Cardinal Jiménez de Cisneros, strongly backed by Ferdinand and Isabella, instituted many reforms in the Spanish clergy at the opening of the sixteenth century. But there was always the danger that reform by a secular power might result in state control of the Church and confiscation of its property.

Failure of Fifteenth-Century Reform Movements

Various schemes for reform had been advanced in the fifteenth century. In the Rhineland, the Brethren of the Common Life, a group of laymen who devoted themselves to communal living and biblical piety, emphasized direct, intimate communion with God in their communities and schools. In Florence between 1494 and 1498 one of the most remarkable preachers of the age, the Dominican monk Girolamo Savonarola, moved multitudes to repentance and encouraged the crowds to follow an old custom of making bonfires of their wigs, makeup, and other "vanities" during Lent. These reformers still held to the medieval conception of reform. According to that conception, the Church itself was divinely constituted and so could not be "reformed," but the individuals who composed it could and should be regenerated. The leaders at the councils of Constance and Basel were reformers of a more modern sort. They meant to reform the institution itself by giving more power to representatives of the clergy, thus making the pope a limited monarch. Hus wanted to reform both the individual and the institution by returning to the Bible as the standard of Christian living and ecclesiastical practice.

Each of these differing conceptions of reform was to take root and bear seed in one way or another during the sixteenth century. But before 1500 the impetus of each movement was soon spent, and the institutional abuses remained untouched. The councils failed to make permanent changes in the constitution of the Church, and both Hus and Savonarola were burned as heretics. Whenever attempts at reform threatened to undermine the status of the clergy as mediators between God and man, or the power of the pope as the Vicar of Christ, they were declared heretical and stamped out. It seemed that the strength of vested interest and the dead weight of authority were so strong that the Church would never be roused from its complacency.

Christian Humanism

A new and hopeful type of reform movement emerged in the sixteenth century—Christian Humanism. Under the inspiration of the classical revival in Italy, a number of scholars in northern Europe began to recommend a return to the best of both the classical and the Christian traditions through a study of the classics and the Bible. They argued that if men could appreciate the ethical perfection of Socrates and Jesus, of Plato and Paul, then the absurdities of theological hair splitting and the irrelevance of many ecclesiastical practices would become evident. Reform would inevitably follow from a better understanding of the simplicity of primitive Christianity—and of the noble ideals of the Greeks and Romans, which they felt to be complementary rather than antagonistic to Christi-

anity. Let the Church take for its guides the Bible and the early Fathers rather than the scholastic theologians of the Middle Ages. Abuses would disappear if laymen and clerics alike would recognize that Christianity was an attitude of mind and a way of life, not a complex set of dogmas and ceremonies.

This program was fundamentally conservative, designed to save the Church from itself. It had a radical element in its demand for lay participation in reform and for vernacular translations of the Bible so that the laity would understand the need for reform. Nevertheless, its leaders were almost without exception loyal to Rome. They were obviously optimistic in their estimate of human nature. They rated the power of reason and education very high, and encouraged historical and literary studies in the hope that they would reveal earlier and purer practices. Cardinal Jiménez in Spain set scholars to producing a monumental edition of the Bible that presented the original Hebrew and Greek texts in parallel columns with the Latin. In Germany, Johann Reuchlin defended the study of Hebrew literature as a means of understanding the Old Testament, even though a group of Dominicans wished to destroy all Hebrew books. In France, Lefèvre d'Etaples studied the Epistles of Paul and translated the New Testament into French (1523) in an effort to enlighten his contemporaries and further the cause of reform. For Sir Thomas More in England, study and reform were also closely related. In his famous *Utopia*, More wrote a searching analysis of the most glaring social, political, and ecclesiastical evils of his day from the point of view of a scholar steeped in Humanism and the Gospels as well as in the monastic tradition of the Middle Ages.

Erasmus

The acknowledged leader of these Christian Humanists was Erasmus of Rotterdam (*ca.* 1469–1536). Erasmus' enthusiasm for the Greco-Roman classics matched his enthusiasm for the Bible and early Christian writings. He devoted his life to scholarship in the conviction that sound learning would help save the Church. He edited the New Testament in the original Greek (1516), with a preface urging that it be translated into all the vulgar tongues, and he published editions of the early Church Fathers. His hundreds of letters and his briefer books were even more influential. In them, with lively humor, underlying seriousness, and an unsurpassed command of the Latin language, he argued for what he called "the philosophy of Christ," the love of God and neighbor that he saw as the essence of Christianity. He insisted that this love be expressed through an active life. He feared that the Church of his day had obscured this essential truth with useless forms and ceremonies. In a typical passage he ridiculed monkish ideas of religion. When the final reckoning comes, one monk will point to his fastings and ceremonies for credit; "another will boast that for sixty years he never touched money, except when his fingers were protected by two pairs of gloves." Christ will interrupt their boasts and say, "Whence comes this new race of Jews [that is, Pharisees]? I promised the inheritance of my Father, not to cowls, prayers, or fasts, but to works of charity." This device of imagining how Christ himself would judge the world of the 1500s was characteristic of Christian Humanism.

Christian Humanism offered the last chance of peaceful reform. But it was a movement that needed time, patience, and understanding to have any impact on the upper classes, and it never had much appeal for the mass of the population. It influenced every effort, both Protestant and Catholic, to reform the Church, but as a practical program it was doomed to failure. It was too aristocratic and too intellectual. The times were revolutionary, and the remedies that Europe was to adopt were both sterner and simpler than Erasmus' "philosophy of Christ."

LUTHER'S
REVOLT FROM ROME

On October 31, 1517, an Augustinian friar serving as Professor of Bible in the little University of Wittenberg in Saxony prepared ninety-five theses, or propositions, for academic debate on the subject of indulgences. The author, Martin Luther (1483–1546), was outraged by the unscrupulous salesmanship of a Dominican friar named Tetzel who had been hawking indulgences in Magdeburg. "So soon as coin in coffer rings," Tetzel was reported as preaching, "the soul from Purgatory springs." The proceeds from this particular sale of indulgences were meant to go toward the building of St. Peter's church in Rome, though half

Portrait of Erasmus
by Albrecht Dürer.

Erasmus' Preface to His Edition of the New Testament

I utterly dissent from those who are unwilling that the sacred Scriptures should be read by the unlearned translated into their vulgar tongue, as though Christ had taught such subtleties that they can scarcely be understood even by a few theologians, or, as though the strength of the Christian religion consisted in men's ignorance of it. The mysteries of kings it may be safer to conceal, but Christ wished his mysteries to be published as openly as possible. I wish that even the weakest woman should read the Gospel—should read the epistles of Paul. And I wish these were translated into all languages, so that they might be read and understood, not only by Scots and Irishmen, but also by Turks and Saracens. To make them understood is surely the first step. It may be that they might be ridiculed by many, but some would take them to heart. I long that the husbandman should sing portions of them to himself as he follows the plough, that the weaver should hum them to the tune of his shuttle, that the traveller should beguile with their stories the tedium of his journey.

From Erasmus, "Paraclesis," *Novum Instrumentum,* trans. by Frederic Seebohm, in *The Oxford Reformers* (New York: Dutton, 1914), p. 203.

O ihr deutschen meidet mich recht/
Des heiligen Vaters Papstes Knecht/
Bin ich/und br ing euch ist allein/
Zehn tausent und neun hundert carein/
Gnad und Ablaß von einer Sünd/
Vor euch/ewer Eltern/Weib und Kind/
Sol ein feder gewehret sein
So viel ihr legt ins Kästelein/
So bald der Gülden im Becken klingt/
Im huy die Seel im Himel springt/

Contemporary caricature of Johann Tetzel hawking indulgences. The last line of the jingle is: "So soon as coin in coffer rings, the soul from Purgatory springs."

of it actually ended up in the pockets of the Archbishop of Mainz and of the Fugger banking firm. Luther's theses were immediately printed and debated not only in Wittenberg but all over Germany. The sensation they caused marked the start of the Protestant Reformation. Luther's chief propositions were:

> There is no divine authority for preaching that the soul flies out of purgatory immediately the money clinks in the bottom of the chest. . . . It is certainly possible that when the money clinks in the bottom of the chest, avarice and greed increase. . . . All those who believe themselves certain of their own salvation by means of letters of indulgence will be eternally damned, together with their teachers. . . . Any Christian whatsoever, who is truly repentant, enjoys plenary remission from penalty and guilt, and this is given him without letters of indulgence.

At the time, Martin Luther was a strong-willed, keen-minded, high-strung man in his early thirties. He was the son of a prosperous peasant turned miner, who had been able to give his boy a university education. The young Luther had experienced several severe emotional crises; the most acute one led him to become a friar. But in his convent he had become increasingly dissatisfied with the

emphasis his teachers laid on good works. He had been a most conscientious friar; he had fasted and prayed and confessed without end. If good works could win a man salvation, surely they should win it for him, he thought. Yet performing the acts commanded by the Church gave him no inner certainty that he was forgiven, only a growing sense of guilt, despair, and deepening spiritual crisis. Peace came to him when he suddenly understood what St. Paul had meant when he said that a man is saved not by doing the works of the Jewish law but by his faith in Christ. The ceremonies and religious practices of the medieval Church seemed to Luther a new Jewish law. Man is too corrupted by sin to meet the demands of such a law by his own efforts, and so he must rely on his faith in God's mercy. It is unthinkable that a man can buy God's favor by doing a good deed or performing some sacramental act. In the matter of saving a man's soul, Luther concluded, God does everything, man can do nothing.

It took Luther some time to work out the revolutionary implications of this thought. If man is saved by faith alone, then ceremonies and sacraments, pilgrimages and indulgences, everything the medieval Church called "good works," are at best irrelevant and at worst dangerous. Indulgences were the first "good work" at which Luther struck. Within a short time after his attack their sales dropped off sharply in Germany. When the Dominicans, chief sellers of the indulgences, persuaded Pope Leo X to condemn his theses, Luther was gradually driven to deny the authority of the pope. Soon afterward, when he came to believe that John Hus had been right on certain matters in spite of his condemnation by the Council of Constance, he denied the authority of general councils as well. By April 1521 Luther was standing before the Emperor Charles V at an imperial diet at Worms and declaring that he was bound by the authority of the Scripture and his own conscience rather than by that of either pope or council. He could not recant any of his writings, he added, because his conscience was "captive to the Word of God" and because it was "neither safe nor right to go against conscience." The

Bible and conscience—these were to be the two chief pillars of Protestant Christianity.

Luther was not burned at Worms, as Hus had been at Constance. His safe-conduct was respected, and he was allowed to return to the protection of his ruler, Frederick, the Elector of Saxony. For twenty-five years, till his death in 1546, he taught, preached, and wrote at Wittenberg. Meanwhile the revolt against the papacy that he had started gathered momentum and spread over northern Europe. In the end, the unity of Western Christendom was permanently destroyed.

Lutheran Principles

In breaking with the papacy, Luther was guided by three main principles: salvation by faith, not by works; the ultimate authority of the Bible; and the priesthood of all believers. The three were closely related. It was through study of the Bible that Luther came to his belief in salvation by faith, and it was to the Bible that he always appealed against the authority of tradition or the papacy. His greatest literary work was a German translation of the Bible (completed in 1534), which he wrote in order that God's Word might be put into the hands of every devout person in Germany who could read. There was no essential difference between a priest and a layman, he insisted. A dedicated layman reverently reading the Scripture was closer to divine truth than a worldly pope proclaiming dogma for the Church. Christ had meant every believer to be a priest to his neighbor; He had not intended a special few to act as mediators between man and God. A Christian can serve God as well by being an honest merchant or a faithful housewife as by becoming a monk or a nun. Thus Luther encouraged the dissolution of the monastic orders, and in order to dramatize his convictions he married a nun and became the happy father of six children.

Luther's original protest had been a purely religious matter, rooted in his own spiritual experience. But to gain support he had to appeal to the nationalistic and financial grievances of his fellow Germans. "What has brought us Germans to such a pass that we have to suffer this robbery and this destruction of our property by the Pope?" he asked in 1520.

Portrait of Martin Luther by Lucas Cranach (1533).

Luther on Justification by Faith

For the word of God cannot be received and honored by any works, but by faith alone. Hence it is clear that, as the soul needs the word alone for life and justification, so it is justified by faith alone and not by any works. For if it could be justified by any other means, it would have no need of the word, nor consequently of faith. . . .

It is evident that by no outward work or labor can the inward man be at all justified, made free and saved, and that no works whatever have any relation to him. And so, on the other hand, it is solely by impiety and incredulity of heart that he becomes guilty and a slave of sin, deserving condemnation; not by any outward sin or work.

Therefore the first care of every Christian ought to be to lay aside all reliance on works, and strengthen his faith alone more and more, and by it grow in the knowledge, not of works, but of Christ Jesus, who has suffered and risen again for him.

From Martin Luther, *On Christian Liberty*, trans. by H. Wace and C. A. Buchheim, in *First Principles of the Reformation* (London: Murray, 1883), pp. 107–08.

"If the kingdom of France has resisted it, why do we Germans suffer ourselves to be fooled and deceived?" Luther appealed to princes eager to confiscate church property, to businessmen unhappy about papal finance, to German patriots resentful of the Italians who dominated the papacy and the College of Cardinals, and to devout laymen and conscientious priests who were shocked by the corruption in the Church. His principles of salvation by faith and of serving God in one's secular calling appealed especially to laymen, who found in them a way of reconciling Christian devotion with an active concern about worldly affairs. High-minded and low-minded motives were inextricably mixed in the minds of those who accepted Luther's arguments.

Luther had no intention of breaking away from the true Church of Christ or of setting up a rival organization. But after 1520 he was convinced that the Church founded by Christ and the Apostles had wandered from the true path somewhere in the Middle Ages, and that the bishop of Rome was not the Vicar of Christ, but rather the Anti-christ. Much of the dogma and ritual of the Church of his day, Luther believed, was the work of men, not of God. Such accretions must be swept away, leaving only the pure faith of the Apostles and the early Church Fathers. In the purified Church there would be only two sacraments (Baptism and Holy Communion) in place of seven, a simplified ritual in German rather than in Latin, and more emphasis on the congregation's participation in the service. But Luther did not want to set up a "new" church; he sought only to reform *the* Church. There could be only one true Church, into which all men were received in baptism. Either Luther was right in defying the pope, or the pope was right in excommunicating Luther. At first there were not two churches, one "Catholic" and one "Lutheran," but an irreconcilable argument over the nature of the one true Church.

The Spread of Lutheranism

Luther's ideas were spread by his students and by the books and pamphlets that poured from the new printing presses. During the early years of the movement, publishers overwhelmingly supported Luther. Leopold Ranke calculated that in 1523 there were almost four hundred books and pamphlets written by Luther and his supporters compared with only twenty or so pro-Catholic works. Many of the younger Humanists supported Luther's ideas and gave his movement intellectual respectability, and even the older Humanists greeted the attack on indulgences with joy. As Luther became more vehement in his criticism of the Church, the older Humanists retreated to the fold of the Catholic Church, but with some reluctance. Even Erasmus, who came to consider Luther a fanatic, broke with him only in 1524, after repeated pleas for moderation had failed.

Many priests and monks, on the other hand, were convinced by Luther's arguments and were among his first converts. These converts were especially numerous in the German cities, and the cities gave Luther his first solid basis of support. The town governments had their own grievances against the Church. The clergy could avoid most local taxes,

Luther on the Church

Thus it may come to pass that the Pope and his followers are wicked and not true Christians, and not being taught by God, have no true understanding, whereas a common man may have true understanding. Why should we then not follow him? Has not the Pope often erred? Who could help Christianity, in case the Pope errs, if we do not rather believe another who has the Scriptures for him? Therefore it is a wickedly devised fable—and they cannot quote a single letter to confirm it—that it is for the Pope alone to interpret the Scriptures or to confirm the interpretation of them. They have assumed the authority of their own selves. And though they say that this authority was given to St. Peter when the keys were given to him, it is plain enough that the keys were not given to St. Peter alone, but to the whole community. . . . Moreover, if the article of our faith is right, "I believe in the holy Christian Church," the Pope cannot alone be right; else we must say, "I believe in the Pope of Rome," and reduce the Christian Church to one man, which is a devilish and damnable heresy. Besides that, we are all priests, as I have said, and have all one faith, one Gospel, one Sacrament; how then should we not have the power of discerning and judging what is right or wrong in matters of faith?

From Martin Luther, "Address to the Christian Nobility of the German Nation," in *Luther's Primary Works,* ed. by H. Wace and C. A. Buchheim (London: Hodder and Stoughton, 1896), pp. 170–71.

and at the same time the financial demands of the Church bore especially heavily on the urban population. The worldly life of the higher clergy and the ignorance of many parish priests were offensive to pious laymen. The towns had already taken over responsibility for most social services (education and charity); why should they not assume responsibility for religion as well? Thus in town after town, with very little violence, the conservative clergy were replaced by followers of Luther. Considering that many towns were in fact independent political entities, they were establishing the first state churches. They did so a decade or more before some of the German princes made Lutheranism a state religion. Luther was not entirely happy about this development (he would have preferred no secular control), but he realized that if the truth, as he saw it, was to prevail, it must be protected by secular rulers.

The peasants were excited by Luther's message at first, but he lost most of them after the Peasants' Rebellion of 1524 to 1525. This was the largest and bloodiest of the many peasant uprisings that resulted from complex economic and social causes during the later Middle Ages. The rebels' chief aim was to abolish serfdom and the burdens of the manorial system. "Therefore do we find in the Scripture that we are free," they argued, "and we will be free." Luther was close enough to his peasant origins to sympathize with their demands, but the freedom he was interested in was an inner religious freedom, freedom from an ecclesiastical system, not from social or political bondage. He felt that the peasants were perverting his message, and their violence further turned him against them. Finally he wrote a bitter condemnation of the uprising. The rebellion was put down with atrocities that went beyond those of the rebels. The peasants felt that Luther had betrayed them, but the middle and ruling classes welcomed his social conservatism. After 1525 he and his followers fought as hard against radicals, who wanted to carry the religious revolt too far, as they did against the Roman Catholics, who wished to wipe out Lutheranism.

There was at first no effective resistance in Germany to the spread of Luther's ideas. The emperor Charles V never wavered in his orthodoxy, but the task of holding together his scattered dominions proved so difficult that he was unable to bring political or military pressure to bear on cities and states that had turned Lutheran. From 1522 to 1559 Charles and his son Philip were caught up in a series of conflicts with France that absorbed much of their energy and income. Meanwhile Charles and his brother Ferdinand were also trying to stem the tide of Turkish conquest in the Mediterranean and the Danube Valley. The French in the West and the Turks in the East, sometimes in alliance with each other, allowed the emperor only a few intervals of peace in which to turn his attention to the religious division of Germany.

By the time of Luther's death in 1546, the German principalities were about evenly divided between the two faiths, while the majority of the free cities supported the Lutheran movement. In 1547, during a peaceful interlude in his international struggles, Charles V finally found an opportunity to attack the Lutheran states. The confused war that followed proved that neither side could destroy the other, and in 1555 the emperor reluctantly allowed his brother Ferdinand, who was ruler of Austria and later emperor, to conclude the Religious Peace of Augsburg. This peace allowed the city-states and princes of the Empire to choose between Lutheranism and Catholicism and bound them to respect each other's rights. *Cuius regio, eius religio*, as someone later summed up the

Title page of the first German translation of the Bible, by Martin Luther, printed in 1534 with the approval of the Elector of Saxony.

Contemporary engraving depicting a noble lady and her son kneeling before peasant rebels to plead for their lives during the Peasants' Rebellion (1524–25).

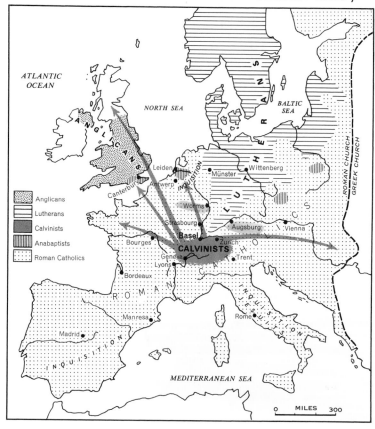

southern Germany remained mostly "Catholic." The division remains today about as it was in 1560. Outside Germany, Lutheran ideas spread widely but took root only in Scandinavia, where Denmark, Norway, and Sweden became Lutheran before mid-century. Perhaps because Luther spoke so forcefully in the German idiom to his follow Germans, his teaching was not so well adapted to export as was the teaching of John Calvin.

CALVINISM

Luther's University of Wittenberg was not the only center from which reform ideas radiated. Other important centers were Zurich, Basel, Strasbourg, and especially Geneva. In these southern German and Swiss cities there developed a type of Protestantism closely related to Lutheranism but different in emphasis. There was more reliance on a highly developed system of theology and church organization and more stress on moral conduct and political action. The members of this second family of Protestant churches are generally called "Reformed" churches, in contrast with the "Lutheran."

Among the early Swiss and south German reformers were the Humanists Ulrich Zwingli of Zurich (1484–1531) and Martin Bucer of Strasbourg (1491–1551). Neither man agreed entirely with Luther. Zwingli took a more radical position on the sacraments, arguing that Communion was essentially a memorial service commemorating the Last Supper. Bucer tried to reconcile various Protestant groups and was more tolerant than most of the other reformers.

More influential than either Zwingli or Bucer was John Calvin (1509–64). Calvin had been trained as a lawyer and a Humanist in his native France before he became converted to Protestantism and settled down as a pastor in Geneva. He learned much from Luther, as well as from Zwingli and Bucer. Through these influences and through his early training, he became the chief theologian and organizer of second-generation Protestantism. His *Institutes of the Christian Religion* served as the basic handbook of Protes-

Sketch of John Calvin drawn by a student, perhaps during a lecture.

principle: the ruler determines the religion for the region. People who disliked the ruler's choice might migrate to another state. Lutherans were allowed to keep any church lands they had seized before 1552, but it was agreed that every Catholic bishop or abbot who turned Protestant in the future would have to resign his title and leave his lands in Catholic hands. This last clause was difficult to interpret and caused trouble later. The chief flaw in the settlement, however, was the exclusion of Calvinists, whose numbers were growing rapidly, from the benefits of the peace.

The Peace of Augsburg was the first official recognition, however grudging, that Western Christendom had been rent asunder and would have to continue as a house divided. It was not religious toleration, but it was a step along the way. In the end, northern Germany became mostly "Protestant" (as Lutherans had been called since 1529, when they presented a "protest" at an imperial diet);

The more rigid Protestants objected to all religious paintings and sculpture as leading to idolatry. In this engraving of 1579, Calvinists are pulling down statues of saints and destroying stained-glass windows.

tant principles for two centuries. It was a clear, well-organized, well-written book in both its Latin and its French versions, and its argument had all the logic a trained lawyer could bring to it. Calvin's two polar principles were the absolute sovereignty of God and the radical depravity of man. No acts of sinful man can merit salvation; God, through his inscrutable will, has destined some to be saved and some to be damned. This doctrine of "predestination," of course, made "good works" in the Catholic sense useless. It did not, however, condone fatalism; men were always God's instruments to carry out His will. Good works might not save a Calvinist—but they might be evidence that God was working through him. Good works were a "sign" that a man was probably one of the Elect.

As time went on, Calvin's church in Geneva became the model for Presbyterian or Reformed churches in France, England, Scotland, the Netherlands, the Rhineland, Bohemia, and Hungary—later in North America and Dutch South Africa. Calvin advocated that each local congregation have a ruling body composed of both ministers and laymen (presbyters, or elders) who were to watch carefully over the moral conduct and beliefs of the faithful. These officials then met in synods that linked up the Reformed congregations of a whole district or nation. Thus in place of the Roman Catholic hierarchy of bishops and priests under the pope, and in place of Luther's state churches, Calvin devised a peculiarly tough and flexible system of church government that resisted control by the state, maintained strict discipline, and, in the lay elders, included a potentially democratic element. Unlike Lutheranism, Calvinism met the two conditions for

Calvin on Predestination

Predestination we call the eternal decree of God, by which he has determined in himself, what he would have to become of every individual of mankind. For they are not all created with a similar destiny; but eternal life is foreordained for some, and eternal damnation for others. . . .

In conformity, therefore, to the clear doctrine of the Scripture, we assert, that by an eternal and immutable counsel, God has once for all determined, both whom he would admit to salvation, and whom he would condemn to destruction. We affirm that this counsel, as far as concerns the elect, is founded on his gratuitous mercy, totally irrespective of human merit; but that to those whom he devotes to condemnation, the gate of life is closed by a just and irreprehensible, but incomprehensible, judgment. . . .

How exceedingly presumptuous it is only to inquire into the causes of the Divine will; which is in fact, and is justly entitled to be, the cause of everything that exists. . . . For the will of God is the highest rule of justice; so that what he wills must be considered just, for this very reason, because he wills it.

From John Calvin, *Institutes of the Christian Religion,* trans. by John Allen (Philadelphia: Westminster Press, 1930), Book III, Ch. 21, pars. 5, 7; Ch. 23, par. 2.

Radical Protestantism: The Teaching of Menno Simons

Menno Simons (1496–1561) was one of the ablest leaders of the radical wing of the Reformation. Simons' followers formed the Mennonite Church, which still exists. His ideas also contributed to the development of the Baptist Church. He never summed up his doctrine in a single document; it has to be put together from scattered pamphlets.

We do not find in Scripture a single word by which Christ has ordained the baptism of infants, or that his apostles taught and practiced it. We say that infant baptism is but a human invention. . . . To baptize before that which is required for baptism, namely faith, is to place the cart before the horse.

Never should any commandment be observed which is not contained in God's holy Word, either in letter or in spirit.

The regenerated do not go to war nor fight. . . . How can a Christian, according to Scripture, consistently retaliate, rebel, make war, murder, slay, torture, steal, rob, and burn cities and conquer countries?

Where have you read in the Scriptures, that Christ or the Apostles called upon the power of the magistracy against those who would not hear their doctrine or obey their words? . . . Faith is a gift of God, therefore it cannot be forced on anyone by worldly authorities or by the sword.

We must be born from above, must be changed and renewed in our hearts and thus be transplanted from the unrighteous and evil nature of Adam into the righteous and good nature of Christ, or we cannot be helped in eternity by any means, divine or human.

From "Selections from the Writings of Menno Simons," in *The Medieval World and Its Transformations*, Vol. II, ed. by G. M. Straka (New York: McGraw-Hill, 1967), pp. 463, 466, 467, 468, 470.

on the Dutch Netherlands. Calvinist minorities formed a kind of revolutionary international society throughout Europe in the later sixteenth century. Like their chief rivals, the Jesuits, the Reformed ministers were often able to elicit a religious loyalty that transcended loyalty to secular rulers and nations. Calvinism was the militant, international form of Protestantism.

THE RADICALS

Some reformers wanted to move much further and faster along the road of religious revolution than Luther, Zwingli, or Calvin. Throughout Germany workers and peasants had been hard hit by the economic changes of the fourteenth and fifteenth centuries. Often their discontent took on a religious coloring, combining easily with what survived of earlier heresies—Waldensian, Lollard, and Hussite, for example. These uneducated men and women took most of Luther's ideas literally—the Bible as ultimate authority, the priesthood of all believers, the freedom of true Christians from man-made ecclesiastical laws and organizations. During the 1520s in Switzerland and in the upper Rhine Valley particularly, little groups of such people came together proclaiming that a true church of Christians was a voluntary association of converted believers, not an official or established institution like that of the Lutherans or Catholics. Most of them believed that until a man came of age and knew what he was doing, he should not be admitted to the church through baptism. Thus, since they had to rebaptize most of their converts, their enemies called them Anabaptists, or rebaptizers. Their ritual was simple, and generally they took the Bible literally. Most of them would not take an oath in a law court, accept public office, or serve as soldiers; some practiced communism of goods on the model described in the second chapter of Acts.

They were cruelly persecuted by Catholics and conservative Protestants alike as dangerous heretics and social radicals. A small but violent minority gave temporary excuse for such persecu-

successful export all over Europe: it possessed a systematic theology, and it offered a practical substitute for medieval church organization.

By the 1550s Calvinism was spreading rapidly. Except in a few cities like Geneva, the nerve center of the movement, and in Scotland, Calvinists never became a majority. But the Calvinist minorities were stubborn, well organized, and widely distributed over Europe. Calvinism left a deep imprint on English society in the form of Puritanism, on France through the Huguenots, on Hungary, and

tion by capturing the city of Münster and conducting a reign of terror there for over a year (1534–35). But generally they were pacifists and eager to suffer as their models, the Apostles, had done. After the 1530s the Anabaptists were to be found mainly in the Netherlands, Bohemia, Poland, and England, having been stamped out in southern Germany, where they had originated.

In addition to such "evangelical" groups, which tried to return to the first-century Gospel even more literally than Luther, there were other religious radicals. Some, like the Quakers in the seventeenth century, continued the medieval mystical tradition by following an inner voice rather than the letter of the Scripture. Others were more rationalistic, anticipating the doctrine that the nineteenth century was to call Unitarianism, the belief that there is only one God, not a Holy Trinity, and that Jesus was not God but man at his best. No one in the sixteenth century went quite this far, but the Spanish physician Michael Servetus (1511–53) combined a rationalistic denial of the divinity of Jesus with a rationalistic ethical program. He was imprisoned by the Catholic Inquisition, escaped, and in 1553 was burned at the stake in Geneva as a result of Calvin's influence.

The ideas of these religious radicals, who went too far not only for Roman Catholics but also for Luther and Calvin, were of great importance in the religious history of the Anglo-Saxon peoples. It was in England during the seventeenth century and later in the English colonies in America that Anabaptist ideas were fully realized. There the doctrine that the church should be a voluntary association, "a free church in a free state," organizing itself and electing its pastor, was accepted without any restrictions. Modern Baptists (who believe in adult baptism only), Congregationalists (who emphasize the autonomy of local congregations of Christians), and Quakers (who rely on the "inner light" and tend toward pacifism) all look back to the religious radicals of the sixteenth century as their remote ancestors. American Protestant conceptions of the place of the church in society derive more from the Anabaptists than from either Luther or Calvin.

ANGLICANISM

The peculiarity of the English Reformation is that it was initiated by a king for reasons that had almost nothing to do with religion. Henry VIII cut England off from the papacy much as the king of France had cut his realm off from the papal obedience in 1395. But in England the jurisdictional breach with Rome was followed by a decisive religious change.

In 1527, ten years after Luther had written his ninety-five theses, both England and its king seemed entirely orthodox. Parliament had restricted papal rights of appointment and jurisdiction in England, but England had not gone so far toward developing a national, or "Anglican," Church as France had in "Gallicanism." Lutheran ideas, strongly opposed by the king, had taken only shallow root in England among a few merchants, monks, and university scholars. There was some anticlericalism and opposition to papal taxation among the people, and

Title page of Daniel Featley's *Description* of 1645, known also as "The Dippers Dipt," a satirical view of the Anabaptists.

some talk of reform among the intellectuals, but no organized movement of revolt. Henry, however, found himself in a personal quandary that was to lead him into direct conflict with the pope, Clement VII. After eighteen years of married life, Henry's wife, Catherine of Aragon, had given him only one living child, a daughter. He knew that the lack of a male heir might well throw England into a new War of the Roses, and he knew that Catherine could bear him no more children. Furthermore, he was infatuated with a lady of the court named Anne Boleyn. Henry therefore asked the pope to annul his marriage with Catherine so that he might marry Anne. It was not hard to find technical grounds for the annulment. Catherine had been married to Henry's short-lived elder brother, and it was against Church law to marry the widow of one's brother. But it was hard to persuade the pope to grant the annulment because he was in the power of the emperor Charles V, and Charles was the nephew of Catherine.

Henry, a strong-willed man convinced that he was right, was skillful in political manipulation. In 1529 he summoned Parliament, determined to make the nation his accomplice in whatever he might have to do. He and his chief minister, Thomas Cromwell, deftly built up anticlerical sentiment in Parliament and forced the English clergy to acknowledge that the king was "Supreme Head of the Church in England." Then Henry threatened to withdraw all revenue and obedience from the pope. When Clement still refused to grant the annulment, Henry carried out his threat. He had the marriage annulled in England by Thomas Cranmer, whom he had just persuaded the pope to name as Archbishop of Canterbury, married Anne, and then, in 1533 to 1534, had Parliament cut all ties between the Roman papacy and England by a series of statutes. Conscientious monks, priests, and laymen who resisted this separation were executed. The most prominent martyr was Sir Thomas More (1478–1535), author of *Utopia* and chancellor of England from 1529 to 1532, who was proclaimed a saint in the twentieth century. Henry was now a kind of pope of the Church of England, except that as a layman he never claimed the power to administer the sacraments. Between 1535 and 1539 he and his agents demonstrated the extent of his authority by dissolving all English monasteries, turning their inmates out into the world, and confiscating their lands. Because Henry needed ready money to carry on a war with France, most of these lands were eventually sold to nobles, gentry, and merchants. The result, probably unforeseen, was to bind a whole new class of landowners to the English crown and to the new religious settlement.

In breaking with the papacy, Henry had no intention of breaking with orthodox Catholic belief and practice. He made it clear to his people that the breach with Rome meant no letting down of the bars against heresy, whether Lollard, Lutheran, or Anabaptist. It was impossible, however, to seal England off from the influx of Protestant tracts and ideas, and Henry himself approved the

A Catholic, Sir Thomas More, on the Church

1557

The true Church of Christ is the common known church of all Christian people not gone out nor cast out. This whole body both of good and bad is the Catholic Church of Christ, which is in this world very sickly, and hath many sore members, as hath sometime the natural body of a man. . . . The Church was gathered, and the faith believed, before any part of the New Testament was put in writing. And which was or is the true scripture, neither Luther nor Tyndale [translator of the New Testament into English] knoweth but by the credence that they give to the Church. . . . The Church was before the gospel was written; and the faith was taught, and men were baptised and masses said, and the other sacraments ministered among Christian people, before any part of the New Testament was put in writing. . . . As the sea shall never surround and overwhelm the land, and yet it hath eaten many places in, and swallowed whole countries up, and made places now sea that sometime were well-inhabited lands, and hath lost part of his own possession in other parts again; so though the faith of Christ shall never be overflown with heresies, nor the gates of hell prevail against Christ's Church, yet in some places it winneth in a new people, so may there in some places by negligence be lost the old.

From *The Workes of Sir Thomas More*, pp. 527, 852, 853, 921.

distribution to churches of an English translation of the Bible. By the time of Henry's death in 1547, the Protestant wing of the English clergy led by Archbishop Cranmer was growing in power. During the brief reign of Henry's sickly son Edward VI (1547–53), the government moved rapidly toward building a church that was moderately Protestant in doctrine and ritual. Cranmer gathered together the most impressive parts of the ancient liturgies of the Catholic Church and translated them into majestic English in the Book of Common Prayer. This collection served as the rallying point of Anglicanism, as Luther's hymns did for Lutherans and Calvin's *Institutes* for Calvinists.

This new official Protestantism had no time to take root among the people. In 1553 Catherine of Aragon's daughter, Mary, the most honest and least politic of all the Tudors, came to the throne. She tried to vindicate her mother and atone for her father's sins by turning the clock back to 1529, abolishing all antipapal legislation, and restoring England to the papal obedience. But she outraged her people's patriotism by marrying a foreigner, Philip II of Spain, son and heir presumptive of Charles V, and she shocked their humanity by allowing three hundred Protestants to be burned for heresy in about three years. The courage with which Cranmer and more obscure victims went to their deaths, together with the arrogance of Philip's courtiers, left an indelible impression on the English people. Patriotism and Protestantism became identified in the public mind.

When Anne Boleyn's daughter, Elizabeth I (1558–1603), came to the throne, there was little possibility that she would keep England in the Catholic camp. Elizabeth cautiously guided her Parliaments and her bishops into a compromise religious settlement. She accepted the title of "Supreme Governor" of the Church in England, but she saw to it that revised articles of the faith and the Book of Common Prayer could be accepted by both moderate Catholics and Protestants. For the rest, she refused "to make windows into men's souls," as she put it; that is, she persecuted only open oppo-

Sir Thomas More, after Hans Holbein (1527).

nents of her policies but not those who quietly dissented from them. After the pope excommunicated her in 1570 she was forced to treat over-zealous Catholics who denied her right to rule as traitors, but unpolitical Catholics were tolerated. Elizabeth was rather more annoyed with the "Puritans," who wished to go much

Henry VIII, after Hans Holbein. (*ca.* 1540).

further than she in purifying the English Church of Catholic traditions. The Puritans were strong in Parliament, but when they became obstreperous, Elizabeth clapped some of them into jail. The idea that patriotism required independence from Rome became dominant during her reign, and in the end England was the largest single state to secede permanently from the Roman obedience. The secession cost less in bloodshed that it did elsewhere, largely because of the firm control that Henry VIII and Elizabeth exercised over the pace of religious change in England.

England under Elizabeth was clearly Protestant, but it accepted a conservative form of Protestantism, a form that looked on Presbyterians with suspicion and on Baptists with contempt. This conservatism grew during the religious disputes of the seventeenth century. Today many Anglicans would follow Henry VIII in insisting that their church is not "Protestant" at all. According to this theory, it was the Roman papacy that in effect had "seceded" from the Catholic tradition during the Middle Ages, and it was Henry VIII and Cranmer who restored the true continuity between the Church of the Fathers and the Church of the sixteenth century. Elizabeth always took the position that the Church of England occupied a middle ground between a Catholic minority that wished to bring England back to Rome and a Puritan minority that wished to build a more radically Protestant church in England.

THE CATHOLIC REFORMATION

Luther, Calvin, Cranmer, and the radical reformers thought of what they were doing as a "reformation" of the Church, and to this day the movement is generally called the Protestant Reformation. To Roman Catholics, however, the movement was a "revolt" against the divine authority of the Vicar of Christ, a religious revolution. From this point of view the only true "reformation" was the successful effort finally made by the Roman Church to reform itself, partly in response to the Protestant attack, partly as a result of internal pressures. Historians call this movement the Catholic Reformation, or the Counter Reformation.

This movement was both a religious revival and a counterattack on Protestantism. Before Luther appeared on the scene, some distinguished members of the clergy founded the Oratory of Divine Love at Rome in the hope of beginning a spiritual revival among the clergy. They directed their efforts toward the monastic orders and the papal court itself. In the course of the sixteenth century they succeeded in transforming the atmosphere at the Vatican. The bloody sack of Rome in 1527 by undisciplined imperial troops practically ended papal hopes of becoming powerful Italian princes. Italy was now effectively under Spanish control. As dreams of temporal power waned, better popes were chosen, who in turn appointed better cardinals. In the second half of the century, several of the popes were zealous, almost fanatical, men who would have seemed utterly out of place in the Renaissance papacy a century earlier. Politics still influenced religion and certain administrative abuses persisted, but the popes of the later sixteenth century were spiritual leaders, not Italian princes.

The driving forces behind the Catholic Reformation, especially the political forces, originated in Spain. Years of crusading against the Moors had given Spanish Catholicism a peculiarly intense quality lacking in the rest of Europe. King Philip II of Spain (1556–98), the son of Emperor Charles V, was a devoted Catholic who felt that it was Spain's destiny to stand as the bulwark of Roman Catholicism against the Protestants in Europe. He tended to give orders to the popes rather than to take orders from them, but during his reign Spanish armies and navies, Spanish diplomacy, and Spanish saints constituted the hard core of a revived and militant Catholicism all over Europe.

The most powerful single agency in restoring papal power, in rolling back the tide of Protestantism, and in carrying Catholic missions overseas was a new order founded by one of the most single-minded and influential saints in Christian history, a Spaniard of Basque descent named Ignatius of Loyola (1491–1556). While he was fighting the French in the service of his king, Ignatius' leg was fractured by a cannon ball. During a long and painful convalescence, he devoured the lives of the saints, which were the only reading matter at hand, and decided to enlist as a kind of Christian knight in the service of the Virgin Mary. During a lengthy period of trial and temptation he perfected the "spiritual exercises" that he later passed on to generations of followers. These exercises consisted in the believer's concentrating his imagination on the most vivid details of hell and of the life and death of Christ in order to strengthen his will and to direct it toward salvation. While Ignatius was a student at the University of Paris (about the same time as Calvin), he enlisted nine friends, who became the nucleus of a new order. This new order, which was approved by the pope in 1540, was the Society of Jesus. Its members became known as Jesuits.

The rules of the new order were designed to develop a flexible, disciplined, and efficient body of ecclesiastical shock troops for the papacy. The Jesuit wore no distinctive habit; he dressed as his job might require, as priest, teacher, missionary, or secret agent. He swore a special oath of obedience to the pope. He was carefully selected and trained for the most dangerous and difficult tasks the Church might require, from serving as confessor to a king, to venturing into Protestant countries where he might be executed as a traitor, to voyaging to foreign lands as remote as Brazil or India. The Jesuits were spectacularly successful. They strengthened the pope's control over the Church itself; they ran the best schools in Europe; and during the late sixteenth century they won back most of Bohemia, Poland, Hungary, and southern Germany from Protestantism.

The Roman Church strengthened itself against the Protestant attack in other ways as well. A general council was held at Trent in three sessions between 1545 and 1563 to define Catholic dogma and to reform abuses. Since the papal representatives and the Jesuits controlled the deliberations from the beginning, there was no danger of a revolt against the papacy as there had been in the councils of a century before. In reply to the central doctrines of Protestantism, the council declared that salvation is by both faith and works and that final religious authority is in the Bible and tradition as interpreted by the Roman Church. A beginning was made at reforming financial and administrative abuses in the ecclesiastical organization (the final and most drastic changes were made by the pope).

Seminaries were set up for the training of priests. The council defined the Church's teachings much more sharply than they had ever been defined before and recognized the absolute supremacy of the pope over the clerical hierarchy. Rome had lost much in the struggle with heresy, but the Catholic Church of 1563 was far better able to cope with future heresies than it had been in 1500. New forms of the Inquisition had been established in Spain (1480), the Netherlands (1523), and Italy (1542), and a system of censorship of printed books (the Index) was instituted by the pope in 1559 and approved, with some additions, by the Council of Trent in 1563. All the faithful were forbidden to read any book on the Index.

The Roman Church had found a new religious vitality and had closed its ranks against the Protestant threat. By the second half of the sixteenth century a relatively monolithic Catholic Church, reorganized from within and backed by Spain, the strongest military power in

Engraving showing the third session of the Council of Trent (1562–63). An amphitheater was set up in the church of St. Maria Maggio.

Europe, faced the divided Protestants on somewhat better than even terms.

SIGNIFICANCE OF THE REFORMATIONS

It is not easy to sum up the significance of the Protestant and Catholic Reformations. They were religious movements, phrased in theological terms, rooted deep in the religious experience of men like Luther and Loyola, and resulting in a religious fragmentation of western Christendom that has lasted to the present day. But Luther's angry protest against indulgences would not have had such far-reaching results had not the economic, social, and political conditions been just right. The religious upheaval was intermingled with the growth of capitalism, of secularism, of national sentiment, and of absolutism in government. It is difficult to say precisely what was cause and what was effect. While German princes, for example, took advantage of purely religious protests to confiscate church property for their own interests, religious reformers also utilized purely secular events, like Henry VIII's desire to get rid of his wife, to advance the Protestant cause.

One thing is clear. The era of reform and revolution in the Church temporarily arrested the trend toward the secularization of culture that had begun in the last centuries of the Middle Ages. The century that followed Luther's death was a religious age; its most serious arguments were religious arguments; its wars were intensified by religious fanaticism; and most of its leading figures were either men of religion or men considerably affected by religion. Intensified interest in religion introduced a new and intolerant "ideological" element into the economic and political causes of conflict in European society. The hatred among Catholic, Lutheran, Calvinist, and Anabaptist was as profound in the sixteenth century as the hatred among fascist, communist, and democrat in the twentieth, and for somewhat the same reasons. No man could believe that he or his family or his society was safe so long as opposing religious groups were allowed to exist. Only in time did it become evident that differ-ing religious beliefs did not necessarily lead to civil war and the collapse of the state. Religious toleration was an eventual result of the Reformation but not of the efforts of the reformers.

For over a century the long-term effects of the Protestant Reformation on the economic, political, and cultural development of Europe have been vigorously debated by historians. It has been argued and denied that Protestantism, with its emphasis on serving God in one's secular calling and with its appreciation of the bourgeois virtues of honesty, thrift, and self-discipline, provided the necessary religious sanction for the development of capitalism. It has been argued and denied that Lutheranism aided the growth of divine-right monarchy, whereas Calvinism provided a spur toward the development of constitutionalism, and Anabaptism toward the development of modern socialism. It has been argued and denied that Protestantism wrecked the development of art by destroying religious sculpture and paintings and by rejecting most religious symbolism. And it has been argued and denied that by dissolving monasteries, the old centers of scholarship and philanthropic activity, Protestants deprived the poor of intellectual and physical support. Both the good and the bad in modern capitalism, modern nationalism, and modern secularism have been attributed to Protestantism by one historian or another.

The historical data are far too complex for dogmatic judgments in such matters. The permanent schism of western Christendom and the temporary intensification of religious motives in European politics can justly be attributed to the Protestant movement. Beyond this, all that can be said surely is that Protestantism allied itself with developments that had their origins far back, sometimes intensified them and accelerated their growth, occasionally blocked or countered their expansion. Capitalism, democracy, nationalism, and the secularization of culture appeared in Catholic as well as Protestant lands, and none of these phenomena can be explained by a simple chain of causes leading back to Luther and his revolt from Rome.

Luther tweaks the beard of Calvin as both of them pull the hair of the pope. This satirical engraving presents a Catholic view of the Reformation controversy.

Suggestions for Further Reading

Note: Asterisk denotes a book available in paperback edition.

Background of the Reformation

For the background of the Reformation, see S. Ozmont, *The Reformation in Medieval Perspective** (1971); G. Strauss, *Pre-Reformation Germany** (1972); and the famous "essay" by J. Huizinga, *The Waning of the Middle Ages** (1924). Huizinga's *Erasmus** (1952), and R. H. Bainton, *Erasmus of Christendom** (1969), are perceptive biographies. Erasmus' best-known writings are available in many modern editions, for example, J. P. Dolan, ed., *The Essential Erasmus* (1964).

The Religious Upheaval

An old, but still useful, work is P. Smith, *The Age of the Reformation** (1920), a lively and opinionated book. H. J. Grimm, *The Reformation Era* (1973), does religious developments fuller justice than Smith and is abreast of recent scholarship, particularly on Luther. H. Holborn, *A History of Modern Germany: The Reformation* (1959), is excellent on Germany. See also B. Moeller, *Imperial Cities and the Reformation* (1972) and Gerald Strauss, *Luther's House of Learning* (1978). There are briefer treatments of the period in general in R. H. Bainton, *The Reformation of the Sixteenth Century** (1952), and E. H. Harbison, *The Age of Reformation** (1955). The best recent work is L. W. Spitz, *The Renaissance and Reformation Movements*, Vol. II (1971). See also O. Chadwick, *The Reformation** (1964), and H. J. Hillerbrand, *The World of the Reformation** (1973). J. Lortz, *The Reformation in Germany*, 2 vols. (1969), is a fair statement of the Catholic position. A. G. Dickens, *The German Nation and Martin Luther* (1972), stresses the urban nature of the Reformation. F. Wendel, *Calvin, The Origin and Development of His Religious Thought* (1963), is excellent. See also G. Rupp, *Luther's Progress to the Diet of Worms** (1964), and R. H. Fife, *The Revolt of Martin Luther* (1957). There are many translations of the writings of Luther, Calvin, and other reformers, for example in the *Library of Christian Classics*. A good anthology of contemporary writings on the movement is H. J. Hillerbrand, *The Protestant Reformation: A Narrative History* (1964).

For the radicals, see G. H. Williams, *The Radical Reformer* (1962). Good introductions to different aspects of the "left wing" of the Reformation are offered in F. H. Littell, *The Free Church* (1958); R. H. Bainton, *The Travail of Religious Liberty** (1951); and C. L. Clausen, *Anabaptism: A Social History* (1972).

The best work on England is A. G. Dickens, *The English Reformation* (1964). See also the brief and authoritative accounts by F. M. Powicke, *The Reformation in England* (1941), and T. M. Parker, *The English Reformation to 1558** (1950). J. J. Scarisbrick, *Henry VIII** (1968), is a brilliant work. A good Catholic account is by P. Hughes, *The Reformation in England*, 3 vols. (1950–54). For the Puritans, see P. Collinson, *The Elizabethan Puritan Movement* (1967).

An excellent discussion of the Catholic Reformation is H. Daniel-Rops, *The Catholic Reformation,** 2 vols. (1961). The best biography of St. Ignatius is by the Jesuit P. Dudon (1949). For a less favorable treatment, see R. Fülöp-Miller, *The Power and Secret of the Jesuits* (1930). Jedin is engaged in writing a definitive *History of the Council of Trent*, the first two volumes of which have appeared in translation (1957). See also A. G. Dickens, *The Counter Reformation** (1969); M. R. O'Connell, *The Counter-Reformation, 1560–1610** (1974); and H. O. Evennett, *The Spirit of the Counter-Reformation** (1968). There is useful material in J. C. Olin, *The Catholic Reformation, Savanarola to Loyola* (1969).

Results of the Reformation

On the economic, political, and cultural consequences of the Reformation there are wide differences of opinion. A famous "essay" by M. Weber, *The Protestant Ethic and the Spirit of Capitalism** (1905), became the starting point of a long controversy about the economic significance of Protestantism, which still continues sporadically. *Protestantism and Capitalism: The Weber Thesis and Its Critics,** ed. by R. W. Green (1973), is a convenient collection of selections from the literature of this controversy. Other collections are L. W. Spitz, *The Reformation: Basic Interpretations** (1972), and R. Kingdom and R. Linder, *Calvin and Calvinism: Sources of Democracy** (1972). K. Holl, *The Cultural Significance of the Reformation** (1911), is inclined to view Luther as the prophet of modern Germany and of twentieth-century culture in general. For a readable and perceptive survey of the period, see A. G. Dickens, *Reformation and Society in Sixteenth-Century Europe** (1966).

18 The Age of Discovery

and the Greatness of Spain

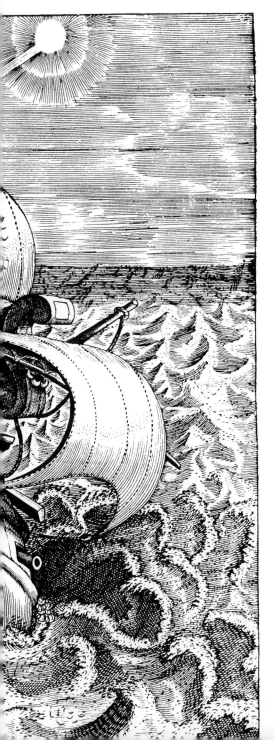

The Protestant Reformation struck a Europe that was already in the throes of a different sort of revolution. That revolution was launched by Portuguese voyages down the northwest coast of Africa; it quickened with the discovery of America and the sea route to India; and it continued unabated throughout the sixteenth century. For Europeans this was an age of discovery without parallel. For the first time they found themselves in direct contact with all the continents on the globe and with all the civilized peoples who inhabited them. That contact began to have a profoundly disturbing effect on the economy and the politics of Europe just as the Peace of Augsburg was bringing a respite from religious strife.

THE DEVELOPMENT OF OCEANIC COMMERCE

In 1400 Europeans knew scarcely more about the earth than the Romans had. The oceans around the Continent were still impenetrable barriers; the only long voyages ever taken by Europeans were the almost forgotten expeditions of the Northmen to Greenland and America. Franciscan friars and the Polos of Venice had shown that China could be reached by land and that the steppes linked Europe and Asia. But after the collapse of the Mongol Empire in the fourteenth

A sixteenth-century sailing ship, with its navigator (left center) sighting the sun to determine his latitude. The foremast (right) is square-rigged for running with the wind. The mainmast and the mizzenmast astern (left) are lateen-rigged for better tacking against the wind.

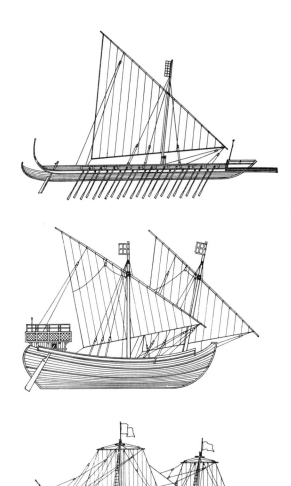

Top: Mediterranean war galley with lateen sail (*ca.* twelfth century); middle: lateen-rigged vessel, much like Columbus' *Niña* (early fifteenth century); bottom: Spanish galleon of sixteenth century, the typical long-distance ship for Spanish commerce.

of world-communication." Europeans had mastered both the technological and the psychological problems of making long voyages over the sea. Their ships had crossed and recrossed the Atlantic Ocean, rounded the southern tips of Africa and South America, pushed into the Indian Ocean, and crossed the Pacific. Before this time men had believed that there was far more land than water on the surface of the globe. Now explorers were discovering that there was far more water than land, and that the water could serve as a highway to any coast in the world for men who knew how to use its winds and ride its waves. The Mongol Empire had rested on mastery of the steppes. The empires of the future would rest on mastery of the oceans. When the first ship to circumnavigate the globe finished its voyage in 1522, Europe had begun to cast a web of communication and influence around the earth. During the next four centuries that web was to draw all the civilizations of the world under the influence of Europe.

Conditions for Maritime Discovery

By the year 1000, Norsemen from Iceland and Greenland had coasted North America in small, open boats. They were too few, however, to make any permanent settlement, and their discoveries were unknown to the rest of Europe. Before Europeans could make a sustained drive to push out across the Atlantic they needed better ships, more reliable aids to navigation, and stronger motivation.

Better ships were long in coming. Oar-propelled galleys had already mastered the Mediterranean, and by the thirteenth century Genoese and Venetian galleys were venturing out into the Atlantic to Morocco and Flanders. But on the open seas mariners needed sails rather than oars and broad, round hulls rather than long, narrow galleys. By the fifteenth century the Portuguese had devised a craft capable of long ocean voyages: the squat, three-masted caravel, with two masts generally square-rigged and one mast lateen-rigged (see the illustration at left). The caravel preserved the advantages of both the northern Eu-

century the routes across the steppes were no longer safe for missionaries or merchants. Arab sailors now became the middlemen between the Orient and Europe. They brought the spices and textiles of India and the East Indies to Alexandria and Beirut, whence the Venetians distributed them to the rest of Europe. The Europeans themselves had no direct contact with the East.

By the end of the sixteenth century an almost incredible geographical revolution had taken place. Arnold J. Toynbee defines it as "the substitution of the Ocean for the Steppe as the principal medium

ropean square-rig, which was better for running before the wind, and the Arab lateen-rig, which was better for sailing close to the wind. It was slower than the galley, but it had more space for cargo and for supplies on long voyages.

Galleys had generally stayed close to land, hugging the shoreline. Before ships could venture straight out to sea, shipmasters needed some way of determining their direction and their whereabouts. The compass (used in Europe by the thirteenth century) gave them a sense of direction in dark weather; the astrolabe (known since the eleventh century) enabled them to determine their latitude with fair accuracy by measuring the elevation of the sun and stars; and the portulan charts (first developed for the Mediterranean) gave them confidence that they could recognize the approaches to most European ports. (No precise way of determining longitude was known until the eighteenth century.)

City-states were the original bases for long-range navigation. Venetian and Genoese merchants linked the Black Sea and Egypt with Italy and England, and the Germans of the Hanseatic League traded from Russian Novgorod to French Bordeaux. But transoceanic exploration, trade, and colonization required a broader base for support. The new monarchies of western Europe were better situated geographically than the Italian

or German city-states to open up the Atlantic. They also had advantages in manpower, resources, and political centralization. After 1400 the western monarchies gradually replaced the cities as the major centers of commercial enterprise.

It is not easy to determine the motives that prompted Europeans—rather than Chinese or Moslems—to "discover" the rest of the world by taking to the sea. The Moslems had been crossing the Indian Ocean for centuries, and the Chinese regularly sailed up and down the East Asian coast and into the Indian Ocean; but neither people tried to go farther. Certainly the crusade ideal influenced Portuguese and Spanish rulers. To convert the heathen and to weaken Islam by placing Christian allies in the Moslem rear was the goal of many explorers. Crusading zeal was not the main impetus of the great discoveries, but it could be used to inspire enthusiasm for dangerous ventures and to sanctify more worldly motives.

Of those more worldly motives, the need to find precious metals was the most compelling. In an age without refrigeration, the spices that helped preserve meats and make them more palatable—pepper from India, cinnamon from Ceylon, ginger from China, nutmeg and cloves from the East Indies—were luxuries that were almost necessities. The

An illustration from a sailing book, *Art de Naviguer* (1583), demonstrating how to determine latitude by observing the sun's height.

long journey from India or the Moluccas and the Arab-Venetian trade monopoly made such spices expensive. But Europeans needed them (and other luxuries such as cotton and silk cloth) more keenly than Asians needed anything Europe had to offer except gold and silver; so there was a steady flow of precious metals from Europe eastward. This drain limited the supply of specie (hard coins) in Europe at a time when it was increasingly needed as currency. Before credit systems became widely used in the seventeenth and eighteenth centuries, the only practical way to provide the money needed by burgeoning commerce and industry was to increase the supply of bullion. European mines had never been very productive and were nearly exhausted by 1400. Fifteenth-century rulers were acutely aware of their need for gold. They knew that they had to have hard cash in their treasury to hire soldiers, equip navies, and maintain bureaucracies, and they knew that European supplies of precious metals were limited.

By the late fifteenth century a restless, energetic, and bold seafaring population was scattered along Europe's Atlantic coastline. Resourceful sailors, fishermen, and merchants had developed the techniques and the ships for making long voyages. They had religious and economic motives strong enough to overcome their superstitious fears of what lay beyond known waters, and their governments were often ready to back them. Europe needed direct contact with Asia, and some Europeans believed that it would not be too difficult to reach Asia by sea. Ptolemy in the second century had underestimated the size of the globe and had overestimated the span of Asia, and the geographers of the fifteenth century, accepting his miscalculations, were convinced that Japan and China lay only a few thousand miles west of Europe. The size of Africa was also underestimated, so that an eastern route did not seem to be too difficult. Either an eastern or a western voyage seemed possible, and the material and psychological environment was favorable for an age of discovery.

Portuguese Exploration

Perhaps the most interesting figure of the whole age stands at its very beginning: Prince Henry the Navigator (1394–1460), the younger son of King John I of Portugal. Prince Henry was obsessed with the desire to learn more about Africa; he devoted his life to organizing, equipping, and sending out fleets that pushed farther and farther down the African west coast. In a remarkable observatory at Sagres on Cape St. Vincent, the southwestern tip of Portugal, he brought together the scientific and the seafaring knowledge of his day. He had vague notions of outflanking Islam by reaching lands that the Moslems had never touched (such as the mythical kingdom of Prester John in East Africa), but his main objective was to find gold. When the Portuguese reached the Gold Coast of Africa in the 1450s this objective was achieved.

After Henry's death the impetus of exploration was lost for a time. Clusters of small islands (the Madeiras, the Azores) were found and settled, but they were not very profitable. (On the other hand, if there was land eight hundred

---

Toynbee on the Age of Discovery

Since A.D. 1500 the map of the civilized world has indeed been transformed out of all recognition. Down to that date it was composed of a belt of civilizations girdling the Old World from the Japanese Isles on the north-east to the British Isles on the north-west. . . . The main line of communication was provided by the chain of steppes and deserts that cut across the belt of civilizations from the Sahara to Mongolia. For human purposes, the Steppe was an inland sea. . . . This waterless sea had its dry-shod ships and its quayless ports. The steppe-galleons were camels, the steppe-galleys horses, and the steppe-ports "caravan cities." . . . The great revolution was a technological revolution by which the West made its fortune, got the better of all the other living civilizations, and forcibly united them into a single society of literally world-wide range. The revolutionary Western invention was the substitution of the Ocean for the Steppe as the principal medium of world-communication. This use of the Ocean, first by sailing ships and then by steamships, enabled the West to unify the whole inhabited and habitable world.

From Arnold J. Toynbee, *Civilization on Trial* (New York: Oxford University Press, 1948), pp. 67–70.

miles out in the Atlantic, there was reason to hope that larger islands existed farther west.) Henry's grandnephew, King John II (1481–95), however, was interested in voyages to the east and speeded up the effort to find an all-water route to India that would short-circuit the Venetian-Arab monopoly. By 1488 Bartholomew Dias had discovered the Cape of Good Hope, and in 1497 Vasco da Gama rounded the cape with four ships, reached Calicut on the Malabar Coast of India in 1498, and was back in Lisbon with two of his ships in 1499. In 1500 a larger fleet, commanded by Cabral, touched the coast of Brazil and then headed for India in Da Gama's wake.

This first contact by sea with India was to have momentous consequences, but neither side was particularly impressed by the other on first meeting. The Hindus had only contempt for the bedraggled sailors who had spent months aboard Da Gama's ships, and the Europeans soon made it clear that they found nothing to respect in the civilization of India. When the Hindus asked Da Gama what he sought in India, he is said to have replied laconically, "Christians and spices."

During the sixteenth century the Portuguese strove to build a commercial empire in the Indian Ocean. Affonso de Albuquerque, the brutal but able Portuguese governor from 1509 to 1515 and the real founder of that empire, understood the relationship between trade, sea power, and strategic bases. He seized Goa on the western coast of India to serve as his headquarters, Malacca on the Strait of Malacca to control the trade between the Spice Islands and the Indian Ocean, and Ormuz to dominate the Persian Gulf. He failed to capture Aden, a base from which he could have strangled the Arab-Venetian trade through the Red Sea. He was as ruthless in disciplining his own men as he was in terrorizing Hindu princes and fighting Arab seamen. At Albuquerque's death in 1515 the Portuguese had a large share of the spice trade (though not a monopoly) and controlled strategic bases all the way from Africa to the East Indies.

It was easy for the Portuguese and other Europeans to seize footholds in India because the Moslem and Hindu princes of the coastal districts were weak, and the Mughal Empire of the North had little power in the South. The Portu-

The Portuguese as others saw them. Above: African bronze sculpture of a Portuguese man. Left: detail from a seventeenth-century Japanese screen painting showing a Portuguese sailor playing a game of *go* with a Japanese friend in a native ship.

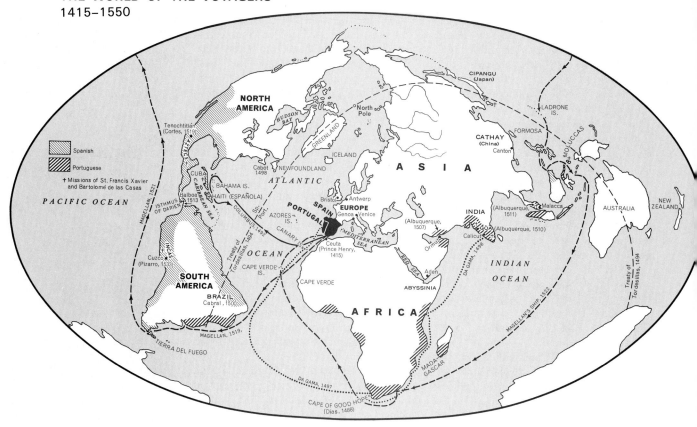

guese, however, established only trading posts, not colonies of settlement, in India, and even the trading posts soon ceased to be very profitable. The early voyages had made large profits for their backers. But the cost to the Portuguese government of equipping fleets and maintaining fighting forces soon ate up the profits. Portugal was a relatively small and poor country, with a small merchant class. Italian, German, and Flemish bankers soon dominated the Portuguese trade, and the spices that arrived at Lisbon were sent on directly to Antwerp, which proved to be a better point from which to distribute them to Europe. The burden of empire was already proving heavy when Portugal fell into the grip of Spain in 1580.

Columbus
and Spanish Exploration

In 1484, before the Portuguese had reached the Cape of Good Hope, a Genoese sailor named Christopher Columbus had tried in vain to persuade King John II of Portugal to back him in a voyage of exploration to the west. Columbus was convinced by all the evidence at hand that it would be comparatively easy to reach Cipangu (Japan) by sailing due west. But for years he was unable to persuade any monarch to back him. At last the rulers of Spain, who had conquered the Moorish Kingdom of Granada in January 1492, were free to turn their attention elsewhere. And so it was under Castilian auspices that Columbus sailed on his famous voyage. It took the Portuguese almost a century of patiently organized effort to reach the Old World eastward, while the Spanish reached the New World westward in one brilliant voyage. There was a large element of luck in the founding of Spain's empire in the New World.

Columbus touched land in the Bahamas on October 12, 1492, thinking he had struck some small islands in the Japanese archipelago. Throughout four voyages and until his death in 1506, he remained convinced, even after touching the mainland, that it was the Old World

Christopher Columbus, the Genoese sailor who sailed west in search of Japan and found the New World. This portrait of Columbus is thought to be the closest existing likeness of him. It is a copy, made in about 1525, of an earlier painting that has been lost.

Vasco da Gama.

of Japan and China that he had discovered. And so, although it was Columbus who named the "Indians" he found on the shores of Haiti and Cuba, it was the Florentine Amerigo Vespucci who gave his name to the continents Columbus had discovered. Amerigo, director of the Medici branch bank in Seville, sailed on both Spanish and Portuguese voyages and described what he saw in letters that were widely read throughout Europe. In one he referred to the great southern continent in the west as *Mundus Novus*, a New World. Later map makers labeled the two new continents "America," after the man who first realized that it was a new, not an old, world that was opening up to view.

The Treaty of Tordesillas, 1494

Since both Spain and Portugal were seeking the same lands, they soon had to appeal to the pope for an adjudication of their rival claims to unoccupied and heathen lands around the globe. The pope, Alexander VI, was a Spaniard, and the line of demarcation that he drew in 1493

a hundred leagues west of the Cape Verde Islands was favorable to Spain, at least in the Western Hemisphere. The Portuguese were unhappy, perhaps because most of the unknown regions of the Atlantic were left to Spain, and in 1494 they persuaded the Spanish to sign the Treaty of Tordesillas. By this treaty a line was drawn from pole to pole 370 leagues west of the Cape Verde Islands, separating Portugal's claims to the east from Spain's to the west. The Portuguese assumed that the line applied only to the Atlantic (it gave them Brazil, though they did not know this in 1494). The Spanish preferred to believe that the line extended round the world, cutting it in half as a knife cuts an orange. They hoped that this interpretation might give them the Moluccas, the heart of the Spice Islands, and, in fact, it would have given them part of what is now Indonesia. But Spain was soon too busy in the Americas to concentrate on the East Indies, and in 1527 it sold all its claims to these islands to Portugal.

Magellan

By 1512 the Portuguese were in the Moluccas, and in 1513 the Spaniard Balboa sighted the Pacific from the Isthmus of Darien in Central America. In the years to come, the Spanish, the English, and others tried again and again to discover a strait through the New World by which they might sail westward into the Pacific and reach the Spice Islands. The Portuguese navigator Magellan was convinced that he could do just that by rounding the southern tip of South America. He knew that Portugal would never back him in such an expedition because it would create a Spanish-dominated route to the islands, so in 1519 he sailed with Spanish backing. It was the third of the truly great voyages—along with those of Columbus and Da Gama. Magellan negotiated the straits that are named for him and got across the Pacific after incredible hardships, only to be killed by natives in the Philippines. His navigator, Sebastian del Cano, brought one of the five original ships back to Lisbon by way of the Cape of Good Hope in 1522, the first ship to sail round the world.

Magellan plotting his position (detail from an allegorical portrait by De Bry).

THE SPANISH EMPIRE IN THE AMERICAS

From 1520 to 1550 the conquistadors of Spain carved out an empire in the Americas. As the Spaniards on the Caribbean islands began to hear exciting tales of wealthy, half-civilized empires, they turned from exploration to conquest. The most notable of the conquistadors were Hernando Cortes, who from 1519 to 1521 conquered the formidable Aztec Empire in Mexico with six hundred men, sixteen horses, and a few cannon, and Francisco Pizarro, who from 1533 to 1534 conquered the Inca Empire in Peru with even fewer followers. Their firearms, steel swords, and horses gave the Spaniards an advantage over the more primitively armed groups that faced them, but it was primarily their daring, their discipline, and their fanatical faith that accounted for their fantastic early successes. Later on, diseases imported from Europe (especially smallpox) reduced native populations to such an extent that revolt was impossible.

Within a generation Spanish soldiers, lawyers, and friars unexpectedly found themselves the undisputed rulers of vast stretches of territory and millions of human beings. Often the new ruling class simply stepped into the place of former conquerors like the Aztecs and Incas, living on the tribute from subject populations that had supported their predecessors. But the Spaniards needed labor to exploit the new lands fully, and the upland Indians already decimated by European diseases could not survive in the rich, but unhealthy, lowlands. Thus when sugar became an important crop, Negro slaves were imported from Africa to do the work. Until the seventeenth century, however, the industry most favored by the Spanish government was the mining of gold and silver. After the discovery of enormously rich silver mines in both Mexico and Peru in 1545, the extraction and shipment of silver became the main business of the Spanish Empire as a whole. Every spring after 1564 the plate fleet of twenty to sixty vessels gathered at Havana harbor to be convoyed by warships to Seville. And every year the Spanish government waited anxiously until the bullion, which everyone agreed was the key to national strength, was safely in harbor.

The empire that grew out of these exploits and these economic activities was a kind of compromise between what the Spanish settlers, the Christian friars, and the Spanish government at Madrid would each have liked to see develop in America. The settlers, many of them former conquistadors, would have liked to set themselves up as manorial lords living on the forced labor of the natives, unmolested by any political direction from Madrid. The Franciscans and other friars, particularly the great Dominican, Bartolomé de las Casas, would have liked to see the natives treated as fellow Christians and fellow subjects of the Spanish crown. Las Casas worked tirelessly to protect both the legal and the moral rights of the Indians in the face of relentless pressure from the settlers to exploit them. The government in Spain was determined to centralize all decision making in Seville or Madrid, and to protect the natives so far as possible, as the friars

Las Casas on the American Indians in the Sixteenth Century

It has been written that these peoples of the Indies, lacking human governance and ordered nations, did not have the power of reason to govern themselves—which was inferred only from their having been found to be gentle, patient and humble. It has been implied that God became careless in creating so immense a number of rational souls and let human nature, which He so largely determined and provided for, go astray in the almost infinitesimal part of the human lineage which they comprise. From this it follows that they have all proven themselves unsocial and therefore monstrous, contrary to the natural bent of all peoples of the world.

. . . Not only have [the Indians] shown themselves to be very wise peoples and possessed of lively and marked understanding, prudently governing and providing for their nations (as much as they can be nations, without faith in or knowledge of the true God) and making them prosper in justice; but they have equalled many diverse nations of the world, past and present, that have been praised for their governance, politics and customs, and exceed by no small measure the wisest of all these, such as the Greeks and Romans, in adherence to the rules of natural reason.

From Bartolomé de las Casas, *Apologética historia de las Indias,* in *Introduction to Contemporary Civilization in the West,* 3rd ed. (New York: Columbia University Press, 1960), Vol. I, p. 539.

y epolính q mexica

Cortes accepting the surrender of Quauhtemoc, last king of the Aztecs. The artist was a Spanish-trained native from Tlaxcala, who chronicled Cortes' conquest of Mexico. Notice the mixture of European and Indian styles.

urged. However, it was difficult to enforce orders when they took weeks to be received and when provincial authorities never had enough manpower to police the vast areas for which they were responsible.

The policy of the Spanish Empire, as it had unfolded by the end of the sixteenth century, was remarkably sensible and humane by contemporary standards. The settlers were allowed to command the forced labor of the subject Indians, but this labor was regulated by public authority, not by private right. There were serious abuses, especially in Mexico, and the long arm of the home government was often exasperatingly slow in dealing with local problems. But as time went on the Spanish came close to ac-

complishing what the Portuguese failed to accomplish in the East and what the English never attempted in North America: the Christianization and Europeanization of a whole population. The Spaniards took seriously the papal bulls of 1493, which gave them the heathen peoples of the New World to convert and nurture in the Christian faith. In theory, the natives were considered Christians and subjects of the king (unlike the unfortunate Negroes, who had been enslaved by West African rulers and who gained no new rights when they were sold to Europeans). The gulf between Spaniard and native was never entirely closed, in either religion or culture. But Spanish and Portuguese in the end became the languages of all but the most

Philip II of Spain, by Titian.

isolated Indians, and Roman Catholicism the dominant religion. Intermarriage was so common that the mestizos, or descendants of mixed marriages, eventually became more numerous than the pure-bred of either race. The Spanish (and the Portuguese in Brazil) made a serious attempt to convert the New World to western civilization.

SPAIN UNDER PHILIP II

In the later sixteenth century Spain was the dominant power in Europe as well as in America. The accession of the Habsburg Charles to the throne of Spain in the early sixteenth century had thrust the Spanish into the full stream of European politics and diplomacy at a moment when the Protestant revolt was beginning to spread, the Turks were expanding up the Danube Valley, and the job of exploring and colonizing America was demanding a huge expenditure of energy. To roll back the threats of heretics and infidels while conquering a new world was a heavy task for a state so recently formed. But for a brief and brilliant time, the Spanish under the Emperor Charles V (1515–56) and his son, King Philip II (1556–98), were almost equal to the challenge. The sixteenth and early seventeenth centuries were the golden age of Spain.

In 1555–56 Charles V divided his family holdings between his brother Ferdinand and his son Philip. To Ferdinand went the Habsburg possessions in Austria, Bohemia and a slice of Hungary, and the imperial crown (still elective in theory, but by now always bestowed on a Habsburg). To Philip went the crowns of Castile and Aragon, with Castile's possessions in the New World, the Kingdom of Naples and the Duchy of Milan (which meant control of Italy), and the Netherlands. Thus for a century and a half after 1556 there were "Austrian Habsburgs" and "Spanish Habsburgs," separate ruling houses but houses that cooperated closely in matters of dynastic policy. Except for the Netherlands, which might well have gone to Ferdinand because of the Netherlands' close cultural and geographical ties with the Empire, the possessions of Philip II formed a more tight-knit and centralized state than his father's holdings.

Philip II was thoroughly Spanish in speech, thought, and character. After the conclusion of peace with France in 1559, he returned from the Netherlands to Spain to remain until his death almost forty years later. He caught the imagination of his people as few of their rulers had done. To the Spanish he is still "Philip the Prudent," one of their greatest kings. Distrustful of his advisers, unable to delegate authority even in minor matters, slow in coming to a decision, strongly Catholic in religion (his enemies would have said "bigoted"), convinced of his divine right to govern Spain as an absolute ruler strictly accountable to God but to no one else, Philip devoted his country to the ideal of a restored Catholic Christendom with the Spanish monarchy as its leading power and defender. For centuries the Spanish had fought the Moors. To Philip, the crusade would continue against half-converted Jews and Moors at home and against Turks and Protestants abroad until the Christian Commonwealth of the Middle Ages had been restored. Meanwhile the Catholic faith would be carried to the New World. Since Spain was the divinely chosen agent of this mission, what was in the interest of Spain was naturally in the

On Philip II of Spain

The pallor of his complexion was remarked on by all observers, and most of them drew the proper conclusion, namely, that it indicated a weak stomach and lack of exercise. Reddened eyes were a penalty of his excessive devotion to the written word both day and night. . . . Reading and writing occupied the major portion of Philip's day. . . . He had taken deeply to heart his father's injunction to direct everything himself, and never to give his full confidence even to the most faithful of his ministers, and the natural result was that his time was completely occupied with receiving and answering reports and letters. . . . Reports, reports, and even more reports; Philip was literally submerged with them in his later years, and moreover he did not stop at reading them; he annotated them, as he went along, with comments on matters as absurdly trifling as the spelling and style of the men who had written them—all in that strange, sprawling hand of his, one of the most illegible hands of an age more than usually replete with chirographical difficulties.

From R. B. Merriman, *The Rise of the Spanish Empire in the Old World and in the New* (New York: Macmillan, 1934), Vol. IV, pp. 21–24.

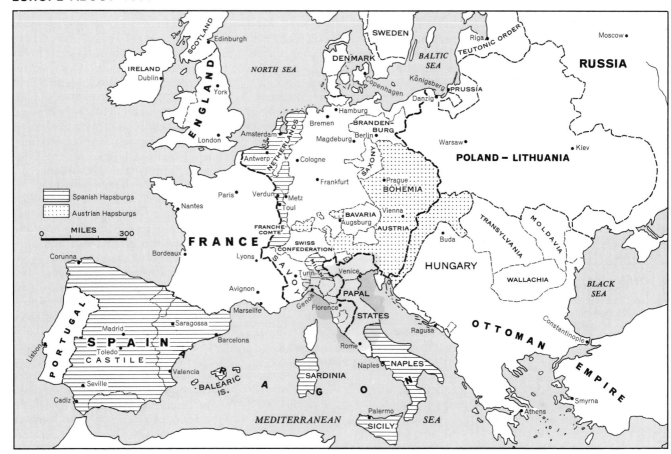

interest of Christendom as a whole. Or so it appeared to Philip and to most of the Spanish nobility.

If ever there was a monarchy and a ruling class with a sense of destiny, it was the Spanish of the sixteenth century. This spirit was evident in the Spanish Jesuits who guided the Council of Trent and helped to reconvert much of central Europe to Catholicism, in the Spanish friars who labored to convert the American Indians, in the conquistadors who toppled native empires in the New World, and in the tough Spanish infantry who, for over a century, defeated every organized army they met in Europe, and gained at least a draw in their struggle with the Dutch guerillas. Philip II's Spain was the strongest military power on the Continent, the strongest naval power in the Atlantic (in spite of the defeat of the Armada in 1588), and the wealthiest state in Europe. Spain was the nerve center of the Catholic Reformation. No wonder the terror of the Spanish name lived on into

the seventeenth century long after Spanish strength had begun to waste away.

Economic Policy

The economic basis of Spain's predominance was the gold and silver that flowed to Seville in a swelling stream from the New World. Early in the sixteenth century the bullion imported was almost entirely gold. But after the discovery in 1545 of the rich mines in Peru and Mexico, it was mostly silver. The value of the treasure that reached Spain rose enormously between 1500 and 1600. In very round figures the average yearly value of bullion imports at the beginning of the century was something under $300,000; by about 1550 the value had increased fifteen times; and by 1600 over forty times, to about $12,000,000. Then a steady decline set in, until about 1660 the average was down to around $1,200,000. The Spanish crown received about a quarter of the total as its share.

Contemporary map showing Spain as the head and crown of sixteenth-century Europe.

This influx of precious metals, combined with internal financial problems, contributed to a steep rise in prices. At first the rise was slow and generally stimulating to Spanish industry and commerce. But it had become precipitous by the middle of the century, amounting to a severe inflation that struck first Spain and then the rest of western and central Europe as the metal flowed out of the Iberian peninsula (in spite of all government prohibitions). It has been estimated that prices quadrupled in Spain in the course of the century. Since prices rose faster than taxes could be increased, Philip II was forced to repudiate his government's debts three times, in 1557, 1575, and 1596. (His successors had to follow the same course in 1607, and 1627, and 1647.) The effect of inflation on Spanish industry was eventually disastrous. Since prices always rose faster in Spain than elsewhere, it was relatively more expensive to manufacture goods in Spain than in other countries. This meant that Spanish producers could not sell their goods abroad and that cheaper foreign products captured the Spanish market.

In the short run, Spain's silver enabled it to maintain supremacy in Europe by paying its armies in cash and buying what goods it needed abroad. In the long run, this policy helped to ruin Spain's industry and commerce, and even to undermine its agriculture. There were other reasons for Spain's economic troubles in the seventeenth century, such as the expulsion of its best farmers, the Moriscoes, as the converted Moors were called. But the influx of precious metals was probably the major reason for both the rapid rise and the equally rapid decline of Spain as the leading power in Europe. Spain lived for a century on the windfall of American treasure, but when the supply of bullion dwindled in the seventeenth century Spain found that the real sinews of its national strength—native industry and agriculture—were ruined.

Religious Policy

Philip II's religious policy was the most narrowly intolerant of his time. He abhorred heresy and unbelief with a holy hatred and said he would rather be king in a desert than in a land of heretics. He feared Islam as the ancient enemy both of Christendom and of his people. In his eyes and in those of most of his countrymen, the Moors who had been forcibly Christianized after the conquest of Granada in 1492 were still Moslems at heart. Furthermore, they were more prosperous than most Spanish farmers, and they were reputedly in league with the Moslems of North Africa. In 1566 Philip ordered them to stop using the Arabic language and learn Castilian, to give up their Moorish dress, and to stop taking hot baths, as was their custom. In 1569 the exasperated Moriscoes broke into a revolt, which was savagely suppressed. They were driven out of Andalusia and scattered over Spain. In the years after 1609 they were driven out of the country entirely. Their numbers and importance have sometimes been exaggerated, but there is no doubt that their loss helped to weaken the Spanish economy.

At the height of the revolt of the Moriscoes in 1570, the Turks captured Cyprus from the Venetians. Once again Europe trembled before the threat of Islamic expansion. Philip II immediately allied himself with the pope and the Venetians to counter the danger, and in October 1571 a Spanish and Venetian fleet won a famous victory over a large Turkish fleet at Lepanto in the Gulf of Corinth. Nothing decisive came of the battle because the Christian forces were unable to follow up their victory. But the event had considerable importance for European morale because it was the first time a Turkish fleet had been defeated.

The Apogee of Spanish Prestige

Philip's prestige probably never stood higher in Europe than in the years immediately following Lepanto. He was popular at home, and his defeat of the Turks gave him the undisputed political leadership of Catholic Europe. France, potentially the strongest monarchy in Europe, was torn by civil war during most of Philip's reign and so was unable to contest his leadership. England seemed weak and divided by religious controversies, and its queen had been excommunicated by the pope in 1570.

Meanwhile the Empire was safely in the hands of Philip's Habsburg cousins. It seemed as if his dream of a resurgent Catholic Christendom dominated by Spain was about to become a reality.

This dream was shattered during the last quarter of the sixteenth century by the revolt of the Netherlands, the rise of English sea power, and the accession of a former Protestant to the throne of France. In his struggle with the embattled forces of Protestantism in northern Europe, Philip overreached himself, exhausted his resources, and started his nation on its long decline.

THE REVOLT OF THE NETHERLANDS

The Netherlands were the wealthiest and most densely populated of Philip II's dominions. The 3 million people dwelling beside the mouths of the Rhine and the Meuse had lived by their industry and commerce since the early Middle Ages. The looms of the southern provinces turned out great quantities of linen and woolen cloth, while the fisheries and shipping of the northern provinces steadily increased in value. The comfortable houses of Bruges, Ghent, Antwerp, and Amsterdam were built with the profits of this flourishing industry and trade.

The seventeen provinces of the Netherlands had been united in a personal union by the dukes of Burgundy. But when Charles V inherited the territories in 1519 through his grandmother, Mary of Burgundy, there was little in the way of national feeling or common institutions to bind them together. Charles, who was brought up in Flanders and spoke Flemish as well as French, was the closest thing to a native ruler the united Netherlands had ever had, but he regularly sacrificed their interests to his broader imperial aims. During his reign the faint beginnings of a Netherlandish national consciousness appeared.

The provinces were a crossroads for ideas as well as for commerce. The Humanism of Erasmus as well as the teachings of Luther took early root in the Netherlands, to be followed by Anabaptist ideas. But in the 1550s a militant, disciplined Calvinism spread rapidly and soon became the dominant form of Protestantism. When Philip II took over the rule from his father in the fall of 1555, Calvinists constituted tight-knit minorities in most of the cities of the seventeen provinces.

Within ten years after his accession, Philip had alienated most of the nobility and bourgeoisie of the provinces. Legally he was not king of the Netherlands, but only duke or count of provinces that had their own individual liberties and customs. Philip paid no attention to these traditional restraints on his power. Native nobles were displaced in favor of Spaniards in the governing council, a policy that hurt the pride of the upper classes. A threat to enforce the laws against heresy with new efficiency and severity sent a chill of terror through the

The baptism of Moslem women, from a Spanish relief (1520).

Calvinist merchants and ministers. Madrid was almost a thousand miles away from Brussels, and Philip's Spanish-Catholic mind was even more remote from the interests and concerns of his busy, prosperous Dutch and Flemish subjects, whether they were Calvinist or Catholic. The revolt that ensued was partly a provincial reaction against centralization, partly a patriotic movement directed against foreign rule, and partly a religious protest against an inquisitorial Catholicism.

In 1566 Calvinist mobs began to break images of the saints and smash the stained-glass windows in Catholic churches throughout the Netherlands. Philip decided to make a frightful example of the iconoclasts. He sent the Duke of Alva and about ten thousand Spanish regulars to the Netherlands with orders to bring the troublemakers either to the block or to the stake. Alva set up what came to be called a "Council of Blood" and boasted (with some exaggeration) that within the six years of his residence in the Netherlands (1567–73) he had executed close to eighteen thousand people. In addition to spilling so much blood, Alva and his council confiscated large amounts of property and imposed a 10 percent sales tax that injured the trade of the country during the year or two it was in force. The Netherlanders never forgot these six years. Instead of crushing the opposition to Philip, Alva's policy solidified the resistance, at least for a time.

William the Silent and Dutch Independence

By 1572 the resistance movement had found a leader in William the Silent, Prince of Orange, the wealthiest landowner in the provinces. William was no military genius—he lost almost every battle he fought against the Spanish—but he had political wisdom, integrity, and patience, a rugged kind of patriotism, and a deep hatred of religious fanaticism, whether Calvinist or Catholic. He tried his best to hold the Calvinists in check, keep all seventeen provinces united against the Spanish, and still find a solution that would leave Philip as titular ruler. For a few years it looked as if he might succeed. In 1576 Calvinist excesses

William the Silent, by Anthony Moro.

provoked a frightful sack of Antwerp by Spanish troops known as the "Spanish Fury." This was enough to frighten all seventeen provinces into an agreement to stick together. The agreement was called the Pacification of Ghent.

Within three years, however, both Protestant and Catholic radicals had got out of hand, moderates had lost influence, and animosity between Catholics and Protestants had begun to undermine the universal hatred of Spain. The almost unanimous opposition to Alva and his successors gradually gave way to a savage civil war in which the Calvinists, the best-disciplined minority, took over leadership of the opposition to Philip. Most of the Catholics rushed back into the arms of Spain for protection. The seventeen provinces split in two as Calvinists fled to the Dutch provinces in the north beyond the great rivers, where they were better able to defend themselves, and Catholics fled to the Walloon provinces in the south, where Spanish troops could be maintained and supplied from the upper Rhine. In 1579 the Dutch provinces in the north formed the Union of Utrecht. This union ultimately became the foundation of the United Provinces, or Dutch Netherlands, which formally declared their independence of Philip II in 1581. And so the unanticipated result of the revolt of 1566 was that the seven northern provinces broke away from Spanish rule, while the ten southern provinces remained under Habsburg control and eventually (in 1830) became the kingdom of Belgium.

The Rise of the United Provinces

The Dutch Netherlands had to fight for their independence for two generations after 1581. They got some help from French and English troops at various times, but the price that the French Duke of Anjou and the English Queen Elizabeth asked for their help was often dangerously high. In the long run it was dogged determination, geography, and the rivalry of their enemies that won the Dutch their independence. William the Silent was assassinated in 1584, but his descendants carried on his tradition of able and disinterested leadership as stadtholders (regents) of one or more of the seven provinces. The "United Provinces" never formed more than the loosest sort of political federation, but the Dutch fought with stubbornness when they had to. The Duke of Parma, who became Philip's representative in the Netherlands in 1578, was one of the best military commanders of his day, but he was unable to reconquer the provinces beyond the bend of the Rhine and the Meuse, especially since he lacked control of the sea. The Dutch "Sea Beggars," or privateers, won as many battles against the Spanish on the water as William's armies lost on the land. When Philip's "Invincible Armada" was broken up in 1588 by the English and the weather, reconquest of the northern provinces became impossible. Finally, in 1648, the king of Spain recognized the independence of his former Dutch subjects.

By this time the new Dutch state had become one of the great powers of Europe. Most long wars exhaust even the victors, but the Dutch came out of this war the most powerful commercial nation in Europe. By the early seventeenth century they were building more ships each year than all other nations combined (two thousand, it was said), and they were better ships than any others. During the first half of the seventeenth century the Dutch captured more and more of the carrying trade not only of Europe but of the world. Their rates were cheaper, their business methods more efficient, their handling of cargo more skillful. Antwerp (in the Spanish Netherlands) had been ruined by the Spanish soldiery and blocked off from the sea through the closing of the Scheldt River by the Dutch. Thus Amsterdam (in the United Provinces) took Antwerp's position as the commercial and financial center of Europe. Until their own vulnerability to attack by land became evident after 1660, the Dutch had no rivals who could contest their power.

The sheer geographical extent of Dutch commercial operations was remarkable. Dutch ships handled much of the grain trade of the Baltic and a large part of the carrying trade of England, France, Italy, and Portugal. When Philip II seized the crown of Portugal in 1580 and stopped the Dutch from visiting Lisbon (whence the Dutch were accustomed to distribute Portuguese spices to the rest of Europe), the Dutch with characteristic daring went out to the source of the spices themselves in the Moluccas. In 1602 the Dutch East India Company was formed and soon established its headquarters at Batavia on the island of Java. By the middle of the century the Dutch had seized the richest part of Portugal's eastern empire—the Moluccas, Malacca, and Ceylon. For over a century the company paid very large dividends, mainly by ruthlessly monopolizing the production of spices and limiting it to keep up

Example of a propaganda badge worn by Dutch "Sea Beggars." The insurgents' hatred of Catholicism is expressed in the inscription: "Better the Turks than the pope."

THE DIVISION OF THE NETHERLANDS   1581

Amsterdam harbor, center of a worldwide trade (detail from an engraving by Pieter Bast, 1597).

prices. In 1652 the Dutch founded a colony at the Cape of Good Hope as a way station to the East. A few decades earlier they had come close to ousting the Portuguese from Brazil. At about the same time (1624) they founded a settlement on Manhattan Island named New Amsterdam that became the center for a large Dutch carrying trade in the New World. When the French and British embarked on overseas trade and colonization, they found not only the Spanish and Portuguese but the Dutch ahead of them all over the world.

So it was an economic giant that Philip II conjured up when he set out to crush his rebellious subjects in the Netherlands. The revolt of the Netherlands may be considered as a kind of dress-rehearsal-in-miniature for those larger popular and patriotic revolts against absolute monarchy, beginning with the Puritan Revolution in England and continuing through the American and French revolutions, that marked the next two centuries. There are many differences among these movements, but there are many similarities in the mixture of economic, patriotic, and religious grievances, the blindness of the absolute monarchs, and the ultimate triumph of "middle-class" interests.

ELIZABETHAN ENGLAND

Philip of Spain was almost as unfortunate in his dealings with England under Queen Elizabeth I as he was in his dealings with the Netherlands. England was crucial to his plans. If he could have added control of England to his control of Spain, Milan, and the Netherlands, France would have been encircled and the vital sea routes between Spain and the Netherlands would have been safer. For a few years (1554–58), while Philip was married to Queen Mary of England, it seemed as if the emperor's dream would be realized: England had been brought within the Habsburg orbit and restored to Roman Catholicism. But Elizabeth's accession to the throne in 1558 changed everything.

Queen Elizabeth I (1558–1603) is generally accounted the greatest of the Tudors and one of England's ablest rulers, though to some critics she was simply a stingy and narrow-minded woman. Whatever the judgment, England was immeasurably stronger at her death than at her accession, and she died beloved by the great majority of her people. At twenty-five, when she came to the throne, she had already lived through disgrace, humiliation, and even danger of execution during her sister Mary's reign. She had seen how Mary had lost the love of her people by marrying a foreigner and by burning heretics. These early experiences left her a strong-willed and shrewd young woman, aware of how precarious both her own situation and that of her nation were, determined to put politics before religion and to follow a purely national policy.

Elizabeth's instinct was always to temporize and compromise. As the daughter of Henry VIII and Anne Boleyn, Elizabeth could never allow England to submit to papal authority. But she wanted a religious settlement that would not alienate patriotic Catholics, and she hoped she could deceive the Catholic powers of Europe for a time into thinking that she could be won back to Rome. On the other hand, she resented the attempt of the left-wing Protestant minority (a group that was gradually gaining the appellation of "Puritan") to dictate a radical religious settlement and a risky, pro-Protestant foreign policy. However, Elizabeth never completely broke with her patriotic Puritan subjects and never lost their loyalty, even when she punished them for advocating radical measures. Elizabeth's policy was nationalist first and Protestant second, but the long-term result was to encourage that fusion of patriotism and Protestantism that became a permanent characteristic of English public opinion.

She compromised and temporized in her foreign policy as well. Her instinct was to avoid clear-cut decisions, to keep a dozen intrigues afoot so that there were always avenues of escape from any policy, and to avoid war at almost any cost. The chief danger at her accession was from French influence in Scotland. The French had long been allies of the Scots, and Mary Stuart, Queen of Scots, was married in 1558 to the heir to the French crown. A year later John Knox, who had become a Calvinist, returned to his native Scotland from Geneva and began a religious revolution. Catholicism and French influence on the Scots were both undermined. Moreover, since Mary Stuart's husband was now king of France, it was clear that France would make every effort to defeat the Calvinists. For once Elizabeth made a rapid decision: to ally with the Calvinist party in Scotland and keep the French out. By 1560 Knox, the Kirk (Scottish Church), and the pro-English party were in control, and the French had lost all influence in Scotland. The way was paved for the union of the English and Scottish crowns in 1603.

Mary, Queen of Scots

Mary Stuart returned to Scotland in 1561 after her husband's death. She was a far more charming and romantic figure than her cousin Elizabeth, but she was no stateswoman. A convinced Catholic, she soon ran head-on into the granitelike opposition of Knox and the Kirk. Her second marriage, to her cousin Lord Darnley, turned out badly, and she became involved in a plot resulting in his murder. In 1567 she was forced to abdicate, and in the following year she fled from Scotland and sought protection in England from Elizabeth. No visitor could have been more unwelcome. Mary, as Henry VII's great-granddaughter, had the best hereditary claim to be Elizabeth's heir, but she was a Catholic and a foreigner. Elizabeth would never formally recognize her as her successor, nor would she marry in order to produce another heir, nor would she do anything to harm her fellow sovereign, except keep a close watch on her through her agents. This policy exasperated Elizabeth's Puritan advisers and left Mary free to become the center of almost every French or Spanish plot against Elizabeth's life during the next twenty years.

The Anglo-Spanish Conflict

Though there were many sources of friction between them, Elizabeth and Philip of Spain remained on relatively good terms for over twenty years. As time went on, however, it became increasingly difficult to keep the peace. England was a small country with less than half the population of Spain, but during the quarter-century of peace that Elizabeth's cautious temporizing gave her people, English industry, commerce, and shipping expanded considerably. For reasons we have already suggested, the Spanish were unable to produce the goods needed by their colonies. And Spanish shipping was incapable of supplying the insatiable colonial demand for African slaves. An aggressive merchant named Sir John Hawkins was the first Englishman to carry both goods and slaves direct to the Spanish settlements in 1562. It was profitable but dangerous work. In 1569 he and his cousin, Sir Francis Drake, were almost wiped out by a Spanish fleet. In revenge, Drake seized the annual silver shipment from Peru on its way across the Isthmus of Panama. From 1577 to 1580 he followed Magellan's route around the world and demonstrated the vulnerability of the Spanish Empire. Meanwhile English sailors were boldly probing the coasts of North America in a vain search for a Northwest Passage that would short-circuit the Portuguese route to the Indies. Like their fellow Protestants, the Dutch, the English were contesting the Spanish-Portuguese monopoly of overseas trade.

It was the revolt of the Netherlands, however, that finally brought England and Spain to blows. For centuries the economic ties between England and the Low Countries had been close. The Eng-

Elizabeth I of England, and her signature. The silver medal commemorates the defeat of the Spanish Armada (1588).

Mary Stuart, Queen of Scots, and her signature. Lead medal by Jacopo Primavera (ca. 1572).

lish people sympathized with Alva's victims, and English Sea Dogs cooperated informally with Dutch Sea Beggars to prey on Spanish shipping and to cut Spanish communications by sea with the Netherlands. Philip's ambassadors in England became deeply involved in one plot after another against Elizabeth's life, usually with the object of setting Mary Stuart on the throne. In 1587 Elizabeth reluctantly consented to Mary's execution when confronted with unmistakable evidence of her complicity in these plots. Philip immediately planned an attack on England. In 1588 he sent his "Invincible Armada" north to hold the Channel while Parma ferried his Spanish veterans across to conquer England for Spain.

The story of the defeat of the Armada has become an allegory of the triumph of a young, vigorous nation over an old and senile nation. The Spanish ships were large and slow, equipped with inferior cannon, and commanded by a landlubber. The fleet was conceived as a means of transporting troops, not of fighting battles at sea. The English ships that put out from Plymouth to harry the Spanish up the Channel were smaller and more maneuverable, trained to fire their cannon at longer range. When the Spanish

reached Calais and anchored there, Parma had still not completed his plans. The English sent in fire ships among the Spanish ships as they lay at anchor, drove them northward in panic, and attacked them fiercely off Gravelines. Stormy weather completed what the English had begun. Hardly half the galleons that had left Spain made their way back northward and westward around Scotland and Ireland. The victory gave a lift to the morale of Englishmen and of Protestants everywhere. It ended all further thought of Spanish conquest of England—or reconquest of the Netherlands, for that matter. It did not mean the end of Spanish sea power, which was still greater than that of any other country. But when peace was finally signed in 1604, the English, with the Dutch, stood close to the Spaniards as powers on the sea.

THE FRENCH WARS OF RELIGION

One obvious reason for Spain's ascendancy in the later sixteenth century was the fact that France, traditionally the chief obstacle to Habsburg expansion, was torn by a series of civil and religious wars that prostrated the monarchy and devastated large areas of the country between 1562 and 1593. Almost overnight France was transformed from an aggressive national monarchy into a victim of intervention by neighboring states.

Background of the Civil Wars

France, with a population about double that of Spain, was the largest nation in Christian Europe under a single government. But, impressive as the French monarchy was, it was far from having absolute power. There was still a powerful and turbulent aristocracy in France, and French provinces clung jealously to local customs and privileges. The country was imperfectly unified; there was no body that could speak for the whole realm, as Parliament could for England. Class differences were sharp, and the bureaucracy was overworked, corrupt, and inefficient. Other countries had the same weaknesses; few other countries had to face the same internal and external threats.

The Armada

When the Spanish Armada challenged the ancient lords of the English on their own grounds, the impending conflict took on the aspect of a judicial duel in which as was expected in such duels, God would defend the right. . . . So when the two fleets approached their appointed battleground, all Europe watched. For the spectators of both parties, the outcome, reinforced, as everyone believed, by an extraordinary tempest, was indeed decisive. The Protestants of France and the Netherlands, Germany and Scandinavia saw with relief that God was, in truth, as they had always supposed, on their side. The Catholics of France and Italy and Germany saw with almost equal relief that Spain was not, after all, God's chosen champion. From that time forward, though Spain's preponderance was to last for more than another generation, the peak of her prestige had passed. . . . So, in spite of the long, indecisive war which followed, the defeat of the Spanish Armada really was decisive. It decided that religious unity was not to be reimposed by force on the heirs of medieval Christendom, and if, in doing so, it only validated what was already by far the most probable outcome, why, perhaps that is all that any of the battles we call decisive has ever done.

From Garrett Mattingly, *The Armada* (Boston: Houghton Mifflin, 1959), pp. 400–01.

Moreover, during the sixteenth century church leaders and political theorists had worked out a formal justification of the right of subjects to resist their rulers when the rulers were doing wrong. Obviously the greatest wrong was to impose a false religion on the people. This doctrine was invoked in the Netherlands against Philip of Spain and in Scotland against Mary Stuart, but it had the most disastrous effects in France. For in a monarchy that was only halfway to absolutism, the strong irritant of religious conflict was injected about the middle of the century in the form of militant Calvinism. The rational theology and disciplined organization of Reformed Christianity—not to mention the superb French style of Calvin's writings—appealed widely to many nobles and bourgeois throughout France. The French Calvinists were nicknamed Huguenots. On the eve of the civil wars they boasted about 2500 churches. They probably never numbered more than a sixth of the population (some scholars say as low as a twelfth), but they were an aggressive and well-organized minority, sure of their faith, and confident of the support of a few men, such as Admiral Coligny, at the very top of the social hierarchy. Arrayed against them were strongly Catholic noble families, and, more important, the University of Paris and the Paris *parlement* (High Court). Most important of all was the fact that the Concordat of Bologna had given the kings of France full control over the appointment of the higher clergy as well as considerable indirect control of papal taxation and jurisdiction. In short, the king and his advisers could see no advantage in religious change, and consequently the Huguenots remained a permanent minority in France.

The Course of the Wars

The wars that broke out in France in 1562 were at once social, political, and religious. When Henry II died in 1559,

the royal authority fell into the hands of the Queen Mother, Catherine de' Medici, during the reigns of her three weakling sons, Francis II (1559–60), Charles IX (1560–74), and Henry III (1574–89). Catherine was an astute woman who put politics before religion and did her best to keep the feuding factions at court and the religious fanatics throughout the country from flying at one another's throats. But she lacked formal authority, and by now the animosities had become bitter. Calvinists allied themselves with discontented nobles and upholders of local autonomy. On the other side were Catholics, royal agents, and defenders of the status quo. Fanatics on both sides appealed for foreign aid, the Huguenots to the English, the Dutch, and the Germans, the Catholics to Spain. Both England and Spain sent troops, mostly at the beginning and again at the end of the wars.

Fighting was of the savage and bitter kind that characterizes civil wars. The Catholics won most of the pitched battles but were unable to wipe out the Hugue-

Massacre of St. Bartholomew's Day, 1572 (detail from a painting by an eyewitness, François Dubois).

nots. In 1572 Catherine was persuaded by the Catholic fanatics that one sharp blow might end all the trouble. At two o'clock on the morning of St. Bartholomew's Day, Catholic armed bands set upon the Huguenots in Paris, where many of their leaders were gathered for the wedding of the king's sister to the Protestant Henry of Navarre. Coligny and many others were killed. The slaughter spread quickly to other French cities, and before it was over probably ten thousand Protestants had been massacred. This was the most spectacular of innumerable atrocities on both sides. It horrified Protestants throughout Europe and, according to one story, made Philip II laugh aloud for the only time in his life. But it had little effect on the conflict in France.

Catherine de' Medici in 1561, by an unknown artist.

Henry of Navarre

The wars dragged on for twenty more years, becoming more and more confused and purposeless until the Huguenot Henry of Navarre came to the throne in 1589 as Henry IV (1589–1610). Though he was the nearest male heir, he was only remotely related to the previous king. He had a difficult time making good his claim to the crown against a Catholic League that held Paris and against troops of Philip II that intervened from the Spanish Netherlands under Parma. In the end he found that the only way he could capture Paris was to renounce his faith and become a Catholic, which he did in 1593. He did not forget his former fellow Protestants, however. By the Edict of Nantes in 1598 the Huguenots were granted freedom of conscience, freedom of worship in specified places, equal civil rights, and control of some two hundred fortified towns throughout France. In short, the edict simply recognized a religious stalemate, and zealots on both sides of the religious fence considered it only temporary. But it constituted the first formal recognition by a European national monarchy that two religions could be allowed to exist side by side without destroying the state, and growing numbers of Frenchmen who preferred civil peace at any price to the anarchy and fanaticism of the past forty

Henry of Navarre in court dress (seventeenth-century enamel).

years supported it. With the conclusion of peace with Spain and the publication of the Edict of Nantes in 1598, France was ready to resume building a strong monarchy.

THE GENERAL CHARACTER OF THE LATER SIXTEENTH CENTURY

The age of Philip II and of Elizabeth of England has been called the Age of Religious Warfare. It is true that religion was often the spark that set aflame the combustible materials of sixteenth-century society, but early nationalism, economic instability, and social unrest also played their part. A more precise description of the period might be the Age of Religious Politics. Until the Reformation, European politics and diplomacy had slowly grown less religious and more secular. Now for a century, thanks to the religious schism, politics and diplomacy became once more strongly motivated and embittered by religion. The monarchies were faced by religious ideologies that often commanded fiercer loyalties than could the dynasties themselves. A Jesuit might scheme and work and die for an ideal that obviously transcended all state boundaries. In the same way a Scottish Presbyterian, a Dutch Calvinist, and a French Huguenot might have more in common than subjects of the same king. Thus religious differences sometimes undermined the power of monarchs, as they did in France and the Netherlands. And sometimes religious zeal reinforced loyalty to the dynasty, as it did in Spain and among English Protestants. Perhaps the best symbol of this Age of Religious Politics was the Escorial, which Philip II built for his residence near Madrid. The building was half-palace, half-monastery; and the private chamber of the king was connected directly with the chapel of the monastery. A century later a palace would be built at Versailles that would express the spirit of a quite different age.

The European Witch-Craze

The Age of Religious Warfare coincided with a tragic episode of western civilization: the European witch-craze. The witch-craze began in the mid-sixteenth century and continued for over a hundred years; before it ended, thousands of persons had been hanged or burned at the stake as convicted witches. The exact number of victims may never be known, but it is certain that the overwhelming majority of them were completely innocent.

Superstitious beliefs and practices—often dating back to pre-Christian times—had always lurked beneath the surface of European life. It was widely believed that some people had occult powers that could be used to assist neighbors in distress—or to harm them. Almost every community had its wizard or cunning woman, someone who offered cures and consolations when the efforts of priest or doctor had proved to no avail. From time to time throughout the Middle Ages, people had also been convicted of malevolent witchcraft; that is, of attempting to use occult means to inflict death or disease on others.

During the sixteenth century, however, the number of people accused of witchcraft began to increase dramatically. In one community after another a single accusation, which formerly might have led to a single witch-trial, triggered a chain reaction of arrests. Most of the victims were females—since witches were popularly assumed to be reclusive old women who had relieved their loneliness by making a "compact" with the Devil—but some men and even children were also arrested. Under torture, the suspects were forced to confess participation in lurid "witches' sabbaths" and diabolical schemes to harm or kill their neighbors. Having confessed, the suspects were then forced to name "accomplices," who in turn would be arrested and convicted. Dozens, even hundreds, of victims were often led to the stake in a single community. (In England, more humanely, the suspects were spared torture, and executions were by hanging.)

Historians are still puzzled about why the witch-craze exploded in sixteenth-century Europe. Certainly its occurrence reflected a growing interest in the "science" of demonology, which had begun to flourish in the late Middle Ages. It is

The Escorial, Philip II's monastery-palace near Madrid.

no accident, however, that the actual increase in accusations and executions coincided with the Age of Religious Warfare. The religious passions unleashed by the Reformation had generated deep hostilities on a level unprecedented in European history. Protestants regarded the pope as Antichrist; Catholics believed that Luther had been spawned by the Devil. Prominent intellectuals, such as King James I of England, felt obliged to publish extensive treatises about the works of Satan and his minions. In such an atmosphere, people of every class could become suspicious of their friends and neighbors, while judges took even the most unlikely accusations seriously,

Religion and Patriotism

A Spanish ambassador reporting the words of a French Catholic in 1565:

Nowadays Catholic princes must not proceed as they once did. At one time friends and enemies were distinguished by the frontiers of provinces and kingdoms, and were called Italians, Germans, Frenchmen, Spaniards, Englishmen, and the like. Now we must say Catholics and heretics, and a Catholic prince must consider all Catholics of all countries as his friends, just as the heretics consider all heretics as friends and subjects whether they are their own vassals or not.

◊ ◊ ◊

An English Protestant writing in 1589:

All dutiful subjects in this land desire with all their hearts the continuance of God's religion; the preservation of Queen Elizabeth; and the good success of the English navy. These particulars, I grant, are not expressed in flat in the Lord's Prayer; but they are contained within the compass of, and may be deduced from the petitions of that excellent prayer. Whosoever doubteth of this is void of learning.

As quoted in Erich Marks, *Die Zusammenkunft von Bayonne* (Strasburg: K. J. Trübner, 1889), p. 14; as quoted in Benjamin Hanbury, *Historical Memorials Relating to the Independents* (London: Congregational Union of England and Wales, 1839–44), Vol. I, p. 71.

and interrogated suspects in the most ruthless possible fashion.

Why did the witch-craze end? In the first place, religious warfare died out in the mid-seventeenth century, and with its passing came a cooling of the religious passions that had inflamed post-Reformation Europe. Even more importantly, the emergence of a modern scientific outlook (see Chapter 21) made the belief in invisible spirits and occult forces increasingly untenable among serious intellectuals. By 1660 the witch-panics were on the wane; by 1700 they all but disappeared. But the witch-craze, like the religious wars themselves, showed the instability of sixteenth-century society.

"Golden Ages"

It is characteristic of the history of civilization that periods of intense political and social conflict sometimes coincide with great creative achievements. Thus the late sixteenth and early seventeenth centuries witnessed a "golden age" of literature and the arts in three of the nations under consideration. Shakespeare's plays and Spenser's poetry in Elizabethan England, Cervantes' *Don Quixote* and Velasquez' paintings in Spain of the early seventeenth century, and Vondel's poetry and Rembrandt's portraits in Holland of the mid-seventeenth century represent a kind of summit of achievement in the history of the arts in these three nations. Shakespeare (*ca.* 1564–1616), Cervantes (1547–1616), and Vondel (1587–1679) are still the greatest figures in the literary history of their native countries, and, though England produced no great painter, Frans Hals (*ca.* 1580–1666) and Rembrandt van Rijn (1606–69) are the towering figures in Dutch painting, as El Greco (*ca.* 1548–1614) and Velasquez (1599–1660) are in Spanish.

In each case the artistic flowering accompanied or, as in Spain, immediately followed a period of heroic national struggle, effort, and achievement. It is tempting to say that ages of national expansion and excitement, times of heroism and "crusade," provide great artists with the stimulation and the receptive audiences they need. On a more mundane level, it is clear that "golden ages" depend on the existence of a class of people with enough education, wealth, and leisure to appreciate luxuries like books and paintings. The historian can record the existence of such classes and the occurrence of heroic national effort in England, Spain, and the Dutch Netherlands during these years. But he cannot account satisfactorily for Shakespeare's extraordinary appreciation of the complexities of human motivation, Cervantes' sympathy for all sorts and conditions of men, or Rembrandt's penetration of the depths of the religious soul. All these are manifestations of purely individual genius. Nor can he account for the appearance in France during a time of troubles of three writers who have profoundly influenced the French mind: Montaigne (1533–92), Descartes (1596–1650), and Pascal (1623–62). The historian can explain something about the conditions and characteristics of "golden ages." He cannot explain the appearance of genius.

Suggestions for Further Reading

Note: Asterisk denotes a book available in paperback edition.

Geographical Discovery Two brief general studies provide a good introduction to the subject: J. H. Parry, *Europe and a Wider World, 1415–1715* (1949), and C. E. Nowell, *The Great Discoveries and the First Colonial Empires** (1954). J. H. Parry gives a more detailed account in *The Age of Reconnaisance* (1963). W. C. Abbott, *The Expansion of Europe*, 2 vols. (1918), is an older but still valuable general account, including consideration of the effect of the discoveries on Europe. John H. Elliott, *The Old World and the New* (1970), is excellent. P. Sykes, *A History of Exploration* (1934), surveys the whole subject from ancient times on; H. H. Hart, *Sea Road to the Indies* (1950), describes the Portuguese exploits; J. B. Brebner, *The Explorers of North America, 1492-1806* * (1933), and A. P. Newton, *The European Nations in the West Indies, 1493-1688* (1933), treat exploration in particular areas. E. Sanceau has written a good modern biography of Henry the Navigator (1947). S. E. Morison, *Admiral of the Ocean Sea,* * 2 vols. (1942), is the best account of Columbus. A shorter discussion by Morison is *Christopher Columbus, Mariner* (1955), and he gives an excellent overall view in *The European Discovery of America* (1971). C. M. Parr, *So Noble a Captain* (1953), is a reliable account of Magellan. E. Sanceau, *The Land of Prester John* (1944), traces Portuguese interest in Abyssinia. The best correctives for older Anglo-Saxon notions of Spanish colonizing are C. H. Haring, *The Spanish Empire in America* (1947), and L. Hanke, *The Spanish Struggle for Justice in the Conquest of America* (1949). R. L. Reynolds, *Europe Emerges* * (1961), is a good analysis of European expansion in general.

The Late Sixteenth Century

J. H. Elliott, *Europe Divided, 1559-1598* * (1968), synthesizes the political history of this era. Volume III of the *New Cambridge Modern History* (1968) is also useful. F. Braudel, *The Mediterranean and the Mediterranean World in the Age of Philip II,* * 2 vols. (1972-73), is a magisterial survey. For an introduction to the witch-craze, see H. R. Trevor-Roper, *The European Witch-Craze of the Sixteenth and Seventeenth Centuries and Other Essays* * (1969). Among the best treatments of the witch-craze in specific countries are K. Thomas, *Religion and the Decline of Magic* * (1971), for England; J. Caro Baroja, *The World of the Witches* * (1965), for Spain; and H. C. E. Midelfort, *Witch Hunting in Southwestern Germany, 1562-1684* (1972). For a general social history of the years 1550 to 1650, see H. Kamen, *The Iron Century* (1971).

Spain

R. B. Merriman, *The Rise of the Spanish Empire in the Old World and in the New,* 4 vols. (1918-34), is a superbly written and scholarly account of Spain in Europe and overseas to the death of Philip II. J. H. Elliott, *Imperial Spain, 1469-1716* * (1964), is a remarkable book. R. Trevor Davies, *The Golden Century of Spain, 1501-1621* * (1937) and *Spain in Decline, 1621-1700* * (1956), are well-informed, interesting, sometimes controversial accounts. J. H. Parry, *The Spanish Theory of Empire in the Sixteenth Century* (1940), studies the effect of empire on the Spanish monarchy. E. J. Hamilton, *American Treasure and the Price Revolution in Spain, 1501-1650* (1934), is the starting point for study of six-teenth-century inflation. G. Parker, *The Army of Flanders and the Spanish Road* * (1972), discusses Spain's military decline, with emphasis on the actual life and problems of Spanish soldiers.

The Netherlands

The most scholarly brief account of the Dutch rebellion and its consequences is in the two books by P. Geyl, *The Revolt of the Netherlands, 1555-1609* * (1932) and *The Netherlands Divided, 1609-1648* (1936). There is a beautifully written popular biography of William the Silent by C. V. Wedgwood* (1944).

Elizabethan England

There is a wealth of well-written, scholarly books on the period. J. Neale, author of three brilliant volumes on the parliamentary history of the reign, has written the best biography of Elizabeth, *Queen Elizabeth I* * (1952). E. Jenkins, *Elizabeth the Great* * (1959), adds insight on the purely personal side. C. Read's thorough biographies, *Mr. Secretary Walsingham,* 3 vols. (1925) and *Mr. Secretary Cecil* (Lord Burghley), 2 vols. (1955, 1960), provide intimate knowledge of the politics of the period. A. L. Rowse has written with zest on Elizabethan society in *The England of Elizabeth* * (1950) and *The Expansion of Elizabethan England* * (1955). J. A. Williamson, *The Age of Drake,* * 3rd ed. (1952), is by a master of naval history, and G. Mattingly, *The Armada* * (1959), is one of those rare books, a definitive treatment of its subject that is at the same time magnificent reading. A good brief survey is S. I. Bindoff, *Tudor England* * (1959).

France

It is more difficult to find good reading in English on France than on England in the sixteenth century. John W. Salmon, *Society in Crisis: France in the Sixteenth Century* (1975), is the best general treatment. L. Batiffol, *The Century of the Renaissance* (trans. 1916), is an older general account of France in the sixteenth century. J. E. Neale, *The Age of Catherine de' Medici* * (1943), is very useful, as is H. Pearson, *Henry of Navarre* (1963). There is a brief modern account of the period in F. C. Palm, *Calvinism and the Religious Wars* (1932). J. W. Thompson, *The Wars of Religion in France, 1559-1576* (1909), is older but still useful. A. J. Grant, *The Huguenots* (1934), is both scholarly and brief. W. F. Church, *Constitutional Thought in Sixteenth Century France* (1941), discusses with discernment the conflict of medieval and modern ideas of government during the civil wars. Social aspects of the wars of religion are well portrayed in N. Z. Davis, *Society and Culture in Early Modern France* (1975).

19 Political and Economic Crises of the Seventeenth Century

The seventeenth century, much more than the fifteenth or sixteenth, is the century in which modern European civilization took on recognizable form. It was also a century that was afflicted by severe political, social, and economic crises, crises at least as dangerous as those that had shaken the medieval civilization of Europe in the fourteenth century. Everywhere the growing power of the state was challenged, and in the 1640s the three strongest European monarchies—Spain, France, and England—were weakened by outright rebellions. War was endemic—the last of the religious wars merged with wars to preserve the balance of power, and these in turn with the first commercial wars. The ravages of war were compounded by bad weather, famine, and plague. Population growth leveled off, and in some areas, notably Germany, population declined. There was also a prolonged economic depression, running through the middle decades of the century. The flow of silver from the New World, which had stimulated the economy, dropped off sharply, and industrial production in Europe increased only slightly, if at all. Only gradually, after 1670, did growth in commerce and industry start spiraling upward again. Meanwhile, poverty exacerbated social unrest, and inadequate revenues limited the capabilities of governments.

Yet out of this unpromising environment a new Europe emerged. Governments, businessmen, and intellectual leaders struggled to keep the gains they had made in the last two centuries. Every challenge was met, at different dates and by different means in different countries. But the net result was that Europe was richer, controlled more of the world's commerce, and had more effective governments in 1700 than in 1600. And, there was at the same time an intellectual revolution, a sharp change in ways of thinking about man and the universe, that did more to change the nature of human life than any of the new ideas that had emerged during the Italian Renaissance (see Chapter 21).

Although seventeenth-century statesmen and writers recognized the importance of economic problems more clearly than had their predecessors, they still felt that political problems deserved primary consideration. They wanted to complete the process that had begun in the thirteenth century, the building of a sovereign territorial state. This process had been interrupted by the troubles of the fourteenth century and the religious conflicts of the sixteenth century; now it was to be pushed to a conclusion. From a theoretical point of view, this meant defining the concept of sovereignty ever more clearly. From a practical point of view, it meant concentrating supreme power in some organ of the state, either in the monarchy (as in France and most other states) or in the representative assembly (as in England).

FRANCE: IN SEARCH OF ORDER AND AUTHORITY 1598–1661

Seventeenth-century France still felt the effects of the anarchy and violence that had prevailed for almost half a century before the Edict of Nantes in 1598. Three weakling kings had tarnished the prestige of the monarchy, and the great nobles had become powerful and unruly. Merchants and manufacturers had been hard hit by the wars, and the peasants had suffered heavily from the ravages of undisciplined soldiers. The mass of the people were eager for security, but still somewhat suspicious of any authority that might violate local privileges and increase the burden of taxation. They could still rebel when they felt that government was pursuing an undesirable course.

Jean Bodin, the most penetrating political thinker of the tragic years just past, had seen what was needed. In his book *The Republic*, which he published in 1576, Bodin argued that in any well-ordered state, supreme power or sovereignty must be clearly lodged somewhere in some organ of the state, preferably the monarchy. Sovereignty he defined as the power of "giving laws to the people as a whole without their consent." Bodin did not think of this power as arbitrary or capricious: the sovereign was still subject to the laws of God and of nature. But he insisted that sovereign power must not be limited by any human agency—that

Opposite: Rembrandt van Rijn, *Syndics of the Cloth Guild* (1662).

417

Triumphal Entry of Henry IV into Paris,
large sketch by Peter Paul Rubens (*ca.* 1630).

Jean Bodin on Sovereignty

Jean Bodin was a sixteenth-century French lawyer who was interested in political and economic problems. The *fact* of sovereignty had been recognized for some time, but Bodin was the first writer to express the *idea* in clear and uncompromising terms.

Sovereignty is supreme power over citizens and subjects unrestrained by laws. . . . A prince is bound by no law of his predecessor, and much less by his own laws. . . . He may repeal, modify, or replace a law made by himself and without the consent of his subjects. . . . The opinion of those who have written that the king is bound by the popular will must be disregarded; such doctrine furnishes seditious men with material for revolutionary plots. No reasonable ground can be found to claim that subjects should control princes or that power should be attributed to popular assemblies. . . . The highest privilege of sovereignty consists in giving laws to the people as a whole without their consent. . . . Under this supreme power of making and repealing laws it is clear that all other functions of sovereignty are included.

From Jean Bodin, *Six Books Concerning the Republic,* from the Latin version of 1586 [the French version of 1576 is less coherent], trans. by F. W. Coker, in *Readings in Political Philosophy* (New York: Macmillan, 1938), pp. 374, 375, 376, 377, 380.

is, it must be "absolute" to be effective. He insisted that it could not be divided. Neither the *Parlements* (the highest French courts) nor the Estates General could veto or modify the decisions of the sovereign. Sovereignty must be recognized as legitimately residing in one person or one political institution. No one had defined sovereignty so clearly before or argued so persuasively for it as the only remedy for insecurity and civil war. Bodin's prescription for France's ills was fulfilled in the French absolute monarchy that became the model and envy of most of Europe.

Henry IV and Sully

The first steps toward restoring the power of the monarchy and the prosperity of the land were taken by Henry IV and his minister, Sully. Henry, first of the Bourbon dynasty, was a popular king—courageous, vigorous, humorous, tolerant, and sound in his judgment of men. But he spent much of his time in hunting and lovemaking and left the routine business of government to Sully and others. Sully was a puritanical Huguenot with a keen sense of economy and a hatred of dishonesty. He improved the financial condition of the monarchy, partly by avoiding expensive wars and partly by patching up the tax-collecting system. The French taxation system was inefficient, corrupt, and inequitable. Many taxes were "farmed"—that is, the right to collect them was granted to private collectors who paid the government a fixed sum and then collected all they could. The burden fell most heavily on the peasants, since the nobles and the upper bourgeoisie were exempt from major taxes. Sully could do nothing to make the system more just (nor could any French minister down to the Revolution), but he could make it work better by discharging dishonest and inefficient tax farmers. (It has been estimated that as a rule hardly half the taxes collected in France at this time reached the treasury.) Moreover, the reestablishment of internal peace and order, which allowed agriculture and commerce to recover, helped to increase the government's revenues, especially from customs duties. When Henry IV was assassinated by a Catholic fanatic in 1610 there was a sizable surplus in the treasury.

The Estates General of 1614

Within a few years the work of Henry and Sully was in ruins. Under the regency of Henry's widow, Marie de' Medici, the treasury surplus was sopped up by rapacious courtiers, and Spain began once more to intervene in French affairs, sometimes in a strange alliance with the Huguenots. In 1614 the Estates General were summoned to one of their rare meetings, but the deliberations soon turned into a struggle between the First and Second Estates (the clergy and the nobility) and the Third Estate (the bourgeoisie, who were represented largely by provincial royal officers). No group was willing to take responsibility; and no group had the power to demand reform. The assembly dissolved with a strong declaration that "the king is sovereign in France, and holds his crown

from God only." It was not to meet again until 1789, on the eve of the Revolution.

Richelieu

In 1614 Henry IV's son, Louis XIII, was only fourteen years old. He was soon to be married to Anne of Austria, daughter of Philip III of Spain, as a symbol of Habsburg influence on France. There was not much to be hoped for from the monarch himself—except that he might choose and support some able first minister. The man was already in sight—a brilliant young bishop named Richelieu—but it took him several years to become a cardinal (in 1622) and head of the king's council (in 1624). From 1624 to his death in 1642 Richelieu was the real ruler of France. Richelieu, rather than any member of the Bourbon dynasty, founded absolute monarchy in France.

There is no mystery about Richelieu, as there is about many other great figures in history. He had the clearest and most penetrating mind of any statesman of his generation. And he made his purpose perfectly plain: to enhance the power and prestige of the French monarchy beyond any possibility of challenge. He came to his task with a marvelous grasp of political and diplomatic possibilities, an infal-

Three studies of Richelieu by Philippe de Champaigne.

lible memory, and an inflexible will unhampered by moral scruples. Richelieu admired Machiavelli's writings, and the heart of his political creed was *raison d'état*—the doctrine that the good of the state is the supreme good, and that any means may be used to attain it. He would coolly send an innocent man to his death in order to frighten other troublemakers, enhance the authority of the monarchy, and so save bloodshed in the end. "In judging crimes against the state," he argued, "it is essential to banish pity." He was not irreligious, but the workings of his mind were overwhelmingly this-worldly. "Man is immortal; his salvation is hereafter," he once argued against some conscientious scruples of the king, but "the state has no immortality, its salvation is now or never." While his cardinal's robes helped protect him against assassination, his policy was that of an astute secular statesman who put public order before religious zeal. His reputation for diabolical cleverness went even beyond the reality and helped him to bewilder his enemies and gain his ends.

Richelieu had three concrete objectives that had to be carried out more or less simultaneously. First, he meant to break the political and military power of the Huguenots. Second, he meant to crush the political influence of the great nobles. And finally, he meant to destroy the power of the Habsburgs to intervene in French internal affairs.

The Edict of Nantes had allowed the Huguenots to garrison about two hundred towns, the chief of which was La Rochelle on the west coast. Richelieu persuaded Louis XIII that he would never be master in his own house until he had wiped out this "empire within an empire." Rumors that the government had decided to attack provoked the Huguenots to rebel, and Richelieu proceeded to besiege and capture La Rochelle. At the Peace of Alais in 1629, which settled the dispute, Richelieu was unexpectedly generous in his terms. He had no respect whatever for what he contemptuously called "the allegedly Reformed religion," but he allowed the Huguenots the right to worship as they pleased once he had attained his primary objective of eliminating their political and military autonomy. He did not wish to alienate Protestants abroad who could help him in a war with Spain and Austria, and he hoped he could make loyal and useful citizens out of the Huguenots. In this he was successful. The Huguenots served the crown in the war that followed against the Habsburgs and loyally supported the monarchy in the crisis of the Fronde.

Richelieu's attack on the political power of the nobility was less successful than his attack on the Huguenots, but it was just as determined. Until the very end of his career, he was constantly threatened by aristocratic intrigues. In response to this threat, he developed a network of spies, set up a special tribunal to try noble lawbreakers, and sternly forbade dueling, a privilege that marked the freedom of the aristocracy from ordinary restraints. He gradually weakened the power of the great nobles who were provincial governors and gave more local administrative responsibilities to direct representatives of the crown. These representatives, called *intendants*, were usually drawn from the *noblesse de la robe*, ennobled officeholders of middle-class ancestry. They were therefore more dependent on the monarchy than the older nobility. Richelieu did nothing to lessen the economic or social privileges of the French nobility, but he did curtail its political power.

Richelieu was no financier, nor did he have any interest in bettering the condition of the common people. He spent large sums on rebuilding the armed forces and even more in actual warfare against Spain. He left the government's finances and the nation's peasants in worse condition than he had found them. But through his subtle diplomacy and his well-timed intervention in the Thirty Years' War (discussed below), he made France, instead of Spain, the leading European power.

Mazarin and the Fronde

Richelieu's death in 1642 (Louis XIII died a few months later, in 1643) put his work to a severe test. Louis XIV was a child of five when his father died, and so his mother, Anne of Austria, was appointed regent. However, she left the business of government to the man whom Richelieu had picked and trained to succeed himself, an Italian cardinal named Mazarin. Mazarin had the subtlety and political skill of his master but not his inflexible will; he was both more adaptable and, as a foreigner, less popular than Richelieu. His two main objectives were to continue the war against Spain until the Habsburgs were defeated and to maintain the prestige of the monarchy at the level to which Richelieu had raised it. The nobility hated him as a foreign upstart, however, and the bourgeoisie hated him for the high taxes he imposed to carry on the war. The result was the last serious rebellion to take place against the monarchy until the French Revolution—a complicated and uncoordinated movement of resistance known as the Fronde (1648–52).

The word *Fronde* referred to a game of slinging clods at passing coaches, which was played by the more unruly children of Paris. The rebellion was like the game; it was annoying, but in the end it did not keep the monarchy from driving along the road to absolutism. The leaders did not want to destroy the French monarchy nor did they wish to upset the established social order. They were composed of several groups—the judges of the *Parlements* (the High Courts) and the chief financial officers, who were practi-

Outbursts during the Fronde in Paris (1648).

cally hereditary bureaucrats, and the nobles led by princes of the blood. Each group wanted to modify the structure of government so that it could have more influence. But no group could agree with others on a joint program, with the exception of the purely negative policy of exiling Mazarin. Thus the *parlements*, which began the struggle, stood for the privileges of the corporations of bureaucrats who controlled the courts and the financial bureaus. They wanted the king to rule with their advice, rather than with that of councilors whom he could make or break as it pleased him. They insisted especially that no tax could be imposed without their consent. The nobles, who joined the rebellion later, had no intention of letting the *parlements* become dominant in government; they wanted to get rid of the *intendants* and regain their old powers as provincial governors. In the provinces, many men rebelled to protect or enlarge local privileges, but they often found it hard to decide whether they should support a *parlement* or a noble governor.

The result might have been different if anyone had dared draw on the deep-seated resentment of the lower classes—a resentment that had been expressed during the first half of the century in many local riots against taxation and misgovernment. But while a few theorists talked of liberty and democracy, no one was willing to take the chance of unleashing forces that might not be controllable. Unlike the contemporary English rebellion, in which the middle and lower classes accepted radical doctrines and defeated the king (see p. 426), the Fronde remained dominated by the nobility and the upper bourgeoisie. Each group approached the brink of making unlimited war on the king even at the risk of social revolution, and each drew back in horror. This innate conservatism, combined with lack of unity among the leaders, led to the disintegration of the rebellion. There was very little hard fighting; by the end of 1652, Mazarin, who had had to flee the country, was once more back in the saddle. Most Frenchmen concluded that a strong monarchy was preferable to futile civil war. The young king, Louis XIV, was to profit from this reaction when he came of age. Meanwhile, he remembered with

loathing the violence and instability of the Fronde. He came to hate Paris, from which he had had to flee in 1648, to despise the mob, and to fear the nobles unless they were restrained by a firm royal hand.

In spite of the Fronde and the tax burden that continued to oppress the common people, Mazarin carried on the war with Spain until the Spaniards were forced to ask for terms in 1659. France gained two Pyrenees counties, and Maria Theresa, daughter of Philip IV of Spain, was married to Louis XIV. Both the treaty and the marriage symbolized the humiliation of Spain and the triumph of France as the leading power in Europe. Mazarin died in 1661, and Louis XIV announced to his ministers that he would henceforth be his own prime minister. Now the work of Richelieu had come to full fruition. The French monarchy no longer had anything to fear from Huguenots and nobles at home or from Habsburgs abroad. It was an absolute monarchy, endowed with a fuller sovereignty than any other yet seen in European history.

ENGLAND: IN SEARCH OF CIVIL AND RELIGIOUS LIBERTY, 1603–60

While Richelieu and Mazarin were laying the foundations of absolute monarchy by divine right, leaders in England were slowly developing a constitutional, parliamentary monarchy. Richelieu could see clearly where he was going, but the goal was never clear to English leaders during their century of conflict with the crown. Englishmen groped their way toward a conception of sovereignty as something rooted in law rather than in personal authority, something to be lodged in the hands of an assembly that represented the community, or at least its more wealthy and influential members. England was not alone in its resistance to absolute monarchy, but the result in most other countries, such as Poland, was anarchy and confusion. Only in England was a representative assembly able to increase its power without wrecking or at least weakening the state. When Queen Anne came to the throne in 1702 the English government was both a stronger and a more popular government than it had been in 1603 when James I succeeded Elizabeth I. The example of England, particularly as reflected in the writings of John Locke, was to have an enormous influence on western history throughout the following two centuries.

England, on the periphery of European civilization, had always been peculiar in its political development. For instance, although the strong monarchy of the Tudors (1485–1603) was part of a general European trend, the survival and strengthening of Parliament under such a monarchy was without parallel elsewhere. The Tudors continued to use Parliament in legislation and taxation, whereas rulers on the Continent felt that representative assemblies were usually either useless or obstructive. Parliament, particularly the House of Commons, slowly acquired a corporate feeling and a sense of being an integral part of the national government. The House of Commons, it will be remembered, represented both the mercantile classes in the towns and the landed gentry (knights and squires) in the country. The gentry had been increasing in numbers, wealth, and political influence since the dissolution of the monasteries. They governed England at the local level as justices of the peace (the English monarchy had no paid bureaucrats like the French *intendants*), and they dominated the lower house of Parliament by sitting as representatives not only of the counties but of many boroughs as well. In any other country they would have been considered members of the lesser nobility; in England they sat in the House of Commons with merchants and lawyers. This House had grown steadily in wealth and influence, until one member could boast in 1628 that the lower house could afford to buy the House of Lords three times over.

Thus the English Parliament in the early seventeenth century represented all the politically active classes of the nation in a way no other representative assembly in Europe did. There were no provincial estates or privileges in England as there were in France, and the class lines among peers, gentry, and wealthy burgesses were not so sharply drawn. The

rigid English rule of primogeniture meant that younger sons of the nobility, who were commoners, often went into the professions. On the other hand, English merchants were continually buying land and becoming gentry. This meant that if the monarch should ever fall out with Parliament—and with the social groups it represented—he would not be able to play class against class or district against district.

The Tudors

Queen Elizabeth had had arguments with her Parliaments, but the threat from abroad and the political good sense of both the queen and the opposition kept these arguments from becoming dangerous. It was generally recognized that only Parliament could make a law or impose a tax. It was also recognized that making policy, especially foreign policy, lay outside the competence of Parliament and within the sphere of what was called the royal prerogative.

The Tudors felt, however, that it was sometimes wise to confirm royal policy

Formal meeting of Parliament in 1625. The Lords are seated; the Commons stand outside the bar.

by parliamentary statute, particularly in the delicate field of religion. Henry VIII used Parliament to break with Rome; Mary had asked Parliament to restore England to the Roman obedience by statute; and Elizabeth had broken with the pope once more by statute. Elizabeth's Parliaments tried more than once to reform the Anglican Church in a Puritan direction and to nudge the queen on foreign policy—presumptuous acts for which Elizabeth scolded them sharply. But she was too popular for Parliament ever to make a real issue of the conflict and too astute ever to demand a clear definition of her prerogative. Tudor "despotism" was a popular despotism, and Tudor rulers found that they could exercise their sovereign power most effectively by seeking the cooperation of Parliament.

James I and Parliament

The Stuarts, who ruled from 1603 to 1714, either could not or would not cooperate with Parliament. James I (king of Scotland and of England, 1603–25), the son of Mary Queen of Scots, was a well-meaning but pedantic intellectual who never understood the social structure or the political realities of the kingdom he inherited from Elizabeth. He had been raised as a Protestant by the regents who ran Scotland after his mother's exile, but he had not greatly enjoyed his Presbyterian upbringing. His aims were praiseworthy—peace with Spain, toleration of the Catholic minority in England, union of England and Scotland, and a strong but benevolent monarchy—but he did not inspire confidence as a political leader. Moreover, many of his ministers were incompetent. Unlike Elizabeth, who often concealed her imperious will in cloudy and ambiguous language, James liked to have things dangerously clear. He had written a book, *The True Law of*

James I, by D. Mytens (1621).

Free Monarchies, in which he insisted that kings owed their position to God alone, were responsible only to God, and in fact were themselves like gods on earth.

His belief in a monarchy "free" of restraints, free to do as it pleased for the common good, did not appeal to the classes represented in Parliament. Some of James's policies might have really helped the poor; others simply transferred wealth from one privileged group to another. In either case, opposition to the king could not endanger the country. The Tudors had long ago ended the threat of aristocratic violence, and peace with Spain in 1604 removed the danger of foreign conquest. Only their own king could now attack the beliefs or interfere with the property rights of the privileged classes. Parliament, fearing royal tyranny, began to criticize James's acts. James, fearing parliamentary intervention in policy matters, began to scold Parliament. The delicate Tudor balance was destroyed.

Friction rapidly developed over three related issues: religion, finance, and foreign policy. The Puritans and their sympathizers in the House of Commons wished to "purify" the Anglican Church of everything that savored of Catholic practice, from "popish" ritual to the authority of bishops. James was convinced that the Presbyterian system of church government, which he had known in his youth in Scotland, would not only destroy royal control of the church, but would threaten the monarchy itself. "No bishop, no king," he remarked within a year of his arrival in England. Parliament, annoyed by the extravagance of James's court and dubious about his policies, denied him enough money to meet the rising costs of government. James replied by raising money without parliamentary approval—for example, by increasing the customs duties on his own authority. When his right to take such actions was contested, the courts ruled in his favor—probably correctly, since the king controlled foreign trade as part of his control of foreign policy. But the seeming subservience of the courts to the royal will further disturbed Parliament.

Meanwhile James was following a foreign policy that exasperated the Puritan majority in Parliament. He was too friendly with Spain for the Puritan taste, he did little to defend Protestants abroad against the rising tide of Catholicism, and he tried in vain to marry his son Charles to the Spanish Infanta. When James chided the House of Commons in 1621 for even discussing his foreign policy, the House bristled and passed a unanimous Protestation defending its right to discuss "the arduous and urgent affairs concerning the King, State, and defence of the realm, and of the Church of England." This was revolutionary talk. James tore the resolution from the Commons' *Journal*, but he could not undo what had been done. The House of Commons, which Queen Elizabeth had kept under the control of her privy councilors, was now taking the initiative under leaders of its own. An aggressive and powerful element among James's subjects was demanding a voice in politics that he was utterly unwilling to grant.

Charles I
and the English Revolution

The situation rapidly worsened during the early years of the reign of Charles I, who came to the throne in 1625. Charles tried to please Parliament by attacking Catholic countries, but his incompetent favorite, the Duke of Buckingham, failed to capture Cadiz in Spain or to relieve the French Huguenots at La Rochelle. Parliament had urged war but had not granted adequate taxes, so the government tried to pay for the wars by levying a forced loan and by imprisoning those who objected to paying. Parliament in 1628 drew up a formal protest in the form of a Petition of Right, which they finally compelled Charles to approve. Its two main provisions were that no one should henceforth be compelled to pay any tax or loan "without common consent by Act of Parliament," and that no one should be imprisoned without cause shown.

By the next year the House of Commons was roused to fury by Charles's assertions of his full control of Church and state. It declared that anyone who introduced anything savoring of Catholic practices in the Anglican Church was "a capital enemy to this kingdom and commonwealth," and that anyone who advised or submitted to the levying of taxes without parliamentary consent was "a betrayer of the liberties of England." The issue of "sovereignty" had finally been raised, and the word itself was being debated by lawyers and parliamentary orators. Where did the supreme power in England lie—in the king or in Parliament? The old answer, that it lay in the "king-in-Parliament," would no longer do. The royal prerogative and "the liberties of England" were not reconcilable any longer.

Charles I now took things into his own hands and ruled without Parliament for eleven years (1629–40). He was less intelligent and more stubborn than his father. James had always yielded before conflict became irreconcilable. Rather than yield, Charles was to resort to duplicity and falsehood in the crises ahead of him, and as a result he ended his life on the block, trusted by almost no one. Trying to duplicate Richelieu's brilliant work across the Channel, he chose tough-minded advisers: Thomas Wentworth, Earl of Strafford, in political affairs, and William Laud, Archbishop of Canterbury, in ecclesiastical affairs. With them and others, Charles devised new methods of nonparliamentary taxation that provided enough money to run the government so long as it stayed out of war. Laud began a movement back toward more ritual and formality in the Anglican service, a movement the Puritans regarded as an attempt to restore Catholicism. All opposition, whether to arbitrary taxation or to innovations in worship, was sternly suppressed by the courts. Everything went well until Laud tried to force the Anglican Book of Common Prayer on stubbornly Presbyterian Scotland. Before long an angry and well-led Scottish army was encamped in northern England. Charles and Strafford,

Charles I, by D. Mytens (1631).

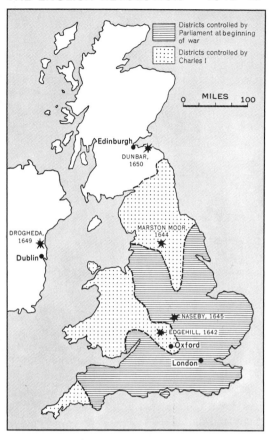

England During the English Revolution 1642–49

Districts controlled by Parliament at beginning of war

Districts controlled by Charles I

MILES 0 — 100

Edinburgh
DUNBAR, 1650
DROGHEDA, 1649
Dublin
MARSTON MOOR, 1644
NASEBY, 1645
EDGEHILL, 1642
Oxford
London

The Dutch view of Cromwell (detail from a print dated April 30, 1653).

ally unanimous. But when the more radical Puritans in Parliament went on to abolish bishops in the Anglican Church and to seek control of the army, a party began to form around Charles in opposition to the parliamentary majority. And thus a civil war broke out in 1642 and lasted until 1649.

Enough has been said to suggest that the English Revolution was primarily a war of ideas, not of classes or of districts or even of interests, although the interests of merchants and gentry who were outraged by nonparliamentary taxation were certainly involved. Generally the towns, the middle class, and the economically advanced southeastern counties of England supported Parliament, while many rural areas, aristocrats, and the backward northwest supported Charles. But nobles, squires, and artisans from all parts of England were to be found on both sides. Unlike the Fronde, in which narrow interest groups failed to work out programs with broad appeal, the English Revolution offered a real alternative to the established order: parliamentary monarchy instead of benevolent absolutism, and a Presbyterian Church governed by elected "presbyters," or elders, instead of an Anglican Church governed by bishops appointed by the crown. Unlike the Fronde again, the English Revolution was able to attract and to accept men with really radical ideas—men who wanted neither a monarchy, nor an established church, nor power in the hands of landlords.

As the civil war intensified, Parliament proved to be more successful than the king in raising money and in building a strong army. A brilliant cavalry officer named Oliver Cromwell formed a "New Model Army" largely from among his fellow Independents, or Congregationalists. The Independents were Bible-reading Puritans of strict morals who believed in independent congregations democratically organized, with little or no national organization. Many of them were of lower economic status than either Anglicans or Presbyterians (though Cromwell and his chief aids would have ranked as gentry). Cromwell and his army finally defeated the king's forces in 1645, only to fall out with the Presbyterians, who had

finding themselves unable to raise an army to fight the Scots, had to summon Parliament to get the money to buy them off.

The Long Parliament, which met in November 1640 and was not dissolved until 1653, became a workshop of revolution. It sent Strafford and Laud to the block. It passed an act stating that a Parliament must be summoned at least every three years. It outlawed all nonparliamentary taxation and abolished the special royal courts (the Court of Star Chamber, which dealt with opposition to the government, and the Court of High Commission, for ecclesiastical affairs), which had been the chief instruments of the "Eleven Years' Tyranny." In other words, in less than a year (1640–41) Parliament had made absolute monarchy impossible in England. This much of its work won unwilling approval from Charles, since sentiment for it was virtu-

dominated Parliament since the Anglicans withdrew in 1642 to join Charles. With Parliament and the army at loggerheads about what to do with the king and about what sort of government to set up in England (many in the army wanted a truly democratic regime), the king was able to escape and make one last bid for victory before being finally defeated by Cromwell in 1648. Cromwell and the Independents in the army were determined now to get at what they considered the root of the trouble. They "purged" Parliament of its Presbyterian members, executed King Charles I in 1649, abolished monarchy and the House of Lords, and set up a republic, or "Commonwealth," with the "rump" of the Long Parliament as its government and Cromwell as its moving spirit.

Cromwell

Cromwell proved to be a revolutionary leader unlike almost any other in western history. He was a deeply religious man who tried in vain to avoid becoming a dictator. Yet he was ruthless and determined when he felt his policies were threatened. He massacred the Catholic Irish when they rebelled, defeated the Scots when they intervened in favor of the son of Charles I, fought a commercial war with the Dutch from 1652 to 1654, and boldly dissolved what was left of the Long Parliament in 1653. In a few short years he had decisively won a civil war, united the British Isles under one government for the first time, made England again the terror of the seas, and apparently wiped the slate clean for any political experiment he wished to try. The rest of his career until his death in 1658, however, was a tragic search for answers to insoluble problems: how to guarantee religious toleration to all kinds of Protestants except determined Anglicans, and at the same time how to develop some constitutional basis for his government. Cromwell tried to rule through a written constitution (the first in the history of any major state) and with the assent of a Parliament. He took the title of Lord Protector instead of king, but he quarreled with his Parliaments as bitterly as the Stuarts had quarreled with

theirs. At one point Cromwell had to set up an open military dictatorship to keep his Parliament from disbanding his army and persecuting his coreligionists. The plain fact was that most Englishmen were not ready for religious toleration, especially toleration of the radical religious minorities that made up a large part of Cromwell's army.

Furthermore, it became more and more evident that it was impossible in England to break utterly with history and to set up a new sort of government simply by writing a constitution. There was already a "constitution" deeply ingrained in the English political tradition, although it was nowhere written down. Soon after Cromwell's death even his own supporters saw that the only possible alternative to military dictatorship was Parliament, and that the only way to restore Parlia-

Oliver Cromwell, painting from the original panel by Samuel Cooper.

Democratic Ideas in the English Revolution

After it was sure of victory, the Parliamentary army began to worry about a proper government for England. A Council of the Army, including representatives of the ordinary soldiers, held a series of debates at Putney in 1647 on a constitution for the country. One of the basic issues was whether all men should be allowed to vote.

Major Rainborough: I think that the poorest he that is in England hath a life to live, as the greatest he, and therefore truly, sir, I think it's clear, that every man that is to live under a government ought first by his own consent to put himself under that government, and I do think that the poorest man in England is not at all bound in a strict sense to that government that he hath not had a voice to put himself under.

General Ireton [Cromwell's son-in-law]: Government is to preserve property. . . . The objection does not lie in the making of the representation more equal but in the introducing of men . . . in this government who have no property in this kingdom. . . .

Sexby [a representative of the soldiers]: I see that though liberty were our end, there is a degeneration from it. We have ventured our lives to recover our birthrights and privileges as Englishmen, and by the arguments urged there is none. There are many thousands of us soldiers that have ventured our lives; we have had little property . . . yet we have had a birthright. But it seems now, except a man hath a fixed estate in this kingdom, he hath no right in this kingdom. I wonder we were so much deceived.

From *Puritanism and Liberty*, ed. by A. S. P. Woodhouse (Chicago: University of Chicago Press, 1951), pp. 53, 62, 69.

The restoration of King Charles II: the crowning in Westminster Abbey (from a contemporary print).

ment was also to restore the monarchy. In 1660 the monarchy, Parliament, and the Anglican Church were all restored when a "Convention Parliament" invited Charles II to return from France and take up the crown.

The Restoration

At first glance nothing more remained in England after twenty years of civil war and revolutionary experiment than had remained in France after the defeat of the Fronde. To this day Englishmen refer to the events just described as the "Puritan Rebellion." They do not call it a revolution because it was succeeded by the "Restoration." But one thing at least had been decided: there was to be no absolute monarchy in England. All acts of the Long Parliament passed before the outbreak of civil war were still valid, and these acts put severe limitations on royal power, even if the balance of power between king and Parliament was still un-

certain. Strafford and Laud had tried to do for Charles I what Richelieu and Mazarin had done for Louis XIV, but all three Englishmen died on the block, while all three Frenchmen died in their beds. The turmoil of the first half of the seventeenth century left most Englishmen with certain half-expressed convictions whose effects can be traced in English history for generations. Among these convictions were a fear of allowing any one individual to acquire too much political power, a deepened respect for government by law rather than by personal command, a reverence for Parliament as the defender of individual rights against arbitrary despotism, and a distaste for standing armies.

The early seventeenth century was a brilliant age in the history of English literature, including Shakespeare's mature work, the Authorized, or King James, Version of the Bible (1611), and Milton's formative years. It was also a brilliant period in political thinking, as statesmen and pamphleteers argued for royalist, parliamentary, or radical principles of government.

Perhaps Thomas Hobbes's *Leviathan* (1651) best represented the political insights and fears, if not the greatest hopes, of these turbulent years. Writing in the midst of civil war and in exile, Hobbes pictured the life of man without government as "solitary, poor, nasty, brutish, and short." Without some authority to enforce law, there is no society, no order, only "a war of every man against every man." Men in general are inclined to "a perpetual and restless desire of power after power." So they set up a sovereign power by agreement or contract (it makes no difference whether the sovereign is a king or a Parliament), by which all men agree to obey the sovereign, but only so long as he is able to maintain order. The sovereign is not bound by anything in the contract. No clearer argument for might as the necessary basis of all right had ever been written. Hobbes took Bodin's argument for a legitimate sovereign authority and subtly transformed it into justification of sheer arbitrary power. His book could be used equally well to support Charles I or Cromwell. In a sense the main effort of Englishmen during the seventeenth century was to find some way to refute Hobbes—to subject political power to the restraint of law and to increase its responsibility to the governed. They finally succeeded in 1688.

GERMANY: DISINTEGRATION AND DISASTER, 1618–48

While France was building the strongest monarchy in Europe and England was undergoing a constitutional crisis from which it was to emerge with new strength, the German-speaking peoples were caught up in one of the most futile and destructive wars in the history of Europe. The Thirty Years' War (1618–48) was really four successive wars that began in Bohemia, spread to the rest of the Empire, and finally involved most of the major powers on the Continent. It was a savage and demoralizing conflict that left "Germany" poorer and weaker than the western European states.

The Causes of the Thirty Years' War

The war sprang out of a complicated mixture of religious and political grievances. Lutherans and Catholics had not fought each other since the Peace of Augsburg (1555), but the Catholics were disturbed by the fact that, in spite of the provisions of the peace, most of the Catholic bishoprics in northern Germany had fallen into Lutheran or secular hands. This gave some grounds for creating an ultra-Catholic movement headed by the Jesuits and the German Catholic princes, particularly Maximilian, Duke of Bavaria. The spread of Calvinism introduced a new source of friction because

Title page of Thomas Hobbes's *Leviathan,* a great landmark in the making of the modern state. Hobbes calls the sovereign power of the state, usually conferred on one man, "that great Leviathan, or rather (to speak more reverently) that mortal God, to which we owe under the Immortal God, our peace and defence."

Calvinists had been excluded from the Peace of Augsburg. When Maximilian roughly disciplined the Protestant town of Donauwörth, Frederick V, the Calvinist ruler of the Palatinate, a small state on the middle Rhine, took the lead in forming a Protestant Union among the German princes and cities in 1608. In reply, a Catholic League was organized the next year under the leadership of Maximilian. By 1609 two illegal military alliances faced each other within the Empire, each afraid of the other and each determined to keep the rival religion from making any further gains.

Revolt in Bohemia

As these examples show, each component of the Empire was a virtually independent state. The Habsburgs, who held the imperial title, realized that the only way to rebuild and expand imperial authority was to establish firmer control over what had been their old family domains—Austria, Bohemia, and Hungary. Thus the Austrian Habsburg, Ferdinand of Styria, got himself elected king of Bohemia in 1617.

Bohemia was a flourishing kingdom in which two nationalities (Germans and Czechs) and several religions (Catholicism, Lutheranism, Calvinism, and remnants of the Hussite movement of two centuries earlier) lived fairly peaceably together under earlier Habsburg promises of toleration. Ferdinand, a zealous Catholic, began systematically to undermine this toleration and to re-Catholicize the country. This action provoked rebellion by the Bohemian Estates, which were dominated by a strong Protestant majority. In May 1618 two of Ferdinand's councilors were tossed from a castle window in Prague, and civil war broke out between the Habsburg ruler and the Estates. The Estates raised an army, deposed Ferdinand, and offered the crown of Bohemia to Frederick V of the Palatinate. When Frederick unwisely accepted, the Protestant Union became involved in defending the Bohemian Estates, while Maximilian of Bavaria brought the Catholic League to the support of Ferdinand. In 1619 Ferdinand was elected emperor. Thus a war that might have remained a local affair soon spread throughout the Empire.

The Bohemian phase of the war was soon ended. The forces of the emperor and the League won an overwhelming victory in 1620. Frederick fled, and the emperor proceeded to work his will on the prostrate Bohemians. Half the property in the country changed hands through confiscation. The Jesuits, with strong secular backing, set out to reconvert the country to Catholicism, and within ten years they had succeeded. The prosperity of the country was ruined, Protestantism was stamped out or driven underground, and Czech nationalism was crushed for two centuries to come. The Habsburgs and their Catholic allies had won the first round decisively.

Danish Intervention

The fall of Bohemia terrified German Protestants and elated the Catholics. The Spanish Habsburgs came to the aid of their fellow Catholics, and the armies of the League were everywhere triumphant. In spite of the common danger, the Protestants could not unite. The Lutherans had been more afraid of a Calvinist victory in Bohemia than of an imperial triumph, and so Lutheran Saxony had ac-

Soldiers and siege artillery of the Thirty Years' War (copper engraving by Merian in "Theatrum Europeam").

tually helped Ferdinand put down the revolt. Although Frederick V was the son-in-law of James I, Protestant England gave no help because James and Charles were too involved in difficulties at home.

In 1625 the Protestant king of Denmark intervened, partly to save the cause of his coreligionists but primarily to pick up some territory in northern Germany. Within a year he was beaten in battle by a large army raised by the most inscrutable figure of the war, a wealthy war profiteer and professional soldier named Wallenstein, who had offered the emperor his services. Wallenstein had no serious religious convictions, and his political aims have puzzled generations of historians. His immediate aim seems to have been to build an imperial Habsburg military machine of such strength that it could not only eliminate all Protestant opposition but could operate independently of all other forces in the Empire, including the Catholic League. Before long Wallenstein and the League were as much at loggerheads on one side as Calvinists and Lutherans were on the other. Religion slowly receded in significance as the war became a struggle for the hegemony of Europe.

The high-water mark of Habsburg triumph and Catholic recovery was reached in 1629. Denmark withdrew from the war, leaving Wallenstein's army supreme. The Catholic League and Jesuit advisers persuaded Ferdinand to issue the Edict of Restitution, which restored to Catholic hands all ecclesiastical lands lost to Protestantism since 1552. It was evident that this edict could not be carried out without more bloodshed, because it meant that Catholic bishops were to be restored throughout northern Germany. Such an act would destroy the rough balance between Catholicism and Protestantism in Germany and weaken the northern states for the benefit of Austria and Bavaria. This threat finally roused the Lutherans inside and outside Germany to a sense of their peril.

Swedish Intervention: Gustavus Adolphus

In 1631 growing Habsburg power was blocked by the intervention of Sweden, a

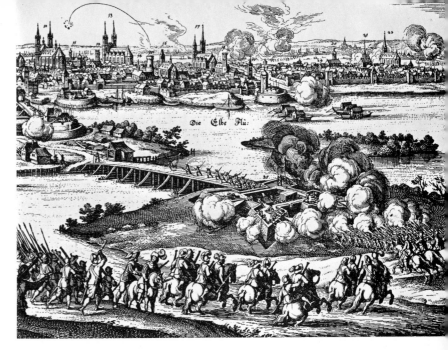

The siege of Magdeburg in 1631 by Habsburg and Catholic forces. This siege resulted in one of the bloodiest massacres of the Thirty Years' War.

country that had not appeared before on the stage of international politics. Gustavus II (Gustavus Adolphus) was the ablest ruler of his generation. His country was sparse in population and resources, but he had cultivated its iron and timber industries, united the nation behind him, and built the best army of the day. It was not large, but it was well

The Sack of Magdeburg
1631

Then was there naught but beating and burning, plundering, torture, and murder. Most especially was every one of the enemy bent on securing much booty. When a marauding party entered a house, if its master had anything to give he might thereby purchase respite and protection for himself and his family till the next man, who also wanted something, should come along. It was only when everything had been brought forth and there was nothing left to give that the real trouble commenced. Then, what with blows and threats of shooting, stabbing, and hanging, the poor people were so terrified that if they had had anything left they would have brought it forth if it had been buried in the earth or hidden away in a thousand castles. In this frenzied rage, the great and splendid city that had stood like a fair princess in the land was now, in its hour of direst need and unutterable distress and woe, given over to the flames, and thousands of innocent men, women, and children, in the midst of a horrible din of heartrending shrieks and cries, were tortured and put to death in so cruel and shameful a manner that no words would suffice to describe, nor no tears to bewail it.

From Otto von Guericke, in *Readings in European History*, ed. by James Harvey Robinson (Boston: Ginn, 1906), Vol. II, pp. 211–12.

equipped (with the first uniforms and an improved musket), well disciplined, and inspired by high morale. Gustavus had already come close to making the Baltic a Swedish lake in wars with Denmark and Poland. He now stepped into the fray as the sincere champion of Lutheranism, hoping apparently to set up a federation of Protestant states in Germany under Swedish leadership.

Gustavus arrived too late to save Magdeburg from a terrible sack by the Habsburg Imperialists in May 1631, but in the fall of 1631 he overwhelmed the Imperialist armies at Breitenfeld in Saxony. He then marched triumphantly to the Rhine. Wallenstein, whom the emperor had dismissed under pressure from the Catholic League, was recalled, only to be beaten by Gustavus at Lützen in 1632. Gustavus himself was killed in the battle, however, and by 1634 his army had finally been outnumbered and beaten. Wallenstein had been murdered by one of his staff, and another phase of the war had come to an end. Swedish intervention had saved German Protestantism but had not gained a decision. The most powerful state of all had been watching the course of events closely and was now about to intervene with decisive results.

French Intervention: Richelieu

Since coming to power in 1624, Richelieu had kept in close touch with the progress of the war through his ambassadors and agents. But for ten years he did not feel that the French army was strong enough to intervene in Germany. His major purpose was to crush the Habsburgs, both Austrian and Spanish, and he was ready to ally with anyone, Protestant or Catholic, who was opposed to them. The Dutch, who went back to war with their old enemies the Spanish, were his first allies, and in 1631 he subsidized the invasion by Gustavus Adolphus. When the Swedes were finally defeated in 1634, Richelieu saw that he would have to intervene directly if he was to check Habsburg expansion in, and perhaps control of, Europe. And so in May 1635 he sent a French herald to Brussels to declare war on the king of Spain.

The Thirty Years' War had lasted for seventeen years with no decisive result, and it was to continue for thirteen more dreary years while French, Swedish, and Dutch armies fought against the Spanish and Austrian Habsburgs. Spain was weakened by the successful rebellion of Portugal and the almost successful rebellion of Catalonia (1640). In 1643 the French finally destroyed the legend of Spanish invincibility by crushing a Spanish army at Rocroi in the Netherlands. It was the first time in 150 years that a Spanish army had suffered a major defeat. The emperor's allies deserted him, and by 1648 the Swedes were threatening Vienna and storming Prague. The dream of Emperor Ferdinand II (who had died in 1637) of re-Catholicizing Germany and establishing Habsburg control over the Empire lay in ruins.

The Peace of Westphalia, 1648

A peace was finally worked out at the Congress of Westphalia (1643–48), Europe's first great peace conference and the first international gathering of importance since the Council of Constance (1414–18). But it was a far different gathering from that of two centuries earlier. The atmosphere and the business at hand were now entirely secular, and the communities represented were sovereign territorial states that recognized no earthly superior and only the most shadowy common interests. "Christendom" had dissolved, and the word *civilization* would not be generally used until the next century to express in secular terms what *Christendom* had once meant to Europeans in religious terms.

Almost every act of the Congress emphasized the importance of the sovereign state. For example, it recognized the right of each German principality to make alliances and to declare war on its own. This constituted practical recognition of the disintegration of the Empire into over three hundred separate sovereignties. Switzerland and the Dutch Netherlands were finally recognized as sovereign states, independent of all ties to the Empire. France acquired some very ambiguous rights to Alsace, Sweden acquired strips of German territory along the

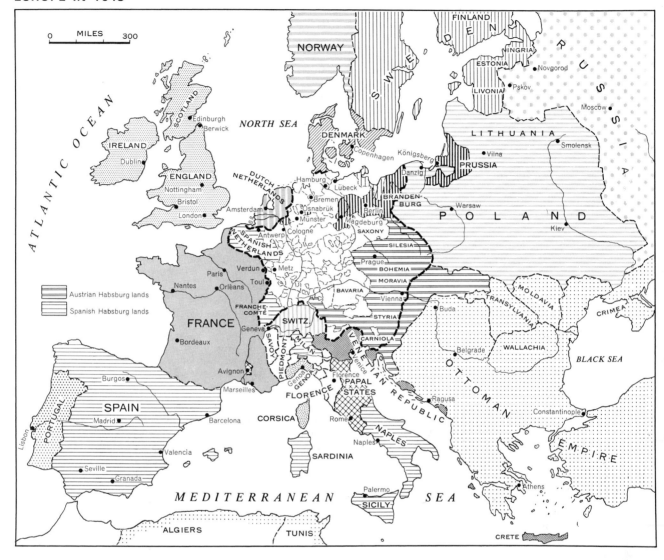

Austrian Habsburg lands

Spanish Habsburg lands

shores of the Baltic and the North Sea, and the two German states of Brandenburg and Bavaria ended up with increased territory and prestige. As for religion, the old principle of *cuius regio, eius religio* was reaffirmed. Calvinism was simply added to Catholicism and Lutheranism as one of the recognized faiths. The ownership of church lands was settled as of 1624, meaning in general that northern Germany remained Protestant and southern Germany, Catholic. France and Spain were unable to reach agreement, so their war continued until French victory was finally recognized in the Peace of the Pyrenees in 1659. France received some territory along the Pyrenees and in Flanders, and the Spanish princess, Maria Theresa, married Louis XIV. In general, the peace settlements of the middle of the century left France the strongest power in Europe, Spain prostrate, the Empire shattered, and a kind of power vacuum in the center of Europe.

The Social Results of the War

The Thirty Year's War was one of the most brutal and destructive wars of which we have record until the twentieth century. Armies robbed, raped, and murdered their way back and forth across Germany. The lack of any modern supply system meant that they had to live off the land. There are gruesome records of towns totally wiped out, cities reduced to a small fraction of their original population, and cultivated land reverting to waste. Destruction of livestock was even more serious than the loss of crops. The fields could be resown when the armies had passed, but work animals took years to replace. Thus starvation and disease killed more than the sword. It is impossible to be sure of the total decline in population, but some historians believe that Germany lost almost a third of its inhabitants. Even if the destruction was not so great as contemporary sources would suggest, the social and psychological effects were certainly frightful. A whole generation grew up accepting violence and brutality as normal. The fragmentation of the Empire into practically independent states hampered economic recovery. Cultural and political provincialism were to go hand in hand for the next two centuries in German history. In fact, it is almost impossible to find any good result of the generation of aimless fighting in Germany known as the Thirty Years' War.

DUTCH UNREST AND SPANISH DECLINE

England, France, and Germany were not the only countries to experience political crises in the first half of the seventeenth century. Political upheavals in this era touched every part of Europe. Even faraway Russia underwent an anarchic "Time of Troubles" before settling down uneasily under the rule of the first Romanov tsar in 1613. In the West, there were violent upheavals in the Netherlands and in Spain.

The northern Netherlands had achieved effective independence from Spain by the beginning of the century and were enjoying enormous economic success. Yet the United Provinces were riven by political and religious conflicts. One party, supported by orthodox Calvinists and led by the House of Orange (William the Silent's family), pressed for an aggressive war against Spain in the southern Netherlands. A second party, supported by the religiously tolerant Arminians (who were unwilling to accept the doctrine of predestination) and led by the mercantile class, favored a policy that might open the way to peaceful trading with Spain. As the Thirty Years' War approached, this tolerant "peace party" was overthrown: war with Spain resumed in 1621 and continued until the Peace of Westphalia. Tensions between the House of Orange and a "regent class" of mercantile interests continued throughout the century. For two decades after 1650 the "regents" dominated Dutch affairs. But when invasion again loomed in 1672—this time France, not Spain, was the enemy—the old conflicts surfaced again. The leading regent, Jan de Witt, was torn to pieces by a mob in The Hague, and the head of the House of Orange—the young Prince William III—was summoned to lead the Dutch war effort.

In Spain, problems that had been building up for decades exploded all at once in 1640. The resumption of warfare in the Netherlands, in Germany, and, finally, with France, put intolerable financial burdens on the Spanish state. Efforts by the leading minister, the Count-Duke of Olivares, to impose a more efficient centralized government and a more effective system of tax collection on the different sections of the Spanish kingdom led to two bitter rebellions in 1640. Portugal (which had been united with Spain since 1580) successfully broke away and regained its independence. And in the same year a revolt broke out in the province of Catalonia. Aided by the French, the Catalans held out for over a decade. Meanwhile unrest also broke out in Spain's Italian provinces.

All of these problems contributed to the decline of Spain and made inevitable its surrender to France in 1659. Yet behind Spain's political troubles lay an even deeper source of trouble: the diminishing strength of Spain's overseas empire. For the decline of Spain was caused largely by changes in the European (and world) economy during the seventeenth century.

THE MERCANTILE ECONOMY OF EARLY MODERN EUROPE

Seventeenth-century kings and ministers were aware that political power depended on economic strength. They sought to increase the wealth of their own countries and to decrease the wealth of rival countries, or at least to prevent its growth. Agriculture, of course, was still the chief occupation in every part of Europe, but very little could be done either to increase home production or to decrease foreign production of food and fibers. Industry was more susceptible to state interference, but none of the major countries was very dependent on industry. On the other hand, the volume and value of European trade had increased enormously. Growth between 1500 and 1600 had been so spectacular that some historians have described it as a "Commercial Revolution." And the countries that were assuming political leadership in Europe were becoming the centers of trade. The main routes now led to Amsterdam, London, and Paris rather than to Venice, Lisbon, and Seville. In the Netherlands, England, and France, the merchant was far more important than the industrialist and far more influential than the farmer.

Therefore, a ruler who wanted to use economic controls as a political weapon thought primarily in terms of altering the patterns of international trade. This policy seemed so natural that no one bothered to give it a name. In 1776, however, Adam Smith, looking at the process with some disapproval, coined the phrase "the mercantile system." This phrase, or its equivalent "mercantilism," has been used ever since.

Problems of Economic Organization

By the end of the sixteenth century it was evident that old forms of economic organization were not able to deal with the vast increase in the volume of trade. The gilds, which controlled production in many towns, could not supply the growing demands of merchants and governments. Most gilds were geared only to local markets and insisted on following traditional, and often inefficient, methods of work. Many governments tried to regulate gilds in order to get uniform, nationwide standards of production, but except for a few luxury articles, this policy proved a failure. It was easier to let the merchants deal with the problem of industrial organization.

One method, already used by the end of the Middle Ages, was called the putting-out system. For example, in the textile industry an entrepreneur might buy wool, pass it out to peasants to be spun into thread, carry the thread to others to be woven into cloth, take the cloth to the dyers, and finally sell the finished product. This system had the double advantage of bypassing the gild restrictions in the towns and of tapping new sources of cheap labor in the countryside. Underemployed peasants with only a few acres were glad to have any extra income; in England they took almost all the work away from the old textile towns. In the same way, English merchants bought Swedish iron, gave it out to Sheffield toolmakers, and sold the product abroad. (The English were the best precision-toolmakers in Europe.) The putting-out system was hard on the laborers, but it increased production and lowered costs.

Another type of organization was the gathering-in system (the factory system). In industries like printing, cannon founding, mining, and shipbuilding, and even in some textile processes such as silk weaving and calico printing, it was more efficient to gather workers together at some central place where their work could be directly supervised and coordinated. There was not much division of labor; each man made a finished or semi-finished article. But transportation costs were cut, and quality could be controlled. In both the putting-out and the gathering-in systems, it was almost invariably a merchant, not the manufacturer or the technician, who did the organizing.

Joint Stock Companies

In commerce an important innovation was the joint stock company. The small partnerships of the Middle Ages (and even the Medici Bank was small by seventeenth-century standards) could not

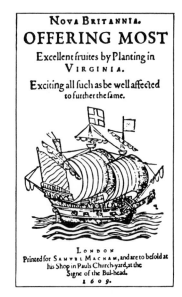

Page from a pamphlet put out by the London Company in 1609 to persuade investors to support its enterprise in Virginia.

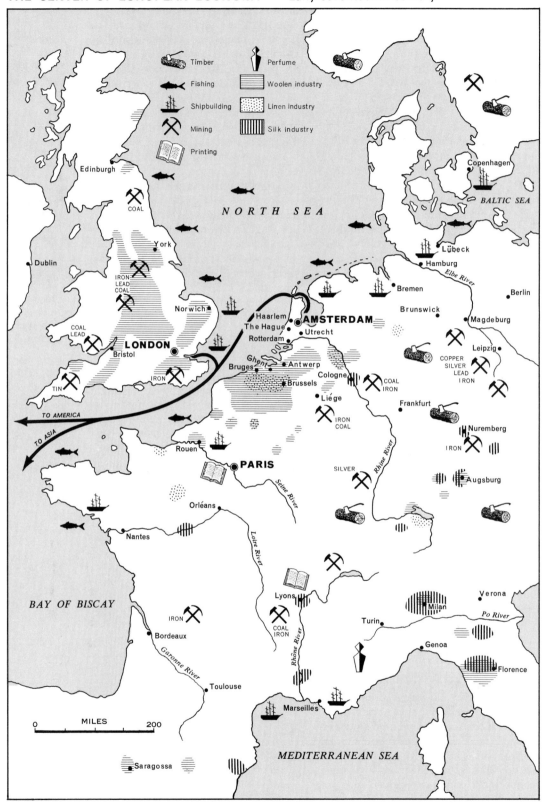

Timber

Fishing

Shipbuilding

Mining

Printing

Perfume

Woolen industry

Linen industry

Silk industry

Edinburgh

COAL

Dublin

York

NORTH SEA

Copenhagen

BALTIC SEA

Lübeck

Hamburg

Elbe River

Bremen

Berlin

Brunswick

Magdeburg

IRON
LEAD
COAL

Norwich

Haarlem

The Hague

AMSTERDAM

Utrecht

Rotterdam

Leipzig

COAL
LEAD

LONDON

Bristol

Ghent

Bruges

Antwerp

COPPER
SILVER
LEAD
IRON

Brussels

Cologne

COAL
IRON

Liège

Nuremberg

TIN

IRON

Liège

Frankfurt

IRON

TO AMERICA

IRON
COAL

Rhine River

IRON

Augsburg

TO ASIA

Rouen

PARIS

SILVER

Seine River

Orléans

Lyons

Verona

Nantes

BAY OF BISCAY

Loire River

Milan

Po River

Turin

COAL
IRON

Genoa

IRON

Bordeaux

Rhône River

Florence

Garonne River

Toulouse

Marseilles

MILES

0   200

Saragossa

MEDITERRANEAN SEA

raise the capital needed for large-scale, overseas voyages. So merchants formed associations called "regulated companies." Governments gave such groups a monopoly on trade to a given area, but each member of the group, while he helped meet common expenses, traded on his own account. They were associations of men, not of capital. What was needed, however, was a type of association that would attract the investments of men who had neither the desire nor the ability to qualify as active traders in a regulated company. The answer was the joint stock company, an amazingly flexible institution that was to be the parent of many other economic and political institutions on both sides of the Atlantic.

The joint stock company began as an association of investors, not of traders. Individuals bought shares in a venture, such as a trading voyage, and shared in the profits in proportion to their investment. When the association continued beyond a single venture, it became a joint stock company. This device had two advantages: it enabled anyone from a modestly wealthy man to Queen Elizabeth to invest in a business enterprise like Drake's voyages, and it associated businessmen with courtiers and statesmen at a time when both business sense and influence at court were necessary to the success of commercial ventures. The joint stock idea originated in southern Europe, but it was first applied to large-scale overseas enterprise in England in the Russia Company of 1553. The English East India Company, the companies that founded Virginia and Massachusetts, and the Bank of England were all joint stock companies. As these examples show, the first joint stock companies were dependent on government support (usually in the form of a trade monopoly) and were not concerned with industry. The joint stock company rapidly became the dominant form of commercial organization; it developed more slowly in industrial production.

The cumulative effect of these changes was to make the king, not the town, the chief regulator of economic activity. The unit of economic activity in the Middle Ages, apart from agriculture, had been the town or the city-state. As stronger monarchs appeared at the end of the Middle Ages, urban economy was steadily absorbed into the national economy throughout much of Europe, except in Italy and Germany. The monarch stepped into the shoes of medieval town officials and regulated trade and production much as municipal governments had done, but on a larger scale.

Mercantilism

The original aim of economic regulation was to advance the common good, not to increase the wealth of individuals. But a king's definition of the common good was the strength and security of his realm, not a general rise in consumption or standards of living. During the seventeenth century monarchs began to believe that their goals could be attained by following the economic doctrine called mercantilism. This doctrine, as applied in the seventeenth century, assumed that there is only a certain stock of wealth in

An Englishman on the Importance of Trade

ca. 1630

Although a kingdom may be enriched by gifts received, or by purchase taken from some other nations, yet these are things uncertain and of small consideration when they happen. The ordinary means therefore to encrease our wealth and treasure is by foreign trade, wherein we must ever observe this rule; to sell more to strangers yearly than we consume of theirs in value. For suppose that when this kingdom is plentifully served with the cloth, lead, tin, iron, fish and other native commodities, we do yearly export the overplus to foreign countries to the value of twenty-two hundred thousand pounds; by which means we are enabled beyond the seas to buy and bring in foreign wares for our use and consumptions, to the value of twenty hundred thousand pounds; by this order duly kept in our trading, we may rest assured that the kingdom shall be enriched yearly two hundred thousand pounds, which must be brought to us in so much treasure; because that part of our stock which is not returned to us in wares must necesarily be brought home in treasure. . . .

Behold then the true form and worth of foreign trade, which is, the great revenue of the king, the honour of the kingdom, the noble profession of the merchant, the school of our arts, the supply of our wants, the employment of our poor, the improvements of our lands, the nursery of our mariners, the walls of the kingdoms, the means of our treasure, the sinews of our wars, the terror of our enemies.

From Thomas Mun, *England's Treasure by Foreign Trade* (New York: Oxford University Press, 1933), p. 5.

the world at any given time, and if one country gains wealth another loses it. (This is a fairly typical assumption in a period of depression; it had already emerged in the fourteenth century and is not unknown today.) To prevent loss, home industries and shipping should be encouraged and colonies founded to provide raw materials that would otherwise have to be bought from foreigners. By regulating trade in these ways a country's stock of precious metals might be increased and surely would not decrease. This was not an unreasonable precaution in an age when credit devices were in their infancy and when, in case of war, a country had to have a reserve of gold and silver to pay its suppliers and soldiers.

The obvious way to build such a reserve—short of discovering new mines or capturing a Spanish plate fleet—was for a nation to export more than it imported. Foreign buyers would have to settle their balances in precious metals. At the very least there should be a balance of trade, so that more money would not leave the country than stayed in it. And so mercantilism called for tariffs to discourage imports and various benefits to encourage export industries. But it was thought that some exports, such as gold and silver, scarce raw materials, and skilled workmen, would weaken a state and should therefore be forbidden. Logically, mercantilist theory called for the abolition of all internal tariffs and all internal barriers to trade in order to build up the home market, though it was impossible to accomplish this except in England. At the core of mercantilism was the conviction that trade is the most important of all economic activities, that the regulation of trade is the government's most important economic concern, and that regulation should result in self-sufficiency and readiness for war.

As we shall see (p. 440), when new colonial policies were developed during the seventeenth century, mercantilists favored tropical colonies that enhanced the strength of the mother country by furnishing products such as sugar and tea and by buying home manufactures. They had no use for colonies that raised crops or produced manufactured goods that competed with the home country's products, nor for colonies that traded directly with other nations. The integration of colonies into the home economy was a cardinal mercantilist principle.

Mercantilism has necessarily been made to seem more clear-cut and consistent than it actually was in practice. It differed from one country to another, in response to the interests of the ruling group. In France the system was often called *Étatisme*, or state-ism. The hand of the government was very heavy in France: government intervention in commercial enterprise was direct and positive; regulation was intense; and relatively little initiative was left to individual enterprise. In England mercantilism also meant regulation of the economy in the government's interest. But even before the Revolution of 1688, and especially afterward, the English government was more responsive to the pressures of businessmen than was the French. It is often very difficult to tell whether English economic policy represented the interest of the state as a whole or the interests of individual entrepreneurs. In the United Provinces, where the federal government was in effect a government of businessmen, the interest of the state and the interests of the business community practically coincided. Dutch mercantilism was not so much the regulation of trade by the state as it was the control of economic policy by organized business. In the rest of Europe, however—in Spain, Portugal, Austria, Prussia, and Sweden—mercantilism represented primarily the interest of the monarchy and so followed the French model more than the Dutch.

Financial Problems

The rise in prices that had marked the sixteenth century slowed down in the seventeenth, and may even have been reversed for a while. It has been estimated that while prices more than quadrupled between 1500 and 1600, they rose no more than 20 percent during the next hundred years, and most of that gain came during the first two or the last two decades of the century. The problems of inflation had been hard enough to handle. With prices rising faster than government income, bankruptcy was always just around the corner. In Spain, with its heavy military commitments, the government had had to repudiate its debts at frequent intervals (see p. 404). But the problems of deflation were even more serious. Taxes brought in less, while government expenditures (mostly for wars) continued to increase. The optimism that comes with inflation, at least to the classes able to profit from it, decreased. The classes that had profited from the inflation of the sixteenth century—merchants, bankers, men who invested in land (like the English gentry)—found the financial atmosphere of the seventeenth century rather chilling. This is one reason why taxation seemed so oppressive after 1600.

Spain never managed to solve its problems and continued to hang on the edge of bankruptcy until late in the century. France did better, partly because its taxes fell most heavily on the peasants, and agricultural prices remained at a higher level than prices of other commodities, thus giving the peasants enough of a surplus to pay for the extravagances of the court and the waste of war. But the French taxation system was antiquated, and trouble was simply postponed to the eighteenth century. In England the Stuarts were never able to build a sound system of government finance because they lost the confidence of Parliament, which controlled the major part of the royal revenue. But after 1688 a government that had gained the confidence of Parliament as well as the business community was able to construct an exceptionally strong system of public finance that included parliamentary taxation, a national bank, and a permanent public debt. In large measure this system was modeled on Dutch governmental finance, the most successful of the age. Since the rulers of the United Provinces were representatives of the business community, they had little difficulty, at least for a century, in raising the money and credit they needed for their overseas empire building and their wars. In an age dominated by trade, a state that had a flourishing commerce and could command the confidence of its merchants could weather any financial storm. A state that had little commerce, or in which commerce was growing slowly while merchants were discouraged, was likely to find itself in financial difficulties.

EUROPEAN COLONIES IN THE SEVENTEENTH CENTURY

European expansion overseas was checked briefly in the seventeenth century, and picked up again only after some fundamental changes were made in patterns of colonial settlement. The earliest and easiest type of colony to establish was a fortified trading post, to which the natives brought readily salable commodities, such as gold, spices, and slaves. This was the Portuguese pattern, and, as the Dutch gradually ousted the Portuguese from the East Indies, it was the pattern that the Dutch tried to follow. But even the Dutch eventually found that they had to go inland and take over responsibility for governing large numbers of people in order to maintain the flow of commodities, and no other colonizing power found it possible to avoid administrative responsibilities for more than a brief period. The Spaniards, for example, could not exploit the wealth of America without taking over the Aztec and the Inca Empires.

Moreover, it became harder and harder to get riches without effort. There was an apparently inexhaustible supply of slaves in Africa, which is why European colonies there could remain at the trading post level. But the market for spices was soon glutted, and, once the pillaging of the American Indians ended, gold and silver could be acquired only by laborious and expensive mining operations. A new type of colony was needed, a colony that produced goods desired by Europeans with its own labor. The first such colonies were the sugar islands of the Caribbean; later came the tobacco, tea, and coffee colonies.

The East

At first the Dutch, the English, and the French tried to cut in on the Portu-

Miniature by an Indian artist of a foreigner, possibly a merchant of the East India Company (*ca.* 1600).

guese trade in India, Ceylon, and the East Indies. The English East India Company was founded in 1600, the Dutch in 1602, the French in 1664. The Dutch discouraged English trade with the Spice Islands—they killed ten English merchants in 1623—so the English withdrew to India. There they set up "factories," or trading posts, on the Portuguese model. Until the breakup of the Mughal Empire in central India early in the eighteenth century, it was never possible for Europeans to penetrate very far into the subcontinent of India. Their footholds on the coast depended entirely on sea power for support; and as Portuguese sea power declined in the seventeenth century and as the Dutch busied themselves farther east, the English were able to establish themselves at Bombay, Madras, and Calcutta. Meanwhile, the French at Pondicherry had become their most important potential rivals. The stage was set for a struggle in the next century between the British and the French East India companies over India's commerce and riches.

The Caribbean

In the Caribbean the Dutch, the English, and the French were all searching for footholds around the periphery of the Spanish settlements. After an unsuccessful attempt to take Brazil from the Portuguese, the Dutch seized Curaçao as a base from which to raid Spanish commerce. The English settled Barbados in 1624 and acquired Jamaica in 1655. Meanwhile, the French settled Guadaloupe and Martinique. These acquisitions were made just as the new colonial model—the colony as a producer of tropical goods—became popular. All the West Indian islands rapidly became rich sugar-producing areas, thanks to slave labor. So the English and the French, who came to the Caribbean to trade and buccaneer in the Dutch manner, stayed on to become plantation owners in the Spanish manner. The English and French sugar islands were the darlings of mercantilists at home. The planters cultivated a crop that could not be grown in Europe; they developed no industries to compete with home industries; and they were entirely dependent on their mother countries for shipping. Not surprisingly, the sugar islands were the center of attention among financiers and diplomats for over a century.

The chronic dearth of manufactured goods and slaves in the Spanish colonies meant that foreign smugglers who could slip by the Spanish navy were always welcome. As Portuguese control of the slaving stations on the western coast of Africa relaxed, the Dutch and English stepped in to supply the Spanish West Indies with the slaves needed on their sugar plantations. The brutality of this trade has become a byword, but it aroused no protest whatever in any European nation during the seventeenth and early eighteenth centuries.

North America

In North America a new wave of colonial expansion was beginning that was to have more far-reaching results than

The Javanese port of Batavia, from a Dutch engraving of 1682. Notice the Dutch architecture, entirely inappropriate for the climate.

West Indian sugar planting, though it was long overshadowed by the economic success of the tropical islands. There were many reasons why the Dutch, the English, and the French became interested in North America at the opening of the seventeenth century. For some time their sailors had been searching for a northwest passage to the Indies. Their ships were already engaged in cod fishing on the Newfoundland Banks. It was evident that North America could supply vast quantities of furs and timber. There might be precious metals, and it might turn out that sugar could be grown farther north than the Caribbean. Permanent settlements could support all these economic activities and at the same time help turn the flank of the Spanish in the New World.

Sir Walter Raleigh's unsuccessful attempt to found a colony in Virginia during the 1580s, however, had revealed some of the difficulties of settling the land the Spanish had left unoccupied. Colder climate, poorer soil, and hostile natives discouraged a plantation type of economy. To plant a permanent colony in North America a whole labor force would have to be transported and supported, perhaps for years, until the settlement became self-sufficient. This called for a large investment of capital and a large number of settlers. Furthermore, it called for strong belief and determination.

The Dutch, the French, and the English

It was the English and, to a lesser degree, the French, not the Dutch, whose determination proved strongest. The Dutch explored the Hudson in 1609 and settled New Amsterdam on Manhattan Island by 1624, but their colony of New Netherland never became more than a center for maritime trade and the export

The Indian village of Pomeiock in "Virginia" (actually North Carolina), watercolor by John White, an artist who took part in Raleigh's attempt to establish a colony at Roanoke in 1585. In his text White notes that mats and the bark of trees were used to cover the dwellings; the town was encompassed by poles instead of a wall.

of furs. Unsupported by the company that founded it, it fell to the English in 1664. The French were more successful. From Cartier, who discovered the St. Lawrence in 1535, to La Salle, who coursed the Mississippi in 1682, their explorers were more adventurous, their fur traders better able to adapt to the country, and their Jesuit missionaries more determined, than the representatives of any other European nation in the New World. In 1605 there were French settlers in Acadia, and in 1608 Champlain founded Quebec. By 1640 there were perhaps three thousand Frenchmen in Canada; by the end of the century about ten thousand.

The growth was slow for several reasons. The settlement of French Canada was marked by paternalism and relatively little individual initiative. Only when the French government actively encouraged Frenchmen to emigrate, as it did under Colbert in the 1660s and 1670s, did the colony grow appreciably. Since land was granted in large blocks, or *seigneuries*, to a few proprietors under semifeudal conditions, there was little inducement for peasants to emigrate. The government strictly prohibited the Huguenots, who wanted to emigrate, from going to Canada (they went to the English colonies instead). A fairly solid block of settlements grew up in the St. Lawrence Valley, but the slow-growing colony of *seigneurs* and *habitants* (as the peasants were called) was soon far outdistanced by the English settlements to the south.

The founding of the English colonies in North America was the result of a peculiarly favorable set of historical circumstances in the mother country. The idea that colonization meant wealth had been skillfully sold to ordinary Englishmen by enthusiasts and businessmen before Queen Elizabeth's death. London and Bristol merchants were ready for colonizing ventures and able to organize such ventures by means of joint stock companies. The constitutional and religious conflicts that troubled England through most of the seventeenth century provided many people with both material and idealistic motives for wishing to emigrate. Finally the English government,

whether it was that of the Stuarts or of their revolutionary opponents, encouraged but did not interfere with colonizing projects. In particular, it put no bar in the way of religious minorities that wished to emigrate.

The first successful colony, planted at Jamestown by the Virginia Company in 1607, had a difficult time until the settlers discovered that by concentrating on a single crop, tobacco, they could buy the goods they needed from England. The little band of religious dissenters who landed at Plymouth in 1620 lost half their number during the first winter and survived only by sheer heroism. But the Massachusetts Bay Company, which founded Boston, was able to profit by the Pilgrims' experience. In 1630 it transported nine hundred settlers across the ocean in a large and well-planned operation. Within ten years the population had increased to about fourteen thousand in Massachusetts and within twenty years there were about twenty thousand in New England as a whole. This population had developed a surplus of food for export, and had plenty of fur, fish, and timber to ship back to the mother country. By the end of the century more colonies had been established, either as offshoots of the original settlements or by royal grants to "proprietors," until there were twelve in all (the thirteenth was added in 1732). It has been estimated that by 1700 there were almost two hundred thousand English settlers in North America, as compared with about ten thousand French. It was already clear that most North Americans would someday speak English.

English and French Colonies

The English colonies were more divided and less well controlled by the home government than were the French. New France was under one central administration at Quebec, whereas the English colonies were under twelve separate governments. Each of the twelve eventually elected representative assemblies that controlled local legislation and taxation. The royal governors were not responsible to these assemblies, but, since they were generally dependent on the assemblies for their salaries, their power was effectively limited. In the 1660s Parliament did its best to impose strict mercantilist theories on the colonies—for example, by ruling that certain exports must be sent directly to England in English or colonial ships. These measures caused complaints, and after the Revolution of 1688 the English government gradually became less insistent on asserting its authority. The colonists accepted parliamentary regulation of their trade so long as the regulations were not too strictly enforced, but they became more and more accustomed to running their own affairs to suit themselves.

Without conscious design, the English in the seventeenth century fashioned a new kind of colonial empire in North America, quite different from either the Portuguese or the Spanish. The Portuguese Empire (and, to a large degree, the Dutch) was based on armed trade. The Spanish Empire was based on the efforts of a ruling class of soldiers, planters, and missionaries to convert the natives and exploit their labor. But the Protestant English (and Protestant Dutch) were never particularly interested in converting the natives. They never felt responsible for the Indians as the Spanish did, partly because there was no possibility of exploiting their labor. So they simply displaced the natives from the land on which they settled. The English transferred a whole European population to a new environment and permitted it to blend the traditional institutions it brought from home with the innovations and improvisations evoked by the new surroundings. Not surprisingly, these innovations tended toward economic, political, and religious freedom. The breeze was blowing in this direction in England, and it was blowing even more strongly in the colonies.

The Russians in Siberia

While the French and the British in North America were pushing westward from the Atlantic seaboard toward the

Codfishing in the waters off Newfoundland (ca. 1720).

A Cossack warrior.

Pacific, the Russians were pushing eastward from the Ural Mountains across Siberia toward the Pacific. The two movements were strikingly similar in many respects, but the Russians had no ocean to cross at the start and they reached the Pacific first. In 1581, groups of Cossacks—"pioneers," or "frontiersmen," who had earlier pushed back the Tartars and Turks and had settled in the lower valleys of the Dnieper, the Don, and the Volga—began to move eastward from the Urals under a leader, Ermak, who became famed in song and story. Like the French in Canada, the Cossacks were mainly in search of furs, particularly sable, and so they followed the dark pine forest, not the steppe to the south. The great rivers of Siberia—the Obi, the Yenisei, and the Lena—flow north into the Arctic Ocean, but in their upper reaches they branch out so that they almost touch one another. Thus the Cossacks could move easily across the continent by water. The movement was not planned or organized. The settlers simply flowed eastward through the sparsely settled wastes of Siberia in search of furs, occasionally stopping to form widely separated settlements, and reached the Pacific in the early 1640s, barely two generations after the movement began. The distance covered was greater than that across North America, but there were no wide mountain barriers until near the end and no serious resistance from natives until the Cossacks met the Chinese in the Amur Valley. There the Russians were checked by a superior, civilized state, and in 1689, by the first treaty concluded between Russia and China, the Russians withdrew from the Amur basin. They remained behind the Stanovoi Mountains for the next 170 years.

Like the English, the Cossacks were in search of freedom as well as furs, and their early communities in Siberia were often wild and lawless, like the later towns of the American "Wild West." But the tsar's government soon reached out across the vast distances to establish its administration and to tax the lucrative fur trade—more like the French than the English government in North America. By 1700 there were perhaps half again as many Russian settlers in Siberia as there were French and British in North America. By the end of the century, Russian traders were venturing across the Bering Strait into Alaska and down the North American coastline in search of seals. Thus long before the English colonists in America had reached the Pacific, the Russians, by a combination of individual daring and government backing, had staked out a claim to the northern half of Asia and had even reached out far enough to touch the shores of the Western Hemisphere.

Suggestions for Further Reading

Note: Asterisk denotes a book available in paperback edition.

General Works on the Seventeenth Century

There are several successful attempts at a synthetic treatment of the period. D. Ogg, *Europe in the Seventeenth Century,** 8th ed. (1960), is a sound and interesting narrative of the major developments on the Continent, arranged by country. G. N. Clark, *The Seventeenth Century** (1931), is a more analytical discussion of different aspects of the period: for instance, population, industries, military organization, political thought, science, religion. C. J. Friedrich's volume in the *Rise of Modern Europe* series, *The Age of the Baroque, 1610–1660** (1952), combines narrative and analysis and makes use of recent interpretations of baroque style. C. J. Friedrich and C. Blitzer, *The Age of Power** (1957), is a brief and thoughtful survey of the century, based on Friedrich's larger work. The essays in T. Aston, ed., *Crisis in Europe, 1560–1660** (1965), are uneven, but the best ones are very good. Geofrey Parker, *Europe in Crisis* (1979) is a new and excellent work on the period.

| **Mercantilism and Economic Growth** | L. B. Packard, *The Commercial Revolution, 1400–1700* (1927), is the briefest reliable treatment of mercantilism. J. W. Horrocks, *Short History of Mercantilism* (1925), and P. W. Buck, *The Politics of Mercantilism** (1964), are somewhat longer studies. The fullest and best treatment is E. F. Heckscher, *Mercantilism*, 2 vols. (1935). H. Sée, *Modern Capitalism* (trans. 1928), is the best extensive discussion of the subject. F. L. Nussbaum, *History of the Economic Institutions of Modern Europe* (1933), summarizes the work of the great German historian of capitalism, W. Sombart. D. Hannay, *The Great Chartered Companies* (1926), is a good introduction to its subject. J. U. Nef, *Wars and Human Progress* (1950), argues that war is a detriment, not a stimulant, to technological and economic progress, particularly in this period. Up-to-date surveys of economic topics are available in C. Cipolla, ed., *The Fontana Economic History of Europe,** Vol. II (1974) and in Cipolla's own book, *Before the Industrial Revolution* (1976). |

| **Expansion Overseas** | In addition to the works cited for Chapter 18 on geographical discovery, the following are useful on special topics: B. H. M. Vlekke, *The Story of the Dutch East Indies* (1945); C. R. Boxer, *The Dutch Seaborne Empire* (1965); C. Gibson, *Spain in America* (1966); and H. A. Wyndham, *The Atlantic and Slavery* (1935). On the rivalry of France and England in America, the many fascinating volumes of F. Parkman dating from the 1860s are still worth reading, especially the earlier ones. G. M. Wrong, *The Rise and Fall of New France*, 2 vols. (1928), is the standard modern account. The *Cambridge History of India*, 5 vols. (1922–37), is useful for reference. Vol. IV of the *Cambridge Economic History of Europe* (1967) emphasizes overseas expansion. |

| **France** | J. Boulenger, *The Seventeenth Century** (trans. 1920), is a standard one-volume account in English. G. Treasure, *Seventeenth Century France** (1966), is a recent survey. F. C. Palm, *The Establishment of French Absolutism, 1574–1610* (1928), and P. R. Doolin, *The Fronde* (1935), are good special studies. Of the many books on Richelieu, the most trustworthy short account is C. V. Wedgwood, *Richelieu and the French Monarchy** (1962). C. J. Burckhardt, *Richelieu: His Rise to Power** (1964), is a solid piece of work. The French social structure is described in P. Goubert, *The Ancien Régime: French Society, 1600–1750** (1973). |

| **England** | The classic one-volume account, Whiggish in sympathy and brilliantly written, is G. M. Trevelyan, *England Under the Stuarts* (1904, 1946). The standard modern account is G. Davies, *The Early Stuarts, 1603–1660,* 2nd ed. (1959), in the *Oxford History of England* series. The detailed narrative history of S. R. Gardiner, published in eighteen volumes (1863–1903) and covering the years 1603 to 1656, is a major achievement of English historical scholarship to which all later accounts are indebted. C. V. Wedgwood has published three volumes of a history of the Puritan rebellion: *The King's Peace* (1955), *The King's War* (1958), and *A Coffin for King Charles* (1964). D. L. Keir, *The Constitutional History of Modern Britain, 1485–1937,** 4th ed. (1950), and J. R. Tanner, *English Constitutional Conflicts of the Seventeenth Century** (1928), together constitute a good introduction to some of the more technical constitutional issues of the period. There are many biographies of Cromwell, but the best is still C. H. Firth, *Oliver Cromwell and the Rule of the Puritans in England* (1900, 1925). W. Notestein, *The English People on the Eve of Colonization, 1603–1630** (1954), is a good introduction to the social history of the period, and B. Willey, *The Seventeenth Century Background** (1934), a good introduction to its intellectual history. A. S. P. Woodhouse, ed., *Puritanism and Liberty* (1951), is a selection of sources illustrating the ferment of democratic ideas during the rebellion. See also W. Haller, *The Rise of Puritanism** (1938); M. Walzer, *The Revolution of the Saints** (1965); and L. Stone, *The Crisis of the Aristocracy, 1558–1642** (1967). For a vivid introduction to the social history of seventeenth-century England, see P. Laslett, *The World We Have Lost,** 2nd ed. (1971). |

| **Germany** | There are good chapters on the Thirty Years' War in Ogg and Friedrich (first section, above), and in H. J. Grimm, *The Reformation Era* (1973), and H. Holborn, *A History of Modern Germany: The Reformation* (1959). Far and away the best general account in English is C. V. Wedgwood, *The Thirty Years War** (1938). The scholars' argument over how destructive the war was may be followed in S. H. Steinberg's criticism of Wedgwood in *History*, Vol. XXXII (1947), pp. 89–102. T. K. Rabb, ed., *The Thirty Years' War** (1964), gives readings on the causes and effects of the war. The Swedish phase of the war is well described by M. Roberts, *Gustavus Adolphus* (1953–58). J. Polišenský, *The Thirty Years War* (1971), examines the social effects of the war, especially in Bohemia. For a wider treatment of the period see Robert W. J. Evans, *The Making of the Hapsburg Monarchy* (1979). |

20 Absolutism and Constitutionalism 1660–1715

During the latter half of the seventeenth century France was the leading nation in Europe. Its population was twice that of Spain and over four times that of England. Its land was fertile and its commerce and industry were growing.

FRANCE UNDER LOUIS XIV

There were no disturbing arguments over forms of government; absolute monarchy was accepted by almost all Frenchmen as necessary, reasonable, and right. By the Peace of the Pyrenees (1659) the French army had displaced the Spanish as the strongest military machine on the Continent. As time went on, it seemed as if not only French generals, French military engineers, and French diplomatists but also French architects, painters, dramatists, and philosophers were the best in Europe. French fashions in dress dominated the Continent; the French language became the leading language of diplomacy and polite conversation, and the French court with its elaborate etiquette and ceremonial became the model for countless smaller courts throughout Europe.

As Florence had been the nerve center of the Italian Renaissance and Spain of the Catholic Reformation, so France was the nerve center of late–seventeenth-century politics, diplomacy, and culture.

How much of this predominance is to be attributed to the long reign of Louis XIV is one of those questions that historians can speculate about but never answer. No one doubts that French (and European) history would have run in different channels had Louis never lived—or had he not lived so long. He was born in 1638, became king in 1643, took the reins of power into his own hands in 1661 at twenty-three, and died in 1715 at the age of seventy-seven, leaving the throne to his great-grandson. By temperament and training Louis was the very incarnation of divine-right monarchy—the idea that hereditary monarchy is the only divinely approved form of government, that kings are responsible to God alone for their conduct, and that subjects should obey their kings as the direct representatives of God on earth. In an age that put its trust in absolute rulers, the achievements of the French people at the peak of their greatness cannot be separated from the personality of their ruler, even if it can be proved that many

Opposite: Louis XIV, by Hyacinthe Rigaud (1701).

The emblem of the Sun King.

of those achievements were unrelated to, or even accomplished in spite of, the ruler.

Louis is said to have remarked, "I am the state." Even if the remark is apocryphal, the words reveal more of the true importance of his reign than anything else he said or wrote. Louis XIV set out early in his reign to personify the concept of sovereignty. He dramatized this aim immediately after Mazarin's death by ordering his ministers thereafter to report to him in person, not to a "first minister."

To be the real head of a large and complicated government required long, hard work, and Louis paid the price. His education was poor, and he had little imagination, no sense of humor, and only a mediocre intelligence. But he had common sense, a knack of picking up information from others, and a willingness to work steadily at the business of governing. "If you let yourself be carried away by your passions," he once said, "don't do it in business hours." Painstakingly he caught up all the threads of power in his own hands. All major decisions were made in four great councils, which he attended regularly. These decisions were then carried out by professional "secretaries" at the head of organized bureaucracies. In the provinces, the *intendants* more and more represented the direct authority of the central government in justice, finance, and general administration. The old French monarchy imposed its authority through judicial decisions and had frequently consulted local and central assemblies. The new monarchy, begun by Richelieu and perfected by Louis XIV, imposed its authority through executive decisions. Louis reduced the importance of the *parlements*, never summoned the Estates General, and, so far as such a thing was humanly possible in his century, built a government that was himself.

Colbert and the Economy

Colbert, Louis XIV's Controller General of Finance, systematically ordered the economic life of the country under royal direction. He was an extreme mercantilist; everything he did was consciously or unconsciously meant to strengthen the country for war. He set up high protective tariffs to help home industry, fostered new export industries, encouraged the French colonies in Canada and the West Indies, and did everything he could to develop a powerful navy and a strong merchant marine. Some historians suspect that his minute regulation of industry and commerce did more to hinder than to help the French economy. But until the burden of foreign wars became heavy in the 1680s, national production and wealth were increasing. Colbert also cut down waste and corruption in the collection of taxes, as Sully had once done, but he was unable to make the burden of taxation much more equitable because of the exemptions held or purchased by members of the nobility and the bourgeoisie, the classes best able

Louis XIV on the Duties of a King   1661

During the early period of his direct rule, Louis XIV prepared notes for the instruction of his son in the art of ruling. He had assistance in this task, and the texts do not necessarily give his exact words. They do express his ideas.

I have often wondered how it could be that love for work being a quality so necessary to sovereigns should yet be one that is so rarely found in them. Most princes, because they have a great many servants and subjects, do not feel obliged to go to any trouble and do not consider that if they have an infinite number of people working under their orders, there are infinitely more who rely on their conduct and that it takes a great deal of watching and a great deal of work merely to insure that those who act do only what they should and that those who rely tolerate only what they must. The deference and the respect that we receive from our subjects are not a free gift from them but payment for the justice and the protection that they expect to receive from us. Just as they must honor us, we must protect and defend them, and our debts toward them are even more binding than theirs to us, for indeed, if one of them lacks the skill or the willingness to execute our orders, a thousand others come in a crowd to fill his post, whereas the position of a sovereign can be properly filled only by the sovereign himself.

. . . of all the functions of sovereignty, the one that a prince must guard most jealously is the handling of the finances. It is the most delicate of all because it is the one that is most capable of seducing the one who performs it, and which makes it easiest for him to spread corruption. The prince alone should have sovereign direction over it because he alone has no fortune to establish but that of the state.

From Louis XIV, *Memoires for the Instruction of the Dauphin*, ed. by Paul Sonnino (New York: Free Press, 1970), pp. 63–64.

1589		1610	1616		1643		1715			1774	1793

Henry IV		Louis XIII				Louis XIV			Louis XV		Louis XVI
	Regency		Richelieu	Mazarin			Regency				

	1624	1642	1661		1723	

to pay. During the crisis of Louis' last war an attempt was made to tax these upper classes in order to stave off bankruptcy, but the attempt set no precedent.

The Nobility

The most dangerous potential opponents of royal absolutism, as Louis XIV knew from his own experience during the Fronde, were the members of the nobility. Louis completed Richelieu's work of destroying the political power of the French nobility. He excluded the nobles completely from all responsible positions in government and cheapened their status by increasing their numbers. An army commission came to be almost the only major outlet for a noble's ambition, which meant that the nobles as a class generally constituted a war party at court. All important positions in Louis XIV's government, such as the secretaryships and intendancies, were filled by men of bourgeois or recently ennobled families. At the same time, he followed earlier precedents in enhancing the splendor of his court and the participation of the nobility in his splendor.

Louis did not attack the social privileges of the nobility; he used them to make the nobles utterly dependent on him. In 1683 he moved the court and government from the Louvre in Paris to Versailles, fifteen miles away. He had hated Paris since the riots of the Fronde, and now in the formal gardens and ornate chateaux of Versailles, which he had built on waste marsh at considerable cost of human lives and treasure, he felt at home. He also felt safe; Versailles was the first royal residence that was completely unfortified. At Versailles, the king lived in an utterly artificial atmosphere, as far removed from reality as Versailles was physically removed from the bustle of Paris. Here the great nobles were compelled to live. Here a ball seemed as important as a battle, and holding the

basin for the king's morning ablutions was a job as much to be coveted as commanding the king's armies. Instead of competing for political power, nobles squandered their fortunes and exhausted their energies in jockeying for social prestige.

The regular rectangular shapes of the gardens, the balanced classical lines of the baroque architecture, the bright glint of mirrors and chandeliers, all these seemed to symbolize and emphasize the isolation of Versailles from nature, from the French nation, from the real world. Through all this Louis moved with impassive dignity. Years of self-conscious practice in kingship had given him a kind of public personality—cool, courteous, impersonal, imperturbable—which carried out perfectly the artificiality of the little world at Versailles. At his death he left to his successors a privileged nobility shorn of all political power and responsibility, demoralized by the empty pleasures and petty intrigues of court life and uneasily aware of its uselessness. It was a dangerous legacy.

Religious Policy

The only other potential opponents of Louis' absolutism were religious groups. The king had his differences with several popes who disliked his Gallican principles, which stressed royal control over the Church in France. These quarrels, however, never led to a real breach. Louis was always a good Catholic in a formal sense. He disliked and persecuted the Jansenists, an austere group of Catholic "puritans" who emphasized the teachings of St. Augustine on original sin, the depravity of man, and the need for divine grace. They felt that the Jesuits were far too optimistic about man's ability to work out his own salvation, and far too ready to compromise with the world. Louis, whose confessors were Jesuits, thought the Jansenists subversive (they

The medal above, issued in 1661, celebrates Louis' accessibility to his subjects. The medal below was struck in 1685 to commemorate the restoration of military discipline in Louis' reign.

Cartoon of 1686 showing a "missionary" of the king (an armed dragoon) "converting" a Huguenot to Catholicism.

pious Catholic whose parents were Huguenots. In 1685 he shocked Protestant Europe by revoking the Edict of Nantes, by which Henry IV had granted religious toleration to the Huguenots.

There were about a million Huguenots out of a total population of perhaps 18 million in France at the opening of Louis XIV's reign. After Richelieu deprived them of their military and political privileges, they had become good citizens and had remained loyal to the crown during the Fronde. Many were successful in industry and the professions, though few had attained the civil and military positions that were theoretically open to them. The French Catholic clergy had long tried to persuade Louis XIV that the continued exercise of the Protestant religion in France was an insult to his dignity and authority, and as the king became more concerned about his salvation the idea of atoning for his sins of the flesh by crushing heresy became more attractive to him. The Edict was "interpreted" more and more strictly. Protestant children were declared of age at seven and converted to Catholicism, and any attempt by their parents to win them back was punished by imprisonment. Money was offered to converts, Protestant chapels were destroyed, and troops were quartered on prominent Huguenots to make life miserable for them. Finally Louis, aided and abetted by his Jesuit advisers, announced that since all the heretics had finally been reconverted to Catholicism there was no further need for the Edict of Nantes, and it was therefore revoked. Protestant churches and schools were closed, and all Protestant children were baptized as Catholics. The Revocation was enforced by imprisonment, torture, and condemnation to the galleys, but many Huguenots continued to practice their faith in secret. Others fled to England, the Dutch Netherlands, Brandenburg, and the New World. The industry and skill of the 200,000 or so Huguenots who escaped contributed appreciably to the economic life of their new homes. To France the Revocation brought both economic and moral loss.

There were only two other examples of such brutal treatment of religious minorities in the seventeenth century: the

had been condemned by the pope) and impertinent (they disapproved of his numerous mistresses). After 1680, though never a particularly religious man, he seems to have become increasingly concerned about the fate of his own soul. When his queen, Maria Theresa, died in 1683, he gave up his mistresses and secretly married Madame de Maintenon, a

Bishop Bossuet on Absolutism

Jacques Bénigne Bossuet was tutor to Louis XIV's son in the 1670s.

The royal power is absolute. With the aim of making this truth hateful and insufferable, many writers have tried to confound absolute government with arbitrary government. But no two things could be more unlike. . . . The prince need render an account of his acts to no one. . . . Without this absolute authority the king could neither do good nor repress evil. . . . God is infinite, God is all. The prince, as prince, is not regarded as a private person: he is a public personage, all the state is in him; the will of all the people is included in his. As all perfection and all strength are united in God, so all the power of individuals is united in the person of the prince. What grandeur that a single man should embody so much! . . . Behold this holy power, paternal and absolute; behold the secret cause which governs the whole body of the state, contained in a single head: you see the image of God in the king, and you have the idea of royal majesty. God is holiness itself, goodness itself, and power itself. In these things lies the majesty of God. In the image of these things lies the majesty of the prince.

From Jacques Bénigne Bossuet, "Politics Drawn from the Very Words of Scripture," in *Readings in European History*, ed. by James Harvey Robinson (Boston: Ginn, 1906), Vol. II, pp. 275–76.

systematic impoverishment and degradation of the Irish Catholics by their English conquerors, and the ruthless suppression of Bohemian Protestantism by the Habsburgs. But in both these cases, unlike that of France, national hatred complicated religious differences. The Revocation of the Edict of Nantes was an anachronistic act of religious intolerance that gained Louis XIV little and lost him much.

Arts and Literature

To dramatize his conception of kingship and to underscore the dependence on the monarch of all other persons and institutions in the state, Louis chose as his emblem Apollo, the sun god. The symbol of the sun, on whose rays all earthly life is dependent, was worked into the architecture and sculpture of the palace of Versailles. The Sun King patronized the arts and gave historians some reason to call his reign the "Augustan Age" of French culture. As befitted such a patron, the prevailing taste was classical, insisting on form, order, balance, and proportion. The ideals of literature and art were "order, neatness, precision, exactitude"—and these were presumed to be the ideals of all reasonable men of all ages.

Pierre Corneille (1606–84) was the father of French classical tragedy. In 1636 he had written *Le Cid*, the first of his powerful dramas that glorified will power

and the striving for perfection. Corneille was still writing when Louis XIV began his personal reign, but he was soon eclipsed by his brilliant younger contemporary, Jean Racine (1639–99). Racine wrote more realistically about human beings in the grip of violent and sometimes coarse passions, bringing French tragedy to its highest point of perfection in the years between 1667 and 1677. Then he underwent a religious conversion and renounced playwrighting as an immoral occupation. Some who thrilled to his and Corneille's tragedies had little respect for the comedian Molière (1622–73), but Molière's wit and satire became the unsurpassable model for future French dramatists. From 1659 to his death in 1673 he was the idol of audiences at Versailles. All three playwrights concentrated on portraying types, not individuals—the hero, the man of honor violently in love, the miser, the hypocrite—embodiments of human passions and foibles who belonged to no particular time or place. As a result, French classical drama of the age of Louis XIV could be understood and appreciated by people everywhere, and French taste in writing came to be the dominant taste of other countries as well. So it was with architecture and the other arts. The baroque style, which ruled the design and decoration of the palace of Versailles, was intelligible and exportable. French artistic and literary standards became the standards of cultivated Europeans everywhere.

Caricature of Molière as an actor.

Engraving of a performance of *Le Malade imaginaire*, Molière's last play (1673). Molière died on stage on the fourth night of the performance.

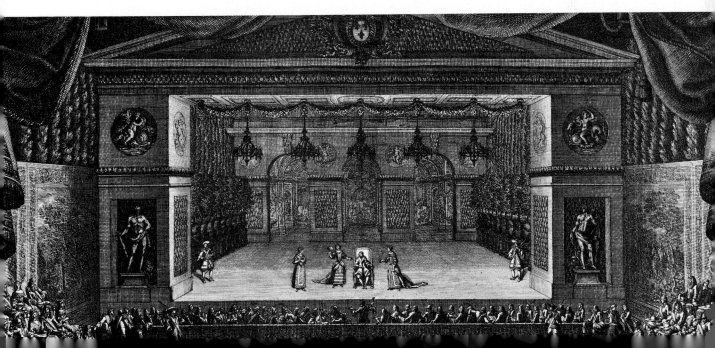

The Wars of Louis XIV

Richelieu and Mazarin had begun the process of strengthening the French army, but French military power reached its peak under Louis XIV. Le Tellier and his son Louvois were the ministers of war for almost fifty years. They subordinated the aristocratic officer class to the royal authority, developed a supply system, coordinated infantry and artillery, and, like Gustavus Adolphus, supplied the soldiers with uniforms. Vauban, one of the great military engineers of history, invented the fixed bayonet and perfected the art of building—and of destroying—fortifications. All in all, Louvois provided his master with the largest and best-equipped army in Europe: one hundred thousand men in peace and up to four hundred thousand in war.

Strengthening the army provided the king with great temptations to use his power in foreign wars. War would please the nobles, who profited by it and who had little outlet for their ambitions at home. War would exercise and justify the enormous standing army. Above all, successful war would enhance the glory of the monarch, raise him still further above his subjects, and perhaps make him the arbiter not only of France but of Europe as well. No one better than Louis XIV exemplified a nineteenth-century historian's dictum, "All power tends to corrupt, and absolute power corrupts absolutely." For half a century Europe was ravaged by wars that were caused by Louis' desire to maintain French prestige and increase French territory. As Louis' thirst for power grew, so did his enemies' fear of him.

The aims of Louis' earlier wars were relatively limited and understandable. With Spain's power broken and the Empire in a state of collapse, he wanted to annex the Spanish Netherlands (later Belgium), Franche-Comté, and bits of western German territories. He fought two wars for these objectives, but each time, after early victories, he found himself thwarted by an alliance of other powers. By 1678 he had gained only Franche-Comté and a few border towns in Flanders.

For a time Louis tried legal chicanery in place of bullets to gain more territory. French courts called Chambers of Reunion were set up to "reunite" to France any land that at any time had been a dependency of a French territory. This process gave Louis control of the independent Protestant republic of Strasbourg in 1681, and it was long before European indignation subsided or Strasbourg became a contented part of France. The Revocation of the Edict of Nantes in 1685 was further evidence to European

The palace at Versailles (1668). Louis XIV is shown arriving in a carriage.

statesmen of Louis' intemperance, and in 1686 the defensive League of Augsburg was formed by the emperor, Spain, Sweden, and several German states. Europe was already at war when William of Orange, ruler of the Dutch Netherlands and Louis' most implacable enemy, became King William III of England in 1689. The circle was closed around France when the English and the Dutch joined the League.

This time France was on the defensive. At the very outset, in 1688, the French united their enemies by perpetrating one of the most senseless atrocities of the century, the systematic devastation of the Palatinate for no good political or military reason just before the occupying French troops withdrew. The War of the League of Augsburg was waged in India and America as well as in Europe, so it may be called the first of the modern world wars. After ten years of fighting, France agreed to the Peace of Ryswick (1697), by which France managed to retain its gains up to 1678 but was forced to renounce nearly all accessions after that date except Strasbourg. England came out of the war considerably stronger as a naval and military power; France came out of it a weaker power than it had been a decade earlier.

The War of the Spanish Succession, 1701–14

At the turn of the century all the fears and hatreds that had been built up during a generation of fighting were concentrated in a fourth struggle, the War of the Spanish Succession (1701–14). This war, like that of 1688 to 1697, was fought in America and India as well as in Europe. In its origins and its course, the older motives of dynastic ambition and preservation of the balance of power were mixed with the newer motives of commercial advantage and national sentiment. Religion now played no important part whatever.

In 1698 Charles II of Spain, who had for thirty years been a kind of walking medical exhibit of half a dozen fatal diseases, was finally dying. He was the last of the Habsburgs who had ruled Spain since 1516, and he had no direct heirs. The question was whether the Spanish

Empire would fall to some member of the Austrian Habsburg family or to some member of the French Bourbon dynasty (both Louis XIV's mother and first wife had been Spanish Habsburg princesses) or would be partitioned or dismembered in some way. The English and the Dutch had obvious reasons for keeping France from gaining control of the Spanish colonial trade or of the Spanish Netherlands. Louis seemed willing to compromise and twice concluded secret treaties with the English and the Dutch to partition the Spanish dominions, but when news of the second treaty reached Madrid the dying king lost his temper. In order to preserve the Spanish Empire intact as a bulwark of Catholicism, he made a will leaving all his dominions to a grandson of Louis XIV. This grandson was proclaimed King Philip V of Spain shortly after the death of Charles II in November 1700.

Louis XIV soon decided to tear up the treaties by which he had accepted a more modest share of the Spanish Empire. He recognized the will of Charles II and sent French troops into the Spanish Nether-

Officer and musketeer of the French Guard (late seventeenth century).

lands. In 1701 William III of England concluded the Grand Alliance of the Hague by which the English, the Dutch, and the Austrian Habsburg emperor bound themselves to fight until they had ended the threat of Bourbon control of Spain and of the Spanish colonies. Louis XIV had made his last and most arrogant bid for the dominance of Europe, but this time he was forced to fight for France's life against enemies who proved as arrogant and unyielding as he. War was now a much more organized and professional use of force. Soldiers were rigidly disciplined, regimental offiers were experienced commanders and not heroic but untrained nobles, and coordination of infantry, cavalry, and artillery had greatly improved the allied forces. Under the brilliant command of Prince Eugene of Savoy and the English Duke of Marlborough, within a few years the allied armies had beaten the French in four bloody battles (Blenheim, 1704; Ramillies, 1706; Oudenarde, 1708; Malplaquet, 1709). The English navy had trounced the French at sea, and the English had seized Gibraltar. An allied army had even dethroned Philip V in Spain for a time.

Louis XIV, his country exhausted, sued for peace on almost any terms, only to be met by an allied demand that he contribute French troops to expel his own grandson from Madrid. This was too much for even a badly beaten monarch, and he refused, backed by a rising tide of national feeling in France. A similar national reaction in Spain in favor of their new Bourbon monarch, Philip V, resulted in the defeat of English and Austrian troops there. In 1710 a victory of the Tories over the Whigs, who had been the war party in England, brought in a government in London favorable to peace. And finally in 1712 the French won their only important victory of the war. In the end the allies paid the price for asking too much from Louis at the moment when he was almost helpless. The Peace of Utrecht (1713–14), which settled the war, was somewhat more favorable to France than it might have been if it had been signed four years earlier. Here at the very end of his career, the balance of power seemed to work in Louis XIV's favor by preventing the elimination of France from the ranks of the great powers.

The Peace of Utrecht, 1713–14

In theory, the Peace of Utrecht gave the French the prize that they had sought at the beginning of the war. Philip V remained on the throne of Spain, but only on condition that the crowns of Spain and France should never be worn by the same monarch. In every other aim, however, the French were thwarted. They gave up all conquests east of the Rhine, failed to win the Spanish Netherlands, and lost their bid for control of the Spanish colonial trade. England was the chief winner. England took Newfoundland, Acadia (modern New Brunswick and Nova Scotia), and Hudson's Bay Territory from France, and Gibraltar and Minorca from Spain. In addition, the English received the *Asiento*—the right to supply black slaves to the Spanish colonies, a privilege that proved very lucrative and provided an excuse for a large-scale smuggling trade with the Spanish Empire.

England came out of the war rich and powerful, in a position to dominate international commerce and with the strongest navy in Europe. France came out of it still a great nation, but with its people badly exhausted by high taxation and its government bankrupt and unpopular. The Austrian Habsburgs gained by being given the Spanish Netherlands (which now became the Austrian Netherlands), as well as Milan, Naples, and Sicily. Austria thus replaced Spain as the dominant power in Italy. Two new smaller powers, Brandenburg-Prussia and the Duchy of Savoy, came out of the war with increased territories and heightened prestige as a reward for having been on the winning side. A century and a half later Prussia was to unify Germany, and Savoy, as the Kingdom of Sardinia, was to take the lead in the unification of Italy. The Dutch kept the Scheldt River closed, thus blocking the trade of Antwerp, the chief port of the Austrian Netherlands. But they had suffered from the long strain of fighting against the French for half a century and were soon to disappear from the ranks of the great powers.

The Peace of Utrecht ended the first attempt by a European state to establish an overwhelming predominance of power since the days of Philip II of Spain. When Louis XIV died in 1715, rulers outside France breathed a sigh of relief; it was even said that the common people of his own land "openly returned thanks to God." His bid for European hegemony had been defeated by the workings of the balance-of-power principle, but the seeds of future war were unfortunately still deep in the European soil.

ENGLAND: THE EMERGENCE OF A PARLIAMENTARY MONARCHY

While Louis XIV was putting the finishing touches on the institution of absolute monarchy in France, the English, without any very clear idea of where they were headed, were completing the foundation of a constitutional monarchy controlled by Parliament.

The restoration of the king, Parliament, and the Anglican Church in 1660 had established a kind of equilibrium between the crown and Parliament, but it was soon evident that it was a very unstable balance. Who was really to control the government—the king or the wealthy landowners and merchants who dominated Parliament? What was the religious settlement to be, and who was to have the last word in making it? Who was to control foreign policy? These three main questions of the past two generations—the questions of politics, religion, and foreign policy—still awaited final answers. It took almost two more generations of domestic intrigue and foreign war for the answers to be found.

Charles II, 1660–85

Charles II was quite unlike his father—witty, worldly-wise, attractive, a man of easy morals and shrewd political sense. He had lived long in exile in France, and his cousin Louis XIV was his model. He would have liked to restore England to Catholicism and to set up an absolute monarchy on the French model, but he was too intelligent to ignore the difficulties in his way and too cautious to persist in the face of determined opposition. He was resolved not to risk exile or execution. He knew that if his goal was to be reached, it would be by intrigue, manipulation, and compromise, not by force or by open proclamation of his aims. The result was twenty-five years of infinitely complex party politics and secret diplomacy in which the issues were never very clear to the people or to the members of Parliament, or even to the king's ministers.

Cavalier Parliament, 1661–79

Parliament held a commanding position at the beginning of the reign. The "Cavalier Parliament," which met in 1661 and was not dissolved until 1679, was dominated by the landed nobility and gentry, who were now restored to their ancient influence in both local and national government. Both groups were strongly royalist for the moment, both determined to stamp out all remnants of religious and political radicalism. But at the same time they were not willing to see the crown recover any real financial independence of Parliament. In place of the old idea that "the king should live of his own," Parliament now granted Charles a regular income from customs and excise duties, but it was not enough. Charles found that he could not meet even the ordinary expenses of government, let alone the expenses of his extravagant mistresses, from his regular revenue. And there was certainly no money for foreign war unless Parliament approved the objectives. So for a time at least, Charles had to let Parliament have its way under the leadership of his father's adviser, Edward Hyde, Earl of Clarendon.

Parliament also had the last word in the religious settlement. The Cavalier Parliament was as strongly pro-Anglican as it was pro-royalist. In a series of statutes passed between 1661 and 1665 and known as the "Clarendon Code," Puritans who dissented from the established church were excluded from local government and Puritan ministers were rooted out of the Anglican clergy. Later legisla-

The House of Commons, on the Great Seal of England (1651).

tion made it illegal for a dissenter to sit in Parliament, to serve in the army or navy, or to attend the universities at Oxford or Cambridge. Behind this attempt to discourage dissent was the fear that Puritans were inevitably political radicals. But while the Clarendon Code lowered the social position and narrowed opportunities for dissenters, it did not greatly decrease their numbers. Presbyterians, Congregationalists, Baptists, and Quakers (also Methodists a century later) formed permanent but peaceful minority groups. The dissenters remained antagonistic to the ruling Anglican majority, but they were even more bitterly opposed to Catholicism.

Charles did not like the Clarendon Code. He would have preferred a policy that tolerated both Puritans and Catholics, but Parliament would not stand for this. In 1672 Charles issued a "Declaration of Indulgence," which suspended the operation of the laws against both groups. But the next year Parliament forced him to withdraw the declaration and accept a severe Test Act excluding all but Anglicans from civil and military office. To the Anglican gentry in Parliament, Puritans were still radicals and Catholics still traitors.

Foreign Policy

Two natural calamities, an outbreak of plague in 1665 and a fire that destroyed much of London in 1666, contributed to general unrest. Uneasiness increased as king and Parliament drifted apart over foreign policy. In 1665 Parliament forced Charles into a commercial war with the Dutch but did not give him enough money to win it. When victories failed to develop, Clarendon was unfairly held responsible and was exiled. After Louis XIV began his attacks on the Spanish Netherlands in 1667, the ordinary Englishman began to see the military power of Catholic France as more of a threat than the commercial rivalry of the Protestant Dutch. But to Charles II, Louis was still the ideal ally—powerful, wealthy, and an old personal friend.

In 1670 England once more allied itself with France against the Dutch, and Charles negotiated with Louis one of the most notorious deals in the history of English foreign policy, the secret Treaty of Dover. By this agreement Charles promised to declare himself a Catholic and to reconvert England to Catholicism in return for French money and, if necessary, French troops. Probably Charles himself was not sure how far he meant to go, but at the least he was ready to adopt a pro-French foreign policy. Between 1675 and 1681 four more secret agreements were concluded between Charles and Louis in which Charles promised he would thwart Parliament's anti-French moves in return for subsidies from France. The close understanding between Charles and Louis leaked out and gradually built up English fears of Catholicism and French dominance. The landed classes represented in Parliament were

---

Pepys's Account of the Great Fire of London
September 2-6, 1666

The fire started near the river, spread to warehouses full of combustible materials, and destroyed most of the old city of London, including St. Paul's Cathedral. This gave Christopher Wren the opportunity to build his famous churches. Samuel Pepys was an eyewitness to the fire and recorded its events in his diary.

[Pepys heard of the fire and took a boat down the Thames.] Everybody was endeavoring to remove their goods, and flinging them into the river or bringing them into lighters; poor people staying in their houses till the fire touched them, and then running into boats. And the poor pigeons, I perceived, were loth to leave their houses, but hovered about the windows and balconys till they burned their wings and fell down. Nobody, to my sight, endeavoring to quench it, but only to remove their goods and leave all to the fire—the wind mighty high and driving it into the city and everything, after so long a drought, proving combustible, even the very stones of the churches.

[That evening Pepys and his wife went out on the river.] We went as near the fire as we could for smoke and all over the Thames; with one's face in the wind, you were almost burned with a shower of fire-drops. This is very true; so that houses were burned by these drops and flakes of fire [even when] three or four—nay five or six—houses from another. When we could endure no more at the water, we went to a little ale-house on the Bankside and there saw the fire grow . . . as far as we could see up the hill of the city, in a most horrible malicious bloody flame, not like the fine flame of an ordinary fire. We stayed till we saw the fire as only an entire arch of fire from this to the other side of [London] bridge and in a bow up the hill for an arch of above a mile long. It made me weep to see it—the churches, houses and all on fire and flaming at once, and a horrid noise the flames made, and the cracking of houses at their ruin.

From *The Diary of Samuel Pepys* (many editions), entry for September 2, 1666.

suspicious of Charles, increasingly less royalist in sentiment than they had been in 1661, and ready to give way to panic if any incident should excite their fear of France and popery.

Whigs and Tories

In 1678 these accumulated fears were fanned into flame by a lurid incident known to history as the Popish Plot. A thoroughly disreputable character named Titus Oates concocted a story, accepted by almost the whole country, that there was a Jesuit plot afoot to murder the king and put his Catholic brother James, the Duke of York, on the throne with French help—"a damnable and hellish plot," Parliament called it, "for assassinating and murdering the king and rooting out and destroying the Protestant religion." Civil war seemed about to break out again.

A "Country Party" led by the Earl of Shaftesbury campaigned at the polls and supported a bill to exclude the Duke of York from the succession to the throne. An Anglican and royalist "Court Party" rallied to the support of Charles II and his brother, though at first without very much enthusiasm. Members of the first group were called Whigs (a name hitherto applied to fanatical Scottish Presbyterians); members of the second group were called Tories (a name for Catholic outlaws in Ireland). The Whigs controlled the three brief Parliaments that followed the dissolution of the Cavalier Parliament in 1679, and innocent men went to their deaths for complicity in the Popish Plot. But the Whig leaders soon overplayed their hand; public opinion swung back in favor of the king, and it was now the turn of innocent Whigs to suffer. By 1681 Shaftesbury had fled abroad, the inventors of the Popish Plot were disgraced or executed, and Charles was stronger than ever before. Until his death four years later he ruled without Parliament, thanks to Louis' subsidies, with his brother James by his side.

The origin of political parties in the modern sense—groups organized for the purpose of electioneering and controlling government through a representative assembly—lies in these chaotic years of English history. Instead of civil war, the eventual outcome was the "two-party system," which came to be characteristic of English and American politics. Whigs and Tories were the remote political heirs of the Parliamentarians and royalists of the 1640s. In turn they became the ancestors of the Liberals and Conservatives, the Democrats and Republicans, of two centuries later.

James II, 1685–88

The Duke of York, who succeeded Charles II as James II in 1685, was a very different sort of person from his brother—a bigoted convert to Catholicism without any of Charles's political shrewdness or tendency to compromise. Within three short years (1685–88) he managed to infuriate almost every group of any importance in English political and religious life, and in the end he provoked the revolution that Charles had succeeded in avoiding. Made overconfident by early successes, he introduced Catholics into the high command of both army and navy and camped a standing army a few miles from London. He surrounded himself with Catholic advisers and attacked Anglican control of the universities. He claimed the power to suspend or dispense with acts of Parliament. In a vain attempt to win the support of Puritans as well as Catholics, he issued a Declaration of Indulgence along the lines of his brother's. By revoking borough charters and browbeating sheriffs he tried to ensure the election of a Parliament favorable to his policies. Louis XIV's Revocation of the Edict of Nantes in 1685 had already terrified Protestants in England. They held back as long as James's immediate heir (his older daughter) was a Protestant, but their fears became unbearable when the hope of a Protestant succession was suddenly destroyed by the unexpected birth of a son to James's Catholic queen.

The "Glorious Revolution" of 1688

In spite of the intense political tension, civil war did not break out in 1688 as it had in 1642. Englishmen still remembered the horrors of civil war, and this time there was only one side. James had literally no support of any signifi-

Engraving of James II, after a painting by Kneller (1688).

Contemporary engraving showing the speaker of the House of Lords offering William and Mary the English crown.

cance, except for a handful of personal friends. He had alienated both Anglicans and nonconformists, Tories and Whigs, nobles and common people. The result, therefore, was a bloodless "revolution," a thoroughgoing political overturn that, as historians look back on it, answered all the main questions of the century in favor of a limited, or parliamentary, monarchy and established the constitutional pattern of English public life that has persisted to the present time.

James II had two daughters by his first wife (Clarendon's daughter), both of whom remained Protestants. The elder, Mary, was married in 1677 to the *stadtholder* of the Dutch Republic, William of Orange, who was Louis XIV's outstanding Protestant opponent on the Continent. In June 1688 a group of prominent and representative Englishmen, both Whigs and Tories, invited William to cross the Channel and save the Protestant cause in England. In the following November William landed on the southern coast of England with a Dutch army and marched slowly on London. There was almost no resistance. James II fled to France, and a Convention Parliament (an irregular assembly of men who had had parliamentary seats) declared that James had "abdicated" the throne by his flight. It then invited William and Mary to become joint sovereigns. A "Bill of Rights" was passed and the "Glorious Revolution" was accomplished.

Q14.

See next pg

Q14b.

The chief result of the Revolution was the establishment of parliamentary sovereignty over the crown. Parliament had made a king and could regulate the right of succession to the throne. Though William was a strong-willed man, especially in matters of foreign policy, he realized, though reluctantly, that Parliament had the final say. And though the supporters of James II and his son intrigued and even staged two abortive rebellions in the eighteenth century, there was no second Restoration. Parliament could criticize, influence, and eventually make the government's policy.

The Bill of Rights emphatically denied the king's right to suspend acts of Parliament or to interfere with the ordinary course of justice. It furnished a base for the steady expansion of civil liberties in the generation after 1688. Religious toleration and freedom from arbitrary arrest were established by law; censorship of the press was quietly dropped. The king had to summon Parliament every year because he could not pay or control his armed forces without parliamentary consent. These regular meetings strengthened the parties and made the king dependent on their support. In 1707 the monarch vetoed a parliamentary bill for the last time.

Struggles for control of policy were now no longer between king and Parliament, but between factions in Parliament. The Revolution did not establish

458

democracy, but it did establish control by the wealthy landed proprietors and merchants over both the central and local organs of English government. Generally speaking, the greater noble landowners, the bankers and the merchants, and most dissenters were Whigs, while the smaller gentry, the Anglican parish clergy, and some great lords were Tories. But parties were still loosely organized, and small factions with selfish interests often held the balance of power. England was governed by shifting alliances among leaders of the propertied classes.

The Cabinet System

It took over a century for parliamentary leaders to work out a smooth and efficient way to run the government. The ultimate answer was to be the "cabinet system"—that is, government by a committee of leaders of the majority party in Parliament, holding the chief executive offices in the government, acting under the leadership of a "prime minister," and acknowledging primary responsibility to Parliament rather than to the crown for their actions. During the reigns of William and Mary (1689-1702) and of Mary's sister, Queen Anne (1702-14), the first fumbling moves were made that led to such a system, though parliamentary leaders had as yet no sense of their goal, and monarchs still considered ministers to be responsible to them rather than to Parliament. The privy council had long been too large and unwieldy for effective action, so that a "cabinet council," or inner circle of important ministers, had developed under Charles II. The members of this "cabinet" slowly found that it was better to discuss major questions among themselves and to present a united front to the monarch on matters of policy. Sometimes a leading member of the "cabinet" was referred to as "prime minister." In order to gain Parliament's indispensable support in war or peace, both William and Anne occasionally found that it was better to choose their ministers not from both parties but from the majority party. By the time Queen Anne died in 1714 it had become evident that the real government of England was slowly falling into the hands of a cabinet of ministers who controlled a parliamentary majority, often by bribery, and felt themselves ultimately responsible to the political interests of this majority.

Religious Toleration

The Revolution also produced a certain measure of religious toleration. Broad-mindedness was becoming fashionable in educated circles, and both Anglicans and Puritans were now more afraid of Catholic France than they were of each other. Puritans had supported Anglicans against James II, and King William, who came from the most tolerant country in Europe, insisted on a religious truce. The result was the "Toleration Act" of 1689, which allowed dissenters to worship as they pleased and to educate their clergy and laity in schools of their own. Dissenters were still legally excluded from all civil and military offices, however, and there was no repeal of the long series of anti-Catholic statutes, although they were not enforced with any great rigor after 1689. Protestant fear that a Catholic might succeed to the throne was finally quieted by the Act of Settlement of 1701, which provided that the sovereign should always be an Anglican. The act also settled the succession, in case James II's two daughters should die without children, on the descendants of that daughter of James I who had married the ill-fated Elector of the Palatinate before the Thirty Years' War. In this way the elector of Hanover came to the throne in 1714, when Queen Anne died without issue, thus bringing the Stuart dynasty to a close.

Growth of English Power

A third result of the Revolution was to unite crown and Parliament on foreign policy as they had never been united under the first four Stuarts, and thus to turn the energies of a generation of Englishmen from domestic conflict to foreign war. Given English fear of Catholicism, King William had no difficulty bringing England into the Grand Alliance against Louis XIV, who was sheltering James II in exile. Parliamentary monarchy soon demonstrated that it was a more formi-

Medal of Queen Anne (1702–14), and her signature.

The *Irish Rebellion.*

One hundred drown'd in a River.

Boys forced to kill the Protestants.

Anti-Catholic woodcuts showing "horrors" of the rebellion by Irish Catholics (1689).

dable foe than the absolute monarchy of the Stuarts had been. The English government was able to raise money to fight its wars in a way that was barred to all other European governments except the Dutch. The founding of the Bank of England in 1694 was an important event in the history of English public finance. Within a few days of its founding, it had raised over a million pounds of investors' money that it promptly lent to the government at 8 percent interest. So long as the government continued to pay the interest, the bank made no demand for repayment of this loan. Thus the present permanent, or "funded," national debt began. The merchants and tradesmen, large and small, who invested their money in the bank obviously had confidence in the government, and their investment bound them still more firmly to support the revolutionary settlement.

Throughout the next century English wealth combined with English sea power was to give the island kingdom a striking power out of all proportion to its area and population. During the reigns of William and Mary and of Anne, trade, which was more and more the foundation of English wealth, increased considerably. The Peace of Utrecht (1713) gave English sea power, the guarantor of English trade, an almost unrivaled position. The solution in 1689 of the chief political

and religious differences between crown and Parliament touched off an almost explosive release of English energies that by 1763 had rocketed England to the hegemony of Europe.

Ireland and Scotland

The Revolution also did something to further the unification of the British Isles, though indirectly. England, Ireland, and Scotland all had the same king from 1603 on, but union went no further than the common crown. The two smaller kingdoms, especially Ireland, suffered greatly during the seventeenth century through involvement in England's religious and political divisions. The native Irish were Catholic to a man, and the Protestant English both despised them and feared them as potential allies of the Catholic Spanish and French. By settling Protestant colonists in Ulster, James I began the policy of creating a Protestant majority in the northeastern region of Ireland. But the Ulster Protestants were Presbyterians and soon became anti-Stuart, while the rest of the Irish were generally loyal to the Stuart dynasty, and for that reason suffered cruelly under Cromwell. After the Revolution, James II tried to fight his way back to his throne by way of Ireland. He was defeated at the Battle of the Boyne (1689), an event whose memory still stirs up bitter feelings between Catholics and Protestants in Ulster. James's defeat led to a savage and systematic persecution of the Catholic Irish by English (and Irish) Protestant landlords, comparable only to Louis XIV's brutal treatment of the Huguenots. The Irish were exploited and bled white economically, their priests were persecuted, and their Parliament was reserved for Protestants only.

The Scots had somewhat better fortune in the end, although they too suffered by being involved in England's troubles through the century. Scotland had gained little by giving a king to England in 1603. It remained a poor but proud neighbor of a larger kingdom, excluded from the benefits of English trade, jealously guarding its own law and its own Parliament, and firmly defending its Presbyterian Church against Anglican

460

attacks. Although it had been the Scots who touched off the revolution against Charles I, there was strong attachment to the native Stuart dynasty in Scotland, especially among Catholic clansmen of the Highlands. After 1649 and again after 1689 Scotland became a base for risings in support of the Stuarts. The Scots accepted the Revolution of 1688, but they did not accept the Act of Settlement of 1701. They threatened to choose a separate king of their own—possibly the exiled pretender James II—in case James's last daughter, Anne, died without issue. This frightened the English into serious negotiations. In 1707 an organic union between the two kingdoms was finally agreed on and was confirmed by an Act of Union. Scotland retained its own law and its established Presbyterian religion, but it surrendered its separate Parliament in return for representation in the English Parliament. Scottish nationalists were (and still are) angry over their loss of independence, but Scotland gained much in the next century by becoming an integral part of the Kingdom of Great Britain. Scottish merchants, administrators, and philosophers were to play a prominent part during the eighteenth century in building the British Empire and in furthering the Enlightenment.

John Locke

The Revolution of 1640 and the Glorious Revolution of 1688 together constituted the first of those revolutions in modern western states that ended absolute divine-right monarchy and eventually put the middle classes in control of government. English leaders did their best to insist to the outside world in 1688 and 1689 that they were doing nothing new or revolutionary at all, but they never succeeded in persuading foreigners that they were merely conservative supporters of ancient English liberties. Europe was more interested in the interpretation of the Revolution by John Locke (1632–1704), a friend of the Earl of Shaftesbury, the founder of the Whig Party. In *Of Civil Government: Two Treatises* (1690), Locke set down in plain, common-sense fashion the general principles underlying the long English strug-

gle for limited monarchy that culminated in the Revolution of 1688. Even if the logic was not always clear, the reasonableness of the discussion had great influence throughout the eighteenth century.

Locke directed his attack explicitly against the divine-right theory of monarchy, and implicitly against the more pragmatic absolute theory of Thomas Hobbes. He began with the rights to "life, liberty, and property," which he said all men possess naturally, and went on to insist that the sole reason for establishing any government is to preserve these rights. Legislative and executive powers are to be strictly separated; if the executive becomes tyrannical and invades the rights of individuals, the people must curb it through their representative assembly—or if all else fails, they may revolt and set up a new government. In other words, an ultimate right of revolution always resides in the people, and the dissolution of government does not necessarily mean the dissolution of society. Locke's book was probably written before 1688 as a sort of program for revolution, but it was not published until after the Revolution and so naturally became a kind of apology for what had been done. Inalienable rights, government by consent, separation of powers,

John Locke (1632–1704), champion of the "natural" rights of man.

the right of revolution—these were the ideas that Locke implied were at the heart of the Glorious Revolution. These were the ideas that seemed self-evident truths to Americans in 1776 and to Frenchmen in 1789 and that formed a link between the English, the American, and the French revolutions.

CENTRAL AND EASTERN EUROPE 1648–1721

The economy of early modern Europe was divided into two sharply defined halves by an imaginary line running north from the head of the Adriatic Sea, around the Bohemian mountains, and down the Elbe River to the North Sea. West of this line was an area that was increasingly affected by the growth of towns and trade. The majority of the population still lived on the land, but most peasants were free workers and many of them small landowners. Most serfs in the West had become agricultural laborers for pay, and most feudal nobles had become landlords who hired labor for wages (particularly in England) or simply lived on rents. Though still a minority, the bourgeoisie were increasingly influential in society and politics.

East of the line was a society still largely agrarian and feudal, an area of few large towns and an insignificant bourgeoisie. Here in Hungary, Bohemia, Poland, Prussia, and Russia, the landed estates were larger and the landed nobility more powerful politically than in the West. During the sixteenth and seventeenth centuries the nobles of eastern Europe managed to reduce the great majority of the peasants to a state of serfdom in which the peasant was bound to the land and forced to work from two to five days a week for his lord. One reason for this drive to enslave the peasant was that grain prices were rising in western markets, and eastern landlords had every inducement to increase the production of their estates. Another reason was that the governments of eastern Europe were either dominated by nobles, as in Hungary and Poland, or favorable to the growth of serfdom because it supported the nobles

The crown of the Holy Roman Empire of the German Nation, used from 961 to 1792.

who served the state, as in Prussia and Russia. In western Europe, command of money was increasingly the key to power and influence; in the East, ownership of land and command of compulsory services were still the secrets of power.

Warfare was as common as in the West, and much more dangerous. States with no natural frontiers on the flat plains of central and eastern Europe could easily be wiped out. Modernized armies were needed, but such armies could be created only by strong, centralized administrations and supported only by effective tax systems. Neither centralization nor taxation was easy. Eastern rulers were facing roughly the same obstacles to the growth of centralized government that western rulers had faced two centuries and more earlier: a powerful landed nobility, a church that held itself above dynastic interests and owned a large portion of the wealth of the land, an agrarian economy with limited commerce and infant industries, a bourgeoisie still too small to bear the weight of heavy taxation, and an ignorant and exploited peasantry tied to the land and thus incapable of meeting the need of new industries for labor. To build a "modern" state in the face of these difficulties was beyond the capacities of all but the ablest rulers.

The Holy Roman Empire

The one large political organization bridging eastern and western Europe was the Holy Roman Empire. But although there was still an emperor, and a Diet, which met "perpetually" at Regensburg after 1663, the Empire was a political fiction. It had no central administration, no system of imperial taxation, no standing army, no common law, no tariff union, not even a common calendar. The Peace of Westphalia had recognized the sovereignty of the individual states, as well as the right of France and Sweden to take part in the deliberations of the Diet. In the welter of political units—free cities, ecclesiastical principalities, counties, margravates, and duchies, together with one kingdom (Bohemia)—that made up the Empire, almost every petty princeling fancied himself a Louis XIV and fashioned a court modeled as closely as possible on Versailles. Already the Empire fitted Voltaire's description a century later as "neither Holy, nor Roman, nor an Empire."

The ruling families of a few of the larger states—Bavaria, Saxony, Hanover, Brandenburg, and Austria—were trying hard to expand their territories by war or marriage and to gain royal titles. Augustus the Strong of Saxony, in addition to fathering (according to legend) more than three hundred children, managed to get himself elected king of Poland in 1696. In 1701 the Elector of Brandenburg obtained the emperor's consent to style himself king in Prussia. And in 1714 the Elector of Hanover became king of England. But only two great powers eventually grew out of the wreck of the Empire. These were Austria and Brandenburg-Prussia.

The Habsburgs and Austria

The attempt of Emperor Ferdinand II (1619–37) to revive and strengthen the Empire under Habsburg control was defeated in the Thirty Years' War. The Habsburgs thereafter turned to a policy that Ferdinand had also furthered: consolidating and expanding the hereditary lands of the family in Austria and the Danube Valley. Thus a centralized Habsburg monarchy might be developed that could hold its own with the states of the West. The Emperor Leopold I (1658–1705) was the chief architect of this policy, aided, and at times prodded, by some capable civil servants and one remarkable general, Prince Eugene of Savoy.

To weld a centralized monarchy together, Leopold had to reduce three separate areas—Austria, Bohemia, and Hungary—to some semblance of unity and obedience. In the Duchy of Austria and neighboring Tyrol, his lawyers were able to establish his ascendancy over a feudal nobility whose economic position was still strong. Bohemia, it will be remembered, had been reduced to obedience to Vienna early in the Thirty Years' War. A new nobility owing its titles to the Habsburg ruler replaced the old, and the crown of Bohemia, previously elec-

tive, was made hereditary in the Habsburg family in 1627.

The real problem was Hungary. Although the Habsburgs had usually been the elected monarchs of the kingdom since early in the sixteenth century, hardly a third of Hungary was actually in Habsburg hands. The rest was either directly or indirectly ruled by the Ottoman Turks. To establish their authority in Hungary, the Habsburg monarchs in Vienna had to deal not only with the powerful Hungarian nobility and the Hungarian Protestants but with the Turks and the French as well. The nobles were wealthy and unruly; the Protestants were numerous and inclined to side with the Turks against the Catholic Habsburgs. The Ottoman Empire was not the power it had been in the sixteenth century, but since 1656 it had been undergoing a revival under a vigorous line of grand viziers of the Kiuprili family, who in the 1660s began a new thrust up the Danube Valley directed at their old enemies, the Habsburgs. Louis XIV, also an inveterate enemy of the Habsburgs, allied himself with the Turks and Hungarian rebels against his Austrian foes. Thus building a monarchy in the Danube Valley was as much a foreign as a domestic problem.

The Siege of Vienna, 1683

The crisis came in 1683. In July of that year a Turkish army of more than one hundred thousand laid siege to Vienna. For two months the fate of Austria seemed to hang in the balance. Then volunteers began to flow in from all over the Continent to help the emperor in his extremity. The greatest pope of the century, Innocent XI, contributed moral and material aid, and King John Sobieski of Poland arrived with an army that helped rout the Turks by September. The retreat continued year after year as the impetus of Europe's last crusade carried on down the Danube Valley, until Eugene of Savoy broke Turkish military power at the battle of Zenta (1697).

The Peace of Carlowitz in 1699 gave the Habsburgs full control of Hungary. The Hungarian Protestants were crushed; many of them were executed for treason.

Emperor Leopold I (above) and Prince Eugene of Savoy, Habsburg commander, detail from a painting by Kupezky.

The landowning nobility was left in full control of its serfs and in possession of many of its old privileges, in return for recognizing the ultimate sovereignty of the chancellery at Vienna. The Habsburgs were thus content with what one historian calls "a loose framework of centralized administration." They left local administration much as they found it, but they had established a strong monarchy in the Danube Valley where none had existed before.

The Treaties of Ryswick (1697) and Carlowitz (1699) marked the appearance on the European stage of two new great powers: England and Austria. Each had risen in response to Louis XIV's bid to make himself the heir of Habsburg power in Spain and Germany. The two illustrated how diverse great powers could be in the seventeenth century: England, a parliamentary monarchy controlled by a commercial and landed aristocracy, its strength based on commerce and sea power; Austria, a bureaucratic monarchy with agriculture and a standing army its most conspicuous sources of strength. At about the same time two more powers were just beginning to appear, each as distinct and different as England and Austria. These were Brandenburg-Prussia and Russia.

The Rise of Brandenburg-Prussia

The story of the rise of the Hohenzollerns in northern Germany is somewhat parallel to that of the Habsburgs in the south, except that the Hohenzollerns started with less and had farther to go. Their achievements owed proportionately more to the genius and patience of one man, Frederick William (1640–88), called the Great Elector.

The Hohenzollerns had been margraves of Brandenburg since 1417 (a margrave was count of a "mark," or frontier province). To this small territory around Berlin they had added by inheritance two other areas: Cleves and some neighboring lands on the Rhine (1614), and the Duchy of Prussia on the Baltic coast to the northeast (1618). When the Thirty Years' War broke out there was nothing to suggest that the ruler of these three scattered territories had any

brighter future than a dozen other German princes. He was an Elector—that is, one of the seven princes who (theoretically) chose the emperor—and thus a member of the highest echelon of German princes. But his lands had no natural boundaries, no traditional ties with one another, poor soil, few resources, and sparse population, about a million and a half in all. Furthermore, they were especially hard hit by the Thirty Years' War. Swedish and Imperialist armies tramped back and forth across Brandenburg without hindrance. Berlin lost over half its population. And the Great Elector's dominions as a whole probably lost almost one-third of their people—a loss that took forty years to make up.

The Great Elector, 1640–88

Frederick William was twenty years old when he became Elector in 1640 during the later years of the Thirty Years' War. Though he was a devoted Calvinist, he nevertheless respected the Lutheranism of his subjects and was genuinely tolerant in an age of intolerance and fanaticism. The helplessness of Brandenburg during the war taught him that his first and foremost task must be the development of an army, and to this end he set himself with unrelenting effort.

"A ruler is treated with no consideration if he does not have troops and means of his own," he advised his son in 1667. "It is these, Thank God! which have made me considerable since the time that I began to have them."

In 1640 he had a poorly equipped and ineffective army of twenty-five hundred men. Before the end of the war in 1648 he had increased it to eight thousand and by his death in 1688 he had a peacetime force of thirty thousand which was once expanded in wartime to forty thousand. It was something of a miracle for a state with the meager population and resources of Brandenburg-Prussia to produce such a large, well-equipped, and well-trained standing army in so short a time. In forty years (1648–88) Brandenburg had become the strongest military power in Germany except for Austria. If there was any explanation, it was the single-minded devotion of the Great Elector to this goal and to any political,

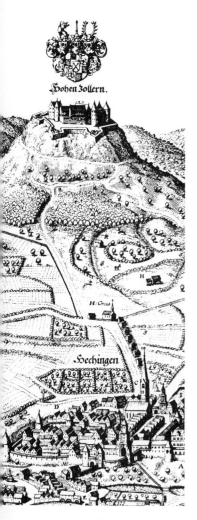

The castle of the Hohenzollerns (detail from a seventeenth-century engraving).

social, or economic policy that would help him reach it.

The first thing he had to do was to establish his authority over the Estates of Brandenburg and Prussia, which had almost complete control of taxation. In Brandenburg the Great Elector was strong enough to imitate the practice of the king of France by simply continuing to raise taxes that had once been granted by the Estates, which were never summoned again after 1653. In Prussia the townsmen were more stubborn and the Junkers (or nobles) more unruly. Their leaders turned to Poland for support, and Frederick soon had a fight on his hands. The fight ended only after he had executed the ringleaders of the resistance. In the end Frederick set up a taxation system for the support of his army that was common to all his territories, administered by civil servants of his own choosing, and independent of local control. The nobility were shorn of their power in the Estates and pressed into service to the Hohenzollern state as officers in the army. In return, the power of the Junkers over their serfs on their own estates was left untouched. Military strength, not social betterment, was the Great Elector's objective.

It could be argued, however, that much social betterment came indirectly from his building of a strong army, even if the Prussian peasants were sinking deeper into serfdom. The devastation of war was even worse than aristocratic oppression, and Frederick William protected a whole generation from invasion. He used his army as a weapon in diplomacy rather than in war by selling his support to one side or another in return for subsidies. The subsidies helped pay for the army, and the alliances seldom required much fighting. By pursuing this policy, the Great Elector and his immediate successors made substantial territorial gains. For example, by playing off Sweden against Russia, the Hohenzollerns gained Stettin and Pomerania in 1720. There was little sentiment and much shrewdness in this foreign policy, which showed its results in the steady growth of the army and the territorial expansion of the state.

Frederick William's economic policy was designed to develop his lands to the point where they could support his army without the need for foreign subsidies. He did much to revive and improve agriculture after 1648, and much to encourage industry and commerce. His tolerant policies made Brandenburg a haven for religious refugees—persecuted Lutherans, German Calvinists, and, above all, French Huguenots after the Revocation of the Edict of Nantes in 1685. These immigrants, together with Dutch, Swiss, and other newcomers, brought new skills in agriculture and industry, helped increase the population, and added considerably to the strength of the state. He welcomed even the more radical Protestant sects and the Jews, drawing the line only at admitting the Jesuits, whom he considered too intolerant.

The recognition of the Great Elector's son as King Frederick I in 1701 symbolized the appearance of a new power in Europe. Prussia (as the Hohenzollern lands came to be known) had devoted relatively more of its population, its resources, and its energies to military purposes than had any other German state during the later seventeenth century. It has been said that in Prussia the army created the state. The army was, in fact, the first institution common to all the Elector's lands, and its bureaus were the

Frederick William, the Great Elector, as a young man; painting by his contemporary Mathias Czwiczeic.

models for many organs of the later civil government. But while the needs of the army were especially important in Prussia, they played a significant role in the development of every great power in Europe except England.

Sweden

While Prussia was growing in strength, its neighbors, Sweden and Poland, were declining, for different reasons. Sweden had burst on the European horizon as a military power of first rank during Gustavus Adolphus' invasion of Germany (1631–32). During the latter part of the century the Baltic became a Swedish lake, and a Swedish empire grew up on both sides of the inland sea all the way from the Gulf of Finland to the North Sea. Copper, iron ore, and agriculture were the Swedes' chief resources, a technically superior musket their chief military advantage.

Swedish power, however, rested on shaky foundations. The country had a population of less than 2 million—not much larger than Prussia or the Dutch Republic. Its lines of empire were over-

extended, and its enemies—from Russia and Poland to Prussia and Denmark—were hungry for revenge.

When young Charles XII (1697–1718) came to the throne, a coalition of Russia, Poland, and Denmark pounced on his Baltic territories. Charles XII proved to be a military genius and crushed his enemies in a series of lightning campaigns. But he became intoxicated by success and engaged in political adventures that far exceeded his country's resources. He marched deep into Russian territory and was totally defeated at Poltava in 1709. He failed to gain Turkish support, though he spent some years at the Ottoman court seeking an alliance. Finally, he lost his life in a raid on Norway in 1718. In the peace settlements of 1719 to 1721, the Swedish empire outside Sweden was divided among Hanover, Denmark, Prussia, and Russia. Sweden settled down gracefully enough in the eighteenth century to its earlier role of second-class power.

Poland

The case of Poland was quite different, though the results were somewhat similar. Poland, formed in 1386 by the union of the crowns of Poland and Lithuania, was, after Russia, the largest state in Europe. Polish prosperity and culture had reached their peak in the sixteenth century, when the Polish people, linked by their Roman Catholic religion to western Europe, had felt some of the effects of the Renaissance, the Protestant revolt, and the Catholic Reformation. By the beginning of the seventeenth century, however, economic and political decline had set in. The Polish monarchy had always been elective. Until about 1572 the nobles had usually elected the legal heirs of their monarchs, but after this they began to choose anyone whom they believed they could control. By 1700 the real power in Poland lay in the hands of the nobility. The monarchy was almost powerless, although petty German princes still sought election to gain the prestige of a royal title. The peasants were the most depressed in Europe, sunk deep in serfdom. There was almost no bourgeoisie, since the towns had not

THE BALTIC: A SWEDISH LAKE 1621–1721

flourished. Political power was concentrated in the diet, which by now represented only the nobility, since representatives of the towns no longer dared to attend.

The diet was notorious for its futility; one negative vote (the *liberum veto*) could block any action. Moreover, by using the *liberum veto* any member might "explode" the diet—that is, dissolve the diet and wipe out everything it had done up to that moment. Of fifty-seven diets held in the century after 1652, all but nine were so "exploded"—one by a member who simply wanted to see what would happen. If legislation did succeed in running the gauntlet of this national assembly, there was still no way of getting it enforced in the provincial assemblies of lesser nobles or on the private estates of the landed barons. John Sobieski (1674–96), a native Pole of high integrity who made a serious effort to lead the country out of its weakness, was the last great king of Poland. After him the Polish crown became simply the prize of foreign intrigue, and Poland started down the path that led to extinction at the hands of more powerful neighbors at the end of the eighteenth century.

Russia

Throughout the seventeenth century there was no great power east of Sweden, Poland, and the Ottoman Empire. The Grand Duchy of Moscow had fallen on evil days after the death of Ivan the Dread in 1584. Disputes about the succession to the tsar's crown led to a "Time of Troubles," and the accession of the Romanovs, who were to rule Russia from 1613 to 1917, at first did little to strengthen the state. In the 1650s a near revolution was provoked by a reforming patriarch of the Orthodox Church, who ordered that the ritual and liturgy be revised in order to bring them closer to

the original Greek text of the Bible. This order exasperated vast numbers of the uneducated masses to whom the Slavonic texts were sacrosanct. For many years after, "Old Believers" resisted the official religious policy of the government in spite of executions and exile.

Russia was a victim state through most of the century, often unable to defend its frontiers against invading Swedes, Poles, and Turks, and still cut off from access to either the Baltic or the Black Sea. English merchants had made contact with Moscow in the 1550s through the White Sea, and German merchants were even more active in the capital. But while Russia absorbed some of the technology (especially the military technology) of the West, it remained relatively untouched by cultural changes in the rest of Europe. The Renaissance, the Reformation, and the scientific revolution, with all the ferment they brought to the West, remained almost unknown to the peoples living east of Catholic Poland.

Peter the Great, 1689–1725

In 1689 one of the most remarkable rulers in all European history came to power in Russia at the age of seventeen. He was a giant of a man, nearly seven feet tall (his enormous boots are still proudly preserved in the Kremlin), with large, skillful hands, inexhaustible energy, insatiable curiosity, and a hot temper. As a boy he had loved to play at war. He had also spent much of his time with the Dutch and Germans who lived in the "German Quarter" of Moscow, listening and learning. In these early years the great passion of his later life seems to have been born: to make Russia a great power by rapidly westernizing its technology, its civil and military institutions, and its popular customs. At his death in 1725 he had aggrandized, upturned, and

Medals celebrating the Treaty of Eternal Peace between Russia and Poland (1686). Above: King John Sobieski; below: personifications of Poland and Russia.

Peter the Great,
by Aert de Gelder.

exhausted his country and had earned the name by which he was to be known to later history: Peter the Great.

Peter's plans at first developed slowly. Using his old-fashioned army, he failed to capture Azov at the mouth of the Don from the Turks in 1695. Next year, after he had built a fleet on the river with Dutch help, Azov fell. Peter had learned a lesson: in order to build a navy and to modernize an archaic army, he would first have to learn a great deal from the West. From 1696 to 1698, thinly disguised as a private citizen, Peter visited Holland, England, and Germany. Here he learned how an utterly different society built its ships, made its munitions, ran its government, and conducted its diplomacy. He alternately shocked and amazed the Dutch and English who came to know him. Direct, spontaneous, and naive in temperament, he always had to try to do things for himself. He

worked in the shipyards, eagerly questioned everyone he met on western technology, and caroused through the night in drunken orgies with his Russian companions. He hired over seven hundred technicians of various sorts to return with him to Russia.

In Vienna word reached him of a revolt of the *streltsi*, the barbarous and undisciplined palace guard, which to Peter represented everything backward and reactionary about Russia. (The *streltsi* were in league with the "Old Believers" and were better at staging palace revolutions than at fighting an enemy.) Peter hastened back to Moscow and made a fearful example of the rebels, executing over a thousand of them and using torture on a scale that shocked even his countrymen, who were used to brutality. At the same time he forbade the wearing of beards and long robes by any Russian, as a sign of his determination to westernize even the personal habits and costumes of his subjects. His subjects wore beards because God was presumed to wear a beard and man was made in His image. But to Peter, beards symbolized the old Russia of reaction, rebellion, and religious fanaticism. The clean-shaven look was western. Typically, the tsar himself took a hand in shaving some of his courtiers.

There was nothing particularly original about what Peter did to reform the military, political, and social institutions of his country. He borrowed his ideas and techniques from what other statesmen were doing at the time in France, England, the Dutch Republic, Brandenburg, and Sweden. But his methods were more casual and informal, more brutal and ruthless, than were those of western countries.

An overwhelming defeat by the Swedes at Narva in 1700 spurred on Peter's efforts to improve his army. With the help of foreign officers and advisers he had trained a formidable force of over one hundred thousand by 1709, the year he annihilated Charles XII's forces at Poltava. At the time of his death the army numbered over two hundred thousand in a population of about 8 million. Years of warfare against the Turks were unsuccessful, and even Azov was lost

Peter the Great Tries to Westernize Russia

The Czar tried to reform fashions, or, to be more exact, dress. Until his time Russians had always worn long beards, which they cherished and preserved with great care. . . . The Czar, to reform that custom, ordered that gentlemen, merchants and all other subjects must each pay a tax of one hundred rubles a year if they wished to keep their beards. . . . Officials were stationed at the gates of the towns to collect that tax, which the Russians considered an enormous sin on the part of the Czar. . . . Many old Russians, after having their beards cut off, saved them to be placed in their coffins, fearing that they would not be allowed to enter heaven without their beards. . . . From the reform in beards, let us pass to that of clothes. Russian garments, like those of [other] Orientals were very long, reaching to the heel. The Czar issued an order abolishing that costume and commanding all the nobles and those who had positions at the court to dress in the French fashion. . . .

As for the rest of the people . . . a suit of clothes cut in the new fashion was hung at the city gates, with an order that everyone except peasants was to have their clothes made on this model. Those who entered the town with clothes in the old style were forced to kneel and have all the part of their garments that fell below the knee cut off. . . . Since the guards at the gates had a good deal of fun in cutting off long garments, the people were amused and readily abandoned their old dress, especially in Moscow. . . .

From Ivan Nestesuranoi, *Memoirs*, 1703, as translated in *Readings in Western Civilization*, ed. by Paul L. Hughes and Robert F. Fries (Paterson, N.J.: Littlefield, Adams, 1960), pp. 130–31.

once again. But decisive victories came in the north. In the Great Northern War Peter gained territory on the Gulf of Finland that had once belonged to Sweden. This gave him the "window on the sea," the direct contact with western Europe through the Baltic, that was his primary aim.

To man his army, Peter developed a conscription system. To pay for it was harder, since he could not borrow money. As expenses increased, he and his advisers taxed anything and everything they could think of: births, marriages, caskets, graves, and beards, among other things. By the end of his reign the combined burdens of heavy taxation, conscription for the army, and forced labor for industry and for building had resulted in a measurable decline in the population.

Political reforms followed military reforms, though more slowly. Peter's method of governing was informal and haphazard. To get something done, he would dash off a hastily written order and set up a commission to carry it out. Slowly, toward the end of his reign, some order was brought out of the resulting chaos. The first provincial governments were set up; the numerous commissions were brought under supervisory "colleges"; and a "senate," or central administrative body, was instituted to interpret the tsar's orders (which were sometimes confusing) and to carry out his will. A secret police also appeared to provide a check on all officials.

In Russia the imperial government did more and individuals or nonofficial groups did less than in any other European country. After 1700 no new patriarch was appointed, and the Orthodox Church was strictly subordinated to the state under a civilian official. When new industries were needed to support the army, government contractors founded them, using forced labor (serfs and criminals) granted by the tsar. One of Peter's most herculean achievements was to compel the ancient hereditary nobility to serve the state. He ordered many of the sons of the nobility to study abroad, then compelled them as well as their parents to serve for life in the army, in the government, or in industry. At the same time

he enlisted commoners for the service of the state, giving them land and titles of nobility. He thus created a "service nobility" out of older and newer classes. To support this service nobility, he allowed them a free hand in dealing with the serfs on their lands. A census for tax purposes resulted in greatly increasing the number of serfs in Russia by classifying doubtful cases as servile. Under Catherine the Great, who came to power a generation after Peter's death, the nobles were freed from the obligation of service to the state, but it took another century for the peasants to become free from the galling form of serfdom prevailing in Russia. In central Europe a serf was usually bound to the land, but in Russia he could be sold apart from the land like a slave and was generally at the mercy of his master—a fact that made it easier for new industries to acquire forced labor but degraded the Russian serf to a level even below that of his counterpart in eastern Germany and Austria.

In 1707 Peter moved the seat of his government to a new city that he had built on conquered territory at the eastern end of the Gulf of Finland and had named in honor of his patron saint. St. Petersburg was a perfect symbol of his work as a whole. It was a city unlike Moscow, without roots in the country's past, built new on a marsh by forced labor. The nobles were ordered to build houses in it, and merchants were ordered to settle in it. This seaport city looked westward to Germany, Holland, and western Europe, not to the interior, as landlocked Moscow had for centuries. The nobility and civil servants hated it at first, but in the end it became their capital—the political center of what has been called "a government without a people," and the social center of a westernized aristocracy out of touch with the Russian peasant. As Versailles came to stand for the France of Louis XIV, so St. Petersburg (later called Petrograd and then Leningrad) came to stand for the Russia of Peter the Great—a powerful autocracy with few vital connections with the people.

Historians still differ sharply in estimating the value of Peter's work, but on some things they are fairly well agreed. The older Russian institutions were

Contemporary cartoon of Peter cutting off the beard of a Russian noble. Those who wanted to keep their beards had to pay a tax and carry a license (below).

bankrupt, and western influences were beginning to have their effect even before Peter appeared on the scene. Peter hastened processes of change that were almost certain to have come in any case. He cannot be blamed for all the evil results that followed, since many of them (such as the intensification of serfdom) had their roots deep in the past and owed much of their growth to Peter's successors. Two things he did accomplish: he transformed Russia from a victim state into a great power, and he involved it irrevocably with the future development of Europe. Since his time, Russia has always been a factor in the European balance of power. Peter's westernizing policy ultimately provoked a strong nationalistic and orthodox reaction, leaving Russia divided to the present day between deep suspicion of everything foreign and eager admiration of western technology and culture. But never again was Russia able to turn its back on Europe.

Even more important than Peter's accomplishments were Peter's methods. His example created a tradition of dynamic autocracy. To future tsars and future dictators his reign was to be the classic example of what might be accomplished by a ruthless and demonic will.

CONCLUSION

The half-century between 1660 and 1715 thus saw significant changes in the political and social structure of Europe. Absolute divine-right monarchy reached the apogee of its development in the France of Louis XIV and was imitated from Madrid to St. Petersburg. It is difficult to imagine two more different personalities than Louis XIV of France and Peter of Russia, but their aims were essentially similar. A few smaller peoples like the Swiss had quietly rejected monarchy in favor of republican government, and the Dutch had become wealthy and powerful as a republic. But it took the English Revolution to demonstrate to Europe that there was a practical alternative to absolute monarchy that could serve great powers as well as small. So by 1715 the political alternatives of absolutism and constitutionalism were each embodied in a great power. At the same time there were important shifts of power within the European state system. The French bid for predominance failed, provoking the rise of England and Austria as great powers. Two great empires of the sixteenth century, the Spanish and the Ottoman, were in decline. Two peoples of limited resources and numbers, the Dutch and the Swedes, had bid strongly for great-power status in the mid-seventeenth century, but by 1715 their strength was spent. Two new powers had appeared in the East to join the balance, the small military Kingdom of Prussia and the vast semibarbarous Tsardom of Russia. The rivalries of these states— England versus France, France versus Austria, Austria versus Prussia, Austria and Russia versus the Ottoman Empire— were to become the dynamic elements in eighteenth-century war and diplomacy.

Suggestions for Further Reading

Note: Asterisk denotes a book available in paperback edition.

General The best general accounts of the period are F. L. Nussbaum, *The Triumph of Science and Reason, 1660–1685** (1953); J. B. Wolf, *The Emergence of the Great Powers, 1685–1715** (1951); and J. Stoye, *Europe Unfolding, 1648–1688** (1969). All three of these books are particularly helpful as introductions to the history of eastern Europe, about which it is hard to find good reading in English. R. Hatton, *Europe in the Age of Louis XIV** (1969), is excellent on the social history of the period. A general study of an important subject begins with this period: E. Barker, *The Development of Public Services in Western Europe, 1660–1930* (1944). On the general theme of this chapter, see J. N. Figgis, *The Divine Right of Kings** (1896, 1922); C. J. Friedrich and C. Blitzer, *The Age of Power** (1957); and F. D. Wormuth, *The Origins of Modern Constitutionalism* (1949).

France Under Louis XIV

There are good chapters on Louis' reign in Ogg and Boulenger, mentioned at the end of Chapter 19. Two excellent short surveys are L. B. Packard, *The Age of Louis XIV** (1914), and M. P. Ashley, *Louis XIV and the Greatness of France** (1946). J. B. Wolf, *Louis XIV** (1968), is a good biography. A. Guérard, *The Life and Death of an Ideal: France in the Classical Age** (1928), is a more thought-provoking and comprehensive discussion, including both politics and culture within its scope. P. Goubert, *Louis XIV and Twenty Million Frenchmen** (1970), relates the career of the king to the social history of France during his reign. N. O. Keohane, *Philosophy and the State in France* (1980), is also useful. J. E. King, *Science and Rationalism in the Government of Louis XIV, 1661–1683* (1949), is an important study. On economic history, the three books of C. W. Cole are the best introduction: *French Mercantilist Doctrines Before Colbert* (1913), *Colbert and a Century of French Mercantilism*, 2 vols. (1939), and *French Mercantilism, 1683–1700* (1943). C. Hill, *Versailles* (1925), is one of many books on the life of the court. W. H. Lewis, *The Splendid Century** (1954), is a popular account of all aspects of the reign, full of fascinating material. The best guides to the literary history of the period are the various works of A. A. Tilley.

England

G. N. Clark, *The Later Stuarts, 1660–1714* (1934), in the *Oxford History of England* series, is a particularly fine synthesis. A more detailed narrative history of the period may be found in three books, all more or less Whiggish in sympathy: D. Ogg, *England in the Reign of Charles II,** 2 vols. (1934); the same author's *England in the Reign of James II and William III* (1955); and G. M. Trevelyan, *England under Queen Anne*, 3 vols. (1930–34). A. Bryant, *Charles II* (1931), is more pro-Stuart. The most recent interpretation of the whole period of revolution in England is C. Hill, *The Century of Revolution, 1603–1714** (1961). There is a good modern biography of James II by F. C. Turner (1948), and of William III by S. Baxter (1966). J. Pollock, *The Popish Plot* (1903, 1945), is the standard investigation of a tangled historical problem. On the economic history of the period, there is a good special study, *The Bank of England*, by J. Clapham, 2 vols. (1944), and a masterly brief sketch by G. Clark, *The Wealth of England, 1496–1760* (1947). C. H. Wilson, *England's Apprenticeship, 1603–1763* (1965), is a remarkable study of England's emergence as a great power. Pepys's *Diary* is the most deservedly famous contemporary account of the Restoration period. It is perhaps read best in the abridgment of O. F. Morshead, *Everybody's Pepys* (1926).

Eastern Europe

In addition to the general accounts in Nussbaum and Wolf (first section, above), two books are very helpful as an introduction to the problems of eastern Europe: S. H. Cross, *Slavic Civilization Through the Ages* (1948), and O. Halecki, *Borderlands of Western Civilization* (1952). For Germany as a whole, see H. Holborn, *A History of Modern Germany, 1648–1840* (1964). On Habsburg history, P. Frischauer, *The Imperial Crown* (1939), follows the history of the house to 1792 and is mostly concerned with personalities. R. W. J. Evans, *The Making of the Habsburg Monarchy* (1979), is even more useful. See also H. G. Hoenigsberger, *The Habsburgs and Europe* (1971). H. F. Schwarz, *The Imperial Privy Council in the Seventeenth Century* (1943), is concerned with constitutional matters. For the events of 1683, see J. Stoye, *The Siege of Vienna* (1964). On Prussia, S. B. Fay, *The Rise of Brandenburg-Prussia to 1786** (1937), is very brief but also very good. J. A. R. Marriott and C. G. Robertson, *The Evolution of Prussia* (1915), and F. L. Carsten, *The Origins of Prussia* (1954), are more detailed. Also, G. A. Craig, *The Politics of the Prussian Army* (1964) is excellent. F. Schevill has written an admiring biography of Frederick William, *The Great Elector* (1947). R. N. Bain, *Scandinavia: A Political History* (1905), and O. Halecki, *History of Poland** (1943), are useful national histories. J. A. R. Marriott, *The Eastern Question* (1917, 1940), is a reliable survey of the slow disintegration of the Ottoman Empire and of the resulting repercussions in Europe. The classic larger history of Russia is by V. O. Kliuchevsky; the standard Marxist account is by M. N. Pokrovsky. There are good one-volume histories by G. Vernadsky, rev. ed. (1944); B. Pares, new ed. (1953); and B. H. Sumner, rev. ed. (1947). B. H. Sumner, *Peter the Great and the Emergence of Russia** (1950), is a well-informed and judicious short account. Kliuchevsky's *Peter the Great* (1958) is an English version of an older but still useful book. R. J. Kerner, *The Urge to the Sea: The Course of Russian History* (1942), contains a valuable account of Russian expansion eastward to the Pacific. J. Blum, "The Rise of Serfdom in Eastern Europe," *American Historical Review*, Vol. LXII (July 1957), is a masterly examination of the differences in the economic development of eastern and western Europe. See also his *Lord and Peasant in Russia from the Ninth to the Nineteenth Century** (1961).

21 The Scientific Revolution and the Enlightenment

Until the seventeenth century the growth of civilized man's knowledge about the natural world around him had been slow, fumbling, and discontinuous. He had made many individual observations of natural phenomena and had derived some useful generalizations from these observations. But many generalizations were poorly stated, and others were entirely erroneous. "Experiments" in the modern sense were all but unheard of, and most people felt that scientific speculation was both unsure and impractical.

THE SCIENTIFIC REVOLUTION

By the eighteenth century a startling change had occurred. A large body of verifiable knowledge about nature had accumulated and has continued to accumulate at an increasing rate down to our own day. This knowledge has had revolutionary effects. Human society today has at its disposal more food, clothing, and shelter, faster ways of moving about the globe, quicker means of communicating across great distances, and more power than anyone could have dreamed of before about 1600. The characteristic mark of our civilization is that it is a "scientific civilization," and this quality began to be noticeable in the seventeenth century.

Discussion of a new method of inquiry—which we call the scientific method—began in the universities in the late thirteenth and fourteenth centuries and came to fruition in western Europe after 1600. The new method was essentially a combination of two elements: careful observation and controlled experimentation, and rational interpretation of the results of this observation and experimentation, preferably by use of mathematics. In A. N. Whitehead's words, science is "a vehement and passionate interest in the relation of general principles to irreducible and stubborn facts."

When Galileo and others began to apply this method in physics and astronomy, other brilliant "discoveries" followed. These discoveries fired the imagination and enthusiasm of European thinkers. Scientific societies were organized, scientific journals began to appear, and "chain discoveries," each one resting on the results of the one preceding it, made their appearance. Science, hitherto the pursuit of occasional lonely individuals, became a social enterprise and has continued so to the present. Furthermore, it became fashionable. The Humanists had been little interested in science, but Newton's work made a profound impression on every writer in Europe. Finally, the gap between the theories of the scholar and the practical knowledge of the technician began to close.

The Medieval Universe

Precisely *why* all this took place when and where it did is still a puzzle. The one thing that can be said is that ever since the twelfth century the people of western Europe had been interested in scientific problems. But the medieval answers to these problems were based on deep-rooted, traditional assumptions about the nature of the universe. For example, it was generally believed that the universe was a finite sphere with the earth at the center. Between the center and the outermost limits were nine transparent spheres that carried the stars, the planets, the sun, and the moon in their daily revolutions around the earth, which remained motionless. On earth all was change, corruptibility, and decay. In the heavens all was perfection and incorruptibility—the perfect sphericity of sun and moon, the unvarying circular motion of the heavenly bodies, and the music of the spheres produced by their motion. And so what was the rule on earth was not the rule in the heavens. There was an earthly physics and a heavenly physics, and the laws of the one were not those of the other.

Even in the Middle Ages, however, not all men were satisfied with this relatively simple picture of the universe. In the thirteenth and fourteenth centuries a small but increasing number of scholars began to question existing explanations. Many of them were Franciscans, inspired perhaps by their founder's sensitive feeling for nature. Stimulated by the current study of Greco-Arabic science, a group of teachers at Oxford and Paris began to apply mathematical reasoning to prob-

Opposite: The Danish astronomer Tycho Brahe's underground observatory was the finest of the sixteenth century. Most of his instruments were under the protective domes.

lems of physics and astronomy, such as accelerated motion. Their speculations were continued by professors at the University of Padua in the fifteenth and sixteenth centuries. At Padua, a center of medical training for three centuries, the proper method of studying nature was vigorously debated in the course of arguments about Aristotle. Medieval universities kept interest in science alive, and the first faint beginnings of the scientific revolution were seen in Oxford, Paris, and Padua.

Most Europeans of 1500, however, did not question the standard Greek authorities. The normal state of everything in the universe was a state of rest: things moved only if they were pushed or pulled by a mover—so said Aristotle. Galen, in the second century A.D. had described the anatomy of the human body so convincingly that doctors still saw the human organs through his eyes. Ptolemy in the same century had worked out such an ingenious mathematical explanation of the observed irregularities in the movements of the planets that no one in 1500 thought it could be improved on. All motion in the heavens was circular, Ptolemy assumed, but there were smaller circles, or "epicycles," whose centers moved around the circumference of larger circles, and on the circumferences of these smaller circles the planets moved. It took about eighty epicycles to do the job, but the system worked quite well in explaining the observed phenomena and predicting their reoccurence with mathematical precision. There seemed to be very little reason at the close of the Middle Ages to try to improve on either the observations or the theories of these ancient writers.

The Background of Change

In the fourteenth, fifteenth, and sixteenth centuries, however, certain forces in European society were preparing the way for a change in the general view of nature. Artisans and craftsmen were becoming more skilled in their techniques. The invention of the lens and the development of the glass industry, to take but one example, gave the promise of vastly extending man's powers of observing natural processes. New techniques in shipbuilding led to voyages of discovery, which in turn stimulated interest in nature and turned men's attention to problems of navigation.

The Renaissance, with its emphasis on literature and art and its veneration for the wisdom of the ancients, was in some of its aspects antiscientific. But the Humanists were interested in Greek scientific texts as well as in Greek literature, and patrons of the arts were also patrons of inventors and technicians. Humanistic study revealed conflicting opinions among the ancients on matters of science, just at the moment when the authority of Galen and Ptolemy was becoming shaky for other reasons. Anatomical studies by artists and the increasing practice of dissection suggested that Galen had made mistakes in observation. Growing skill in mathematics exposed the clumsiness of Ptolemy's explanations. In the opening years of the sixteenth century, conditions were ripe for change.

The Scientific Revolution

ALFRED NORTH WHITEHEAD

A brief and sufficiently accurate description of the intellectual life of the European races during the succeeding two centuries and a quarter up to our own times is that they have been living upon the accumulated capital of ideas provided for them by the genius of the seventeenth century. . . . It is the one century which consistently, and throughout the whole range of human activities, provided intellectual genius adequate for the greatness of its occasions. . . . The issue of the combined labors of four men [Descartes, Galileo, Huyghens, and Newton] has some right to be considered as the greatest single intellectual success which mankind has achieved.

HERBERT BUTTERFIELD

The so-called "scientific revolution," popularly associated with the sixteenth and seventeenth centuries, but reaching back in an unmistakably continuous line to a period much earlier still . . . outshines everything since the rise of Christianity and reduces the Renaissance and Reformation to the rank of mere episodes, mere internal displacements, within the system of medieval Christendom.

From Alfred North Whitehead, *Science and the Modern World* (New York: Macmillan, 1925), pp. 57–58, 67; from Herbert Butterfield, *The Origins of Modern Science* (London: Bell, 1949), p. vii.

1543: Vesalius and Copernicus

In 1543 two notable scientific works heralded the end of medieval science and the beginnings of a revolution in western man's conception of nature. Vesalius' *On the Structure of the Human Body* was for its day a marvelously careful description of human anatomy based on direct observation in dissection and illustrated by graphic and accurate plates. Vesalius did not free himself completely from the authority of Galen, nor was there much theory in his book. But it was an influential example of the power of observation. Copernicus' *On the Revolutions of the Heavenly Bodies* was a brilliant mathematical treatise that showed that the number of Ptolemy's epicycles could be reduced to thirty-four if one assumed that the earth turned on its axis once a day and moved around the sun once a year. Unlike Vesalius, Copernicus was not primarily an observer. He learned during his study at Padua in the early years of the century that there was an ancient opinion that the earth moved, and he found that this assumption made everything simpler to explain mathematically. Since medieval theory decreed that "nature always acts in the simplest ways," the simpler explanation must be the truer. And so with little experimental or observational proof, Copernicus presented his readers with a theory of a universe in which the earth was no longer the center. The experimental and the theoretical sides of the modern scientific method were perfectly exemplified in Vesalius' and Copernicus' books, but they were not yet conjoined in one man or one work.

In 1600 a monk named Giordano Bruno was tried as a heretic, condemned, and burned at the stake for preaching that the universe was not finite but infinite in extent, that it was filled with numberless suns and planets like our own, and that God was equally in every planet or atom in the cosmos. Bruno had been inspired by Copernicus, although Copernicus himself believed in the finite sphere of the fixed stars and the uniqueness of the earth. Nevertheless, this intuition of the infinity of the universe spread gradually among scientists.

The medieval cosmos based on the earth-centered Ptolemaic conception. Ptolemy's explanation of the universe as a closed and defined system seemed so perfectly put together that it was not criticized for fourteen centuries—until the discoveries of Copernicus and Galileo.

Bacon and Descartes

Two major prophets of the Scientific Revolution were Francis Bacon (1561–1626) and René Descartes (1596–1650). Bacon, an English lawyer, statesman, and essayist, waged a vigorous battle in his books against the deductive method of Scholasticism, which started from premises usually taken on authority and then deduced all the logical consequences. This method might help men to organize truths already known, he said, but it could never help them to discover new truths. Only inductive reasoning, which starts from direct observations of phenomena and goes on to develop the principles that explain these observations, can produce new truth. Bacon was as interested in controlling nature as in knowing its processes. He pictured an imaginary society of scientists whose end was to benefit mankind by conducting hundreds of experiments and discovering useful facts. Bacon failed to appreciate the importance of mathematical models

Scientific revolutionaries of the seventeenth century: Francis Bacon (above) and René Descartes.

in theoretical analysis (he was unconvinced by Copernicus), and although he praised experimentation, he performed almost no experiments but collected his data, in the traditional way—from books. Nevertheless, his writings did dramatize the importance of empirical research. The founding in 1662 of the Royal Society of London, the first scientific society in England, owed much to Bacon's inspiration, and in a sense he was the remote ancestor of the great research laboratories and research teams of today.

Descartes, a French mathematician and philosopher, was a more important figure than Bacon, but he lacked Bacon's intuitive understanding of the need for careful observations. To Descartes, the excitement of science lay in mathematical analysis and theory. In a famous autobiographical account, he told how the literature and philosophy he studied as a youth left him unsatisfied because they reached no certain conclusions, how mathematics charmed him by its precision and certainty, and how he set out to discover a "method of rightly conducting the reason and discovering truth in the sciences." In November 1619, in a moment of intuition, he saw the exact correspondence between geometry and algebra: the truth that any equation can be translated into a curve on a graph, and that any regular curve can be translated into an equation. This intoxicating vision suggested to him a new way of grasping ultimate truth. If only men would systematically doubt all notions based on authority or custom and start with clear and precise ideas they know to be true, the whole universe might be deduced from a few simple principles and thus comprehended as clearly as the coordinate geometry he had discovered.

Descartes was one of the first to believe that science could save humanity. His enthusiasm was infectious, but he moved too fast. He reduced the universe, including the body of man, to a mathematically intelligible machine. To do this he had to take mind out of the world of matter entirely and define it as a separate substance that comprehended the world of matter but did not exist in it. His generalizations in astronomy, physics, and anatomy were often premature, and his passion for system building went beyond his capacity to check by experiment. (He did do important work in optics, but this was hardly enough to justify his basic theories.) But his enthusiasm for scientific "method," his belief that everything could be reduced to mathematical terms, and his insistence on systematic doubt of all earlier theories left a profound mark on the thinking of scientists in the next two centuries. Descartes made it easier for his successors to reject old ideas, and they gradually came to accept his belief that the language of science must be mathematics.

Experiment and Mathematics

Both Bacon and Descartes were overoptimistic. Bacon thought that a generation of determined experimentation would establish a solid structure of knowledge about the universe. Descartes thought that a universal science could be deduced fairly soon from a few basic mathematical axioms. He also believed that the universe was much less complicated than it is; it was one of Descartes' pupils who described the world as a gigantic piece of clockwork.

Meanwhile, experimentation and mathematics were developing slowly and steadily in the hands of a growing host of scientists. William Gilbert used what little was known of the mysterious force of electricity to deduce that the earth itself was a great magnet (1600). William Harvey, who had studied at Padua, proved that the blood must circulate from arteries to veins to heart to lungs and back to heart and then arteries again. He did this by estimating the amount of blood pumped out by the heart in a minute and arguing that it must go somewhere (1628). Later in the century the new microscope revealed the tiny capillaries that actually connect arteries to veins. Torricelli, Pascal, and others investigated the ancient proposition that "nature abhors a vacuum," a proposition that had long been believed by most scholars. In order to prove the falseness of the proposition, the new investigators created vacuums in test tubes, invented the barometer, and discovered the pressure of the atmosphere. All these advances evidenced a growing precision in observation and an increasing sophistication both in controlling experiments and in quantifying their results.

At the same time, mathematics was making rapid strides. The invention of decimals and of logarithms early in the century facilitated calculation; Pascal inaugurated the study of probability; and at the end of the century Newton and Leibniz crowned the work of many others by simultaneously inventing the calculus, which provided the first method of analyzing regularly accelerating or decelerating motion.

Kepler

It was in astronomy and physics that observational techniques and mathematical methods found their most fruitful union. The German astronomer Johannes Kepler (1571–1630) was troubled by discrepancies in Copernicus' theory, which he nevertheless believed to be true. He worked from the observations of his master Tycho Brahe, which were far more accurate than those available to Copernicus. Copernicus had clung to the old belief that all heavenly bodies moved in circles. But to Kepler it was obvious that the planets' orbits were not circles. For years he worried about the geometry of these orbits and finally decided that the ellipse might be a good model. The properties of the ellipse had been studied since the time of the Greeks, and Kepler quickly saw that this solution fitted the observations. The planets' orbits, he announced, are elliptical, with the sun in one of the two foci of the ellipse. Further, a line from the sun to a planet sweeps out equal areas of the ellipse in equal times, and the cube of the distance of each planet from the sun is proportional to the square of the time of its revolution. Here was astounding proof of the intuition of Descartes and others that nature in some mysterious sense was mathematical. A geometrical figure, studied for centuries as an abstract form, was found to "fit" the facts of nature. The implication was that nature was perhaps really a machine, intelligible to careful observers equipped with the tools of mathematics.

Galileo

The first fruits of Kepler's work appeared in 1609. During the same year an Italian, Galileo Galilei (1564–1642), professor at Padua and Pisa, turned a newly invented instrument, the telescope, on the heavens and soon afterward published an account of what he saw. The changeless perfection and perfect sphericity of the heavenly bodies had dissolved before his gaze. The moon had craters and mountains; there were moving spots on the sun; there were rings around Saturn; and Jupiter proved to have four moons of its own. A bright new star had already appeared and been noted in 1572, and in 1577 a new comet had cut a path through what should have been crystalline spheres. The finite, spherical universe of the Middle Ages was shattered, and thoughtful men suspected strongly that they were looking out into boundless space, sparsely populated by stars like the sun and possibly by other solar systems as well. The old distinction between terrestrial and celestial physics was apparently dissolving. The moon and sun were not perfect globes, and the stars were not changeless. Perhaps the same forces and laws operated both on earth and in the heavens. Nor was the earth any longer the motionless center of the universe. The earth was a planet circling the sun like Jupiter or any other, and round about the solar system were infinite, silent spaces.

This was too much for obscurantists in the Church. The Copernican theory had been denounced in 1616, and in 1632 Galileo himself was condemned by the Roman Inquisition, threatened with torture, and forced to recant. Nevertheless, his brilliantly written dialogues contributed mightily to the overthrow not only of Ptolemy in favor of Copernicus, but also of Aristotle in favor of a new physics.

Galileo's physics was inspired by the speculations of the fourteenth-century Franciscans, but he went much further and was much more accurate in developing mathematical formulas to describe the laws of motion. He worked out the law of falling bodies. The result was a simple mathematical formula again: the distance covered increases as the square of the time. He saw that the path followed by a projectile is a regular curve, a parabola, produced by the operation of two forces on the projectile—the initial

Two of Galileo's telescopes.

Harvey Discovers the Circulation of the Blood
1628

Since calculations and visual demonstrations have confirmed all my suppositions, to wit, that the blood is passed through the lungs and the heart by the pulsation of the ventricles, is forcibly ejected to all parts of the body, therein steals into the veins . . . flows back everywhere . . . from small veins into larger ones, and thence comes at last into the vena cava and to the auricle of the heart; all this too in such amounts that it cannot be supplied from the ingesta [food] and is also in greater bulk than would suffice for nutrition.

I am obliged to conclude that in all animals the blood is driven around a circuit with an unceasing, circular sort of motion, that this is an activity of the heart which it carries out by virtue of its pulsation, and that in sum it constitutes the sole cause for the heart's pulsatile movement.

From C. C. Gillispie, *The Edge of Objectivity* (Princeton, N.J.: Princeton University Press, 1960), p. 71.

impetus and the pull of the earth. He came close to formulating the key concept of modern mechanics, the law of inertia: that all bodies tend to remain at rest or to continue in motion in straight lines unless acted on by outside forces. From this deceptively simple proposition—so fundamentally different from Aristotle's conception of motion as the result of some mover's action—was to spring the law of gravitation. Galileo prepared the way, but the actual formulation of the law was to be reserved for one who was born in the year Galileo died, 1642.

Newton

It was the genius of an Englishman, Sir Isaac Newton (1642–1727), that related Kepler's astronomy to Galileo's physics, destroyed all distinction between celestial and terrestrial physics, and accomplished at least part of Descartes' dream of establishing a "universal science." The basic intuition came to Newton while he was still a student in his twenties at Cambridge University. The thought occurred to him that the force that keeps the moon from flying off at a tangent and bends it into an orbit about the earth must be exactly the same force that pulls an apple from its branch to the ground. There must be a reciprocal force of attraction between every body in the universe, and this force must be calculable—even if we do not know exactly what it is in itself. Newton's earliest calculations came close enough to mathematical proof to persuade him that it was in truth the same force that operated on the moon and the apple, and that this force varied "directly as the product of the masses" involved and "inversely as the square of the distance" separating the bodies. For some time he seems to have lost interest in his "law," but twenty years later a friend, the astronomer Edmund Halley, urged him to work out and publish his theory. Newton developed the necessary mathematics (the calculus) to prove his theory to his own satisfaction and published his conclusions, in Latin, in *The Mathematical Principles of Natural Philosophy* (1687). This proved to be one of the most influential books ever written in the history of science as well as in the history of human thought.

To scientists Newton's law of gravitation provided a single, simple explanation of a growing mass of data in astronomy and physics and laid the foundations of future research in both these sciences. Further, Newton gave scientific method its classic formulation in his "Rules of Reasoning":

> In experimental philosophy (i.e., science) we are to look upon propositions collected by general induction from phenomena as accurately or very nearly true, notwithstanding any contrary hypotheses (theories) that may be imagined, till such time as other phenomena occur, by which they may either be made more accurate or liable to exceptions.

Newton's support of the experimental, or inductive, approach was aimed at the premature generalizing of Descartes and his followers. But obviously he did not underestimate the value of mathematical theory, as Bacon had. In Newton the slow growing together of empirical observation and rational interpretation reached full maturity.

The Newtonian Universe

To the layman, who learned about Newton's work through popularizers, a new universe began to open up. It was a far cry from the small and finite medieval universe. It was a universe in which the significant objects were bodies or masses moving about in infinite space in response to regularly operating forces. Mass, force, and motion were the key concepts, and mathematics was the means of understanding them. Medieval man had been obsessed by the question "Why?" and had felt he understood whatever he encountered in nature once he had discovered its end or purpose. Seventeenth-century scientists limited themselves to asking "How?" and were satisfied when they found what appeared to be the regular patterns in natural processes. The world of Kepler, Galileo, and Newton was a vast machine, working according to laws that could be mathematically expressed, laws that were intelligible to anyone who followed the proper experimental and mathematical methods.

What was the place of God and of man in this universe? We shall see what the answers to this question were in the next century. But here it must be observed that no seventeenth-century scientist of prominence thought that he was reading God or man out of the universe. Descartes considered himself a good Catholic and was apparently not troubled by the dangers inherent in his sharp separation of the world of matter from the world of mind. Newton spent most of his energy in his later years in religious speculation. Contradictions between faith and science were not necessarily evident to the first modern scientists and their readers.

Still, the religious view of life was weakening in the later seventeenth century, and the development of science was in part the result of this decline. The charters of the scientific societies and academies that sprang up throughout Europe during the century usually contained clauses stating that purely theological or political discussion would not be tolerated and that "ultimate" or "final" causes were no part of the group's concern. In the earliest history of the Royal Society of London, published in 1667, it is clear that scientific discussions had offered a peculiar attraction to thoughtful men during a fanatical and bitter civil war like the Puritan Revolution. Science was impartial politically and theologically; it did not stir men's tempers; it would not start religious wars; and above all, it was useful—it could benefit mankind. Scientific truth was an alternative to theological truth that was more verifiable, more practical, more peaceful—or so at least some men argued. It was more than coincidence that modern science arose in a century that saw Europe's last violent struggles over religion.

One supremely sensitive philosopher felt the religious awe implicit in the new mechanistic picture of the universe. This was an obscure Dutch lens grinder, Baruch Spinoza (1632–77). To Spinoza the new universe of mass, force, and motion, operating in strict obedience to inexorable laws, was God. There was no need, he thought, to consider God as above, behind, or beyond nature. God is not a "free cause" apart from natural law. He is not "Creator" or "Redeemer." He is natural law. "God never can decree, nor ever would have decreed, anything but what is; God did not exist before his decrees, and would not exist without them." Nature is "a fixed and immutable order," with "no particular goal in view." Man, like everything else, is part of this order. So Spinoza could write a book called *Ethics Demonstrated in the Geometrical Manner* and say, "I shall consider human activities and desires in exactly the same manner as though I were concerned with lines, planes, and solids." The wise man contemplates this natural order with serenity and delight. This was Spinoza's religion. Naturally such arguments were called atheistical, and Spinoza was considered a dangerous radical by his contemporaries.

For most men, however, the new science did not destroy the traditional religion. Rather it compelled them to consider the religious significance of a greatly expanded and complicated universe. The telescope was revealing the immense size of the cosmos, displacing the earth and even the sun from the

Newton's design for a reflecting telescope.

center of the universe. The microscope was beginning to reveal the wonders of the world's minutiae—the capillaries, the bacteria, the cells, the foundations of life. No one felt the two infinites—the infinitely great and the infinitesimally small—so keenly or speculated so profoundly about their religious significance as Blaise Pascal (1623–62). "The whole visible world is only an imperceptible atom in the ample bosom of nature," he wrote. The universe, he said, is "an infinite sphere, the center of which is everywhere, the circumference nowhere." "The eternal silence of these infinite spaces frightens me." Yet to examine a mite—"with its minute body and parts incomparably more minute, limbs with their joints, veins in the limbs, blood in the veins, humors in the blood, drops in the humors, vapors in the drops"—is equally astonishing. "What is man in nature? A Nothing in comparison with the Infinite, an All in comparison with the Nothing, a mean between nothing and everything." And yet man is greater than anything in the universe because he comprehends all this, and because Christ died on the cross for him. In this way, Pascal related the new universe to Christianity. Other Christians were not so concerned about the new science, and other scientists were not so concerned to articulate a Christian interpretation.

THE CULTURE OF THE SEVENTEENTH CENTURY

The Baroque Style in Art

The age of the scientific revolution was also the age of the "baroque" style in art—a style that sprang up in the later sixteenth century, reached its climax about the middle of the seventeenth, and came to its end around the middle of the eighteenth. The term *baroque* (French for "odd" or "irregular") was invented by eighteenth-century critics who regarded seventeenth-century art as a grotesque corruption of Renaissance art. But modern critics consider the baroque a great achievement; one of them has called it "the high-water mark of European crea-

View of the baroque interior of the church at Weiss in Germany.

tive effort." As a style it is difficult to define because it reflected all the contrasts and contradictions of seventeenth-century culture in general: its religious ecstasy and its sensual worldliness, its credulity and its rationalism, its violence and its respect for order. Baroque painters and sculptors were influenced by all these contradictions. They portrayed voluptuous women in repose, military heroes in battle, and saints in ecstasy with equal skill and zest.

In general, the dominant notes of the baroque were a sense of tension and conflict and a liking for the grandiose and dramatic. The conflicts of man and the universe, of man and man, and of man within himself were conceived on a more heroic, and often a more tragic, scale than they had been in the Renaissance. Renaissance painters and writers had been interested in man himself. Baroque painters and writers were fascinated by man in his environment—typical men torn by conflicting passions, confronted by human and supernatural enemies, buffeted by elemental forces beyond their control.

There were instructive parallels between the thought-worlds of the artists and the thought-worlds of the scientists of the period. To Galileo and Newton, bodies or masses moving through space in response to conflicting forces such as gravitation and centrifugal force were the objects of study. To the great French dramatists of the age—Corneille, Racine, and Molière—the objects of study were typical human beings acting and reacting in response to conflicting passions such as love and duty. Baroque painters were intrigued by space. Vermeer portrayed figures in a space that was bathed and suffused with light; Rembrandt spotlighted them in the midst of darkened space; and others pictured them floating through apparently infinite space (to baroque artists the supernatural was natural). The scientists' concern with "mass, force, and motion" seems closely related to the painters' and poets' concern with men caught in the tension between elemental forces in their whole natural or supernatural environment. The typical hero of baroque literature, it has been said, is Satan in Milton's *Paradise Lost.*

"To reign is worth ambition though in hell:/Better to reign in hell than serve in heav'n." So speaks Satan after the Fall, swayed by colossal passions, moving through vast three-dimensional spaces, commanding many of the natural forces in the universe, but ultimately checked and frustrated by God.

The most typical product of baroque architecture was the royal palace: Versailles in France, Schönbrunn in Austria, or Blenheim, Marlborough's regal residence in England. The style was fundamentally Renaissance classical, but grander, more ornate, and more complicated. These palaces were designed to be the stage settings of worldly greatness. The vast reception rooms, the halls of mirrors, the great sweeping staircases, and the long vistas of the formal gardens were designed to enhance the drama of royalty and aristocracy. Even the churches of the period—such as Bernini's colonnades framing St. Peter's in Rome—suggested the majesty of God rather than his mercy.

But it was the operas that originated in Italy early in the seventeenth century that were the most original creation of the baroque. The union of dramatic action and a less polyphonic, more direct musical style was a great popular success, and opera continued to grow as a distinct form of art down to the twentieth century. The grandiose and palatial stage settings (sometimes outdoors), the dramatic conflicts of the action, and the emotive power of the music exactly suited the taste of the period. Italian composers led the way until the end of the seventeenth century: Monteverdi, the father of the opera, Frescobaldi, Scarlatti, and Vivaldi. But an Englishman, Henry Purcell, wrote the most moving opera of the century, *Dido and Aeneas* (1687).

SEVENTEENTH-CENTURY THOUGHT ABOUT MAN

The seventeenth century developed conceptions about man that were based on Renaissance views but went beyond them. These conceptions may be conveniently summed up under three heads:

Opera singers of the baroque period. Detail from a drawing for an opera setting by Ludovico Burnacinia, Vienna (1674).

individualism, relativism, and rationalism tempered by empiricism. We are speaking here of the thought of the most adventurous and best-educated minds, not of the many, whose thought-world was still conventional and in many ways "medieval."

Individualism

Radical thinkers of the seventeenth century took an increasingly individualistic view of man in society. The most intense Christian piety of the period—whether it was the Catholic devotion preached by St. François de Sales, the stern conscience of Puritans and Jansenists, or the warm inner conviction of German Pietists—was highly individualistic. The trend was equally evident in political theory. The fashion was to start with the individual and then to ask how society and the state could have originated and how they could be justified. Supporters of the divine right of kings were still numerous, but advanced thinkers were arguing that the state was based on a contract, either explicit or implicit, between the people and the ruler. Some, like Hobbes, argued that this contract, once made, was irrevocable. Others, like Locke, insisted that if the ruler broke the terms of the contract, which were usually thought to provide for good government, the people might depose him and set up a new ruler in his place. This idea of a "political contract" between ruler and people had some basis in the Old Testament and had been reinforced by feudal "contracts" between lords and vassals. It had been revived as a fighting idea by religious minorities when they were resisting the tyranny of rulers.

As time went on, the idea of a "social contract" took its place by the side of the "political contract." This was the idea that society itself was the result of a voluntary agreement among individuals who had been absolutely independent in their original "state of nature." The two ideas were mixed, somewhat confusedly, in Locke and later theorists. In both contracts, the individual with his rights and his natural independence logically came first; then came society or the state. In contrast, the Middle Ages had thought of society as an organism or a "body" in which individuals were mere "members." The more radical thinkers of the seventeenth century were coming to think of society as an artificial organization of independent individuals based on voluntary agreement or consent.

Relativism

The greatest thinkers of the Middle Ages were sure that the people of Christendom were God's chosen people and that the truth had been revealed once and for all to Christians. During the sixteenth and seventeenth centuries, Humanism, the voyages of discovery, and the development of science greatly weakened this assurance.

Humanism had shaken this assurance by revealing Greco-Roman civilization in clearer historical perspective. Here—in a society long since dead, but still alive in its literature, its art, and its historical records—was an alternative to the medieval Christian view of life. Modern historical studies—history, archeology, philology—were born during the Renaissance and were carried on with even greater skill during the seventeenth century. This steady development of the "historical sciences," as they would be called today, slowly impressed on thoughtful Europeans that there had been other societies in other times with values, beliefs, and institutions quite different from those of the present. Thus the idea of relativism in time was born and grew. What had been right behavior for a Roman was perhaps not right behavior in other times.

The idea of relativism in space resulted from the geographical discoveries, as we have seen. The discovery in America of societies far less civilized than Europe and of societies in Asia more civilized in many respects than Europe had the effect of shaking European provincialism. Perhaps the "noble savages" of the New World were happier than the more cultured but more corrupt Christians of Europe. Perhaps Christians had something to learn from Persian sages and Chinese philosophers. Each society had different standards; was any set of standards absolutely right? So at least increasing numbers of Europeans began to think in the seventeenth and eighteenth centuries.

As the temporal and geographical horizons of the European imagination widened, the vision of man's place in nature was complicated by scientific discovery, as we have seen in considering Bruno and Pascal. European Christians were not unique in time and space, as they had once thought; nor, perhaps, was man himself unique.

The intellectual results of historical study, geographical exploration, and scientific discovery are best seen in the work of Pierre Bayle (1647–1706), the great scholarly skeptic of the later seventeenth century. Bayle, originally a Huguenot, was briefly converted to Catholicism, but he renounced all orthodox belief when his brother died in a dungeon during an attempted forced conversion. He took up residence in the relatively tolerant Dutch Netherlands and devoted the latter part of his life to a crusade against superstition, religious intolerance, and dogmatism in general. In 1697 Bayle published a huge rambling book, a *Historical and Critical Dictionary*, which had enormous influence on eighteenth-century thinkers. Into this book he poured all the relativism and skepticism that he had acquired through his extensive historical study, his amateur knowledge of science (he was an admirer of Descartes), and his personal experience. He argued that atheists might be good citizens and that there was no necessary connection between a man's religious beliefs and the way he behaved. Bayle insisted that there is nothing more abominable than to make religious conversions by force. He ridiculed the idea that stars and planets could influence human life and mercilessly attacked superstition on every front. He distrusted all historical authorities, including the writers of the Old Testament, unless he was sure that their account of events was inherently credible. His test of truth was reason—and few if any accounts of miracles met this rigorous test. All in all, Bayle was the most thoroughgoing skeptic and the most destructive critic of his generation.

Rationalism and Empiricism

The leading thinkers of the seventeenth century were predominantly rationalistic. Reason was the faculty that distinguished man from the beast, and the triumphs of seventeenth-century science proved that reason could be trusted. And so the conclusion was drawn that the man of reason could know and understand the world into which he was born if he made the right use of his mind.

This optimistic attitude was reflected in the growing belief in "natural law." The idea of a law of nature that served as a standard of moral behavior for all men at all times in all places originated with the Stoics and was developed by medieval scholars. During the Renaissance and the Reformation this idea went into eclipse, but the discovery of scientific "laws of nature" (like Kepler's laws of planetary motion) helped to revive the belief that natural laws of human behavior also existed. Cicero had given the idea classic formulation: "There is in fact a true law—namely, right reason—which is in accordance with nature, applies to all men, and is unchangeable and eternal. By its commands this law summons men to the performance of their duties; by its prohibitions it restrains them from doing wrong." This law was implanted in the minds of men by God himself. Its content was hazy, but it was understood to include respect for life and property, good faith and fair dealing, giving each man his due. These principles could always be discovered by reason, just as reason could discover the proof of a geometrical proposition. Hugo Grotius, a Dutch jurist and statesman, in his book *On the Law of War and Peace* (1625), turned to the law of nature in an attempt to find some basis for a "law of nations" that would transcend the religious fanaticisms of the Thirty Years' War. And in more general terms, if natural law is the same for all men, then it lessens the contradictions caused by the relativism in time and space that was perplexing seventeenth-century men.

The most influential example of this kind of thinking was John Locke's faith

Title page of John Locke's *Essay Concerning Human Understanding* (1690).

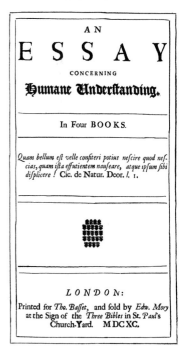

AN
ESSAY
CONCERNING
Humane Underſtanding.

In Four BOOKS.

Quam bellum eſt velle confiteri potius neſcire quod neſcias, quam iſta effutientem nauſeare, atque ipſum ſibi diſplicere ! Cic. de Natur. Deor. *l.* 1.

LONDON:
Printed for *Tho. Baſſet*, and ſold by *Edw. Mory* at the Sign of the *Three Bibles* in St. *Paul's* Church-Yard. M DC XC.

that there are certain "natural rights" vested in every individual in the "state of nature," notably life, liberty, and property. From this it follows logically, as conclusion from axiom, that men form societies and set up governments mainly to preserve these rights. Descartes had hoped to be able to deduce the universe from a few central mathematical principles; Locke in his *Second Treatise of Government* (1690) assumed that he could deduce society and government from a few simple axioms about man and natural law.

This enthusiastic rationalism in the study of man and society was qualified by an undercurrent of empiricism, of respect for sense-experience. Here again Locke led the way in his *Essay Concerning Human Understanding.* Many of its readers thought that it did for the study of man what Newton had done for the study of nature. Locke argued that all our ideas come from experience. The mind at birth is a *tabula rasa,* a clean slate, on which our sense-experiences gradually imprint conceptions. There are no "innate ideas," and no self-evident axioms (as Descartes had assumed). The mind and its ideas can be explained only by the outside forces that act on it.

This was the purest empiricism. Locke hoped that it would provide a weapon for getting rid of all the superstitions and prejudices that cluttered men's minds, but it could destroy many things besides superstitions, including some of Locke's own doctrines. Logically, Locke's theory of the mind did away with original sin (which was held to be born into all men), with revelation (which did not come through the senses), with mathematical axioms, and with all "natural rights" (which were considered innate and not based on experience). And so the rationalism of Locke's theory of society clashed with the empiricism of his theory of the mind—as the mathematical tendency clashed with the fact-finding tendency in seventeenth-century study of man in general. The eighteenth century was to inherit both: a strong faith in reason and natural law, together with a firm confidence in the value of sense-experience. Out of these two a new blend was to come in the "Enlightenment."

THE ENLIGHTENMENT

The task that the leading thinkers of the eighteenth century set themselves was to popularize the methods and principles of seventeenth-century natural science and to apply these methods and principles to God, man, and society. Scientific discovery continued, but the work that attracted the most brilliant writers of the age was that of applying the new scientific methods to long-festering human ills—economic, social, political, and ecclesiastical. Their concern was not so much to discover new truth about nature as to use the methods of natural science to reform society.

The eighteenth century's own name for this movement was the "Enlightenment." This term suggested the dawn of an age of light after a long night of darkness—the darkness of ignorance, superstition, intolerance, and slavery to the past. This new light was the light of science, as the poet Alexander Pope suggested:

> Nature and nature's laws lay hid in night;
> God said, "Let Newton be," and all was light.

There were "enlightened" writers and readers in every country of Europe from Russia to Spain and from England to Italy. Correspondence, exchange of publications, and travel linked these men together. Even in far-off America, Franklin and Jefferson were in close touch with and accepted by leaders of the Enlightenment. Nevertheless, this international movement was centered in France, and more particularly in Paris. There were good reasons for this. After the death of Louis XIV (1715) the French government became steadily more inept and ineffective, while the social tension between the privileged aristocracy and the less privileged, but powerful, wealthy bourgeoisie became more acute. Many leaders of the Enlightenment were bourgeois, and their writings often reflected bourgeois interests. These men of letters were angered by bureaucratic stupidity and aristocratic arrogance; they wanted to get rid of privilege and obscurantism. They learned to write with clarity and wit so that they influenced not only their fellow bourgeois but many members of the nobility as well. Government censors were either stupid or secretly in accord with critics of society. They could stop only the most blatant attacks; they were quite incapable of checking the criticism and satire that poured from the presses, particularly in the second half of the century.

For someone interested in ideas, Paris was the most exciting place in Europe during the eighteenth century. Here the intellectuals were in close touch with one another, excited by the feeling that they were helping to guide a revolution of ideas without precedent in European history, and bound together in a crusade to put an end to all the barbarities and absurdities of the old order. Such an intellectual conspiracy could develop only in Paris, capital of the largest and most civilized state in Europe. Other countries were too small or too backward to become major centers of "enlightened" thought and agitation. England, which had had its own Enlightenment or pre-Enlightenment with Hobbes and Locke, was a little too complacent to become a center of the Enlightenment. But the Scots delighted in stirring up their duller neighbors to the south; David Hume and Adam Smith were major Enlightenment figures, and Edinburgh in the eighteenth century was one of the great European intellectual centers.

Voltaire

As a movement the Enlightenment is often dated from Voltaire's visit to England (1726–29). Voltaire (1694–1778)—his real name was François Marie Arouet—became the central figure and moving spirit of the Enlightenment, in part at least as a result of this trip. He already had reason to dislike the old regime in France, having been imprisoned for a short time in the Bastille. In England he read Newton and Locke, and he sensed the relative freedom of English society compared with his own. After his return to France he published his *Philosophical Letters on the English* (1733), in which he passed on to his readers Newton's main principles in watered-down form, as well as Locke's theories of human nature and

An assembly of *philosophes:* Voltaire (1), Adam (2), Abbé Maure (3), d´Alembert (4), Condorcet (5), Diderot (6), and Laharpe (7). Contemporary engraving by Jean Huber.

political freedom. He skillfully contrasted the rationality of Newton's method and the reasonableness of the English way of life with the more unreasonable aspects of church, state, and society in France.

These letters set the tone of "enlightened" propaganda in France for the next half-century or so. They were "philosophical"—that is to say, they reflected on the facts of life to discover their meaning, and they searched constantly for general principles that might be useful to mankind as a whole. And so the men of the Enlightenment called themselves *philosophes*, observers of the human scene with breadth of view and a sense of the practical. They were popularizers in the best sense of the word, crusaders for the application of the best intellectual tools of the century to the most vexatious social problems of their own day. Voltaire was the greatest of them—the most prolific, the wittiest, the most readable, and perhaps the angriest. His prime targets were religious intolerance, religious bigotry, and superstition. The close union in France of religious persecution and theological obscurantism with a capricious monarchical despotism exasperated him.

"*Ecrasez l'infâme*" (crush the infamous thing), he cried, in letters, pamphlets, stories, and satires. In an essay on "religion" he described a vision he had had of a desert covered with piles of bones, the bones of "Christians slaughtered by each other in metaphysical quarrels." He went on to report a "philosophical" conversation with the shades of Socrates and Jesus, who both deplored the spectacle he had just seen. And he attacked intolerance in his own day as vigorously as the barbarism of the past.

When Voltaire died in 1778, he was the most widely read author in Europe, the first writer to have made a fortune from the sale of his own writings. He was buried in Paris in a ceremony worthy of a king.

Montesquieu

Another leading figure of the Enlightenment, Montesquieu (1689–1755), tried to institute a "social science" by applying the methods of the natural sciences to the study of society. In *The Spirit of the Laws* (1748) he suggested that forms of government were related to climate and other environmental factors, and he tried to discover what form of government best fitted a given set of environmental conditions. The book was not "scientific" by later standards, but it was the first serious attempt since the Greeks to try to show the relationship of a system of government to its environment. (Voltaire later elaborated the concept in his *History of Civilization*, 1754). Montesquieu, like Voltaire, was impressed by Locke's theories about the English constitution. As a French nobleman he wished to limit the excesses of royal absolutism. He concluded that the ideal political form was a separation and balance of powers within government. This conclusion was to have great influence on the authors of the American Constitution.

Diderot and the Encyclopaedia

A third major figure of the Enlightenment was Denis Diderot (1713–84), co-editor of a huge *Encyclopaedia* designed to sum up human knowledge and provide a kind of handbook of enlightened philosophy for the educated world. Diderot was an enthusiast for science, and he saw

the relationship between science and technology more clearly than most of the *philosophes*. The plates showing machinery and industrial processes are one of the most remarkable features of the *Encyclopaedia*. Diderot was also full of confidence in man and his abilities, a kind of prophet of a this-worldly religion of man. His interests were reflected in the titles and content of the *Encyclopaedia*, which appeared in thirty-five volumes over the course of thirty years (1751–80). Much of the most trenchant writing of Diderot, Voltaire, and other *philosophes* (or Encyclopedists) was done in articles for the *Encyclopaedia*. The book succeeded in becoming a bible of the "enlightened" everywhere. Through it ran faith in man's reason, pride in his accomplishments, contempt for his follies, and confidence in his future.

Leading Ideas of the Enlightenment

No intellectual movement is successful unless it has followers as well as leaders, and the Enlightenment, like the Renaissance, produced its full quota of earnest, but dull, disciples and literary hacks who used Enlightenment language to create sensations or to attack their enemies. But the silent supporters of the Enlightenment were even more numer-

ous than the writers who jumped aboard the bandwagon. As Robert Darnton has shown, the sales of the *Encyclopaedia* in tiny, provincial towns were astonishing. The main ideas of the Enlightenment struck root all over Europe and produced

A plate from Diderot's pictorial *Encyclopaedia* illustrating different kinds of domestic spinning devices, from the clumsy spindle and distaff (at left) to the more productive treadle-operated spinning wheel (fig. 2).

Key Words in History

If we could discover the little backstairs door that for any age serves as the secret entranceway to knowledge, we will do well to look for certain unobtrusive words with uncertain meanings that are permitted to slip off the tongue or the pen without fear and without research; words which, having from constant repetition lost their metaphorical significance, are unconsciously mistaken for objective realities. In the thirteenth century the key words would no doubt be *God, sin, grace, salvation, heaven,* and the like; in the nineteenth century, *matter, fact, matter-of-fact, evolution, progress;* in the twentieth century, *relativity, process, adjustment, function, complex.* In the eighteenth century the words without which no enlightened person could reach a restful conclusion were *nature, natural law, first cause, reason, sentiment, humanity, perfectibility.* In each age these magic words have their entrances and their exits. And how unobtrusively they come in and go out! We should scarcely be aware either of their approach or their departure, except for a slight feeling of discomfort, a shy self-consciousness in the use of them.

From Carl L. Becker, *The Heavenly City of the Eighteenth-Century Philosophers* (New Haven, Conn.: Yale University Press, 1932), p. 47.

a generation that had new ideas about religion and social organization. These ruling ideas may be summed up in five words, each of which bore a heavy freight of meaning in the eighteenth century: reason, nature, happiness, progress, and liberty.

The eighteenth century believed as passionately in reason as the seventeenth, but with a difference. Voltaire's "reason" relied more on experience and less on mathematics than Descartes'. It was a weapon of skeptical inquiry based on observed facts (or what he thought were facts) rather than an instrument of deduction from axioms. To the men of the Enlightenment, reason was the alternative to superstition and prejudice; it was the only sure guide to the principles that governed man and nature. Man's reason could discover the fundamental rationality of the universe, and it could also make human society more sensible. The *philosophes*, as shown by their writing for the *Encyclopaedia*, were less interested in "pure science" than in its applications, less concerned with system building than with specific reforms. Reason was now a pragmatic instrument, applicable not only to astronomy and physics but to agriculture, government, and social relations as well.

Nature was one of the favorite words of the Enlightenment. It was not always clear just what the *philosophes* meant by it, but it was clear enough that to nearly all of them "nature" or "the natural" were the proper standards for measuring God and man. If a thing was according to "nature," it was reasonable and therefore good. Voltaire and his contemporaries brought the idea of natural law to the peak of its prestige and the beginning of its decline. One of them devised this definition of natural law:

> The regular and constant order of facts by which God rules the universe; the order which his wisdom presents to the sense and reason of men, to serve them as an equal and common rule of conduct, and to guide them, without distinction of race or sect, towards perfection and happiness.

There is order and law, then, throughout the universe—laws of economics, of politics, of morality, as well as of physics and astronomy. These laws can be discovered by reason. Men may ignore or defy them, but they do so at their peril. To the enlightened, the way to happiness lay in conformity to nature and nature's laws. The man who broke nature's laws was looked on by the enlightened of the eighteenth century somewhat as the heretic who broke God's laws was looked on by the clergy in the Middle Ages: as a rebel against the order of the universe.

The end in view now was happiness, not salvation—happiness here in this world, not joy in the next. The Enlightenment was thoroughly secular in its thinking. When Jefferson included "the pursuit of happiness" along with life and liberty as an inalienable human right, he

Historical Relativism in Montesquieu: The Effects of Climate and Geography

In Asia they have always had great empires; in Europe these could never exist. Asia has larger plains; it is cut out into much larger divisions by mountains and seas . . . and the rivers being not so large form more contrasted boundaries. Power in Asia, then, should be always despotic; for if their subjugation be not severe they would soon make a division inconsistent with the nature of the country.

In Europe natural divisions form many nations of moderate extent, in which ruling by laws is not incompatible with the maintenance of the state: on the contrary, it is so favorable to it that without this the state would fall into decay. It is this that has formed a genius for liberty that renders each part extremely difficult to be subdued and subjected to a foreign power. . . .

Africa is in a climate like that of the south of Asia and is in the same servitude. America, being lately destroyed and repeopled by the nations of Europe and Africa, can scarcely display its genuine spirit, but what we know of its history is very conformable to our principles. . . .

Monarchy is more frequently found in fertile countries and a republican government in those which are not so, and this is sometimes a sufficient compensation for the inconveniences they suffer by the sterility of the land. Thus the barrenness of the soil of Attica established a democracy there.

From Charles de Secondat de Montesquieu, *The Spirit of the Laws*, Book XVII, Chs. 6, 7; Book XVIII, Ch. 1 (in the Bohn Standard Library edition), Vol. I, pp. 289–91.

was expressing the general agreement of the enlightened. The tendency of medieval Christianity to ignore misery in this life because it would be compensated for in the next angered the *philosophes*, who insisted that Christian ideals, if they were worth anything at all, must be realized here and now. Voltaire and his fellows were humanitarians. They abominated torture and cruelty, slavery and the callous treatment of the insane. An Italian, Beccaria, was the first to point out that savage penalties do not stop crime and to demand more rational treatment of criminals. The *philosophes* were also cosmopolitan and even pacifist in temper. Some of the bitterest passages ever written about the insanity of war and the absurdity of blind patriotism were penned by Voltaire. The "happiness" that he and others talked about was often materialistic. But it corresponded closely with Christ's injunction to feed the hungry, clothe the naked, and visit the sick and imprisoned. To the enlightened this was far more important than saving anything so vague as one's own soul.

The *philosophes* were the first sizable group of educated Europeans to believe in progress. They took the older Christian idea of the spiritual progression of mankind from the Creation through the Incarnation to the Last Judgment and secularized it. The progress of civilization, they believed, was now out of God's hands and in man's own. Once man had found the clue to discovering and using nature's laws in government, economics, and technology, progress was sure, if only research could prevail. There was some pessimism about this, but certainly both man and society were perfectible. On the whole, they thought that time was on man's side, not against him.

This was a major revolution in western thought. The Middle Ages could not have conceived of purely secular progress unrelated to God. Men of the Renaissance still felt themselves inferior to the heroic Greeks and Romans. But in a literary battle between "ancients" and "moderns" that began in 1687 the idea appeared that the "moderns" were as good as, and probably better than, the "ancients." By 1750 a French *philosophe* and economist, Turgot, suggested that the essential element in history was man's slow struggle upward to his crucial discovery of the scientific method. In 1794 Condorcet, a mathematician under sentence of death during the French Revolution, wrote a *Sketch for a Historical Picture of the Progress of the Human Mind*, which summed up all the optimism of his century. He saw "the strongest reasons for believing that nature has set no limit to the realization of our hopes" and foresaw "the abolition of inequality between nations, the progress of equality within nations, and the true perfection of mankind." Progress, he concluded, was now "independent of any power that might wish to halt it" and "will never be reversed." The scientific method cannot be lost, scientific knowledge of natural law will accumulate, and so progress can never cease. It was an intoxicating vision, a vision shared by the majority of the enlightened.

All the French *philosophes* were concerned about liberty. They were acutely aware of the limitations on liberty that prevailed inside France: restrictions on freedom of speech, freedom of religion, freedom of trade, freedom to choose a job, and freedom from arbitrary arrest. Looking at England through slightly rose-colored glasses, they envied Englishmen their economic, political, and religious liberty. Their concern about liberty was potentially the most explosive part of their thinking, but almost none of them felt that violence was necessary. Their belief in liberty was tied to their belief in reason. Reason would soon reveal the true natural laws governing everything from trade and government to religion. The artificiality of French society, French government, and French religious practices would become evident, and a benevolent despotism, enlightened by this knowledge, would set things right. Or so at least Voltaire and the majority of the Encyclopedists believed.

The Enlightenment and Religion

These ideas inevitably affected the religious thought of Europe. The fashionable belief among educated persons in the eighteenth century came to be

Deism, the belief in a God who is Creator but not Redeemer. Like a watchmaker who designs and constructs a complicated piece of machinery to keep perfect time, so God created the universe and started it going and then stepped aside to let it run according to its natural laws. God does not concern himself with redeeming men or society. The essence of religion is awe and reverence before the rationality and perfection of the universe—a feeling reflected in the hymns of Isaac Watts, which are still sung in many Protestant churches. To a Deist (Voltaire was a good example) all talk of revelation or miracle, all belief in the special intervention of God in the natural order, was false. All dogma and ritual were superstition, since man needed only his reason to understand God. The heart of natural religion was the morality common to all mankind. "Light is uniform for the star Sirius," Voltaire wrote, "and for us moral philosophy must be uniform." Obviously, Deism tended to undermine orthodox Christianity and to substitute for it a rational belief in God as First Cause and natural law as man's moral guide. A few of the French *philosophes* went further and pushed beyond Deism to atheism. Baron d'Holbach, for example, argued that there is nothing but matter in the universe, that man himself is a conglomeration of atoms, and that everything that happens is determined by natural law. But in the end many Protestants were able to find a compromise between Christian beliefs and the Enlightenment's rationalism, humanitarianism, and tolerance. The result in the nineteenth century was Protestant Liberalism.

Others reacted against Deism in the direction of more intense piety. To the enlightened, religious fervor of any sort savored of the fanaticism that had caused the wars of religion, and so all enthusiasm was frowned on. But Deism could be understood only by the educated, and its cold rationality had no appeal to emotional natures. Hence the wide popularity of two warmly emotional Protestant movements, Pietism in Germany and Methodism in England and America. Both emphasized the importance of inner religious experience, of individual "conversion." Pietism was a second and

milder Protestant Reformation, directed this time not against the pope but against both the dogmatically orthodox and those who were inclined to Deism in Germany. Individualistic, tolerant, and unconcerned about creeds or ceremonies, the Pietists attracted followers among both Catholics and Protestants.

John Wesley (1703–91) was the leader of a somewhat parallel revival of a warm, personal Christian piety in England in the years following his conversion in 1738. Finding his efforts resisted by the respectable Anglican clergy, he took his message directly to the people, addressing huge congregations outdoors or in remote chapels, teaching them to sing their way to heaven with the hymns of his brother Charles, and sending out streams of pamphlets from his printing presses to the congregations he had established. In the end Wesley was forced to establish a new denomination outside the Anglican Church—the Methodist (originally a term of derision directed at the "methodical" piety of Wesley's followers). Methodism touched thousands upon thousands of Englishmen at home and in the colonies who cared nothing for the arid intellectualism of many of the Anglican clergy in the eighteenth century. More than one historian has suggested that it was Methodism that kept the English lower classes from turning to revolutionary violence during the first impact of the Industrial Revolution.

Social and Political Thought

The *philosophes* were interested in social and political problems, but they were reformers, not revolutionists. Their formula for reform was simple: discover by reason and experience the natural laws that should operate in any given situation, clear away all artificial obstacles to their operation, and the result will be progress toward happiness and freedom. The first "economists" in the modern sense used this formula to launch an attack on mercantilism. In 1758 François Quesnay published his *Economic Survey*, which argued for the existence of natural economic laws that must be allowed to operate freely. In 1776 the Scot Adam Smith published his *Wealth of Nations*,

John Wesley preaching in a private house.

which argued in parallel fashion that all nations would be wealthier if they removed restrictions on trade and let the natural law of supply and demand govern the exchange of commodities. Quesnay was primarily interested in agriculture and Smith in commerce, but both came to the same conclusion: that economic laws, like other natural laws, should be respected, that interference with these laws is dangerous, and that the greatest happiness and freedom come from allowing these laws to operate freely.

The same line of reasoning in political theory led to the theory of enlightened despotism. The *philosophes* hoped that divine-right monarchy would become benevolent monarchy, that monarchs would gradually become "enlightened" (or perhaps engage enlightened *philosophes* as advisers) and so govern their people according to natural law rather than according to their own caprice. To Voltaire and most of his fellows, government should be for the people but not necessarily by the people. A smaller group believed that reason pointed in the direction of a constitutional monarchy like the English, a government based on natural rights and contract, with a separation of powers as a further guarantee of political liberty. Finally, to enlightened despotism and constitutional government there was added a third theory, the theory of democracy, still too radical to be of much immediate influence but of enormous importance for the future. This was the theory obscurely but excitingly preached in *The Social Contract* (1762) by Jean Jacques Rousseau (1712–78).

Rousseau

Rousseau, a native of Geneva, turned up in Paris after a troubled and wandering youth, came to know Diderot and others of the *philosophes*, and for a time tried to become one of them. He was never easy in their company, however. He trusted reason, but he relied even more on emotion. He trusted nature, but to him nature was the unspoiled simplicity of precivilized man, "the noble savage." In a kind of conversion that he experienced in 1749, he became convinced that mankind had lost more than it had gained by cultivating the arts and sciences, and so he surrendered his faith in progress. He grew more and more irritated by the artificiality of Paris society and finally broke with his former friends. Voltaire thought him mad, and Rousseau was haunted in his miserable later years by the illusion that he was being persecuted by everyone.

Rousseau was the great critic of the Enlightenment. By temperament he was a shy and sensitive misfit who vainly wanted to "belong." Deep down he knew himself to be good, but he felt that he had been corrupted and humiliated by an artificial society to which he did not and could not belong. To what kind of society or state could he give himself, then? Only to a society in which there were no hereditary rulers, no privileged aristocracy, no one with any right to lord it over others, none but those who had freely consented to become members of the society and had given up to the group all their individual rights. Perhaps Rousseau had an idealized Geneva in mind as he wrote *The Social Contract*—a community in which all the citizens knew and trusted one another—in which the minority accepted the majority's view with good grace because both felt themselves part of the same community. At any rate, he developed a theory of liberty as willing obedience to laws that the individual himself had helped to make as an active and loyal citizen, even though he might have been in the minority on any given issue. Locke and Montesquieu had thought that the way to obtain political liberty was to guarantee individual rights and to separate the organs of government so that no one of them could gain unrestricted control. Rousseau thought he would never feel free until he could find a community to which he could give up everything, on condition that all others did the same. In such a community there would be no division between rulers and ruled; the people would rule themselves. What magistrates there were would be mere servants of the community who could be instantly removed if they failed to carry out the people's will. If the people really governed themselves, there should be no checks and balances, no

Jean Jacques Rousseau.

Rousseau on the Social Contract

The problem is to find a form of association . . . in which each, while uniting himself with all, may still obey himself alone, and remain as free as before. This is the fundamental problem of which the Social Contract provides the solution: . . . the total alienation of each associate, together with all his rights, to the whole community. . . . Each man, in giving himself to all, gives himself to nobody. . . . Each of us puts his person and all his power in common under the supreme direction of the general will, and, in our corporate capacity, we receive each member as an indivisible part of the whole. . . . In order that the social compact may not be an empty formula, it tacitly includes the undertaking, which alone can give force to the rest, that whoever refuses to obey the general will shall be compelled to do so by the whole body. This means nothing less than that he will be forced to be free.

From Jean Jacques Rousseau, *The Social Contract* (New York and London: Everyman's Library, 1913), Book I, Chs. 6, 7, pp. 14–18.

separation of powers, no protection of rights.

Rousseau was picturing democracy in its purest and simplest form: a tight-knit community of loyal and active citizens, unhampered by any checks on their collective will because they unreservedly accepted this general will as their own. His book was highly abstract and difficult to understand. But when revolution actually flared up in France after his death, *The Social Contract* came into its own. It was not a work of the Enlightenment; its full force could be felt only in the new age of democratic revolution, nationalism, and Romanticism. And when romantic nationalism reached its peak, Rousseau could be used to justify dictatorship (which after all is supposed to embody the common will) as well as democracy.

So the two centuries that saw the Scientific Revolution and the Enlightenment might well be called the most revolutionary centuries in western intellectual history. The true watershed between what we call "medieval" and "modern" thought about God, man, and nature runs somewhere through these two centuries. The world of Luther and Loyola, of Charles V and Philip II, was still or-

ganically related to the Middle Ages. The world of Newton and Locke, of Voltaire and Rousseau, was unmistakably the father of our own.

ARTS AND LETTERS IN THE EIGHTEENTH CENTURY

The pervasive faith in the rationality, intelligibility, and order of the universe displayed by the scientists and philosophers of the age was reflected in the art and literature of the later seventeenth and early eighteenth centuries. Rationalism blended easily with classicism. The regularity and harmony of Newton's universe seemed to accord with the balance and proportion that Greek architects had admired as artistic ideals and with the rationality and restraint that the leading Greek and Roman writers had held up as literary ideals. The dictators of literary and artistic taste at the close of the seventeenth century were classicists, and when *philosophes* like Voltaire wrote dramas they accepted classical standards as unquestioningly as Corneille and Racine. Architects accepted classical rules of balance and unity with equal zeal in the "Georgian" buildings of England and the beautifully proportioned Place de la Concorde in Paris. Enthusiasm for classical antiquity reached its post-Renaissance climax in 1748, when the remains of the Roman city of Pompeii were discovered in startlingly well-preserved condition under the lava of Mt. Vesuvius.

An Age of Prose

The age of reason was an age of prose. Essays, satirical tales, novels, letters, and histories were the characteristic literary forms of the eighteenth century. Authors bent their energies to description and narrative rather than to suggestion and imagination. The essays of Addison and Steele, which began to appear in 1709, sketched a delightful picture of English rural society, while Jonathan Swift's *Gulliver's Travels* (1726) and Voltaire's *Candide* (1759) were more biting and satirical commentaries on human society. As the century progressed, the novel emerged as the favorite form of literary expression; the most mature example was Henry Fielding's *Tom Jones* (1749). Besides fiction, men read philosophy, economics, and history—of which Edward Gibbon's majestic *History of the Decline and Fall of the Roman Empire* (1776–88) was the most enduring example. Everything that could be done in prose—argument, satire, realistic description, historical narrative—was tried and done well by some French or British writer.

The elegance and aristocratic flavor of eighteenth-century society can be seen in its painting, and especially in the portraits, which were the most characteristic form of the art. The delicate-featured and exquisitely groomed women who look coolly down on the observer, and the worldly, sometimes arrogant, faces of their husbands under their powdered wigs suggest the artificiality of their society and sometimes the hardness of their characters. Furniture, tableware, and the great town and country houses of wealthy merchants and nobles reflect the same elegance and aristocratic spirit.

Not all the books, the arts, and the crafts were meant for the enjoyment of the aristocracy, however. The eighteenth century saw the appearance of the first newspapers, written for a wide audience of educated readers. William Hogarth (1697–1764) made engravings of his realistic satirical sketches of English society and sold them by the thousands. Above all, the novelists, the dramatists, and the musicians began to appeal to a middle-class audience that went far beyond the limits of the aristocracy. After the 1770s the plays and operas in Paris were apt to have a keen, satirical edge and to be directed at bourgeois listeners. The heroes and heroines of the novels were more often of middle-class origins than either upper- or lower-class. Music began to move from the aristocratic salon into the public auditorium.

Music

The greatest cultural achievement of the eighteenth century was its music. The musical world of the early eighteenth century was dominated by two great Germans: Johann Sebastian Bach (1685–1750) and George Frederick Handel (1685–1759) (who spent most of his life in England). Together they realized all the dramatic and emotive possibilities of the baroque style: Handel in his oratorios for chorus and instruments, Bach in his richly varied works for keyboard instruments, chamber groups, orchestras, and choruses. In the latter part of the century the orchestra, which had originated in the seventeenth century, was expanded and strengthened, the pianoforte invented, and music brought more and more into touch with a wider public. Franz Joseph Haydn (1732–1809), who wrote for both chamber groups and orchestras, developed the musical forms known as sonatas and symphonies. The other outstanding musical personality of the latter half of the century, Wolfgang Amadeus Mozart (1756–91), was possibly the most gifted musician who ever lived. A child prodigy, he lived only thirty-five years and died in poverty, but within this short span of time he produced string quartets, concertos, symphonies, and operas that were masterpieces of invention and form.

Wolfgang Amadeus Mozart, unfinished painting by Joseph Lange.

The Beginnings of Romanticism

Beneath the dominant tendency to respect rational structure and classical balance, however, there were countercurrents of revolt. Some evidence of these currents was seen in Pietism and Methodism, and in Rousseau's distrust of an exclusive reliance on reason. More clearly than Rousseau, the Scottish philosopher David Hume (1711–76) criticized reason as a method of knowing truth and defended the validity in human experience of feeling, conscience, and habit. French and English novelists developed sentimentalism to a fine art, putting their heroines through heart-rending misfortune and mistreatment and trying at every turn to arouse the reader's anger, pity, love, or terror. The most influential example was Samuel Richardson's two thousand-page tear-jerker, *Clarissa* (1748), which influenced Rousseau in writing his *Nouvelle Héloise* (1761). The strange, the unusual, the off-beat, and the fantastic began to come into fashion. Gothic architecture and literature began to be appreciated once more, and a collection of poems (1762) ostensibly by a medieval poet named Ossian was very popular, though it turned out to be a forgery.

In Germany, which never came totally under the sway of the French Enlightenment, a "Storm and Stress" (*Sturm und Drang*) movement in literature emphasized the great elemental emotions and denied the supremacy of reason. Johann Gottfried von Herder (1744–1803) worked out a philosophy of history that emphasized the uniqueness and peculiarity of each nation or race, the individuality of its genius, and the falsity of any view that denied this uniqueness in the name of universal reason. Johann Wolfgang von Goethe (1749–1832) at the start of his long literary career published *The Sorrows of Young Werther* (1774), a morbid tale ending in a suicide, which appealed to lovers of sentiment and sensibility.

The greatest philosopher of the age, Immanuel Kant (1724–1804), a man who never traveled more than a few miles from Königsberg, his native city in East Prussia, launched a powerful attack on the rationalism of his age as too narrow and too dogmatic. Starting from David Hume's criticism of reason, Kant distinguished carefully between speculative (or scientific) reason and practical (or moral) reason in his very difficult book, *Critique of Pure Reason* (1781). The effect of his work was to enable Christians and idealists to make a new case for religion and morality based on the fact of man's conscience.

Taken together, these various tendencies heralded the beginnings of what was to be called Romanticism. The "Age of Reason" thus contained within itself the seeds of an age that would rely for its artistic, philosophical, and even social insight on emotion and conscience rather than on reason.

Suggestions for Further Reading

Note: Asterisk denotes a book available in paperback edition.

General J. H. Randall, *The Making of the Modern Mind* (1926, 1940), is the most successful one-volume survey of the course of western thought, by a philosopher with a sense for historical context. To Randall, "the modern mind" is essentially the scientific mind. C. Brinton, *Ideas and Men** (1950)—the material since the Renaissance has been published as *The Shaping of the Modern Mind** (1953)—is a more informally written and engaging narrative by a historian. Both books are particularly good on the seventeenth and eighteenth centuries. G. R. Sabine, *A History of Political Theory* (1938), is the most penetrating one-volume survey, particularly full on English political thought in the seventeenth century and French in the eighteenth. A. O. Lovejoy, *The Great Chain of Being** (1936), is a classic account of the underlying western conception of the universe as a hierarchical structure of being, from the Greeks to the nineteenth century. M. Ashley, *The Golden Century* (1968), is a well-written survey of seventeenth-century social and cultural history. J. Bronowski and Bruce Mazlish, *The Western Intellectual Tradition* (1974) puts the period in a general perspective.

The Scientific Revolution E. A. Burtt, *The Metaphysical Foundations of Modern Physical Science** (1924, 1955), and A. N. Whitehead, *Science and the Modern World** (1925, 1948), are famous philosophical inquiries into the origins of modern science, not easy reading, but rewarding to the serious student. A. R. Hall, *The Scientific Revolution** (1954), is the best modern account, well informed and critical. H. Butterfield, *Origins of Modern Science, 1300–1800** (1949), is a more readable discussion of the subject for the lay reader written by a general historian. A. Koyré writes absorbingly about the cosmological implications of the "revolution" in *From the Closed World to the Infinite Universe** (1957). C. C. Gillispie, *The Edge of Objectivity** (1960), is a brilliantly written essay on the growth of objectivity in the study of nature from Galileo to Einstein. T. S. Kuhn, *The Copernican Revolution** (1957), describes the transformation of astronomical thought. *The Structure of Scientific Revolutions** (1962), by the same author, is a controversial but brilliant discussion of scientific change in general. R. G. Collingwood traces the chief western conceptions of the natural order from the Greeks to the present in *The Idea of Nature** (1945). C. J. Singer, *From Magic to Science** (1928), is still valuable for its interpretation of the origins of modern science. On the social background of scientific development, three books are particularly valuable: M. Ornstein, *The Role of Scientific Societies in the Seventeenth Century* (1928); D. Stimson, *Scientists and Amateurs: A History of the Royal Society* (1948); and G. N. Clark, *Science and Social Welfare in the Age of Newton* (1937). See also R. K. Merton, *Science, Technology and Society in Seventeenth Century England* (1970). There are biographies and special studies, too numerous to list here. of every scientist mentioned in the text. But two studies of a famous case are worth noting: G. de Santillana, *The Crime of Galileo** (1955), and F. S. Taylor, *Galileo and the Freedom of Thought* (1938). The effect of scientific discovery on literature is the theme of M. Nicolson, *Science and Imagination** (1956). R. Hooykass, *Religion and the Rise of Science* (1972) is a good study of this topic.

Culture of the Seventeenth and Eighteenth Centuries

There is no full and reliable discussion in English on the baroque style in art, the basic studies being in German. The best introductions are in C. J. Friedrich, *The Age of the Baroque, 1610–1660** (1952) in the *Rise of Modern Europe* series, and Chapter 6 of H. Leichtentritt, *Music, History, and Ideas* (1938). The Pelican *History of Art** has good studies of individual countries for the period from 1600 to 1880. The latter third of G. N. Clark, *The Seventeenth Century* (1931), is devoted to art, literature, and philosophy. B. Willey's two volumes, *The Seventeenth Century Background** (1934) and *The Eighteenth Century Background** (1940), sketch a broad background for the study of English literature in the period. F. Fosca, *The Eighteenth Century* (1953), is probably the best introduction to the painting of the age. In addition to Leichtentritt, M. F. Bukofzer, *Music in the Baroque Era* (1947), is particularly interesting. There is no satisfactory general account of religious developments, but A. C. McGiffert, *Protestant Thought Before Kant* (1911), is a brief reliable account. M. J. Bradshaw, *The Philosophical Foundations of Faith* (1941), is illuminating on the religious attitudes of prominent seventeenth-century figures like Descartes. M. L. Edwards, *John Wesley and the Eighteenth Century* (1933), is one of many books on Methodism. See also G. R. Craig, *The Church in the Age of Reason* (1961).

Contemporary Literature

The best way, as always, to gain a firsthand knowledge of the thought and feeling of the period is through a study of some of the paintings, the buildings, the literary and philosophical writings, and the musical works of the age. This becomes increasingly easy to do after the sixteenth century because of the availability of reproductions, records, and inexpensive reprints. The student will have to make his own selection, but some of the following should be on any reading list (there are many editions of each except where specified): Descartes, *Discourse on Method;** Bacon, *New Atlantis;* Pascal, *Pensées;** Galileo, *Dialogue on the Great World Systems,* ed. by G. de Santillana (1953); John Bunyan, *The Pilgrim's Progress;** John Locke, *Second Treatise of Government** and *Essay Concerning Human Understanding;**Selections from Bayle's Dictionary,* ed. by E. A. Beller and M. D. Lee (1952); Beccaria, *Essay on Crimes and Punishments** (trans. 1953); *The Portable Voltaire,** ed. by B. R. Redman (1949); Rousseau, *Social Contract;** Henry Fielding, *Tom Jones;** Samuel Richardson, *Clarissa* (abridgment, Modern Library, 1950). *The Portable Age of Reason Reader,** ed. by C. Brinton (1956), is an excellent selection of readings from the *philosophes.*

The Enlightenment

The most significant study of the transition from the seventeenth century to the eighteenth, from the Scientific Revolution to the Enlightenment, is P. Hazard, *The European Mind: The Critical Years, 1680–1715** (trans. 1952). There are excellent chapters on the Enlightenment in W. L. Dorn, *Competition for Empire, 1740–1763** (1940), and in the *New Cambridge Modern History,* Vol. VII: A. Cobban, *The Old Régime, 1713–1763* (1957). The most searching interpretation of the movement as a whole is E. Cassirer, *The Philosophy of the Enlightenment** (1932, trans. 1951), which emphasizes the break with older ways of thinking accomplished by the eighteenth century. C. L. Becker's charming lectures, *The Heavenly City of the Eighteenth-Century Philosophers** (1932), emphasize the continuity with the past. G. R. Havens, *The Age of Ideas: From Reaction to Revolution in Eighteenth-Century France** (1955), is a sound study. On the idea of progress, besides Becker, see J. B. Bury, *The Idea of Progress** (1920, 1932); R. F. Jones, *Ancients and Moderns** (1936); and C. Frankel, *The Faith of Reason: The Idea of Progress in the French Enlightenment* (1948). C. R. Cragg, *Reason and Authority in the Eighteenth Century* (1964), is an excellent account of the Enlightenment on the English side of the Channel, and D. Mornet, *French Thought in the Eighteenth Century* (1929), of Enlightenment on the other. P. Gay, *The Enlightenment: An Interpretation** (1966–69), is an attempt to pull all aspects of the movement together. For the political thought of the *philosophes,* see K. Martin, *French Liberal Thought in the Eighteenth Century** (1929); and for the historical thought of Voltaire, Robertson, Hume, and Gibbon, see J. B. Black, *The Art of History* (1926). Two unfamiliar aspects of the Enlightenment are brought to light in R. Darnton, "The High Enlightenment and the Low-Life of Literature in Pre-Revolutionary France," *Past and Present,* no. 51 (1971), and *Mesmerism and the End of the Enlightenment* (1968).

22 Aristocracy and Empire, 1715–1789

The seventy-five years between the death of Louis XIV (1715) and the outbreak of the French Revolution (1789) have a character of their own. This was a period of stability and equilibrium. There were no religious wars and no social upheavals (except for an uprising of serfs in far-off Russia), and there appears to have been somewhat less social mobility than in the seventeenth century. Monarchy was the most prevalent form of government, with divine-right monarchy evolving into "enlightened despotism."

Closely examined, however, the governments of the European states in the eighteenth century, both monarchies and republics, are better described as "aristocracies." Everywhere landed or moneyed minorities controlled or strongly influenced the governments of Europe. The Whig nobles and merchants who dominated the English Parliament, the French nobles and lawyers who dominated the royal councils and the law courts of France after the death of Louis XIV, the Junkers who commanded the Prussian armies, the landed nobles who made a farce of the Polish Diet, the "service nobility" that ceased to serve any but its own interests after the reign of Peter the Great in Russia, the wealthy bourgeois who directly controlled the governments of the Dutch Republic and the German free cities—all were rich, well-born, and privileged, and thus fitted the eighteenth-century definition of aristocrats. Everywhere "aristocracy" was resurgent against absolute monarchy, and many of the gains of seventeenth-century monarchies were lost or compromised. Only where the monarch or the chief minister was a man of unusual ability was this revival of aristocratic influence turned to the benefit of the central government.

In this undeclared war between monarch and aristocrat a kind of compromise was generally reached. Eighteenth-century governments maintained an uneasy balance between centralization and decentralization, between absolute monarchy and aristocratic privilege. This might have been illogical, but strict adherence to basic principles had caused the bloody religious and civil wars of the last two centuries. Most men were glad to accept the structure of society and government as they found it after 1715. It was a glorious age to be alive in—if you were an "aristocrat." There was much abject poverty, injustice, and brutality in European society, but these could be forgotten if one centered one's attention on the brilliant "civilization" (the word first appeared in the 1770s) of the Paris salons or the London coffeehouses. To men who remembered the devastation of the Thirty Years' War or the fanaticism of Cromwell's "saints," social stability and political equilibrium were worth a fairly high price in injustice.

INTERNATIONAL RELATIONS

Equilibrium was also the rule in international relations. The defeat of Louis XIV's bid for a preponderance of power in Europe had been bloody and costly, and European statesmen were tacitly agreed that all such attempts to become "top dog" should be stopped at the outset. The balancing of power among the "great powers" of Europe—France, Britain, Austria, Prussia, and Russia (Spain, Holland, Sweden, Poland, and the Ottoman Empire could no longer qualify)—became the chief concern of diplomats.

The balance, of course, seldom remained steady for very long. Every country was constantly on the lookout for additional territory or for new colonies and trading opportunities abroad. In order to avoid large-scale wars like those needed to curb Louis XIV's ambitions, it became the custom for all the great powers to expect "compensation" whenever one of them was fortunate or daring enough to acquire new territory. This was hard on the weaker states, which were carved up to provide the "compensation," but it admittedly preserved the balance and often maintained the peace.

There were wars, and they were fairly frequent. But they were not so bloody or so exhausting as those of the seventeenth century. Generally they were "limited wars"—in two senses. First, they were limited in the numbers of persons who took part in them or were affected by them. Eighteenth-century armies were

Opposite: Frederick II of Prussia in 1778.

497

professional armies, often recruited or kidnaped from the dregs of society or composed of foreign mercenaries. Except in Russia, where serfs made up most of the army, there was no general conscription, and the civilian was usually little affected by wars. Warfare consisted of elaborate maneuvering by highly disciplined professional units rather than bloody mass combat. There was little pillaging, even in enemy territory, because it was bad business to devastate a territory that might be annexed.

Wars were limited also in their objectives. There were no wars of annihilation. The enemy of today might be the ally of tomorrow, and it was thought well not to defeat any power too thoroughly because that would disturb the balance. The reli-

gious hatreds of the seventeenth century had cooled, and the passions of revolutionary liberalism and nationalism had not yet sprung into flame. The statesmen and generals fought for comparatively definite and concrete political and economic objectives, not for ideologies. When the objectives were attained—or when it became clear that they could not be attained immediately—the statesmen made peace or arranged a truce. There was no need to fight through to unconditional surrender. In spite of cutthroat competition for "empire"—in the form of land, population, colonies, or trade—the monarchs, bureaucrats, and aristocrats of the eighteenth century felt themselves part of a common civilization. The competition was a jockeying for power

EUROPE IN 1715

among cousins rather than a fight for survival against deadly enemies.

The picture of a stable, well-balanced eighteenth-century society sketched here could of course be compared to Newton's picture of the universe—a beautifully stable order of perfectly balanced gravitational pushes and pulls in which every mass moved along discoverable lines of force. But this picture must not be exaggerated. The eighteenth century was also a dynamic age. Its precarious equilibrium was an equilibrium among rapidly expanding forces. Wealth and trade were increasing; something like a revolution in agriculture was in the making, and a revolution in industry had begun. European economy and diplomacy were rapidly becoming global rather than continental, and the struggle for empire was reaching the farthest corners of the earth. For the first time, battles fought in America, Africa, and Asia began to tip the balance of power in Europe. And in trying to keep the balance, each country accentuated its own particular sources of strength. England relied more and more on naval power and commerce, Prussia on its army and bureaucracy. Russia intensified its reliance on serfdom, while Austria made up for weakness in Germany by increasing its power in southeastern Europe. France, the one country that did not want to specialize, found itself coming out second-best in most fields—naval power, military power, and industrial growth. Its intellectual and cultural leadership masked, but did not remedy, these weaknesses. In short, differences in the bases of power among European nations increased rather than decreased during the period and made it harder to keep the balance. With growing political rivalry added to rapid social change, it can be seen that the eighteenth century was not all order and stability. It was pregnant with revolution as well.

The years from 1715 to 1789 may conveniently be divided into three periods of about twenty-five years each: (1) a generation of peace and prosperity, 1715–40; (2) a period of worldwide warfare, 1740–63; and (3) an interval of enlightened despotism, aristocratic resurgence, and revolutionary stirrings, 1763–89.

PEACE AND PROSPERITY 1715–40

After the peace settlements of 1713 in western Europe and of 1719 to 1721 in eastern Europe, both governments and peoples were weary of war. The age that followed was unheroic, unexciting, and corrupt, like many other postwar periods. But peace restored law and order, and order stimulated an enormous expansion of trade, particularly in western Europe.

Increase of Trade and Wealth

Seaborne commerce was the key to wealth in the eighteenth century. Thanks to the enterprise of their merchants and the technical skill of their mariners, the foreign trade of Britain and France increased about five times during the eighteenth century. In the case of Britain the sharpest increase was in colonial trade. This meant that Britain needed a

The Baron, caricature of a member of the French nobility (1785).

Engraving from a
seventeenth-century history
of the West Indies showing
the workings of a sugar
plantation.

larger merchant marine than its rivals
and forced the British to build the
strongest navy in the world to protect its
overseas trade. In the case of France the
greatest increase was in trade with other
European nations. In both cases the ac-
cumulation of wealth in the hands of the
upper classes was spectacular. For the
first time the wealth of Europe began to
eclipse the wealth of Asia. The two preceding centuries of exploration and establishment of overseas trading connections had begun to pay off handsomely
in material benefits. The dinner table of a
merchant of Liverpool, for instance, was
graced by sugar from the West Indies,
wine from Portugal, and tobacco from
Virginia. His wife might wear calico from
India in summer and furs from Canada
in winter. Their daughter might be married to the heir of a nobleman whose
capacious Georgian house had been built
on the combined profits from his land
and his mercantile investments.

But many of the commodities on
which this thriving trade was based were
derived from the labor of slaves or serfs.
Only African slaves could be forced to
do the kind of work required on the
sugar plantations of the West Indies, and
even they survived only about seven
years, on the average. There was an almost insatiable demand for black slaves
in the sugar islands, a demand that was
met largely by English slave traders, who
procured their victims from the petty
kings of the west coast of Africa, exchanged them for sugar in the West Indies, had the sugar converted into rum,
then used the rum to debauch native
rulers and village leaders and thus to
secure more slaves in Africa. The serfs
who toiled without recompense for their
noble landlords in the grain-producing
regions of eastern Europe were in much
the same position in the economic order
as the slaves of the West Indies. In short,
a large part of the European economy

was still based, as the economy of Greece and Rome had been, on servile labor.

There were signs in England, however, of the beginnings of revolutionary changes in both farming and industry. Eventually these changes were to result in an unprecedented expansion in the amount and variety of food, clothing, shelter, and luxuries that Europeans could produce. Historians speak of these changes as the "Agricultural Revolution" and the "Industrial Revolution," but these two revolutions picked up speed very slowly. For example, the first workable, though inefficient, steam engine was in use by 1700; the greatly improved Watts engine appeared three-quarters of a century later but was not widely used until after 1800. Since the results of the Agricultural and Industrial Revolutions were seen most clearly in the nineteenth century, they will be discussed in later chapters.

Mississippi and South Sea Bubbles

European commercial capitalism was still expanding its field of operations in the early eighteenth century. The period of peace after 1713 encouraged both private financial speculation and wildcat commercial ventures. The years 1719 and 1720 saw the first large-scale example of a typically modern phenomenon, a cycle of boom-and-bust, or, as contemporaries called it, a "bubble."

The wars of Louis XIV had burdened both the French and the English governments with large debts. When a Scottish promoter named John Law showed up at the court of France after the death of Louis XIV and offered to solve the government's financial troubles, he was given *carte blanche* to manage the French economy as he saw fit. He set up a bank to issue paper currency and organized a Mississippi Company to trade with France's colony in Louisiana. The company boldly took over the government's debt, accepting government bonds in payment for shares of its own stock. Then it promoted a boom in the price of its stock by spreading tall tales of its commercial prospects. When the price finally reached forty times its original

value, investors began to sell in order to cash in on their profits. Before long the price had plummeted, the bubble had burst, and Law had fled the country.

A similar episode occurred across the Channel in London. A South Sea Company had been organized to exploit the trade with the Spanish colonies provided for by the Peace of Utrecht. It too took over much of the government's debt, and it too deliberately promoted a boom in its own stock. In 1720, a few months after Law's failure, the South Sea bubble burst.

The collapse of the Mississippi and South Sea bubbles in 1719 and 1720 hampered the development of joint stock companies and ruined a good many individual investors. But the two companies had shown how to mobilize vast amounts of capital and how to find new sources of support for the public debt. Deliberate encouragement of speculation had tarnished both objectives, but the underlying commercial purposes of the two companies were essentially sound. When they were reorganized, both continued to make money for their investors for many years. French trade, particularly, was stimulated, although investors lost confidence in the French government. In contrast, the English government came to acknowledge the national debt as a public obligation and never again permitted private interests to assume responsibility for it, thus gaining the confidence of investors.

England Under Walpole

During the generation of peace that followed the death of Louis XIV, the English worked out some of their internal political problems. As had been determined by the Act of Settlement, the Elector of Hanover succeeded Anne as ruler of England in 1714. Compared with the Stuarts, the first two Hanoverian monarchs, George I (1714–27) and George II (1727–60), were colorless figures. Both were stupid men who spoke little or no English. They interfered constantly in minor details of government, but neither was capable of grasping the larger issues. As a result, the "inner cabinet" of ministers became more and more

George I of England (1714–27), and his signature. Medal by John Croker.

Caricature of George II drawn by a British officer about 1760.

responsible for policy decisions. Legally, the king was still free to choose his own ministers. Actually, he had to select men who could influence elections and control a majority in Parliament. These leading ministers had to meet frequently in order to concert policy. They began to force out of office colleagues who disagreed with the group's majority, and they usually accepted the leadership of the ablest or most powerful among them in presenting their policy to the king. These informal practices vaguely foreshadowed the "cabinet system" and "prime minister" of the nineteenth century.

Sir Robert Walpole (left), leader of the Whig government from 1721 to 1742, talking to the speaker of the House of Commons. Engraving after a painting by Hogarth.

Robert Walpole, a country squire who had family connections with both the landed and the commercial aristocracies, is generally considered the first prime minister in English history, though he would not have acknowledged the title. For some twenty years, from 1721 to 1742, he was the manager of the Whig party in Parliament and the leading minister in the government. The first two Hanoverians by necessity chose their ministers from Whigs, since the Tories were tainted by affection for the Stuarts and had little strength in Parliament.

Walpole was a good-natured, hardheaded politician who understood the landed and financial "interests" represented in Parliament and knew how to hold a parliamentary majority together by tact, persuasion, and, if necessary, bribery and corruption. The fact that he was addicted to hard drinking and off-color stories helped rather than hurt him in managing the Whig merchants and landed gentry who controlled Parliament and ran local government as justices of the peace. Walpole's motto was, "Let sleeping dogs lie." He took care never to stir up any issue, at home or abroad, that might arouse passion and conflict. In 1733, for instance, he proposed a sensible scheme for raising more revenue from excise taxes and less from customs duties in order to discourage smuggling and encourage legitimate trade. But when his scheme was met by a storm of irrational abuse ("No excise, no popery, no wooden shoes" was one slogan), he dropped it. So far as the colonies were concerned, he followed a policy of "salutary neglect," leaving them to grow in population and wealth by their own efforts. In foreign affairs he preserved the peace until 1739, when the London merchants and their spokesmen in Parliament forced him into a commercial war with Spain. Even then he tried to keep the war as limited as possible.

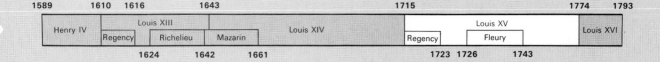
On the whole, Walpole's ministry was a fruitful one for England. Both England and its colonies prospered; the credit of the government was never better; and the ruling aristocracy of landed and commercial wealth governed with a loose rein. When Voltaire visited England from 1726 to 1729 he may have idealized English society and government somewhat. But there was without question more equality before the law in England, more personal freedom, more sense of public obligation in the ruling class, more security of property, and more widespread prosperity than anywhere else in Europe.

Louis XV and Cardinal Fleury

The generation of peace that brought strength to Britain brought weakness to France. Louis XIV's great-grandson Louis XV (1715–74) was a child of five when he came to the throne. The Regency that governed in his name for eight years had to make concessions to all the powerful elements in French society that had been kept in leash by the Sun King. The result was an aristocratic reaction in French government. Nobles began to reappear as policymakers on the royal councils, and the *Parlement* of Paris boldly reasserted its ancient claim to register and enforce royal legislation or not, as it saw fit. The French monarchy remained as absolute as ever in theory, but after Louis XIV there was no strong hand to make the theory work. French government became inefficient and inconstant. Aristocratic privilege exasperated the middle classes and in the long run made it impossible for the government to avoid financial insolvency.

For a time the decline was arrested by Cardinal Fleury, the leading minister from 1726 to 1743. Fleury had ability, but he was no Richelieu. He was past seventy when he came to power, and his policy,

much like Walpole's, was to preserve the peace, make cautious compromises, and avoid direct confrontation with the holders of power—in this case the nobility. He dissociated himself from the statesmanlike attempt of another minister to tax the nobility like everyone else, but he stabilized the currency, encouraged trade, and did all he could to make the old system of tax-farming work. His monarch was too debauched and incapable to set a more constructive course.

Fleury lost power in his last years, and when he died at the age of ninety, Louis XV decided that he would govern for himself without a prime minister. This simply meant that France now had a king who could neither govern himself nor let anyone else govern for him. Louis XV's best-known remark, "After me, the deluge," perfectly expressed his attitude. The aristocracy naturally took full advantage of this situation and greatly increased its influence. France remained the largest and potentially the most powerful nation in Europe. French trade and industry were growing at a rapid rate, but the government was run by royal mistresses and favorites (Mme. de Pompadour was the most prominent), and the French state could not make full use of its resources.

Declining Monarchies and Empires

Elsewhere in Europe, with few exceptions, monarchical institutions were in decline as they were in France during the generation after the Peace of Utrecht.

In Spain the Bourbon whom Louis XIV established on the throne, Philip V (1700–46), managed to curb the nobility somewhat and to encourage trade and industry. But the dry rot had eaten too deep into Spanish society and government to allow a real revival of the nation's greatness. Neither the Spanish

Arms of Louis XV, from Diderot's *Encyclopaedia*.

Maria Theresa of Austria with her husband, Emperor Francis I, and eleven of their children.
The future Emperor Joseph II stands in the right center. Painting by Meytens.

economy, nor the army and navy, nor the colonies made any significant gains.

Austria was an imperfectly united empire composed of three separate kingdoms (Austria, Bohemia, and Hungary) and two dependencies of quite different cultures and traditions (northern Italy and the southern Netherlands). The Habsburg Emperor Charles VI (1711–40) had to spend years in persuading his own subjects and foreign governments to accept a "Pragmatic Sanction" that provided that his daughter Maria Theresa (Charles had no sons) should succeed him as ruler of all his various lands. By the time of his death he had the agreement on paper of everyone concerned, but no one was sure just how long the agreement would be respected by greedy neighboring monarchs or restless Hungarian nobles.

Farther to the east, the Polish and Ottoman empires continued to decline. A desultory and trivial war over the succession to the Polish crown was fought between 1733 and 1738 by France and Spain against Austria and Russia. The Russian candidate for the throne won out, and all the losers were "compensated" by being given scraps of territory elsewhere—Spain in Naples and Sicily, for instance. At the same time Austria and Russia were once more at war with the Ottoman Turks. The Turks were never completely dominated by their neighbors, as were the Poles, but it was evident that neither state counted for much in the European power structure.

In the generation after Peter the Great's death in 1725 a series of palace revolutions placed the Russian crown successively on the heads of half a dozen children or incompetent women. German, particularly Prussian, influence was very strong at the court. As in France, the nobles managed to free themselves from many of the restrictions placed on them by earlier and stronger monarchs. The Russian nobles extended the power that Peter had given them over their own serfs but tried to renounce the obligation to serve the state that he had imposed on them in return. In Russia, as in Hungary and Prussia, the peasant sank deeper and deeper into serfdom during the eighteenth century, while the governments made one concession after another to the hereditary nobles in order to gain their favor. Until the accession of Catherine the Great in 1762 there was no strong hand at the helm of the Russian state, but Peter's work in raising his country to the position of a great power in European war and diplomacy proved to be permanent.

Frederick William I of Prussia

Probably the most successful ruler of his generation apart from Walpole—and for quite different reasons—was King Frederick William I of Brandenburg-Prussia (1713–40). While absolute monarchy seemed to be in decline elsewhere, this strange, uncouth, and furious man, who smoked tobacco and drank beer in Gargantuan quantities, continued the work of transforming one of the smallest and poorest states of Europe into a great military power. Following in the footsteps of the Great Elector, he centralized the administration in a so-called General Directory, pared civil expenditures to the bone, and worked his subordinates remorselessly, all with the object of building the best-disciplined and most formidable army in Europe. "Salvation is from the Lord," he remarked, "but everything else is my affair." When he was through he had increased the size of his army to over eighty thousand men, twice what it

Frederick William I, by Antoine Pesne.

505

had been under his father. But while Frederick William built the fourth largest and the most efficient army on the Continent, he drew back whenever he might have used it. He left his son a full treasury, an efficient civil bureaucracy, and a highly trained army—one that had not fought a battle in over a generation.

He despised his son, Frederick, for his unmilitary habits and his taste for reading Voltaire and playing the flute. On occasion he would break the flute, burn the books, and even have the young man publicly beaten. When Frederick finally tried to flee the country with a friend, his father had the friend beheaded before his son's eyes and put the young man to work in the bureaucracy. Strange to say, the treatment worked. Without losing his taste for literature and music, Frederick grew interested in administration and the army. He succeeded his father in 1740 as Frederick II (1740–86), better known to history as Frederick the Great.

WORLDWIDE WARFARE 1740–63

The peaceful generation just described was followed by a generation dominated by two wars, the War of the Austrian Succession (1740–48) and the Seven Years' War (1756–63), separated by a few years of intensive diplomacy. These wars grew out of two irreconcilable rivalries for power. One was the rivalry between the rising Hohenzollerns of Prussia and the more established Habsburgs of Austria for territory in central Europe. The other was the rivalry between Great Britain and France for trade and colonial empire in North America, the West Indies, Africa, and India. Twice these two rivalries became entangled with each other, although the partnerships changed between the wars. And in the final peace of 1763 England and Prussia gained at the expense of France and Austria.

The British Navy and the Prussian Army

These wars were to demonstrate that the most efficient fighting units in eighteenth-century Europe were the British navy and the Prussian army. The most obvious explanation of superiority in each case was the unrivaled excellence of the officers. But behind the two military arms were two sharply different societies and political systems, each well adapted to the particular sort of competition in which the nation found itself.

Great Britain had many advantages in the race for sea power. It was an island, safe from invasion by land, and therefore able to pour into ships the men and money that continental states had to pour into armies. Maritime enterprise was both profitable and patriotic; a seafaring career attracted enterprising younger sons of the nobility and gentry as well as yeomen and artisans. The reservoir of experienced sailors was larger in England than in France, its nearest rival, because the British had the largest merchant marine in the world. Finally, the government and the ruling classes recognized the importance of trade and sea power, and in spite of periods of neglect they supported naval construction and encouraged British shipping.

Britain's rival, France, had almost all the advantages England had—experienced sailors, a large merchant marine, warships superior in design even to the

Figures from recruiting signs for the Prussian army (1740).

British, and colonial bases overseas. But France had long land frontiers and a tradition of pushing those frontiers to the east and of intervening in the affairs of central Europe. This situation created an impossible dilemma. France could not be both the greatest land power and the greatest sea power, and if the army was favored, as it usually was, then the navy suffered.

The Prussian army was the creation of the Hohenzollerns, who had shaped a society and designed a state to support it. The Prussian bureaucracy and fiscal system had grown out of institutions devised to provide direct support to the army. The Junkers had been taught that their calling was to serve the king, in the army by preference, in the civil service if necessary. In return for their service they were given wide powers over the serfs who supported them. Enterprising members of the small middle class were also enlisted into the civil service, and serfs were conscripted when needed into the army. The proverbial discipline of the Prussian army pervaded to some degree both the society and the government. In England, central government by Parliament, local government by amateurs, and a considerable amount of freedom proved to be a good formula for producing sea power. In Prussia, centralized professional administration with an absolute monarch leading a disciplined aristocracy proved to be a successful formula for producing land power.

The War of the Austrian Succession, 1740–48

In 1740 Maria Theresa, a beautiful but inexperienced young woman, succeeded her father in the Habsburg dominions, to which her right of succession had been guaranteed by the Pragmatic Sanction. Frederick II of Prussia almost immediately threw his army into Silesia, one of her richest provinces, on the northeastern frontier of Bohemia. Frederick had published an anonymous little book against the immorality of Machiavelli, but he had learned some of the Florentine's precepts well. Silesia, with its million inhabitants, its linen industry, and its iron ore, would finally make Brandenburg-Prussia a great power. Both Maria Theresa and the European powers were caught off guard. Frederick seized what he needed and spent the next twenty years defending his gain.

For a time it was not too difficult. Frederick's boldfaced aggression encouraged every enemy of the Habsburgs to join in the attack: Bavaria, Spain, and finally France. Strangely enough, Hungary, which resented Habsburg rule, proved to be Maria Theresa's salvation. When she went to Budapest with her infant son and made an emotional appeal to the Hungarian Parliament, the chivalrous nobility rose tumultuously to her support. During the wars that followed, an able minister, Count Haugwitz, centralized the Habsburg administration and reorganized the army. Austria, a helpless victim state in 1740, was able to revive and become a formidable antagonist to the king of Prussia. Frederick's armies fought brilliantly, however, and the combined pressure of France, Bavaria, and Prussia—shaky though the alliance was—proved to be too much for Maria Theresa to overcome. In 1748, at Aix-la-Chapelle, she agreed to a peace treaty that left Silesia in Frederick's hands.

Meanwhile the Anglo-French rivalry had also broken out into war. When war began between England and Spain in 1739, it was only a question of time before France would be drawn in. France and Spain cooperated closely in the eighteenth century. Both had Bourbon rulers, and France had a large economic stake in the Spanish Empire since France supplied the Spanish colonies with most of their manufactured goods. English and French interests clashed in America and in India. In North America the English felt threatened by the French military hold on Canada and Louisiana, while the French felt threatened by the pressure of the English colonies expanding northward and westward. In the West Indies there was rivalry over the sugar islands. In India the death of the last strong Mughal emperor in 1707 had led to the collapse of all central administration. Both the French and the British East India companies were trying to influence native principalities, particularly around Madras and Pondicherry. From Canada

to the Carnatic Coast of India uneasy Frenchmen and Englishmen were ready to fly to arms.

In 1744 France declared war on Great Britain, and immediately the war in Europe and the war overseas merged into one. In 1745 the American colonists captured Louisbourg in Canada, and in 1746 the French seized Madras. Nothing decisive came of the conflict, however, because the English could not yet make up their minds whether to concentrate their efforts on a land war on the Continent against France or on the war overseas. The former policy was denounced by the "Patriots" in Parliament as "Hanoverianism"—that is, a pandering to the interests of the monarch, George II, who was Elector of Hanover in Germany. The English navy defeated the French; the French army defeated the English on the Continent; but neither side pressed its successes very far, either on sea or on land. A typical "limited" war, the War of the Austrian Succession ended in a stalemate so far as Britain and France were concerned. The French gave up their conquest of Madras, and the English government, much to the disgust of the American colonists, gave back Louisbourg. The French came out of the war with no gains over either Austria or England. The English came out of it with a clearer sense of how they should fight their next war with France.

The Diplomatic Revolution

England had fought in the War of the Austrian Succession in loose agreement with its old ally, Austria. France had fought in a still looser alliance with Prussia (Frederick deserted his ally twice to make truces with Austria). During the years between 1748 and 1756, a "diplomatic revolution" took place in which the chief antagonists in the first general war of mid-century changed partners in preparation for the second. This "revolution" illustrates nicely the main characteristics of eighteenth-century diplomacy.

The chief instigator of the "revolution" was Count Kaunitz, the Austrian chancellor. Burning with desire to crush Frederick and recover Silesia, he decided that the only practical way was to heal the ancient antagonism between Bourbons and Habsburgs and to gain the support of France—and if possible of Russia as well—in a new war against Prussia. Prussia, he was sure, could not last long against the three strongest powers on the Continent. Kaunitz worked carefully to bring the mistress of Louis XV, Mme. de Pompadour, around to his side, but it was a chain of calculations and miscalculations by other statesmen that finally persuaded France to agree to the alliance. The English ministry became worried about whether Austria had the will and ability to help England defend Hanover against France. Prussia was obviously better placed to defend Hanover, but when Frederick agreed to do so in return for British subsidies, the French were irritated. Since Frederick had made an agreement with France's ancient enemy, England, the French were now ready to reach an understanding with Frederick's enemy, Austria. Soon a coalition of France, Austria, and Russia was arranged, and it looked as if Prussia's situation was hopeless. Frederick saw that his only chance was to catch his enemies off guard, and, characteristically, he started the war with an offensive in 1756, almost a year earlier than his opponents had planned.

Conflict Overseas

War had already broken out between the British and the French overseas. In India, Joseph Dupleix had been trying since 1749 to make the French East India Company a political as well as a commercial power. By dominating native states, he hoped to increase the company's revenue and hamper British trade. The English East India Company soon became alarmed, and there were some armed clashes in which Dupleix's forces were defeated. In 1754 the company directors, afraid that Dupleix was leading them into serious conflict with the British, recalled him to France. Ironically, his idea of increasing the company's revenue through domination of native states was adopted by the British East India Company under its brilliant local leader, Robert Clive, and became the foundation of British territorial rule in India.

The situation in America was even more tense than in India. The French in Canada had used the interval of peace to build a chain of forts from the St. Lawrence down the Ohio to the Mississippi, and the British government had countered by sending ships and troops to the American colonies. The time was approaching when the two expanding empires of the North American continent were going to clash, and there were now perhaps a million and a half British subjects (including slaves) in North America and only about sixty thousand French—the ratio had grown to 25 to 1. British troops and colonists began to strike at the French forts. An attempt to capture Fort Duquesne, the most important link in the chain (on the site of modern Pittsburgh), was disastrously defeated in

Bengal miniature of about 1760 showing a British East India Company employee adapting to his Indian environment.

1755, and England and France were at war.

So in 1756 Europe was once more deep in conflict—this time France, Austria, and Russia against England and Prussia. The largest navy in the world had little to fear, but the odds were very great against the best army in Europe. If Prussia were defeated and partitioned, as seemed likely, any British gains overseas might well be wiped out at the peace conference. The Anglo-French and the Austro-Prussian rivalries had become inextricably mingled.

The Seven Years' War*
1756–63

England made no headway in the war until the summer of 1757, when William Pitt became virtual prime minister. Pitt, one of Britain's greatest war ministers, shrewdly focused the nation's war efforts on conquests overseas. His policy repre-

*This war, in its American phase, is known as the French and Indian War.

sented the commercial aims of the London business community, but it also appealed to the pride of the ordinary Englishman in the navy and the growing colonial empire. Pitt concentrated power in his own hands, and his energy and his enthusiasm stimulated his subordinates to unheard-of efforts. The "year of miracles" (1759) demonstrated Pitt's remarkable ability to direct a complex series of operations and to choose first-rate commanders. In this one year Quebec fell, Guadaloupe was taken, French military power in India was broken, and the French fleet was crushed off Quiberon Bay. England's control of the seas enabled it to hold both Canada and India, a classic example of the strategic importance of sea power.

While Britain was destroying the French Empire abroad, Prussia was fighting for its life on the Continent. England's "year of miracles" was a year of near disaster for Prussia. Its army was badly defeated by the Russians at Kunersdorf in 1759; the Prussians now needed a miracle just to survive. Only

View of the taking of Quebec by British forces in 1759. This eighteenth-century engraving is quite accurate in its depiction of military positions.

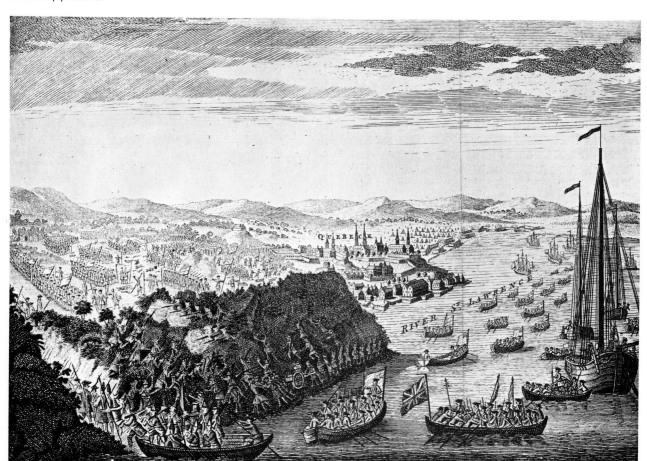

the divisions among his enemies allowed Frederick to prolong the war. Kaunitz had not promised enough of the spoils to France and Russia to stimulate an all-out effort from either country. Pitt's subsidies to German forces were just enough to pin the French down in bloody fighting in Westphalia. The war was unpopular in France and was putting a heavy strain on the already shaky French financial system. Austrian armies were poorly led, and the Austrian government was almost as afraid of the Russian army in the Oder Valley as it was of the Prussian. So Frederick held on, though his resources were almost exhausted, until the "Hohenzollern miracle" occurred. Empress Elizabeth of Russia died in 1762 and was succeeded by her nephew, Peter III, a warm admirer of the king of Prussia. Peter promptly withdrew from the war, and Austria now had only a crippled and sulky France as a major ally. With no hope of winning a decisive victory, Maria Theresa decided to end the war. Peace was made in 1763, leaving Prussia in permanent possession of Silesia. To have preserved the status quo was a moral victory for Frederick. Prussia had clearly established itself as one of the great powers.

The death of an empress saved Frederick the Great from possible defeat. The death of a king indirectly robbed Britain of some of the fruits of victory. When George III succeeded his grandfather in 1760 he wished to prove himself thoroughly English, unlike the first two Georges. This meant withdrawing from all involvement in German affairs, contrary to Pitt's advice. By October 1761, Pitt had been forced out of office. Lord Bute, George's Scottish favorite, deserted Frederick II and set himself to get peace with France at almost any price.

The Peace of Paris, 1763

The peace finally signed at Paris in January 1763 was overwhelmingly favorable to Great Britain, but it was not so severe on the French as Pitt would have wished. France received back from its conqueror most of its purely economic stakes around the world: trading posts in India, slave stations in West Africa, the rich sugar islands in the West Indies, and fishing rights off Canada, together with two tiny islands off Newfoundland, St. Pierre and Miquelon. But in India and in North America the new colonial system required control of large territories to supply the trading posts. Sugar islands could produce great wealth in a few square miles, and the French were happy to retain their possessions in the Caribbean. But in the long run it was the continents that counted. With the collapse of its political and military power in India and on the North American continent, the first French colonial empire was permanently broken. France agreed to maintain no more troops in India and to recognize the native rulers whom the British had set up. France ceded the whole of Canada and everything east of the Mississippi to Britain and handed over Louisiana west of the Mississippi to Spain. Henceforth the British had no serious competitors in North America.

"ENLIGHTENED" DESPOTISM 1763–89

During the twenty-five years that followed the Peace of Paris, the "enlightened" ideas and practices of a number of European monarchs fired the imagination of educated men. The ancient institution of monarchy seemed to take a new lease on life. It looked as if the major ideas of the Enlightenment—reason, natural law, happiness, progress, liberty—were filtering through to the rulers. The later *philosophes* had questioned aristocratic and ecclesiastical privilege, unequal taxation, and the unfair treatment of certain social classes. Was it reasonable? Was it natural? These were the fashionable questions in "enlightened" quarters, and some of the crowned heads of Europe became troubled by them. Further, the mid-century wars had left almost every European state in need of reform and reconstruction. Law and order had to be restored, trade revived, and government treasuries refilled. So the practical needs of a postwar era, added to the ferment of new ideas, produced what was known as "enlightened despotism."

This apparently new kind of monarchy was in many ways a revival of older monarchical ideas, and a reaction against the power that the aristocracy had gained in the eighteenth century. In rooting out irrational customs and vested interests, enlightened despots could curb the power of the nobility and the clergy and attack local and provincial privileges just as monarchs before them had been doing for several centuries. The difference was in the way the enlightened despots justified what they did. They talked little about divine right or hereditary title and a great deal about following reason and serving the public. Frederick the Great called himself "merely the first servant of the state," liable at any moment to render an account of his service to his subjects. But this did not mean that he or any other monarch felt he was really responsible to his people. Monarchs might be "enlightened," but they were still "despots." As one contemporary economist observed, "Whenever old disorders have been eradicated speedily and with success, it will be seen that it was the work of a single enlightened person against many private interests." *

* Quoted in R. R. Palmer, *The Age of the Democratic Revolution* (Princeton, N. J.: Princeton University Press, 1959–64), p. 105.

Catherine the Great, on a gold medal struck to celebrate her accession as empress of Russia.

Few of the rulers who dominated the political horizon in the later eighteenth century measured up to the ideal of an enlightened despot. George III of England (1760–1820) did not even pretend to be "enlightened," and the English would not have been pleased if he had; they were satisfied with the status quo. Louis XV of France (1715–74) was hardly enlightened in any sense of the word, although some of his policies were. Among the minor monarchs, Gustavus III of Sweden (1771–92) and Charles III of Spain (1759–88) had good claims to the title, but the three rulers whom the *philosophes* cited most often as enlightened despots were Catherine the Great of Russia, Frederick the Great of Prussia, and Joseph II of Austria.

Catherine the Great of Russia

Catherine II (1762–96) was a German princess who became empress of Russia through a conspiracy of her friends that led to the assassination of her husband, Tsar Peter III (1762). Uneasily conscious of being a usurper, she tried to make Russia great in an effort to endear herself to her people. She had to make concessions to preserve the support of the nobility, including lavish gifts to a long succession of lovers whom she used as her chief officers of state. She read the books of the French *philosophes*, corresponded with Voltaire, persuaded Diderot to visit her court, and made much of her "enlightenment" for publicity purposes. In 1767 she excited her admirers by summoning a legislative commission to codify the laws of Russia and to give the nation a sort of constitution. The representatives were elected by every class in the land except serfs, and they came armed with statements of grievances. Very little came out of their deliberations, however: some slight religious toleration and some limitation of torture in legal proceedings. The members went home in 1768, and the Russian government was to make no further attempt to summon a representative assembly until the twentieth century.

The net result, in fact, of Catherine's reign was not enlightened government but the strengthening of the nobility and the extension of serfdom. From 1773 to

1775 a vast and dangerous uprising of serfs broke out in the valley of the Volga, led by a Cossack named Pugachev. The revolt was directed at the local landlords and officials; and after it was broken and Pugachev had been brought to Moscow in an iron cage to be drawn and quartered, it was these landlords and officials who profited by the reaction. Peter the Great's idea of a service nobility had long been weakening. In 1785 Catherine freed the nobles from both military service and taxation and gave them absolute control over the serfs on their estates. Further, she gave away large tracts of crown land to noble favorites, thus subjecting hordes of relatively free peasants on these estates to serfdom. At the end of her reign it has been estimated that 34 million out of a population of 36 million Russians were in a state of serfdom—a state that was not very different from that of slaves in the American colonies. The net result of Catherine's reign was to encourage the forces that were making Russia a state built on slavery.

Catherine was called "the Great" not because of her enlightenment—if she had any—but because of her conquests. Peter the Great had pushed his possessions out to the Baltic Sea in the northwest at the expense of Sweden. Catherine expanded the frontiers of her state many hundreds of miles to the west and south at the expense of Poland and the Ottoman Empire. Russians were concerned about the large Orthodox minority in Catholic Poland. Furthermore, during a large part of the seventeenth century, the Poles had threatened Moscow, and the Polish frontier was still only about two hundred miles from the old Russian capital when Catherine came to the throne. The ancient Russian thirst for vengeance on the Poles was to be richly satisfied after 1763 when Catherine put one of her favorites, Stanislaus Poniatowski, on the Polish throne. From that time on, Russia and Prussia made it their business to see that the anarchy and confusion of Polish politics continued and that any suggestion of constitutional reform or revival of the national spirit was snuffed out.

The Partitions of Poland

In 1772 Catherine and Frederick the Great arranged the first partition of Po-

RUSSIA'S GROWTH IN EUROPE 1462–1796

land. Frederick took West Prussia and so joined Prussia to Brandenburg territorially for the first time. Catherine took a generous slice of northeastern Poland. To preserve the balance of power they thought it wise to give Maria Theresa a share of the loot (Galicia). The pious empress hung back at first, but Frederick remarked that the more she wept for Poland, the more she took. This first partition shocked the Poles into a nationalistic revival. King Stanislaus himself was swept along by the patriotic fervor and forgot that he owed his throne to Catherine. In 1791 after the outbreak of the French Revolution, a remarkable reform constitution was instituted setting up a strong monarchy and abolishing the *liberum veto*. Catherine's answer was swift and ruthless. Early in 1792 she called off the war she was fighting against the Turks, rushed an army into Poland, abolished the new constitution, restored the old anarchy, and arranged a second partition of Polish territory in 1793, this time with Prussia alone.

These events were followed by a

THE PARTITIONS OF POLAND

genuinely popular uprising in what was left of Poland, led by a Pole who had fought for the Americans in their revolution, Thaddeus Kosciuszko. The end was inevitable. Kosciuszko was captured by the Russians, the revolt collapsed, and Stanislaus was forced to abdicate. The Kingdom of Poland was wiped off the map in a third partition in 1795 among Russia, Prussia, and Austria. In the three partitions, Russia took almost two-thirds of the original Polish territory, and Prussia and Austria divided the remainder.

Catherine's successes against the crumbling Ottoman Empire were almost as decisive. In a series of wars running from 1768 to 1792 Catherine gained the Crimea and most of the northern shore of the Black Sea. The Treaty of Kuchuk Kainarji (1774) also gave Russia vague rights to protect Orthodox Christians in the Ottoman Empire—rights that were to be used later as excuses for Russian intervention in Turkish affairs. The Ottoman Empire escaped the fate of Poland because it was stronger internally and because its two chief enemies, Austria and Russia, were jealous of each other. But when Catherine died in 1796 there seemed to be little obstacle to a Russian advance to Constantinople and the Mediterranean.

Frederick the Great of Prussia

Frederick II of Prussia (1740–86) had a somewhat better claim than Catherine to be considered "enlightened." He had a first-rate mind and a real grasp of what the *philosophes* were talking about. He invited Voltaire to Potsdam, and although they soon fell to quarreling over the merits of Frederick's poetry, they both agreed that it was the job of a king to combat ignorance and superstition among his people, to enhance their wel-

Maria Theresa on the First Partition of Poland

This letter to a diplomat is doubtless sincere, but as Frederick the Great said, "Maria Theresa wept, but she kept on taking."

This unfortunate partition of Poland is costing me ten years of my life. . . . How many times have I refused to agree to it! But disaster after disaster heaped upon us by the Turks, misery, famine and pestilence at home, no hope of assistance from either France or England, and the prospect of being left isolated and threatened with war both by Prussia and Russia—it was all these considerations that finally forced me to accept that unhappy proposal which will remain a blot on my reign. God grant that I be not held responsible for it in the other world! I confess that I cannot keep from talking about this affair. I have taken it so to heart that it poisons and embitters all my days.

This abbreviated version of the letter is from *Readings in Western Civilization,* ed. by Paul L. Hughes and Robert F. Fries (Paterson, N.J.: Littlefield, Adams, 1960), p. 134.

fare, and to promote religious toleration. Frederick welcomed religious exiles of all sorts—even Jesuits expelled from France and Spain. He treated the Jews badly, but his general tolerance in religion was the best evidence of his enlightenment. He was a mercantilist in his economic policies; he sought national self-sufficiency and used protective tariffs to foster infant industries. Interested in the new scientific agriculture, he tried to encourage new methods by bringing foreign farmers to his kingdom. Some three hundred thousand immigrants entered Prussia during his reign. Finally, he rationalized and simplified the Prussian laws and court procedures—another typical objective of enlightened despotism.

In some respects, however, Frederick was not at all enlightened, though he was always a despot. He believed firmly in social rank and privilege. The Junkers served him well as officers in his army, and the army was the most important organ of the state. In return for their services, he allowed the nobles to keep full control over the peasants on their estates. He strictly defined the ranks of noble, bourgeois, and peasant and made it difficult if not impossible for a man to move from one class to another. Prussian serfs were not so badly off as Russian and Polish serfs, but those who lived on private estates were almost as much at their lord's mercy. Frederick did something to improve the lot of serfs on his own estates, but otherwise he showed no taste for social reform.

In some respects the discipline, the machinelike efficiency, and the strict centralization of power in the Prussian monarchy were the results of a long Hohenzollern tradition, quite unrelated to the influence of the Enlightenment. The powerful state that Frederick II erected in twenty-three years of war (1740–63) and consolidated in twenty-three years of peace (1763–86) was the most striking political achievement of his time. But twenty years after the strong hand of the despot was removed, Prussia proved to be an easy victim for Napoleon. The weakness of enlightened despotism, as well as its strength, lay in the fact that everything depended on the monarch.

Joseph II of Austria

The monarch with the best claim to be called an enlightened despot was Joseph II of Austria. Although he professed contempt for the *philosophes*, he

THE GROWTH OF BRANDENBURG-PRUSSIA   1640–1795

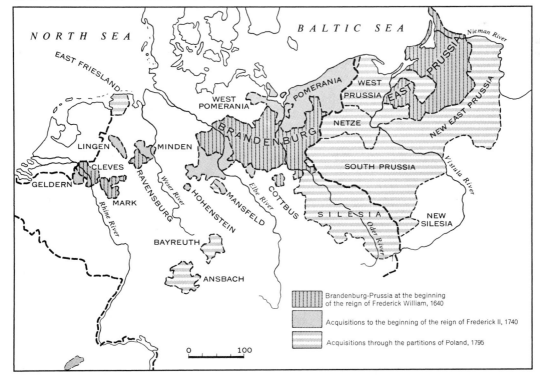

was more thoroughly converted to the main tenets of the Enlightenment than any of his fellow monarchs. And he was probably more sincerely devoted to his people's welfare than any of the others.

Frederick II's seizure of Silesia in 1740 was the signal for a reorganization of the Habsburg Empire. During Maria Theresa's long reign (1740–80) an imperial bureaucracy was developed that was able to centralize in Vienna the administration of all the divisions of the empire except Hungary. All parts of the empire but Hungary were brought into a tariff union in 1775. The nobles were compelled to assume at least some of the burden of taxation. Maria Theresa did more for the serfs in her kingdom than any other ruler

of her time by limiting the amount of labor they owed their lords and by curbing the lords' power to abuse them. In much of this she was aided and abetted by her son, Joseph, who became emperor and coregent after the death of her husband in 1765. But Joseph wished to move much further and faster than his mother. Until her death in 1780 he chafed under the compromises and conservatism that characterized Maria Theresa's policies, particularly in religion.

In the ten years of Joseph II's own rule (1780–90), literally thousands of decrees poured out from the imperial chancellery in Vienna. He proclaimed religious toleration for all Christians and Jews. He dissolved monasteries devoted solely to contemplation and turned their revenues over to the hospitals that were to make Vienna the medical center of Europe in the next century. He applied a system of equal taxation in proportion to income to everyone in the Habsburg dominions, regardless of rank or nationality. He imposed one language for official business, German, on all parts of the empire, including Belgium, Italy, and Hungary. Most significant of all, Joseph abolished serfdom. Early in his reign he issued a number of decrees that gave all serfs in the Habsburg dominions personal freedom—freedom to leave the land, to marry whom they pleased, to choose any job they liked. This much of Joseph's work was permanent. In later decrees he tried to relieve peasants who stayed on the land of all forced labor and to turn them into property-owners, but these decrees were repealed by his successors.

Joseph II made more and more enemies by his policy of centralization and reform: the clergy, the landed nobility, non-German parts of his empire like Hungary, even peasants who failed to understand his intentions. In 1789, when revolution broke out in France, peasants in the Austrian Empire began to plunder and to murder landlords to gain the rights Joseph had held out to them. In 1790 both Belgium and Hungary were in revolt against his rule. The Church was bitterly hostile to him. Joseph felt lonely and deserted. "I am the only one holding to the true course," he wrote his brother

Joseph II, an Enlightened Despot

The following two extracts show both sides of enlightened despotism. Joseph wanted to reform the state, but he could do so only by autocratic methods.

I have not confined myself simply to issuing orders; I have expounded and explained them. With enlightenment I have sought to weaken and with arguments I have sought to overcome the abuses which had arisen out of prejudice and deeply rooted customs. I have sought to imbue every official of the state with the love I myself feel for the wellbeing of the whole. . . .

The good of the state can be understood only in general terms, only in terms of the greatest number. Similarly, all the provinces of the monarchy constitute one whole and therefore can have only one aim. It is necessary therefore that there should be an end to all the prejudices and all the jealousies between provinces [and] all races which have caused so much fruitless bickering. [Circular letter of Joseph II, 1783.]

◆ ◆ ◆

Unity and the end of prejudices, however, were to be achieved by dictates of the monarch. A common language was needed; Joseph II determined what it should be.

The German language is the universal tongue of my empire. I am the emperor of Germany. The states which I possess are provinces that form only one body—the state of which I am the head. If the kingdom of Hungary were the most important of my possessions, I would not hesitate to impose its language on the other countries. [Letter to a Hungarian noble, 1783.]

From T. C. W. Blanning, *Joseph II and Enlightened Despotism* (London: Longman Group, 1970), pp. 131–32; from Louis Léger, *Histoire de l'Autriche Hongrie* (Paris, 1879), p. 373.

Leopold, "and I am left to labor alone. . . . I am without any assistance whatsoever." Worn out, he died in 1790, choosing as his own epitaph: "Here lies Joseph II, who was unfortunate in everything that he undertook."

It is clear why Joseph II has been called "the revolutionary Emperor." Like Peter the Great he had shown what a single determined will could accomplish in the face of stubborn private interests. Unlike Peter, he had been guided by the principles of reason, tolerance, and humanitarianism. But Joseph was a revolutionist without a party. He had to depend on an unimaginative bureaucracy and on the secret police that he found it necessary to set up. Enlightened despotism in his hands might have formed a bridge between divine-right monarchy and democratic revolution. But it also suggested that permanent revolution demanded a broader base of popular understanding and support than he had been able to command.

FRANCE, ENGLAND, AND THE AMERICAN REVOLUTION 1763–89

France and Great Britain were the centers of the Enlightenment, but neither had an enlightened despot as monarch. Perhaps as a result (such large generalizations are very difficult to prove), each suffered a revolution from below. The American colonists won their independence from England in the name of reason and natural rights, and the French bourgeoisie, fired by the same ideals, destroyed aristocratic privilege in France.

Abortive Revolution from Above in France

When the Seven Years' War ended in 1763, both the French and the British governments needed more revenue to carry the burden of their war debts and to meet the rising costs of administration. Louis XV proposed to continue a war tax that fell on nobles and commoners alike and to institute a new tax on officeholders. It was a statesmanlike proposal, but Louis' program was greeted by a storm of

opposition from nobles and wealthy bourgeois alike. The *parlements* resisted the new taxes on the ground that they went against the "fundamental laws" of the kingdom and the "natural rights" of Frenchmen. Louis answered by abolishing the *parlements* and instituting a new system of law courts. It looked like a minor "enlightened" revolution, but it did not last. Louis XV died in 1774, and his son, Louis XVI, was neither strong enough nor determined enough to continue the fight against privilege. The old *parlements* were restored, the new taxes were dropped, and the financial problem was passed on to more cautious ministers. In the end, Louis XV's abortive reforms resulted in a further aristocratic reaction. After 1774 the nobility and the *parlements* came back so strongly from their temporary defeat that the Bourbon monarchy became in effect their prisoner.

The Revolt of the British American Colonies

The political and social situation was different in England, but the course of events was somewhat similar. A reasonable attempt by the government to raise new revenue was met by a storm of opposition in the American colonies. As a result, the attitude of the English governing classes stiffened. Concessions either to the colonists abroad or to reformers at home became impossible, and an irreconcilable conflict broke out that ultimately split the British Empire.

For nearly half a century before the Seven Years' War the policy of the British government toward its American colonies, as we have seen, had been one of "salutary neglect." For all practical purposes, the thirteen colonies governed themselves. Governors were appointed by the ministry in London, but their salaries were paid by colonial legislatures that were in fact quite independent of the British Parliament. These legislatures were also elected more democratically than Parliament or than almost any other representative body in Europe. Before 1763 Parliament never tried to tax the colonies. It did impose customs duties on colonial trade, but the intent of these levies was not to raise revenue but to force trade to flow toward the mother country.

The Seven Years' War, by eliminating French military power from North America, made the colonists feel more confident and less dependent on Great Britain for protection. At the same time it induced Parliament to tax the colonies in order that they might carry a fair share of the financial burden of imperial defense. The colonists had not done much of the actual fighting against the French. English troops had carried the brunt of the war, and after its close it was English troops that had to put down an Indian uprising under the Ottowa chief Pontiac across the Alleghenies. The taxes paid by the average American colonist were less than one-twenty-fifth of those paid by an Englishman. It seemed only fair to ask British Americans to carry some of the cost of maintaining English troops in North America.

In March 1765 Parliament imposed a stamp tax on paper of all sorts, including legal documents, commercial agreements, and newspapers. Familiar to Europeans as such a tax was, it aroused furious opposition in America among lawyers, merchants, and editors—the most articulate groups. A congress of delegates from nine of the colonies urged "that no taxes be imposed on them but with their own consent," and went on to argue that there was no practical way for the British Parliament to get American "consent" to any taxation. A year after its passage, Parliament repealed the Stamp Act but at the same time declared that crown and Parliament had the right to tax the colonies if they wished to. In 1767 Parliament returned to the attack with an act imposing duties on imports into the colonies of tea, paper, paint, lead, and glass. This was met by a determined colonial boycott, and in 1770 all the duties but those on tea were withdrawn.

Up to this point the colonists had shown little appreciation of the financial and military problems of the Empire, and Parliament had shown little appreciation of the factors that made the colonists doubt or fear its authority. But so far there had been no irrevocable break. Beginning in 1773, however, matters came to a head. In that year Parliament took over political responsibility in India from the East India Company and set up a Governor General, thus founding British rule in India. In order to compensate the company for its loss of political power, it was allowed to sell its surplus tea directly to American retailers. This move would presumably lower prices, increase sales, and thus increase in turn the revenue from the tea duty. The idea that the British government might get more in taxes from the colonies so infuriated a radical minority in Massachusetts that a party of Bostonians disguised as native Indians boarded three East Indiamen in Boston harbor in December 1773 and dumped thousands of pounds' worth of tea into the water. Parliament reacted with a violence out of all proportion to the incident. The port of Boston was closed, and

George Washington at Princeton. Portrait by Charles Willson Peale.

the Massachusetts legislature was deprived of much of its power (1774). This reaction drove the twelve other colonies to rally behind Massachusetts out of fear for their own charters.

To make matters worse, an otherwise statesmanlike measure, the Quebec Act of 1774, was passed at a moment when it appeared to be a further attack on the English-speaking colonies by Parliament. The act guaranteed the preservation of the French language and the Catholic religion in Canada and defined Canada as including all territory north of the Ohio River and west of the Allegheny Mountains. Settlement beyond the mountains was forbidden, an act that annoyed both rich speculators and poor pioneers. By now the breach was irreparable. To George III, to a large majority in Parliament, and probably to a majority of Englishmen, the American colonists had proved to be thoroughly irresponsible rebels who must be taught a lesson. To a majority of the colonists, the policy of Parliament was leading directly to unbearable tyranny—the kind of tyranny that they now felt it had been their main purpose to escape when they had originally emigrated to America. Fighting broke out at Lexington and Concord in 1775. A Continental Congress was summoned to meet in Philadelphia, and on July 4, 1776, the colonies formally declared their independence of king and Parliament in a declaration whose words rang like a tocsin summoning the people to rebellion throughout the Old World.

The American War of Independence

The American War of Independence was in a certain sense a civil war within the British dominions on both sides of the Atlantic. The colonists had friends in England, and the Irish sympathized with American grievances. The Whig faction to which Edmund Burke belonged tried in vain to induce George III and his prime minister, Lord North (1770–82), to follow a more moderate policy. A group of true "radicals," inspired by a rather unlovable champion of freedom of speech and parliamentary reform named John Wilkes, attacked the king's influence in Parliament, urged the publication of Parliamentary debates, and agitated for more democracy in the election of members. These radicals were too small a minority to carry any weight, but their political faith was that of the Declaration of Independence: that government must be by consent of the governed. Conversely, there were "Tories" in the colonies who agreed with Parliament and deplored the breach with England. In all, sixty thousand of them were to emigrate to Canada, never to return.

The War of Independence (1775–83) was won by the American colonists with French help. Following the principles of balance of power, France wanted compensation for the loss of Canada by depriving Britain of its American colonies. French supplies before the battle of Sar-

George III of England.

atoga (1777) and French troops and ships after the battle were of inestimable help to General Washington in his struggle to wear down the British forces in the colonies. In the peace treaty of 1783 the thirteen colonies gained their independence and won title to all the land east of the Mississippi, north of Florida, and south of the Great Lakes.

During the war most of the colonies had summoned conventions and drafted written constitutions with bills of rights to form the basis of their new governments. In 1787 a constitutional convention of delegates from all the colonies met in Philadelphia and drafted a constitution that bound the colonies in a federal union. This union was so successful that in mid-twentieth century the government founded on it could boast the longest continuous political tradition of any in the world except the British. In the same year, in the Northwest Ordinance, the colonists decided momentously to extend the principles for which they had fought to their still unsettled western territories. When these territories became populated, they would become not colonies or dependencies but "states," equal in status to the thirteen original members of the union.

The Significance of the American Revolution

The success of the American Revolution had profound effects on Europe and eventually on other parts of the world.

As the liberals in Europe saw it, a people had taken its destiny into its own hands, had revolted against its established rulers, and had set up a government and governors of its own choosing. It had gained its liberty without falling into license. John Locke's ideas—natural equality, unalienable rights, government by consent of the governed, and the ultimate right of revolution—had been vindicated. Montesquieu's theory of a separation of powers had been written into both state and federal constitutions across the Atlantic. The constitutional conventions of the former British colonies appeared to demonstrate that a people could create a society and a government by formal contract. Furthermore, events in America seemed to demonstrate that smaller political units could be federated into a larger union without recourse to despotism. In sum, the American Revolution dramatized and passed on to the western world two political ideas of great importance for the future: the idea of limited, or constitutional, government (which had a long history reaching far back into the ancient and medieval worlds), and the idea of popular sovereignty, or democracy (which was relatively new in an age still strongly aristocratic in its thinking).

The quarter-century between the Peace of Paris and the outbreak of revolution in France apparently opened to the western world three possible roads for future development: enlightened despotism, aristocratic domination, and democratic revolution.

Suggestions for Further Reading

Note: Asterisk denotes a book available in paperback edition.

General The best general account of the century in English will be found in the three relevant volumes of the *Rise of Modern Europe* series, each with excellent critical bibliographies: P. Roberts, *The Quest for Security, 1715–1740** (1947); W. L. Dorn, *Competition for Empire, 1740–1763** (1940); and L. Gershoy, *From Despotism to Revolution, 1763–1789** (1944). M. S. Anderson, *Europe in the Eighteenth Century* (1961), is a good recent survey. Volume VII of the *New Cambridge Modern History*, A. Cobban, *The Old Régime, 1713–1763* (1957), has good articles on every major aspect of the period but is not for continuous reading. A. Sorel, *Europe under the Old Régime** (1947), is a translation of the introduction to a famous larger work of 1895 to 1904. R. R. Palmer, *The Age of the Democratic Revolution* (1959–64), is a major work of interpretation that sees the American and French Revolutions, together with the smaller disturbances of the period, as manifestations of a single great "democratic revolution." Other useful studies are C. B. A. Behrens, *The Ancien Régime** (1967), and Leonard Krieger, *Kings and Philosophers* (1970).

Economic and Social See the works on mercantilism and economic history noted for Chapters 18 and 19; E. Williams, *Capitalism and Slavery* (1944), argues that mercantilism was compatible with slavery, but that the new industrial capitalism undermined it. On the aristocracy, see *The European Nobility in the Eighteenth Century,** ed. by A. Goodwin (1953), a collection of essays by various authors, and F. Ford, *Robe and Sword: The Regrouping of the French Aristocracy after Louis XIV** (1953), a study of the French aristocracy. For the other end of the social spectrum, see O. Hufton, *The Poor of Eighteenth-Century France* (1974). A. Young, *Tours in England and Wales* (1932), is a selection from the journals of a very keen observer of the eighteenth-century countryside. As brief introductions to the Agricultural and Industrial Revolutions, the general economic histories of Europe by H. Heaton, rev. ed. (1948), and by S. B. Clough and R. T. Rapp (1975) are useful.

Expansion Overseas W. B. Willcox, *Star of Empire: A Study of Britain as a World Power, 1485–1945* (1950), and H. I. Priestley, *France Overseas Through the Old Régime: A Study of European Expansion* (1939), are good general works. J. R. Seeley, *The Expansion of England* (1883), is a very influential older account. C. G. Robertson, *Chatham and the British Empire** (1948), is a brief modern discussion. On India, see H. Dodwell, *Dupleix and Clive* (1920); E. Thompson and G. T. Garratt, *The Rise and Fulfillment of British Rule in India* (1934); and H. Furber, *John Company at Work: A Study of European Expansion in India in the Late Eighteenth Century* (1948). On America, in addition to the books cited for Chapters 19 and 20, see L. B. Wright, *The Atlantic Frontier: Colonial American Civilization, 1607–1763* (1947), and M. Kraus, *The Atlantic Civilization: Eighteenth-Century Origins* (1949). On the economic history of the British colonies, see C. P. Nettels, *The Roots of American Civilization* (1938). On social history, see J. Henretta, *The Evolution of American Society, 1700–1815** (1973).

Political and Diplomatic J. Lough, *Introduction to Eighteenth-Century France* (1960), is a very good starting point for study. The best brief introduction to England is J. H. Plumb, *England in the Eighteenth Century** (1951). B. Williams, *The Whig Supremacy, 1714–1760* (1939), in the *Oxford History of England,* is a more extended topical treatment. Two other books by J. H. Plumb offer interesting reading: *Sir Robert Walpole* (1956) and *The First Four Georges** (1957). The serious student of the English political system and how it operated should examine the various studies of L. B. Namier. On Prussia, there is excellent material in Dorn (first section, above); a first-rate biography of Frederick William I, *The Potsdam Fuehrer,* by R. Ergang (1941); biographies of Frederick the Great by P. Gaxotte (1941) and G. P. Gooch (1947); and an expert general account by W. H. Bruford, *Germany in the Eighteenth Century** (1952). See also H. Rosenberg, *Bureaucracy and Autocracy, the Prussian Experience* (1958). C. L. Morris, *Maria Theresa: The Last Conservative* (1937), is probably the best of several biographies, S. K. Padover, *The Revolutionary Emperor* (1934), and T. C. W. Blanning, *Joseph II and Enlightened Despotism* (1970), are both good on Joseph II. On Joseph's most important reform, see E. M. Link, *The Emancipation of the Austrian Peasant, 1740–1798* (1949). There are many biographies of Catherine the Great, but G. S. Thomson, *Catherine the Great and the Expansion of Russia** (1950), is the most informative from the historian's point of view. On the enlightened despots as a group, G. Bruun, *The Enlightened Despots** (1929), is brief but extremely good. The best accounts of the war and diplomacy of the age will be found in the *Rise of Modern Europe* series, but there is a very brief account in A. H. Buffinton, *The Second Hundred Years' War, 1689–1815* (1929); C. Petrie, *Diplomatic History, 1713–1933* (1946), helps provide the continuity lacking in separate volumes.

The American Revolution Two volumes in the *New American Nation* series provide the best up-to-date introduction: L. H. Gibson, *The Coming of the Revolution, 1763–1775** (1954), and J. R. Alden, *The American Revolution, 1775–1783* (1954). L. Gottschalk, *The Place of the American Revolution in the Causal Pattern of the French Revolution* (1948), and E. S. Morgan, *The Birth of the Republic, 1763–1789** (1956), offer a somewhat broader perspective. On the origins of the Revolution, see C. Andrews, *The Colonial Background of the American Revolution* (1924); B. Bailyn, *Ideological Origins of the American Revolution** (1967); and E. S. Morgan and H. Morgan, *The Stamp Act Crisis* (1953). M. Beloff has selected an interesting set of contemporary sources in *The Debate on the American Revolution, 1761–1783** (1949). On the side of ideas, C. L. Becker's study of the text of *The Declaration of Independence** (1922, 1942) is consistently illuminating. The best recent studies include P. Maier, *From Resistance to Revolution** (1972), and R. M. Calhoon, *Revolutionary America: An Interpretive Overview** (1976).

23

The French Revolution and Napoleon

The French Revolution marked a turning point in European history. The events that began in 1787 and ended with the fall of Napoleon Bonaparte in 1815 unleashed forces that altered not only the political and social structure of states but the map of Europe. Many attempts were made, in France and elsewhere, to undo the work of the Revolution and to repress the ideas of liberty, equality, and nationalism that the Revolution had inspired. But the Old Regime was dead, in France at least, and a Europe dominated by monarchy and aristocracy and by a hierarchical social order could never be fully restored. With the coming of the French Revolution, then, we enter into a more modern world—a world of class conflict, middle-class ascendancy, acute national consciousness, and popular democracy. Together with industrialization, the Revolution reshaped the institutions, the societies, and even the mentalities of Europeans.

THE ORIGINS OF THE FRENCH REVOLUTION

By the last half of the eighteenth century, France appeared to have overcome the dismal cycle of famine, plague, and high mortality that, in the preceding century, had inhibited both demographic and economic growth. The majority of Frenchmen who lived in the villages and tilled the fields were better off than their counterparts in most of Europe. French peasants, for example, owned some 40 percent of the country's farmlands. The mild inflationary trend that characterized much of the eighteenth century increased the wealth of large landowners and surplus wealth in agriculture served to stimulate the expansion of the French economy as a whole. Modest advances in the textile and metallurgical industries, the construction of new roads and canals, and urban growth were other indications of economic development.

Yet, despite evident signs of prosperity, there was great discontent and restlessness in France in the 1780s. French institutions were obsolete, inefficient, and uncoordinated. They were controlled by the nobility and by self-perpetuating corporations of hereditary officeholders. To anyone touched by the ideas of the Enlightenment they seemed irrational and unjust. The middle classes, especially, were offended by the legal and social distinctions that kept them from attaining high office or exerting political influence. Every bishop in France was of noble birth; only nobles could receive commissions in the army; bourgeois

The French peasant supports the clergy and the nobility in this eighteenth-century cartoon. The rabbits and doves eating the peasant's grain were protected by law for the sport of the upper classes.

plans for economic reform were constantly thwarted by the privileged classes. The economy, particularly in agriculture, remained unstable and subject to fluctuations that could drive the peasants and urban poor to starvation. An inefficient and inequitable tax system yielded too small an income to support the state, discouraged economic growth, and fell most heavily on the poor. On the eve of the Revolution, France faced a conjuncture of crises. Three of these crises—agrarian distress, financial chaos, and aristocratic reaction—were particularly acute.

Agrarian Distress

Wretched weather and poor harvests in 1787 and 1788 weakened the agricultural economy. The poorer peasants lived at a subsistence level at best; with poor crops they starved. The purchasing power of well-to-do peasants declined. Grain shortages led to sharp increases in the cost of bread. Moreover, from the late 1770s the long-term growth of the French economy had been interrupted in several important areas, such as the wine trade, and between 1776 and 1787, agricultural profits generally declined, though not to the low levels of the first part of the century. Nevertheless, noblemen and other large landowners, who had become accustomed to high profits, sought to save their declining fortunes by demanding from their tenant farmers dues and obligations that had long been neglected. The countryside was ripe for revolution.

Financial Chaos

The finances of Louis XVI's government were a shambles. By 1787 one-half of the nation's tax revenues went to service the massive public debt that Louis XIV had left to his successors. France's involvement in the Seven Years' War and in the American War for Independence had driven the government further along the road to bankruptcy. Without a reform of the tax system the king could not meet his obligations. But such a reform would mean an attack on the privileges of the upper classes, and this Louis could

never quite summon the courage to do.

Three ministers in succession struggled with the problem. The first, the Swiss banker Necker, was dismissed by the king in 1781 after he had proposed some modest reforms. Necker's successor, Calonne, thought he could carry on without much change. But as the deficit mounted he grew alarmed, and in 1786 he proposed a much more radical reform program than Necker's. The most striking provision of Calonne's program was a direct tax on all landowners—noble and commoner, lay and clerical. To oversee the assessment of the new tax, Calonne suggested that the king create local and provincial assemblies in which all men of property would be represented regardless of social status. In addition, older taxes, such as the *taille*, which weighed on the lower orders, were to be reduced. Calonne's reforms struck at the very heart of the system of privilege and the social hierarchy of the Old Regime.

Calonne, aware that there would be bitter opposition to his plans, persuaded Louis XVI to call a conference of notables in the hope that they could be induced to back his program. But the members of this assembly, which met in February 1787, were drawn largely from the privileged orders and refused to support Calonne.

The king now dismissed Calonne and put in his place one of Calonne's chief opponents, Lomenie de Brienne, Archbishop of Toulouse. This prelate, though a member of both the higher nobility and the higher clergy, soon came to the same conclusions as Calonne. He tried to enact a similar reform program, but the *Parlement* of Paris, the most privileged of all the corporations of officeholders, refused to register the royal edicts. It declared that only the Estates General could approve such measures. When Brienne tried to break the opposition by exiling the magistrates of the *Parlement* and by abolishing the high courts, he touched off furious protests by many members of the upper bourgeoisie and the nobility. In the face of these attacks, the government backed away from its reform program. In July 1788, the king yielded to the opposition and ordered a meeting of the Estates General for May 1789.

Aristocratic Reaction

During the 1780s, then, aristocratic demands on the peasantry were aggravating the distress of the countryside, and aristocratic resistance to tax reform was hampering the government in its attempts to revamp the nation's financial structure. These were two facets of the aristocratic reaction that was directly responsible for the coming of the French Revolution.

The tremendous strength of the French privileged classes had been built up steadily during the reigns of Louis XV and Louis XVI. At every turn the poor, the aspiring middle class, and enlightened reformers in government confronted the fact of privilege. Some men of the Enlightenment, in particular Voltaire, and such royal ministers as Turgot and Calonne encouraged the king to rationalize state finance and to bring a measure of justice to French society at the expense of the privileged groups. Louis XVI supported several of these plans for reform, but he always backed down when the privileged classes protested. By the 1780s it appeared that the French king was the prisoner of the nobility and that he would do nothing to displease them.

Moreover, the nobles were particularly skillful in confusing the issue. Certain privileges, such as those that protected the laws, institutions, and customs of the provinces from encroachments by the central government, limited the arbitrary power of the king. These privileges, or liberties, were compared with the restrictions on royal power in England, and the English were regarded as the freest people in Europe. Thus the nobles could resist royal attacks on privilege by asserting that the king was simply trying to get rid of all restrictions on his power. Through this argument, the nobility and the *parlements* were able to gain wide support and considerable sympathy when they resisted the arbitrary orders of the king, even when those orders were directed toward desirable ends.

There were those, however, who were not deceived by the rhetoric of the privileged orders. The hesitations of the king and the intransigence of the aristocracy increased the bitterness of large sections of the population. They wanted to put an end to privilege, and they felt that the unreformed monarchy would not help them in this struggle. The attack on privilege and the demand for equality before the law were the driving forces in the Revolution from beginning to end. Privilege, it seemed, could be destroyed only by attacking aristocracy and monarchy.

THE FRENCH REVOLUTION AND THE KING

The Estates General, which had not met since 1614, was convened by the king at Versailles on May 5, 1789. The electoral process by which deputies were selected was a relatively generous one: all adult French males had the right to vote, indirectly, for representatives to the Third Estate, which served the interests of the commoners. Moreover, following some recent examples in provincial assemblies, the Third Estate was given twice as many representatives as the other two Estates. The First and Second Estates (the clergy and the nobility, respectively) represented the privileged orders. The king had asked that all local electoral assemblies draw up *cahiers de doléances*—lists of grievances—to submit to the Estates General when it met. Thus in the months preceding the convening of the Estates General, a great political debate occurred. Almost all politically minded men agreed that the monarchy should yield some of its powers to an assembly and seek consent to taxation and legislation. By 1788 some noblemen were willing to go part way in abolishing privileges and in equalizing taxation. But the early debates in the Estates General revealed that the lawyers and bourgeois who represented the Third Estate were bent on a much more drastic reform.

The Estates General and the National Assembly

The mood of the Third Estate was best expressed by one of its deputies, the Abbé Sieyès. In a famous pamphlet, *What Is the Third Estate?*, Sieyès argued that the real French nation was made up of people who were neither clergymen

Caricature of the Abbé Sieyès.

nor noblemen, and that this majority should have the decisive voice in all political matters. This idea was translated into action during the opening debate on voting procedures in the Estates General. Since the Third Estate had as many representatives as the other two combined, it wanted the three Estates to meet and vote together. A few liberal nobles and a number of the lower clergy were sure to support the Third Estate. The king and the privileged orders, on the other hand, demanded that the Estates vote separately. This was traditional procedure, and it assured that the first two Estates would retain control.

The Third Estate not only rejected the king's plan for separate meetings: on June 17 it declared itself the National Assembly of France and invited the other Estates to sit with it. The National Assembly then assumed the right to approve all taxation and to withhold all taxation if its political demands were not met. In the face of this bold initiative, the king hesitated but finally resorted to a show of force. On June 20 Louis XVI had the Third Estate barred from its usual meeting place. The deputies then convened in a nearby indoor tennis court and took an oath not to disband until they had drafted a constitution. This Tennis Court Oath was the first great act of the bourgeois revolution in France.

The Tennis Court Oath
June 20, 1789

The National Assembly, considering that it has been summoned to establish the constitution of the kingdom, to effect the regeneration of public order, and to maintain the true principles of monarchy; that nothing can prevent it from continuing its deliberations in whatever place it may be forced to establish itself; and finally, that wheresoever its members are assembled, *there* is the National Assembly:

Decrees that all members of this Assembly shall immediately take a solemn oath not to separate, and to reassemble wherever circumstances require, until the constitution of the kingdom is established and consolidated upon firm foundations. . . .

From *A Documentary Survey of the French Revolution*, ed. by John Hall Stewart (New York: Macmillan, 1951), p. 88.

In a dreary repetition of the political ineptitude he had shown in previous crises, Louis missed his chance to act as impartial mediator between the hostile Estates. On June 23 he went before the Estates General and offered a program of reform that only partly satisfied the demands of the Third Estate for tax reform and did nothing to abolish the privileges of the nobility. At about the same time, the king began to concentrate troops around Versailles and Paris. By now, however, neither partial reform nor brute force was a sufficient answer to the political crisis. The revolution had become a battle between those who desired a more equal and open society and those who wanted to preserve the privileges of the aristocracy.

The Popular Revolt

Most of the deputies in the Third Estate were lawyers, professional men, and lesser officeholders. Their aspirations were those of the French bourgeoisie. In the urban centers and the countryside resided yet another element of the Third Estate—the mass of artisans, shopkeepers, and peasants who lived in poverty or on the edge of it. Their aspirations and needs were not identical with those of the deputies at Versailles. But in the summer of 1789 a series of spontaneous popular disturbances and revolts broke out that linked, for the moment at least, the bourgeoisie and the common people in an uneasy alliance against the aristocracy.

Notable among these uprisings was an attack on July 14 (still France's national holiday) on the Bastille, a royal fortress and prison in Paris. By the end of June the city of Paris had grown tense. The economic depression of the 1780s and the poor harvests of 1788 and 1789 had reduced the urban poor to misery, and to misery was now added the fear that the king and the aristocrats were conspiring to dissolve the Estates General. When the king's troops appeared on the outskirts of the city, the immediate reaction of the citizens was to arm themselves. It was their search for arms that brought the leaders of the Parisian electoral assembly and a crowd of journey-

men and workers to the Bastille. The commandant at first barred the gates and fired on the crowd. He then lost his nerve, opened the gates, and the crowd stormed in and slaughtered the garrison.

The fall of the Bastille was an event of small consequence in itself, but its implications were immense. The attack was regarded as a blow against royal depotism. It demonstrated that the Revolution was not simply a debate over a constitution. Of greatest importance, it brought the city of Paris and the political leaders of Paris to the forefront. A new, revolutionary municipal government was formed; henceforth Paris would shape the direction of the Revolution. Finally, the events in Paris set off revolts in the provinces.

The French peasants, also disappointed with the slow pace of reform, now began to take action of their own. Like the poor of the cities, the peasants had been heartened by the political promise of the winter of 1788/89. They had patiently drawn up their *cahiers* and they had chosen their electoral committees; then they had waited confidently for relief to follow. The Estates General met in May. Spring passed and summer came, but the peasants were still poor;

they were still not allowed to till the unused land of the nobles; and they still had to pay their customary dues.

Then, during July 1789, the month of the storming of the Bastille, rumors spread through rural France that there would be no reforms and that the aristocrats were coming with troops to impose reaction on the countryside. The result was panic and rioting throughout the country. During the "Great Fear," as it is called, frightened peasants gathered to defend themselves against the unnamed and unseen enemy. Once assembled and armed, however, they turned against the enemy they knew—the local lord. Though the lords themselves were rarely in residence, peasants burned their châteaux, often tossing the first brand into the countinghouse, where the hated records of their payments and seigneurial obligations were kept.

The Destruction of Privilege

The popular revolts and riots had a profound impact on the king, the aristocracy, and the deputies of the Third Estate alike. Already in June, before the storming of the Bastille, Louis XVI had recognized the National Assembly and

The Oath at the Jeu de Paume, by Jacques Louis David. The deputies of the Third Estate, joined by some of the clergy and nobility, swear not to disband until they have drafted a constitution.

Storming the Bastille (July 14, 1789). The revolutionary leader is accepting the surrender of the prison.

French Women Become Free. Print from the General Collection of Caricatures about the Revolution (1789).

ordered the clergy and the nobles to sit with the Third Estate. He also recognized the revolutionary government of Paris and authorized the formation of a national guard composed largely of members of the bourgeoisie. But the king received no credit for his concessions from the revolutionary leaders, who felt, quite rightly, that his sympathies were still with the nobles. At the same time, Louis' indecision had discouraged many of the strongest supporters of the Old Regime. The most reactionary noblemen, headed by the king's brother, the Count of Artois, began to leave the country. Other members of the aristocracy sought to preserve their property by making dramatic concessions to the call for reform.

On the night of August 4, one nobleman, the Viscount de Noailles, stood before the Assembly and proposed that all feudal levies and obligations be abolished. In a performance at once impressive and bizarre, nobles, clerics, and provincial representatives arose to renounce noble privileges, clerical tithes, and pro-

vincial liberties. In effect, the Old Regime was dismantled in one night, and the way seemed clear for the Assembly's main business—to draft a constitution. The implementation of the concessions of August 4, however, was half-hearted. The structure of aristocratic privilege was indeed abolished along with tax exemptions and hereditary officeholding, but peasants were to continue paying customary dues to their lords until they had redeemed them. Only when the Revolution reached a more radical stage was this obligation abolished.

The Declaration of the Rights of Man

On the whole, the National Assembly had succeeded in wiping out the privileges of the upper classes, the corporations of officeholders, and the provinces. Now it faced the task of creating new political, legal, and administrative structures for the country. The ideological framework for this task was set forth by the constitution-makers in the Declaration of the Rights of Man, which they adopted on August 27, 1789.

In this preamble to a constitution, the members of the National Constituent Assembly (that is, the National Assembly acting in its constitution-making role) established a set of principles idealistic enough to sustain the enthusiasm of the mass of Frenchmen for the Revolution and sweeping enough to include all humanity. The basic ideas of this document were personal freedom, equality under the law, the sanctity of property rights, and national sovereignty. The first article declared that "men are born and remain free and equal in rights." There were to be no class privileges and no interference with freedom of thought and religion. Liberty, property, and resistance to oppression were declared inalienable and natural rights. Laws could be made and taxes levied only by the citizens or their representatives. The nation, not the king, was sovereign. Thus was established the framework for a system of liberty under law. The Declaration was a landmark in the fight against privilege and despotism, and it had a great appeal to revolutionary and democratic factions throughout Europe.

The Declaration of the Rights of Man

August 27, 1789

1. Men are born and remain free and equal in rights; social distinctions may be based only upon general usefulness.
2. The aim of every political association is the preservation of the natural and inalienable rights of man; these rights are liberty, property, security, and resistance to oppression.
3. The source of all sovereignty resides essentially in the nation; no group, no individual may exercise authority not emanating expressly therefrom.
6. Law is the expression of the general will; all citizens have the right to concur personally or through their representatives in its formation; it must be the same for all, whether it protects or punishes. All citizens, being equal before it, are equally admissible to all public offices, positions, and employments, according to their capacity, and without other distinction than that of virtues and talents.
10. No one is to be disquieted because of his opinions; even religious, provided their manifestation does not disturb the public order established by law.
11. Free communication of ideas and opinions is one of the most precious of the rights of man. Consequently every citizen may speak, write, and print freely, subject to responsibility for the abuse of such liberty in the cases determined by law. . . .

From *A Documentary Survey of the French Revolution,* ed. by John Hall Stewart (New York: Macmillan, 1951), p. 114.

The October Days

The Declaration of the Rights of Man was not simply a page lifted from John Locke, the *philosophes*, and the Americans. It was a highly political document hammered out in an Assembly that was showing itself to be increasingly divided. There were those among the moderate leaders of the Assembly who found the Declaration too radical and sweeping. These men desired to reconcile Louis XVI with the Revolution and to construct a constitutional system on the English model with a monarch guided by an assembly controlled by the rich and the well-born. The issues that divided the crown and the country could not, however, be compromised. Louis simply refused to give formal approval to the decrees and the Declaration that followed the night of August 4.

The king's recalcitrance, the divisions in the Assembly, and the food shortages combined to produce yet another popular explosion. On October 5, 1789, a crowd of some twenty thousand armed Parisians, including a large number of women, marched on Versailles, demanding bread and insisting that the royal family return to Paris. The king considered flight, but he was persuaded by Necker, who had been recalled to the government, and by Lafayette, leader of the National Guard, to appease the crowd and leave Versailles. On October 6 the royal family drove into Paris surrounded by shouting crowds, and established themselves at the Tuilleries palace. A few days later, the National Constituent Assembly followed.

The Parisians seemed satisfied with the king's capitulation, and the Assembly, together with the king and his ministers, turned to the question of the constitution. Henceforth, however, the deliberations of the Assembly were to take place in the heated atmosphere of Paris. Here in the capital many political clubs were formed to debate the issues and settle on policy. Here too were political agitators, journalists of all opinions, and, above all, crowds that could be mobilized to bring pressure on the Assembly. From the autumn of 1789 on, the Revolution became more and more a Parisian affair.

The Achievements of the National Constituent Assembly, 1789–91

It took two years to make the constitution. By the end of that time the government had been reorganized, the Church had been dispossessed of its lands, and the rights of Frenchmen had been more clearly defined. These are the main results of the Assembly's complex and lengthy deliberations:

The Monarchy. By acts passed in September 1789, Louis XVI was reduced from his position as a king by divine right to the role of a constitutional monarch. He was given the right of suspensive veto over legislation that allowed him to delay the passage of laws for two years. The monarchy remained hereditary, and the king retained control of military and foreign affairs.

The Legislature. The Constitution of 1791 provided for a unicameral Legislative Assembly, elected for two years. The Assembly had the power to initiate and enact legislation and to control the budget. It also had the exclusive right to declare war. Members of the Constituent Assembly were forbidden to serve in the new legislature, an unfortunate decision that barred experienced men from a body that had few precedents to guide it.

The Electorate. The Constitution did not provide for universal manhood suffrage. It divided Frenchmen into active

The three Estates "hammer out" a new constitution in this contemporary engraving.

Playing cards of the French Revolution. Personifications of Liberty and Equality have taken the place of kings and queens.

and passive citizens. Only the former, who met a property qualification, had the right to vote. The active category comprised some two-thirds of the adult male population. Active citizens voted for electors, who in turn elected the Legislative Assembly. These electors, as well as officeholders in the Assembly, were drawn from some fifty thousand of the country's wealthiest men. Even with these restrictions, a far larger percentage of the population could vote and hold office than in England.

The Administration. The elimination of aristocratic privilege invalidated most of France's local administration, which had been controlled by the nobility or small oligarchies of officeholders and rich bourgeois. The Assembly completed the process of dismantling the administrative apparatus of the Old Regime by abolishing all former provinces, intendancies, and tax farms. On a clean administrative map they drew eighty-three departments, roughly equal in size, with uniform administrative and judicial systems. Administration was decentralized and put in the hands of some forty thousand local and departmental councils, elected by their constituents.

The Church. The reorganization of the French Church was decreed by the Civil Constitution of the Clergy, promulgated in August 1790. It was one of the most important and fateful acts of the Revolution. The Assembly confiscated the lands of the Church and, to relieve the financial distress of the country, issued notes on the security of the confiscated lands. These notes, or *assignats*, circulated as money and temporarily relieved the financial crisis. Clergymen henceforth became paid officials of the state, and priests and bishops were to be elected by property-owning citizens.

The Constitution of 1791, together with the Declaration of the Rights of Man, summed up the principles and politics of the men of 1789. In its emphasis on property rights, its restrictive franchise, and its fiscal policy, the Constitution had a distinctly bourgeois bias. To look upon the document simply as a product of selfish interest, however, would be to underestimate its achievements. A new class of peasant proprietors had been created. The framework

for a society open to talent had been established. Administrative decentralization, it was thought, would overcome the prevailing fear of despotism. Equality before the law, if not political equality, had been made a fact. These were impressive and revolutionary changes. But to succeed and mature, the new order needed peace, social stability, and the cooperation of the king. None of these was forthcoming. Within a year the Constitution of 1791 had become a dead letter, and the Revolution had entered a new phase.

The Failure of Constitutional Monarchy

The Constitution of 1791 was most certainly an imperfect instrument. The Civil Constitution of the Clergy, for example, offended the pope. Many bishops and priests refused to accept it, and they found broad support in the country. Schism in the Church became a major factor in the eventual failure of the Assembly to create a stable government. Moreover, the restrictive franchise opened the constitution-makers to the charge that they wanted to substitute a wealthy oligarchy for an aristocracy. Such obvious defects, however, were not alone responsible for the failure of constitutional monarchy. The principal culprit was the monarch himself.

At the head of the government stood a king who was thoroughly discredited. In June 1791, Louis XVI tried to escape from France in order to join the forces of counterrevolution abroad. He very nearly succeeded but was caught at Varennes, near the eastern frontier, and was brought back to Paris. This humiliating episode destroyed what little authority Louis still possessed. He now swore to obey the new constitution; but he was only a figurehead.

At this point the situation was complicated by outside pressures. Louis' fellow monarchs were unhappy over the way in which their royal colleague was being treated. The privileged orders in other countries feared that the leveling principles of the Revolution would spread. The English, many of whom had sympathized with the Revolution so long as it seemed to be following an English model, began to denounce the radicalism and violence of the French. Edmund Burke, in particular, saw clearly the radical nature of the Revolution. In his *Reflections on the Revolution in France* (1790) he insisted on the importance of tradition in preserving an orderly society and declared that it was folly to abandon time-tested institutions in favor of new ones based on abstract ideas. He did not convince radical writers or some of the articulate craftsmen, but he convinced almost everyone in power in England. Hostility to France was an old tradition; Burke gave new reasons for continuing it. And everywhere French refugees spread counterrevolutionary propaganda urging Europe's monarchs to intervene.

The Legislative Assembly
September 1791–September 1792

The Legislative Assembly met in an atmosphere of intrigue, fear, and factional strife. There were two issues on which it was almost impossible to find a solid majority. The first was the position of the king. He could not be trusted, and he would not commit himself to the principle of equality, on which everyone did agree. Was it worth compromising with the king in order to preserve the constitution and the unity of the country? If not, how far should the Assembly go in restraining or in punishing the king?

The second problem, which caused even sharper divisions, was that of defining "equality." Was the emphasis to be on equality before the law, or on equality of opportunity, or on political equality, or on economic equality, or on a mixture of two or more of these ideals? Here there was not only no clear majority, but no consistency within groups and even within individuals.

There were no parties in the Assembly, but there were the "clubs," loosely organized associations with affiliates in the provinces. One of the largest and best-organized groups was the Jacobin Club, with 136 members out of the 745 representatives. The Jacobins were republicans and wanted to get rid of the king. But they were also well-to-do bourgeois. They were far from agreement on political and economic equality, or on the pace at which change should take place. They were divided into at least two

factions. One faction was led by Brissot de Warville, the ablest politician in the Assembly. The other, composed mainly of Parisians, eventually found a leader in Maximilien Robespierre.

As it turned out, the issue that temporarily united the Assembly was that of declaring war on Austria. Inept diplomacy by European monarchs, even more inept politics in the French royal court, and a very real threat of counterrevolution convinced millions of patriotic Frenchmen that the forces of reaction were about to destroy all that had been gained since 1789 and that war was the only way to save their country and their freedom. The emperor of Austria and the king of Prussia in the Declaration of Pillnitz (August 1791) proclaimed that European monarchs must unite to restore order and monarchy in France. This was largely bluff, but it sounded ominous. Some conservative ministers thought that a victorious war against Austria would strengthen the king and allow him to end the Revolution. However, Louis XVI and his Austrian queen, Marie Antoinette, apparently hoped for a French defeat that would lead to the restoration of royal authority.

External threats and court plots played into the hands of Brissot's republican faction. Brissot believed that a crusade to unseat the monarchs of Europe would rekindle the revolutionary fervor of the French people and rally them around his plan to establish a republic in France. He was opposed in the Jacobin Club by Robespierre, who feared that a war would strengthen the conservatives and lead to dictatorship. But Brissot proved the stronger, and the powerful Jacobin Club passed a resolution advocating a declaration of war. Brissot took the issue before the Assembly, and in April 1792 all but seven deputies voted for war with Austria.

The First War
of the Revolution

The declaration of war transformed the Revolution. With war came the end of the monarchy and the constitution. With it also came terror and dictatorship. France became not simply the home of the Revolution but the exporter of revolutionary ideals. Finally, under the stress

Anonymous contemporary portrait of Robespierre.

and emotions of war, France became a modern, unified nation-state.

The war began badly. The French army lacked leadership and discipline. The government was short of money and hampered by factional disputes. The royal family and their supporters encouraged the enemy. It is not surprising that the Austrians and their allies, the Prussians, were soon able to advance along the road to Paris.

Two things saved the Revolution. The Austrian and Prussian generals, who were at least as incompetent as the French, delayed and divided their forces. And there was a genuine outburst of patriotic and revolutionary enthusiasm in France. It was during this crisis that the *Marseillaise* was composed, a stirring appeal to save the country from tyranny. The French kept on fighting, despite their failures. As a result, when the Austro-Prussian army was checked at Valmy, one hundred miles from Paris, in September 1792, its cautious commander decided to call off the invasion. The allies had lost their best chance to crush the Revolution before it gathered strength.

THE FRENCH REPUBLIC

During these gloomy months, when everything seemed to be going wrong, the radical politicians of Paris gained a commanding position in the government. These Jacobins—Robespierre and Georges-Jacques Danton were the most important—based their power on national guards summoned to protect the capital, on the Parisian crowds, and, from August 10, 1792, on an insurrectionary Paris Commune that replaced the legal municipal government. The poorer classes were suffering from economic depression and political uncertainty, and they were afraid that the Old Regime might be revived. The bourgeois radicals in the Assembly never fully sympathized with the desire of Paris artisans and workers for economic equality, but they could agree with them on the need for drastic political changes. In August the Jacobins touched off an uprising in Paris that forced the Legislative Assembly to suspend the king from office and to issue a call for a revision of the constitution. A

National Convention, elected by universal manhood suffrage, was to determine the new form of the French government. The events of August triggered what is often called the Second French Revolution. This revolution began with the deposition of Louis XVI; it ended in a bloody terror that consumed its own leaders. In many ways it confirmed Edmund Burke's most dire prophecies. And yet the Second French Revolution did not follow inexorably upon the first. War created its own necessities, survival being the most pressing.

The Convention and the Jacobins

The National Convention met in Paris on September 21, 1792, in the wake of a fierce bloodletting earlier in the month—the so-called September massacres. These massacres, which took the lives of some thirteen hundred prisoners in Paris, were part of a pattern of fear, terror, and revolutionary justice that persisted throughout much of the Convention's three-year rule.

The delegates to the Convention were elected by a minority of Frenchmen, despite universal manhood suffrage. Many citizens were repelled by the deposition of the king and the violence of the summer of 1792. Others were intimidated. Some were excluded from the electorate by governmental decree. Thus the most radical elements of the French population had disproportionate strength in the elections. Not surprisingly, many of the delegates were Jacobins.

The Jacobins, however, were divided. The followers of Brissot, now called the Girondists, made up one faction. They dominated the Convention in its early months. In general, the Girondists represented the interests of provincial republicans, and they were bitterly opposed to the Paris Commune. Their foreign policy was aggressive and expansionistic. It was they, for example, who issued a manifesto in November 1792 offering France's aid to all revolutionaries throughout Europe. In domestic affairs, the Girondists were relatively moderate—at least when compared with their Parisian enemies. On the prime issue of 1792, the fate of the king, the Girondists urged that Louis

XVI be imprisoned for the duration of the war. There was little doubt then—and less now—that Louis was guilty of treason. But the resolution condemning him to death passed by only one vote. He was guillotined on January 21, 1793. This victory for the so-called Mountain—Robespierre and Danton's faction—was followed by a purge of the Girondists in June 1793. The architects of France's war policy were among the first victims of that policy.

The Jacobins and the War

The Girondists fell before their Jacobin opponents in the wake of crushing French defeats by an overwhelming new coalition of European powers. The execution of Louis XVI, France's designs on Holland, and its annexation of Savoy and Nice prompted England, Spain, Portugal, and several lesser states to join Austria and Prussia in the war against France. In the face of such a formidable combination, the French armies suffered a series of reversals. The victor of Valmy, General Dumouriez, was badly defeated in Belgium, and, in the spring of 1793, he defected to the enemy.

Now the government, under the direction of a Committee of General Defense (later the Committee of Public Safety), undertook to organize the entire nation for war. It applied conscription on a nationwide scale for the first time in modern European history. It raised huge armies, far larger than those that could be called up by the old-fashioned monarchies against which France was fighting. And it supported those armies by means of confiscation and heavy taxes. The armies were organized by a military genius, Lazare Carnot, an engineer who made a science out of the service of supply.

The monarchies of Europe, which were used to fighting limited wars with limited resources for limited gains, were overcome by a French nation organized for war. They could not afford to arm all their people; they still depended on the old officer corps for their leaders. And, much as they despised the Revolution, they were still not prepared to sacrifice all their resources to put it down. Other problems distracted the crowned heads

Portrait of Louis XVI during his imprisonment at the time of the Revolution, by Joseph Ducreux.

The Execution of Louis XVI

The carriage proceeded thus in silence to the Place de Louis XV,* and stopped in the middle of a large space that had been left round the scaffold: this space was surrounded with cannon, and beyond, an armed multitude extended as far as the eye could reach. . . . As soon as the King had left the carriage, three guards surrounded him, and would have taken off his clothes, but he repulsed them with haughtiness: he undressed himself, untied his neckcloth, opened his shirt, and arranged it himself. The guards, whom the determined countenance of the King had for a moment disconcerted, seemed to recover their audacity. They surrounded him again, and would have seized his hands. "What are you attempting?" said the King, drawing back his hands. "To bind you," answered the wretches. "To bind *me*," said the King with an indignant air. "No! I shall never consent to that: do what you have been ordered, but you shall never bind me. . . ."

Many voices were at the same time heard encouraging the executioners. They seemed reanimated themselves, in seizing with violence the most virtuous of Kings, they dragged him under the axe of the guillotine, which with one stroke severed his head from his body. All this passed in a moment. The youngest of the guards, who seemed about eighteen, immediately seized the head, and shewed it to the people as he walked round the scaffold; he accompanied this monstrous ceremony with the most atrocious and indecent gestures. At first an awful silence prevailed; at length some cries of "Vive la République!" were heard. By degrees the voices multiplied, and in less than ten minutes this cry, a thousand times repeated, became the universal shout of the multitude, and every hat was in the air. . . .

*Now the Place de la Concorde.

From *English Witnesses of the French Revolution*, ed. by J. M. Thompson (Oxford: Basil Blackwell, 1938), pp. 230–31.

of Europe: England was seeking colonial conquests, and the eastern powers were still concerned with the Polish problem. So the French recovered from the blows of 1793 and by the late spring of 1794 had broken through into the Low Countries. When the Convention ended its work in 1795, France was stronger and held more territory than it had under Louis XIV at the height of his power.

The Instruments of Jacobin Rule

Military success was achieved only through the intensive and often brutal organization of the French people. The Constituent Assembly's program of administrative decentralization had left France without any effective chain of command linking the National Convention in Paris to the provinces. Moreover, the Convention was an ungainly body, incapable of swift action. Into this void moved the radical Jacobins. In the provinces, Jacobin clubs virtually replaced local governing bodies and through their committees of surveillance controlled public life. At the center, executive power was entrusted to two committees—the Committee of Public Safety and the Committee for General Security. The former wielded almost dictatorial power over France from July 1793 until July 1794. It had twelve members, of whom Robespierre was the most prominent.

The genuine achievement of the twelve capable men who composed the Committee of Public Safety, in coping with internal unrest and external war, is often overlooked because of the "Reign of Terror" they imposed on France. The Terror must be put into the context of the problems that confronted Robespierre, Carnot, and their colleagues. From early 1793 there had been a series of internal rebellions against the government. Conservative peasants of the Vendée, a region in the west of France, had revolted

against the national conscription and in favor of their priests who opposed the Civil Constitution. Later in the year, the Girondists, who opposed what they thought was excessive centralization, stimulated local uprisings in some large provincial towns. In the heat of war, such rebellions appeared treasonable, and the Terror was used as a political weapon to impose order. Also, during much of the Committee's tenure, Parisian politicians, both to the left and to the right of Robespierre, maneuvered to secure power. Terror, against Danton among others, was a weapon in these internecine conflicts. There was an economic terror directed against war profiteers and hoarders. Finally, there were local terrors, uncontrolled from the center, in which Jacobins and undisciplined representatives of the government took revenge on their enemies. In the end, the Terror gained a certain momentum of its own, and the list of suspects grew. Among the factors in Robespierre's fall was the fear of the Convention that its remaining members would soon become victims of revolutionary justice.

In all, some forty thousand people were killed by the government and its agents. The largest number of victims were peasants; next came rebellious citizens of provincial towns, and politicians. Some hundreds of thousands of suspects were imprisoned. Even the Committee of Public Safety finally divided over the excesses of the Terror. When military successes restored a measure of stability to France, the National Convention reasserted its authority. Among its first acts was the arrest and execution of Robespierre in July 1794.

Jacobinism and French Society

The militant phase of Jacobinism was relatively short. The Committee of Public Safety ruled for a year, and Robespierre had complete authority for only four

Here Lies All of France. An engraving of Robespierre guillotining the executioner after having guillotined everyone else in France.

months. Thus, beyond the brilliant organization of the national defense, the Jacobins made few permanent contributions to French institutions and society. Certain of their acts, however, have remained of symbolic significance to the French Left. Among these were the guarantees of the right to a public education for all and the right of public welfare for the poor; these guarantees were set forth in an abortive constitution drawn up in 1793. In addition, the Jacobins were responsible for price controls and for the division of confiscated property among the poor. These decrees, however, were not the product of a conscious social philosophy; they were opportunistic acts designed to win over the disaffected crowds in the cities and the landless peasants in the countryside. The Jacobins were radical democrats who believed deeply in political equality; they were not socialists. With their fall in the summer of 1794, the Revolution fell back into the hands of the propertied bourgeoisie. It was this class that in the end gained most from the Revolution.

The Thermidorian Reaction and the Directory, 1795–99

The demise of Robespierre and the Jacobins touched off a wave of reaction against the excesses of the Terror. This "Thermidorian reaction," named after the month in the revolutionary calendar when Robespierre was executed (Thermidor/July), turned against the austerity of Jacobin rule and at times took the form of a "white terror" against the radicals in Paris and the provinces.

In 1795 the Convention finally presented France with a constitution, the third since 1789. It provided for a five-man executive board, called the Directory, and a two-house legislature. Even the republican-oriented Convention had been sufficiently sobered by the Terror to abandon its promise of universal suffrage, and the franchise was weighted in favor of the propertied classes. Once in office, the Directory proved both corrupt and incompetent. It maintained a militantly aggressive foreign policy and allowed the French economy to deteriorate disastrously. A more or less communistic movement led by "Gracchus" Babeuf received some support from the poor, but was easily suppressed. The French poor were still largely artisans and peasants—property owners and not wage-earners. More dangerous was a royalist revival. Elections in 1797 demonstrated such an upsurge in royalist sentiment that the results had to be cancelled. The Directory's single source of strength was the army. With the economy foundering and popular unrest increasing, the Directory was ripe for the *coup d'état* that in 1799 brought one of its most successful generals, Napoleon Bonaparte, to power.

NAPOLEON'S RISE TO POWER

Napoleon Bonaparte was born on the island of Corsica in 1769, shortly after the

---

The Thermidorian Reaction

In two days after the execution of Robespierre, the whole Commune of Paris, consisting of about sixty persons, were guillotined in less than one hour and a half, in the Place de la Révolution; and though I was standing above a hundred paces from the place of execution, the blood of the victims streamed under my feet. What surprised me was, as each head fell into the basket, the cry of the people was no other than a repetition of "*A bas le Maximum!*"* which was caused by the privations imposed on the populace by the vigorous exaction of that law which set certain prices upon all sorts of provisions, and which was attributed to Robespierre. The persons who now suffered were all of different trades; and many of them, indeed, had taken advantage of that law, and had abused it, by forcing the farmers and others who supplied the Paris market, to sell at the maximum price, and they retailed at an enormous advance to those who could afford to pay. I did not see Robespierre going to the guillotine; but have been informed that the crowd which attended the wagon in which he passed on that occasion, went so far as to thrust their umbrellas into the wagon against his body. . . . It now became a measure of personal safety, to be able to declare that one had been imprisoned during Robespierre's tyranny. It was dangerous even to appear like a Jacobin, as several persons were murdered in the streets, by *La Jeunesse Parisienne*,† merely because they wore long coats and short hair.

*"Down with price controls!"
†"The (gilded, aristocratic) Paris youth."

From *English Witnesses of the French Revolution*, ed. by J. M. Thompson (Oxford: Basil Blackwell, 1938), pp. 248–49.

The interior of the Great Pyramid, as depicted in the *Description of Egypt* (1809–26), published by the scholars who accompanied Napoleon on his campaign in Egypt. They explored ancient monuments and provided the first modern survey of Egypt.

island had been annexed by France. The Bonapartes were members of the minor nobility, and at the age of nine Napoleon was admitted to a military school in France. From that time on, he knew no other life than the army. When most of the aristocratic officer corps left France after the fall of the monarchy, Napoleon stayed on to serve the Republic. He rose to become a brigadier general in 1793 at the age of twenty-four. He helped to reconquer Toulon—one of the towns that rebelled against the Convention in 1793—and he suppressed a royalist riot in 1795. By 1797, when the Directory felt its power slipping, Barras, one of the Directors, realized that Napoleon's support could be valuable. He sought Napoleon's friendship first by introducing the young general to one of his cast-off mistresses, Josephine Beauharnais (whom Napoleon married), and then by giving him command of an army that was preparing for an invasion of Lombardy, a province in northern Italy under the control of Austria.

The Italian campaign of 1797 removed Austria from the war, gave France control of northern Italy, and established Napoleon's reputation as an outstanding general. After the defeat of the Austrians only England was still at war with France. In 1798 Bonaparte took an army by sea to Egypt, where he hoped to sever England's lifeline to India. He easily defeated the Egyptians, but the English admiral Horatio Nelson sank the French fleet near the mouth of the Nile. Napoleon's army, trapped in Egypt, was soon decimated by disease. In the midst of this crisis, Napoleon heard that the Directory was in danger of falling and that some of the Directors wanted to create a military dictatorship. Leaving his army in Egypt, he made his way secretly back to France to offer his services to the conspirators.

The most important Director was the Abbé Sieyès, and it was with this former leader of the First French Revolution that Napoleon conspired. On November 9, 1799, he used military force to compel the legislators to abolish the Directory and substitute a new government in which a board of three consuls would have almost absolute power. The conspirators asked Napoleon to serve as one of the consuls. They hoped he would provide the personal popularity and military power needed to support a regime that would be dominated by the other two consuls. But when the new constitution was written—at Napoleon's orders—the general emerged as First Consul and virtual dictator. When the French people were invited to endorse the constitution in a plebiscite, they voted overwhelmingly to accept it. To Frenchmen exhausted by years of revolution, terror, and economic instability, Napoleon seemed to be the guarantor both of the gains of the Revolution and of order.

NAPOLEON AND DOMESTIC REFORM

Bonaparte was, above all, a soldier, and his fortunes always hinged on military success or failure. Yet his domestic reforms were profound and enduring. If the French Revolution gave the country an ideology that, henceforth, would both inspire and divide Frenchmen, Napoleon gave France many of its characteristic institutions. Better than any eighteenth-century monarch, Bonaparte fulfilled the *philosophes'* dream of an enlightened despot.

Between 1799 and 1801 Napoleon led a series of successful campaigns against the coalition that England, Austria, and Russia had formed to defeat him. He wanted to win a favorable peace so that he could devote himself to consolidating his position in France. Hostilities ended in 1801 and did not break out again on any major scale until 1805. Napoleon used those four years to restore domestic concord and economic stability and to establish a network of administrative institutions that gave coherence and uniformity to his government.

Perhaps Napoleon's most characteristic contribution was the *Code Napoléon*. From the laws left by the several legal systems of the Old Regime and the succession of revolutionary governments, Napoleon's advisers compiled a uniform legal code that is still the basis of French law. The *Code* maintained in theory the revolutionary concept of equality before the law, but it was in fact far less egalitarian than the laws of the revolutionary era. It emphasized, for instance, the authority of the government over its citizens, of employers over their employees, and of male heads of families over their wives and children. Property rights received particularly strong protection under the *Code.*

Other Napoleonic reforms followed a similar pattern. They often upheld in principle the ideals of the Enlightenment and the Revolution but served in practice to strengthen France's new authoritarian state. Napoleon retained, for instance, the division of France into eighty-three uniformly administered departments. He used the departmental system, however, not to foster local responsibility, as had been intended, but to create a highly centralized administration controlled directly by the First Consul through field administrators called prefects. He also instituted a nationwide system of public schools that not only educated the young—an ideal of the *philosophes*—but imbued them with an exaggerated patriotism and devotion to their ruler.

In reforming France's finances Napoleon followed the British and American examples by chartering a privately owned national bank as a depository for government funds and a source of credit for French businessmen. With government deposits as security, the bank issued paper money as legal tender. Increased currency, a stable franc, and improved credit helped to strengthen France's shaky economy. Napoleon also resolved that perennial problem of the Old Regime—taxation—by developing uniform taxes collected directly from each individual by paid officials.

Although Napoleon was far from devout, he understood better than his republican predecessors that domestic peace could not be achieved until the religious question had been settled. Accordingly, he signed with Pope Pius VII the Concordat of 1801, which regularized the situation created by the Revolution. Although the document recognized that the majority of Frenchmen were Roman Catholics, the Catholic Church was not to be the established church in France. Church properties confiscated during the Revolution were not restored. Moreover, the First Consul retained the right to appoint bishops. Through the Concordat of 1801, Napoleon regained the loyalty of French Catholics and at the same time won the gratitude of owners of former church properties.

Although Napoleon brought a form of enlightened despotism to France, he did so at the expense of much of the individual liberty that had been a basic principle of the Enlightenment. The legislative institutions created by the Constitution of 1799 were a sham. Political opposition was punished and the press was strictly censored. Napoleon's training was military, and too often his solution to political and social problems was force. Nevertheless, his government in its early years was popular. He preserved the property of those who had gained from the Revolution. He satisfied the

Unfinished portrait of Napoleon by Jacques Louis David, the imperial court painter.

Political Maxims of Napoleon

These extracts from communications to the Council of State (1801–04) come from the period when Napoleon was First Consul and was trying to construct a civilian government.

We have finished the romantic period of the Revolution; we must now start to make it into history, to see only what is real and possible in applying its principles and not what was speculative and hypothetical. To follow any other policy today would be to philosophize and not to govern.

I shall respect public opinion when its judgments are legitimate, but it has whims that must be scorned. It is the duty of the government to enlighten public opinion, not to follow it in its errors.

One can lead a people only by promising it a future; a chief of state is a seller of hopes.

Constitutions should be short and obscure. . . . A constitution should be drafted in such a way that it will not hinder the actions of a government and not force the government to violate it. . . . If there are problems with a government that is too strong, there are many more with a government that is too weak. Things won't work unless you break the law every day.

My system is very simple. I believe that in the circumstances, it is necessary to centralize power and increase the authority of the government in order to build a nation. I am the constitution-making power.

Translated from Edouard Driault, *Napoléon: Pensées pour l'Action* (Paris: Presses Universitaires de France, 1943), pp. 30–34.

social ideal of the Revolution by maintaining legal equality, equality in taxation, and careers open to talent. In his administration, he incorporated royalists, constitutionalists, and Jacobins. With such accomplishments, he easily won popular approval when he declared himself First Consul for life in 1802. And two years later, on December 2, 1804, the nation rejoiced when, in the presence of the pope, he crowned himself Emperor of the French.

THE NAPOLEONIC EMPIRE

Napoleon did not create French imperialism; he inherited and had been an agent of the aggressive expansion undertaken by the Convention and the Directory. A satellite republic had already been established in Holland in 1795, and during the victorious campaigns against Austria toward the end of the decade, French armies had extended French power to Switzerland and parts of Italy. This burst of French expansion had come to an end when Napoleon signed peace treaties with Austria in 1801 and England in 1802. Large-scale hostilities were resumed in 1805, and from that time until Napoleon's ultimate defeat ten years later, France was almost constantly at war.

If Napoleon could have avoided war he might have consolidated his European empire. But his own ambition and the continuing enmity of England made war almost inevitable. England was determined to keep France from becoming the dominant political and economic power in Europe. French control of the Low Countries had already violated a basic rule of English foreign policy—namely, to keep these invasion bases and commercial centers out of the hands of a strong power. The British and their ablest statesman of the period, William Pitt the Younger, furthermore, were convinced that Napoleon was using the peace to ready France for yet another war. Pitt soon was able to persuade other continental states that they must join England to restore the balance of power and resist the spread of French influence in central Europe.

Napoleon was just as ready for war as was England. He felt that his empire could never be secure and that his plans for Europe could never be achieved until England had been thoroughly defeated. The two states drifted into war in 1803, and other continental powers—Austria, Russia, and finally Prussia—joined England.

It was a difficult war for the two major contestants. Napoleon could not gain control of the sea, and without this control he could not subdue England. He made his greatest effort in 1805 when he concentrated his army at Boulogne and tried to entice the British fleet out of the Channel by an elaborate set of naval feints in the Atlantic. But the English were not deceived. While one fleet guarded England against invasion, another, under Nelson, caught the French off Cape Trafalgar and annihilated them (October 21, 1805). Napoleon was never again able to threaten England with invasion.

The English, on the other hand, could not defeat the French on the Continent and were dependent on the armies of their allies. By the fall of 1805 the armies of the Russian and Austrian emperors assembled in central Europe for a combined assault. Instead of waiting for the attack, Napoleon marched an army deep into central Europe and took the Austrian and Russian generals by surprise. He defeated the Austrian and Russian forces first at Ulm, and then again in the most spectacular of all his victories, at Austerlitz, on December 2, 1805.

With Austria defeated and Russia in retreat, Napoleon followed up his victory

1789		1795		1799	Napoleon	1814

Revolutionary Governments	Directory	Consulate	First Empire

1804

with a complete reorganization of the German states. He helped end the Holy Roman Empire and eliminated most of the small German principalities. Out of these petty states he created a satellite system composed of fourteen larger states that were united in a Confederation of the Rhine, with Napoleon as protector.

Prussia, which had not at first joined the coalition against Napoleon, entered the fray in 1806 and was soundly defeated at Jena in October of that year. King Frederick William III was forced to accept a humiliating peace and to become an ally of France. The following spring, Tsar Alexander I of Russia again sent an army against Napoleon, only to have it defeated at Friedland in June 1807. In three campaigns in three successive years, Napoleon had defeated the three strongest powers on the Continent and established his position as master of Europe. Russia was too large to occupy, but Napoleon had taught Tsar Alexander the futility of opposition. A few weeks after Friedland, Napoleon and Alexander held a dramatic meeting near Tilsit in eastern Prussia. Alexander recognized Napoleon's supremacy in the West, and Napoleon agreed not to intervene in Russia's internal affairs or to prevent Alexander from extending Russian influence into the Ottoman-controlled Balkans.

Napoleonic Europe and the Continental System

Napoleon had reached the summit of his power. All Europe, save England, was under his control (see color map "Napoleonic Europe"). France, Belgium, Germany west of the Rhine, and parts of Italy and Illyria constituted a French Empire ruled directly by Napoleon. Holland, Westphalia (a Napoleonic creation in Germany), and southern Italy were theoretically independent kingdoms, over which Napoleon placed three of his brothers as kings. Northern Italy was also a kingdom, with Napoleon himself as king. The Grand Duchy of Warsaw was carved out of Prussia's Polish territories and given to France's ally, the king of Saxony. In 1808, the Bourbon monarch of Spain was overthrown and replaced by Napoleon's brother Joseph.

England alone resisted the tide of French expansion. From 1806 on, Napoleon tried to weaken England by wrecking British trade with the Continent. This so-called Continental System imposed heavy penalties on anyone trading with England and put a heavy strain on the economies of the continental countries. England made the strain worse by blockading all countries that subscribed to the French system. The English blockade drove Denmark into a close alliance with France and helped cause the War of 1812 with the United States. But the blockade caused less ill will than Napoleon's decrees. It was impossible for the European economy to function properly without English trade. Smuggling became a highly organized and profitable business, and attempts to enforce French regulations strengthened the opposition to Napoleon everywhere. Most important of all, the blockade led to a quarrel between Napoleon and Alexander of Russia.

Tsar Alexander had not been happy with the results of his alliance with Napoleon. France had gained vast territories; Russia had acquired only Finland and Bessarabia. Napoleon's creation of the Grand Duchy of Warsaw menaced Russia's control of the Polish lands it had seized in the 1790s. But the greatest grievance of the Russians was the Continental System. Russia needed English markets for its grain, and Alexander would not and could not enforce the rules against trade with England. Napoleon, bent on the destruction of England,

Contemporary engravings of French soldiers of Napoleon's era. Left: a sharpshooter of the Imperial Guard; right: a cannoneer.

hailed as liberators. Napoleon took full advantage of this feeling. He was able to break the archaic political and social structures of many states. Within the Empire, the *Code Napoléon* was established, the privileges of the Church and aristocracies were abolished, and fetters on local industry and commerce were removed. Napoleon saw himself as the "revolution on horseback" and sought to impose a new order on Europe—a new order that was enlightened, rational, and French.

This vision of Napoleon's was, at best, only partially achieved, and even those who had most enthusiastically received the invading French armies soon perceived that imperialism was a more important component of the Napoleonic system than was liberation. The Continental System contributed to a general economic crisis in Europe that alienated the commercial and industrial interests. High taxes and conscription were imposed on the tributary states. And the French system was enforced by tight police surveillance. Napoleonic tutelage, even at its most benevolent, appeared incompatible with the libertarian and nationalistic ideals of the French Revolution.

Increasingly, Napoleon was beset by the growth of nationalistic feelings and national resistance to his rule. In Germany, Italy, and Spain, national awakening was intimately linked to opposition to French hegemony. This opposition took many forms. In Italy and Germany cultural movements gained momentum that emphasized the common history, language, and literature shared by these fragmented countries. In Spain resistance was expressed more violently when rebellions broke out in 1808 against the regime of Joseph Bonaparte. In was here that Napoleon first confronted guerrilla warfare and encountered serious failure. A Spanish victory at Baylen in 1808 was the initial break in the emperor's record of invincibility. By 1813, the Spanish rebels, with the help of an English army under Wellington, had driven the French from Madrid and had organized a constitutional government that controlled more than half the country.

The appearance of a well-organized

could not tolerate this breach in his system. He requested Alexander to stop the trade; when Alexander refused, Napoleon prepared to invade Russia.

The Weaknesses of the Napoleonic Empire

When Napoleon undertook his Russian campaign in June 1812, his hold on Europe and even on the French had begun to weaken. French expansion had at first been greeted with enthusiasm by many of the inhabitants of the Low Countries, Germany, and Italy. Enlightenment ideas were strong in these regions, and their governments were unpopular. In the northern Netherlands there was opposition to the domination of the House of Orange and the urban oligarchy. In the Austrian Netherlands (Belgium), nationalist feelings had led to a revolt against Austrian rule as early as 1789. Italy was dominated by Spain and Austria, and growing nationalism and spread of the Enlightenment made the ideas of the French Revolution attractive to many Italians. In Germany the writings of the *philosophes* had been eagerly read, and there was general disgust with the archaic structure of the Holy Roman Empire and the stodgy governments of the petty principalities. In short, there had been serious political unrest in much of Europe in the 1780s and 1790s, and the invading French armies had often been

English army on the Continent was one indication that the balance of power in Europe was shifting against Napoleon. There were other signs, the most important of which was the recovery of France's nominal ally and potential enemy, Prussia. After the humiliating defeat at Jena, the process of reconstructing the kingdom was begun. Under Generals Gneisenau and Scharnhorst, the Prussian army was modernized and universal military training was introduced. To revitalize the country, another reformer, Baron vom Stein, persuaded the king to abolish serfdom and to grant a large measure of liberty to Prussian municipalities. Stein's social reforms were limited in their effects, but the military reforms allowed Prussia to play a significant role in the final defeat of Napoleon.

As his enemies were strengthening themselves and challenging the French monopoly of force, Napoleon began to lose his grip at home. Economic domination of Europe, which had been the goal of the Continental System, failed to materialize, and France, like the rest of the Continent, suffered from the economic crisis that marked the last years of Napoleon's rule. Internally, the regime grew more repressive, and Napoleon became increasingly intolerant of criticism. After his divorce from Josephine and his marriage to Marie Louise of Austria, Napoleon more and more took on the airs of an Old Regime monarch. Those Frenchmen who had provided him with his magnificent and spirited army were now exhausted by the burdens of empire.

The Invasion of Russia and the Fall of Napoleon

In June 1812 Napoleon marched into Russia with six hundred thousand men, the largest army ever assembled up to then. Most had been recruited in the German states or in other dependencies. Napoleon expected to deliver a fast and decisive blow, but the Russians, greatly outnumbered, did not give battle. Instead they retreated, drawing Napoleon behind them. After one costly but inconclusive engagement at Borodino, Napoleon occupied Moscow in September and waited for Alexander to offer peace terms. But no message came.

After five weeks Napoleon realized that he could not keep so large a force in Russia through the winter, and in October he began the long march westward. Since the land through which he passed had already been devastated, he lost thousands of men to disease and starvation. When the cold weather came, the weakened soldiers were no match for the elements. As the remnants of Napoleon's army stumbled closer to the frontier, Polish and German soldiers deserted and headed homeward. When Napoleon reached the German border in December, he could not muster one hundred thousand men. If Austria or Prussia had chosen to launch an attack at this time, the war could have been ended. But the allies did not know the extent of the disaster.

Once in German territory, Napoleon hurried to Paris and organized a new army that he marched eastward in the spring of 1813. But defeat had ended Napoleon's glory, and he was badly beaten by the combined armies of Austria, Prussia, and Russia at Leipzig in October. Napoleon lost about two-fifths of his men and retreated back across the

---

Napoleon I: A Self-Assessment   1817

In spite of all the libels, I have no fear whatever about my fame. Posterity will do me justice. The truth will be known; and the good I have done will be compared with the faults I have committed. I am not uneasy as to the result. Had I succeeded, I would have died with the reputation of the greatest man that ever existed. As it is, although I have failed, I shall be considered as an extraordinary man: my elevation was unparalleled, because unaccompanied by crime. I have fought fifty pitched battles, almost all of which I have won. I have framed and carried into effect a code of laws that will bear my name to the most distant posterity. I raised myself from nothing to be the most powerful monarch in the world. Europe was at my feet. I have always been of opinion that the sovereignty lay in the people. In fact, the imperial government was a kind of republic. Called to the head of it by the voice of the nation, my maxim was, *la carrière est ouverte aux talents* without distinction of birth or fortune. . . .

From *The Corsican*, ed. by R. M. Johnston (Boston: Houghton Mifflin, 1910), p. 492.

Retreat of Napoleon's army across the Beresina River (1812), by an anonymous painter.

cated for the second time. The allies now exiled him to St. Helena, a small and remote island off the Atlantic coast of Africa. The era of the Revolution and Napoleon had ended.

The era had ended, but it could not be effaced. The allies could restore a Bourbon to the throne of France, but the new king, Louis XVIII, could not restore the Old Regime. He had to keep many of Napoleon's officials. He had to preserve the Napoleonic administrative system and the Concordat with the Church. He had to accept both the revolutionary principle of equality under the law and the revolutionary land settlement. He had to grant a constitution to his people. It was a conservative constitution with a very limited electorate, but it meant that the king's rule was not absolute. And throughout Europe the great ideas of the Revolution—liberty, equality, and nationalism—lived on, and with them the new and dangerous concept of revolution as a means of attaining social and political goals. These ideas were only partially recognized in some countries and totally suppressed in others, but they persisted everywhere—smoldering coals that were to burst into flame again and again during the nineteenth century.

The political balance of power in Europe had been permanently altered. No one could restore the petty states of Germany or the feeble republics of Italy. No one could ignore the claims of Russia to have, for the first time, a voice in the affairs of western Europe. No one could fail to recognize the tremendous strides that England had made in industry and commerce during the wars. Conversely, for the first time in two centuries, France was no longer the richest and strongest European state. These were some of the new political facts with which the diplomats at Vienna had to deal.

Rhine. Meanwhile, Britain's general Wellington defeated another French army in Spain and crossed the border into southern France. On March 31, 1814, the allied armies entered Paris, and one week later Napoleon abdicated. After some debate, the allies restored the Bourbons to the throne of France and then called a conference in Vienna to settle the fate of the rest of Europe.

Napoleon was exiled to the island of Elba, off the Italian coast. But he still had one battle to fight. In March 1815 he escaped and landed in the south of France. The army proved loyal to the deposed leader, and Napoleon was soon in control of France once again.* But the allies were prepared. Napoleon was conclusively defeated at Waterloo on June 18, 1815, and three days later he abdi-

*The three months spanning Napoleon's escape from Elba, resumption of power, and second abdication following his defeat at the battle of Waterloo are known as the Hundred Days.

Suggestions for Further Reading

Note: Asterisk denotes a book available in paperback edition.

General   The best general work on the French Revolution is the authoritative study by G. Lefebvre, *The French Revolution* (1962–64). A somewhat different interpretation may be found in F. Furet and D. Richet, *The French Revolution* (1970). C. Brinton, *A Decade of Revolution, 1789–1799** (1934), in the *Rise of Modern Europe* series, is still a fine introductory summary. See also A. Soboul, *The French*

*Revolution: 1787–1799** (1975), and M. J. Sydenham, *The French Revolution** (1966). Valuable source material may be found in J. H. Stewart, ed., *A Documentary Survey of the French Revolution* (1951), and P. Dawson, *The French Revolution* (1967). J. M. Thompson, *The French Revolution** (1943), is a solid standard work. R. R. Palmer, *The Age of the Democratic Revolutions*, 2 vols. (1959–64), places the French Revolution in its broad European perspective. He published a revised and shortened version as *The World of the French Revolution* (1971). The same is done in N. Hampson, *The First European Revolution: 1776–1815** (1969), and, with a neo-Marxian approach, in E. J. Hobsbawm, *The Age of Revolution: 1789–1848** (1962). W. Doyle, *Origins of the French Revolution** (1980), assesses the literature since 1939.

The Social History of the Revolution

An excellent brief introduction to the social history of the Revolution is N. Hampson, *Social History of the French Revolution* (1962). The essays in J. Kaplow, ed., *New Perspectives on the French Revolution** (1965), are indispensable for an understanding of the social movement. A. Cobban, *The Social Interpretation of the French Revolution* (1964), is an important revisionary statement. On the role of the masses, see G. F. E. Rudé, *The Crowd in the French Revolution** (1959). E. Barber, *The Bourgeoisie in XVIIth Century France** (1955), discusses the background of bourgeois discontent.

Major French Interpretations of the Revolution

Alexis de Tocqueville's *The Old Regime and the French Revolution** (1956) presents the classic view of the Revolution as the continuation of the centralizing tendencies of the Old Regime. G. Lefebvre, *The Coming of the French Revolution* (1947), gives an excellent picture of France in the first year of the Revolution and states precisely and clearly the nature and problem of the French Revolution as a whole. For a treatment from the republican side, see F. V. A. Aulard, *The French Revolution*, 4 vols. (1901, 1910). A. Mathiez, *The French Revolution** (1928), is a sympathetic leftist interpretation of the Revolution.

Special Topics

B. Stone, *The Parlement of Paris, 1774–1789* (1981), deals with this important institution. Perhaps the best introduction to the Convention and the Reign of Terror is the brief study by J. M. Thompson, *Robespierre and the French Revolution** (1953). R. R. Palmer, *Twelve Who Ruled** (1941), is a fascinating account of the Reign of Terror written from a biographical approach. D. M. Greer, *The Incidence of Terror During the French Revolution* (1935), is a statistical account of who was actually executed and how. The role of Paris in the Revolution is the subject of A. Soboul, *The Parisian Sans-Culottes and the French Revolution* (1964). C. Tilly, *The Vendée** (1964), is a sociological analysis of the counterrevolution. On party politics during the Legislative Assembly and the Convention, see M. J. Sydenham, *The Girondins* (1961) and *The First French Republic, 1792–1804* (1973). The fall of the Jacobins and the period of the Directory are dealt with authoritatively in G. Lefebvre's *The Thermidorians** (1937) and *The Directory** (1946). For a more recent treatment, see M. Lyons, *France under the Directory* (1975). A. Forrest, *The French Revolution and the Poor* (1981), is an important contribution.

Napoleon and the Napoleonic Empire

G. Bruun, *Europe and the French Imperium** (1938), in the *Rise of Modern Europe* series, is a good general introduction. Among the many biographies of Napoleon are those of J. M. Thompson, *Napoleon Bonaparte* (1952), and F. Markham, *Napoleon** (1966). The best guide to interpretations of the period and perhaps the best book on Napoleon in English is P. Geyl, *Napoleon: For and Against** (1949). The best treatment in any language are the two volumes by G. Lefebvre, *Napoléon* (trans. 1969). On Napoleon's domestic policy, see R. Holtman, *The Napoleonic Revolution** (1967). See also, I. Collins, *Napoleon and his Parliaments, 1800–1815* (1979). Both R. B. Mowat, *The Diplomacy of Napoleon* (1924), and H. C. Deutsch, *The Genesis of Napoleonic Imperialism, 1801–1805* (1938), remain standard works on foreign policy. See also S. T. Ross, *European Diplomatic History 1789–1815: France Against Europe** (1969). The best recent treatment of Napoleon's military career is D. Chandler, *The Campaigns of Napoleon* (1966). O. Connelly, *Napoleon's Satellite Kingdoms* (1965), deals with the rule of Napoleon and his relatives over most of Europe. G. H. Lovett, *Napoleon and the Birth of Modern Spain*, 2 vols. (1965), tells a dramatic story. Napoleon's relations with the two peripheral powers of Europe are treated in C. Oman, *Britain Against Napoleon* (1944), and in A. Palmer, *Napoleon in Russia* (1967). On the end of Napoleon's career, see C. Hibbert, *Waterloo: Napoleon's Last Campaign* (1969).

Index

A

Abbasid Caliphate, 176, 218, 301–05, 309
Abdul-Hamid II, 690
Abelard, 222–24, 225; *Sic et Non,* 222, 223
abortion, 844
Abraham, 18–19, 170
Abu-Bekr, 171, 173
Abu'l Abbas, 176
Abul Fazl: quoted, 326
Abyssinia, 681, 715
Acadia, 442, 454
Acaemeneid Empire (Persia), 126
Acre, 229, 307, 308–09
Acropolis, 43
Action Française, 657
Actium, battle of, 77
Act of Settlement (1701), 459, 461, 501
Act of Union (1707), 461
Adams, Henry, 648
Addison, Joseph, 492
Adelaide, 197
Aden, 397
Adenauer, Konrad, 788, 800–01
Adler, Victor, 660
Admiral Graf Spee (battleship), 773
Adrianople, 316; battle of, 113; Treaty of (1829), 556, 595
Adua, battle of, 661, 681
advertising, 649
Aegean Sea: ancient trade and settlements, 12, 13, 14, 16, 26, 28–31
Aehrenthal, Aloys von, 690
Aeschylus, 43; *Oresteia* trilogy, 44
Aëtius, 116
"affirmative action" program, 845
Afghanistan, 175, 324, 683, 684, 815, 825, 835
Afghan Lodi Dynasty (India), 325
Africa, 506, 589; central, 680–81; east, 687; European imperialism in, 633, 636, 643, 679–83; explorations in, 393, 396–97; famine in, 844; nationalism in, 836; Roman expeditions in, 93; slaves from, 400–01, 409, 439, 440, 500; and Third World, 791–92, 841; west, 511, 600, 681. *See also* North Africa; South Africa
African Groundnut Council, 841
Agadir, 691
Agincourt, battle of, 284
Agnew, Spiro, 806
agriculture, 435; in ancient Middle East, 4–6, 9, 10; and capitalism, 364–65, 629, 631; improved technology for, 581, 649; land reclaimed for, 209; open-field system, 572; revolution in, 499, 501, 571–73; three-field system, 206, 572. *See also* individual countries
Agrippa, 77, 80
Agrippina, 85
Ahmose, 15, 16
Ainu, 339–40
Aix-la-Chapelle, 548–49; Treaty of, 508
Ajanta, 130
Akbar, 326–28
Akhnaton, 16
Alais, Peace of (1629), 420
Alamanni, 153

Alaska, 555, 628
Ala-ud-Din, Delhi sultan, 325
Albania, 690, 692–93, 702, 759, 769, 775, 789, 810
Alberti, Leon Battista: *On the Family,* 353
Albigensian heresy, 245, 253, 255
Albuquerque, Alfonso de, 397
Alcuin, 183
Alexander III, Pope, 242
Alexander VI, Pope, 363, 372, 399
Alexander I, Tsar of Russia, 539–40, 541, 546, 548–49, 556, 558
Alexander II, Tsar of Russia, 596, 616–17, 662, 705
Alexander III, Tsar of Russia, 662
Alexander the Great, 24, 50–51, 54, 57, 63, 126
Alexandra, Empress of Russia, 664, 703
Alexandria, 50, 52, 54, 76, 88, 92, 96, 112, 159, 176, 229, 394
Alexius Comnenus, Byzantine Emperor, 305–06, 307
Alfonso X, King of Castile, 241; *Siete Partidas,* 241
Alfred the Great, 190–91, 200
Algeciras, Act of (1906), 689, 691
Algeria, 317, 600, 679, 781, 799, 836–37
Ali, 173, 174, 176
Allende (Gossens), Salvador, 807, 841
Allen of Hurwood, Lord, 761
Alliance for Progress, 807
Allied Control Council, 785
Allied Military Control Commission, 712, 715, 718
Allied Powers: First World War, 699–705, 707–20, 748; post-Second World War, 784–91; Second World War, 773, 774–77, 779–83
alphabets, 17–18, 31, 168. *See also* writing
Alsace, 188, 432
Alsace-Lorraine, 187, 610, 658, 688, 700, 708
Alva, Ferdinand Alvarez de Toledo, Duke of, 406, 410
Ambrose, St., 114, 119
America, 363, 365, 408, 450, 453; Catholic Church in, 400–03; discovery of, 393, 398–99; metals from, 400, 403–04, 417
American Federation of Labor, 630, 730
American Indians, 399, 400–02, 403, 439, 443, 624, 632
American Revolution, 408, 517–20, 588, 623; ideals of, 462, 520, 529
Amiens Cathedral, 232
Amin Dada, Idi, 837
Amorites, 8
Amos, 18, 21
Amsterdam, 365, 405, 407, 435
Anabaptists, 384–85, 390, 405
Anagni: attack at, 264, 271
Analects of Confucius, The, 136
anarchism, 591, 617, 662
anatomy, 359, 474, 476
Anaxagoras, 45
Andalusia, 404
Anderson, Thornton: quoted, 315
Andropov, Yuri, 809–10
Angkor Wat, 131–32

Angles, 145. *See also* Anglo-Saxons
Anglicanism, 385–88, 424–28
Anglo-German Agreement (1935), 761
Anglo-German Heligoland Treaty (1890), 687
Anglo-Russian Entente (1907), 684, 689, 695
Anglo-Saxon Chronicle, 200, 211, 212
Anglo-Saxons, 155; Britain under, 116, 143, 145, 151–53, 199–202, 210–12; literature, 200. *See also* Germanic kingdoms; Germanic tribes
Angola, 837, 838–39
Anjou, 235, 238, 239
Anjou, François Hercule, Duke of, 406
Ankara, 316
An Lu-shan, 331, 332
Anna Comnena: quoted, 307
Anne, Queen of England, 422, 459–60, 461, 501
Anti-Comintern Pact (1936), 760
Anti-Corn Law League, 566
Antigonus, King of Macedon, 51
Antioch, 52, 112, 159, 176, 305–06
anti-semitism, 655, 758–59
Antoninus Pius, Roman Emperor, 87
Antony, Mark, 75–77
Antwerp, 365, 398, 405, 406, 407, 454
apartheid, 814, 838, 845
Apollonius, 52
Apuleius: *Golden Ass,* 95
Aquinas, St. Thomas, 250, 263–65, 294, 303, 353; quoted, 263
Aquitaine, 156, 181, 235, 238, 239, 255, 267, 269, 270, 281
Arab Empire: Abbasid dynasty, 176, 218, 301–05, 309; aristocracy, 174, 176; conquests of, 51, 118, 164, 167, 173, 175–76, 299; culture, 167, 168, 174–75, 176; decline, 303–05, 309; government and administration, 174–75, 299, 303–04; military, 303, 304; North Africa under, 162, 175; Ommiad dynasty, 173–76, 304; philosophers, 302–03; scholars, 174–75, 247, 263, 299, 302–03, 317–18; science, 53, 167, 168, 198, 224, 245–46, 294, 302, 473; Spain under, 155, 175, 204, 259, 366–67; trade and commerce, 175, 176, 179, 301, 330, 394, 395–97. *See also* Moslems
Arabia, 7, 81, 167–68, 170, 173, 317; religion, 168–73
Arabic numerals, 129, 302
Arab League, 831
Arabs: conflict with Jews, 735, 791, 814, 831, 833–34; invasion of India, 323; nationalism, 831–32; terrorists, 833
Arafat, Yasir, 833
Aragon, 240, 289, 366–68, 402
Arakcheiev, Alexis, 556
Aramaeans, 17
Arberry, A. J.: quoted, 170
Arcadius, Roman Emperor, 115
archeology: in China, 132; in Crete, 12–13; in Egypt, 15; in Greece, 28; and Hebrew scriptures, 18, 19; in India, 3; in Pompeii, 3, 492; in Rome, 58, 92; Stone Age, 4

Archimedes, 53

architecture: baroque, 451, 481; Buddhist, 127, 331; church, 120, 162, 219, 220–22, 231–33, 263, 291; classical, 492; Egyptian, 11, 15, 32, 42; functional, 631, 743; Georgian, 492; Gothic, 220–22, 231–33, 263, 291–92, 494; Greek, 32, 42, 67, 94; Hindu, 326; medieval, 219, 220–22, 231–33, 263, 552; of Mesopotamia, 6, 7, 11; Moslem, 175, 303; Roman, 67, 94, 118, 162, 355; Romanesque, 222; Turkish, 317. *See also* individual countries

Argentina, 632, 798, 839–40

Arianism, 108, 114, 117–18, 119, 144, 145, 149, 154, 155

Aristarchus, 53

aristocracy, 208, 235, 499; vs. monarchy, 497, 512, 517. *See also* nobility; individual countries

Aristophanes, 46, 52; *Clouds, The,* 44; *Lysistrata,* 44

Aristotle, 46, 49, 53, 145, 146, 167, 223, 245–47, 263–64, 294, 300, 302, 353, 474, 477–78; *Politics,* 292

Arius, 108, 114

Arkwright, Richard, 573

Armenia, 167, 173, 687

Arminians, 434

Arminius (Herman), 81

Armstrong, Neil A., 816

Arnold, Matthew, 671

art: baroque, 480–81; Buddhist, 127, 130; Christian, 120; "golden ages" of, 414; manuscript illumination, 292, 300; and Romanticism, 553; and science, 669–71; Stone Age, 4. *See also* painting; individual countries

Arthurian legend, 234

Artois, Charles Philippe, Count of, 528, 556–57. *See also* Charles X, King of France

Ashoka (Mauryan emperor), 127

Asia, 633; East, 122; imperialism in, 683–84; nationalism in, 643, 824; and Third World, 792. *See also* Southeast Asia; individual countries

Asia Minor, 14, 16, 30, 713; Byzantine reconquest of, 299, 305–06, 308; conquered by Persia, 23, 39–40, 50; Greek city-states in, 26, 31, 38, 40, 41, 48, 49, 51, 71; religions of, 54, 57, 90–91, 124; under Rome, 64, 71, 72, 87, 117, 159, 162, 166; under Turks, 217–18, 305–06, 307, 310, 316

Association of Southeast Asian Nations (ASEAN), 830–31, 841

Assyrian Empire, 16, 18, 22, 30

astrolabe, 395

astronomy: in ancient Middle East, 8, 45; Arabs, 168, 198, 246, 302; Greek, 53, 130, 246; Indian, 129–30; medieval, 198, 246; Roman, 95–96; in Scientific Revolution, 473–77

Asturias, 155, 156, 240

Aswan Dam, 832–33

Atatürk, Kemal, 835

Athens, ancient, 30, 34–36, 38, 40–42, 52, 54, 64, 71; arts, 42–43; drama, 36, 43–44,

46; festivals of Dionysius in, 36, 43, 53; government, 33, 34–35, 38, 41–42, 47, 48–49; historians and philosophers, 44–49; imperialism of, 47; navy, 34, 38–39, 40, 47, 48; Peloponnesian War, 46–47; Persian Wars, 24, 26, 36, 38–40, 44–45. *See also* Greece, ancient

Atlantic Charter, 784

atomic weapons, 742, 783–84, 791–92, 797, 846. *See also* nuclear power

Atoms for Peace Program, 816

Attica, 35, 38

Attila, King of the Huns, 116

Attlee, Clement, 786, 798

Attu, 783

Augsburg, Peace of (1555), 381–82, 393, 429–30

Augustenburg, Duke of, 607

Augustine of Canterbury, St., 152–53, 153n

Augustine of Hippo, St., 145, 449; *City of God, The,* 115, 119; *Confessions,* 119

Augustus (Octavian), Roman Emperor, 75–77, 79–84, 89

Augustus II (the Strong), King of Poland, 463

Aurangzeb (Mughal emperor), 327–28

Aurelian, Roman Emperor, 100, 103

Auschwitz, 779

Austerlitz, battle of, 538

Australia, 613, 633, 634, 647, 649

Austria: *Anschluss,* 755, 759, 764, 765–67; foreign affairs, 497, 499, 505, 513–14, 557, 559, 596, 598, 612, 617, 676–78, 687, 688–93, 716, 762; and French Revolutionary Wars, 531–32, 533; government and politics, 604, 607, 659, 709, 759; in Habsburg Empire, 290–91, 295, 367, 370, 402, 430, 431, 432, 453–54, 463–64, 470, 505, 516, 540, 547–50, 554, 557–58, 562–66, 598, 601–03; industrialization, 574–76, 660; and Italian unification wars, 601–03, 606–07; labor, 652, 661; mercantilism, 438; and Napoleonic Wars, 536, 538–39, 542; nationalism in, 559, 563, 568, 604; post-First World War, 712, 713, 714, 720, 727, 731; post-Second World War, 787, 812; and Prussia, 598, 603, 604–09, 610; Seven Years' War, 509–11; socialism in, 660–61; social reform, 659, 660, 661; War of the Austrian Succession, 507–09

Austria-Hungary, 604, 659–61, 674, 677, 689, 693; First World War, 693–95, 699–704, 706, 708–09; nationalities in, 647, 659–61, 674, 708. *See also* Austria; Hungary

Austrian Netherlands, 454, 505, 516. *See also* Belgium authoritarianism, 747, 759, 807

Avanti, 753

Avars, 165, 183

Averroës, 302–03

Avicenna, 302

Avignon: papacy in, 271–72, 277–78, 359–60

Axis Powers, 763, 769, 773–76, 779–83

Ayub Khan, Mohammed, 822

Azores, 396

Azov, 468

Aztec Empire, 400, 439

B

Babeuf, "Gracchus," 535

Babur, 326

Babylonian Captivity, 22, 272n; and Avignon papacy, 272, 277, 278, 344

Babylonian civilization, 6–8, 22; architecture, 6–7; legal code, 8; mathematics and astronomy, 8, 45; religion, 6, 8. *See also* Mesopotamia

Bach, Johann Sebastian, 493

Bacon, Francis, 475–76, 478

Bacon, Roger, 264

Bactria, 54

Badoglio, Pietro, 781

Bagehot, Walter, 648; *Physics and Politics,* 634, 667

Baghdad, 175, 176, 301–02, 309; Pact (1955), 831–32

Bahamas, 398

Bahmini dynasty (India), 325

Bakunin, Mikhail, 591, 617, 651

balance of power: European, 347, 417, 454–55, 470, 497–99, 519, 541–42, 545, 547, 595, 598, 612, 618, 674–78, 686–89; international, 793, 796, 812

Balboa, Vasco de, 399

Baldwin, Count of Flanders, 308

Baldwin, Stanley, 733

Baldwin of Lorraine, 305

Balfour Declaration, 735

Balkan League, 692

Balkans, 162, 165, 244, 316, 781, 785; Byzantine influence in, 301, 308; early history, 51, 61, 98, 113–14, 115, 117, 159, 166; European imperialism in, 674, 676–78, 689–91; First World War, 700, 702; nationalism in, 676, 678; under Ottoman Empire, 539, 595, 676; Second World War, 775–76; Wars, 692–93

Baltic states, 229, 466, 469, 662, 704, 727, 748, 774; post-Second World War, 785, 787

Balzac, Honoré de, 590, 670

Bancroft, George, 621

Bandung Conference (1955), 841

Bangladesh, 824–25, 841

Bani-Sadr, Abolhassan, 835

banking: European, 348, 365, 398; government control of, 630; medieval, 230, 253, 275

Bank of England, 437, 460, 798

Bannockburn, Battle of, 267, 281

Baptists, 385, 388, 456

Barani: quoted, 325

Barbados, 440

barbarians: and Roman Empire, 109–19; ruled North China, 140–41

Barcelona, 240

baroque style, 480–81

Barras, Paul, 536

Bartók, Béla, 743

Basel, 382; Council of, 376

Basham, A. L.: quoted, 126, 127

Basil I, Byzantine Emperor, 299

640; science and technology, 132, 137, 138, 294, 302, 334; Second World War, 783, 786, 787; Sino-Japanese War, 639, 642, 688, 779; and Soviet Union, 737, 765; Sung dynasty, 332–36, 337; Taiping Rebellion, 637–38; T'ang dynasty, 329–39; trade and commerce, 93, 137, 139–40, 175, 176, 330, 335, 395–96, 613, 636–38. *See also* People's Republic of China

Ch'in dynasty (China), 137–38

Ch'in Shih Huang-ti (Ch'in emperor), 138

Ch'ing dynasty, 338–39

chivalry, 235, 281, 345, 354

Chola kingdom (India), 320, 322

Chou dynasty (China), 133–34

Christian IV, King of Denmark, 431

Christian Democratic Party (Italy), 802

Christian Democratic Union (West Germany), 800, 801

Christianity, 18, 24, 482–83; beginnings of, 89–92, 669; conflicts between state and, 109, 114, 117; culture of, 118, 120; doctrinal disputes in, 108, 112, 152, 163–64, 166; in East, 111–12, 159, 163–64, 166; and Holy Land, 595; and Islam, 164, 324; and Jews, 89–90, 92; and papacy, 112, 116; persecution of, 85, 91, 95, 100, 106, 107–08, 163, 172, 175; and philosophers, 303; in Roman Empire, 103, 104–09, 111–12, 114, 149, 163; in Rome, 85, 88, 89–91, 95, 96, 100, 103, 104–09, 111–12, 114, 149; in Spain, 240–41; theology of, 145. *See also* Arianism; individual religions

Christian Socialists, 590–91, 652

Chronicle of Moissac, 185

Chuang Tzu, 136; quoted, 137

Chu Hsi, 336, 338

Chun Doo Hwan, 828

Cimon, 42

Circus Maximus, 92

Cistercians, 219–20

cities: riots and crime in U.S., 804, 805; rural movement to, 572, 577–78, 649. *See also* city-states; towns; urbanization

city-states: emergence of, 4, 6; Mesopotamian, 6–7; of Rome, 61, 65, 80, 87–88; spread of, in Fertile Crescent, 7. *See also* Greece, ancient; Italy

Civil Constitution of the Clergy, 530, 534

civilization: beginnings, 6–7; cycles in, 741; early spread of, 14; and population growth, 739. *See also* Middle Ages, new civilization of

Civil Rights Act (1964), 805

civil rights and liberties: in England, 458, 845; Locke on, 461–62; in U.S., 626, 628, 629, 804, 805, 845

civil service: in China, 329, 333

Civil War, U.S., 621, 622, 627–29

Clairvaux monastery, 219

Clarendon, Edward Hyde, 1st Earl of, 455–56, 458

Clarendon Code, 455–56

Clark Memorandum (1930), 737

Claudius, Roman Emperor, 84–85

Cleisthenes, 38

Clemenceau, Georges, 655, 703, 710

Clement V, Pope, 271–72

Clement VII, Pope, 278, 349, 363, 386

Cleopatra, Queen of Egypt, 76–77

Clermont, Council of (1095), 217

Cleveland, Grover, 685

Cleves, 464

Clive, Robert, 509

clock: invention of, 295

Clovis, King of the Franks, 153–55

Cluny monastery, 214, 219, 224

Cobden-Chevalier Treaty (1860), 599

Code (Justinian), 165

Code of Hammurabi, 8

coexistence, 797, 811, 815–16

Coimbra University, 247

coinage: Greek, 31; Roman, 118; U.S., 631

Colbert, Jean Baptiste, 442, 448

Cold War, 788–93, 797, 800, 802, 803–05, 811–15, 821

Coligny, Gaspard de, 411, 412

Colombia, 686

colonies: and economy, 438, 439–40, 443, 633, 643; governments, 442–43, 517–20; nationalism in, 736–37. *See also* imperialism; Third World; individual countries

Colosseum, 92

Columban, St., 155

Columbus, Christopher, 293–94, 363, 368, 398–99

Cominform, 790

Comintern, 714, 718, 748–49, 759, 790

Committee of National Liberation, 785

Commodus, Roman Emperor, 98

Common Market (European Economic Community), 798, 799, 800, 803, 816, 836

Commonwealth of Nations, 798

communication, 571, 575, 622, 648

communism, 586–87, 747, 846; international (War), 714, 747–49, 759, 784–85, 808–11, 813–14, 829–31; and nationalism, 747; spread of, 788

Communist China. *See* People's Republic of China

Communist Information Bureau. *See* Cominform

Communist League, 586–87

Communist Manifesto (Marx and Engels), 567, 587–89

Communist Party, 759; Chinese, 737, 825, 826; French, 734, 799, 800; German, 726; Italian, 802; Russian, 749, 750, 808; in western Europe, 811

Comneni dynasty (Byzantine), 305

compass, 302, 395

Compiègne: surrender at, 774

Compromise of 1850, 626

Comte, Auguste, 665, 740

compurgation, 146, 147–48

concentration and extermination camps, 758, 778–79

Concordat of Bologna (1516), 370, 411

Concordat of 1801, 537–38, 542, 656

Condorcet, Marie Jean, Marquis de: *Sketch for a Historical Picture of the Progress of the Human Mind*, 489

Confederate States of America, 627

Conference of Ambassadors, 692

Confucianism, 134–39, 335–36, 338, 342, 638

Confucius, 135–36; *Analects*, 136; quoted, 136

Congo Free State, 680

Congregationalists, 385, 426, 456

Congress of Troppau (1820), 549

Congress of Vienna (1815), 545–48, 595, 598, 612, 710

conquistadors, 400, 403

Conrad, Joseph, 742

conservatism: European, 545; and nationalism, 552–53; and Romanticism, 550

Conservative Party (British), 457, 613–14, 652–54, 718, 725, 733, 797–98

Constable, John, 550

Constance, Council of (1414–18), 360, 361, 376, 378

Constantine, Roman Emperor, 107–09, 127; conversion of, 107, 181

Constantine XI, Byzantine Emperor, 317

Constantinople, 108–09, 112–14, 117, 145, 159–67 *passim*, 176, 299, 300, 316; fall of (1453), 54, 317, 329; Moslem siege of, 176; sack of (1204), 306, 307–08; viking attacks on, 189–90, 310

Continental Congress, 519

Convention of 1841, 595

Convention of Gastein (1865), 607

Coolidge, Calvin, 729

Cooper, James Fenimore, 621

Copernicus, Nicolaus, 294, 477; *On the Revolutions of the Heavenly Bodies*, 475

Coral Sea, battle of, 783

Corbulo, 85

Corcyra, 47

Corfu, 715, 755

Corinth, 31, 39, 47, 64

Corneille, Pierre, 481, 492; *Le Cid*, 451

Corn Laws, 558, 566, 630, 653

Cornwall, 17, 116

Corporation Act, 559

Corpus Juris, 164–65, 166, 224, 352

Corsica, 65, 535

Cortenuova, battle of, 260

Cortes, 369

Cortes, Hernando, 400

Cossacks, 444

Council of Europe, 803

Council of Nicaea (325), 108

Council of People's Commissars, 706, 749

Counter Reformation. *See* Catholic Reformation

Courageous (carrier), 773

Courçon, Robert de: quoted, 247

Courland, 702

courts: ecclesiastical, 242–43, 272; feudal, 192–93, 195, 211–13, 236, 255–56; Germanic, 146–47; and Inquisition, 245; trial by inquest, 212–13; trial by jury, 236, 257. *See also* law

Craig, Gordon A.: quoted, 676

Cranmer, Thomas, 386–87, 388

Crassus, 71, 72–73, 74

Crécy, 281

Quebec, 442, 510, 633; Conference, 784
Quebec Act (1774), 519
Quemoy, 813
Quesnay, François: *Economic Survey,* 490–91

R

Racconigi Agreement (1909), 691
race, 15
Rachmaninoff, Sergei, 743
Racine, Jean, 451, 481, 492
racism, 668, 778, 798, 816–17, 836–37, 845
Radetzky, Joseph, 562
railroads, 574–75, 576, 599, 601, 629, 630
Rajputs, 322, 323, 326
Raleigh, Sir Walter, 441
Rama, 128, 132
Ramayana, 128
Ramses II, 16
Ranke, Leopold, 380
Rapallo, Treaty of (1922), 717
Raphael, 357
Rashatrakuta Empire, 320, 323
Rasputin, Gregory, 664, 703
rationalism, 483–84, 492, 743; and Enlightenment, 488–89, 493–94, 545, 550, 554, 576; and faith, 263–64, 265
Ravenna, 115, 155, 161
Rawlinson, H. G.: quoted, 323, 325, 326, 327
Reagan, Ronald, 806, 807
Realism, 669
Realpolitik, 604, 606, 675
Redistribution Bill (1885), 653
Reed, John: quoted, 707
Reform Act (1867), 653
Reform Bill (1832), 566–67
Regensburg, 462
Regulation Act (1773), 634
Reign of Terror, 532, 534–35
Reims: surrender at, 783
Reinsurance Treaty (1887), 678, 687
relativism, 482–83, 488
religion: atheism, 490; conflict with philosophy, 302–03; Deism, 490; and Enlightenment, 489–90; ethical monotheism, 18, 19–21; European age of, 390, 412–14; literature of, 292–93; Marx's attacks on, 590; mystery cults, 53–54, 66, 91, 100, 104–06, 115, 669; and nationalism, 379–80, 387–88, 390, 408, 413; revival of, 213–18, 744, 846–47; and Romanticism, 551–52, 668; and science, 477, 479–80, 482, 667–69; and skeptics, 483; toleration in, 381–82, 390, 465, 483, 515; western, and Aristotelian logic, 49. *See also* Christianity; individual countries and religions
Rembrandt van Rijn, 414, 481
Renaissance: arts and literature, 344, 352, 355–57; concept of man in, 349, 352–57 *passim;* education, 345, 350–51, 359; Humanism, 350–52, 357, 359; in Italy, 291, 344–45, 352–59; papacy, 362–63, 372; philosophy, 353, 355; revival of, 833; and science, 359, 474; and secularism, 350, 355, 356–57; society, 345, 348–52, 353–55
Renan, Ernest, 668; *Life of Jesus,* 668
Renoir, Auguste, 670
reparations: First World War, 711, 712,

716, 718, 719–20, 729; Second World War, 787
Republican Party (U.S.), 457, 626, 710, 730–31, 733, 803–06, 812
Reuchlin, Johann, 376
Reuter's news agency, 575
revolution, 492, 542; causes of, 545, 549, 553, 555, 560, 563, 568, 590; failure of, 567–68; and middle class, 408, 461, 566, 567; right of, 461–62, 520; and socialism, 651, 705
Rhee, Syngman, 793, 828
Rhineland, 279, 375, 383, 540, 710–11, 718, 761–62, 783
Rhodes, Cecil, 649, 682
Rhodes, 51, 52
Rhodesia, 798, 816–17, 821, 830
Rhodes Scholarships, 644
Ricardo, David: *On the Principles of Political Economy and Taxation,* 581–82
Ricci, Matteo, 339
Richard I (Lion-Heart), King of England, 233, 237, 239, 307
Richard II, King of England, 282–84, 287
Richardson, Samuel: *Clarissa,* 493
Richelieu, Armand de, 419–21, 422, 425, 428, 432, 448, 449, 450, 452
Riga, 229; battle at, 706; Peace of, 748
Rig veda, 125
Rilke, Rainer Maria, 742
Rio Treaty (1947), 807
Robespierre, Maximilien, 531–32, 534–35
Rocco, Alfredo, 755
Rochau, A. L. von: quoted, 606
Rockefeller, John D., 630, 649, 666
Rocroi, 432
Roentgen, Konrad, 741
Roger II, King of Sicily, 210
Rohl, J. C. G.: quoted, 658
Romagna, 603
Roman Catholic Church, 167, 759; Babylonian Captivity, 271–72, 277, 278, 344; canon law, 225, 243; clergy, 183, 186 and n, 213, 229–30, 237, 242–44, 249, 253, 262–63, 269–70, 373, 388; conflicts with secularism, 253–72, 350, 366, 369–70, 375; corruption in, 213, 372–75, 377–78; courts of, 243, 272; criticisms of, 244, 249, 253, 254, 266, 269–72, 279–80, 344, 349, 377–85; and Darwinism, 668–69; dogma and ritual, 380, 389, 551–52; and education, 179, 184, 246–47, 250, 389, 390, 552; and feudalism, 192, 209; financial policies, 182, 184, 242, 254, 272, 372–75; and French Revolution, 530; Great Schism, 275, 277–78, 344, 359–60; and heresy, 163, 172, 175, 244–45, 253, 260, 262–63, 359, 360–61, 367, 389, 402, 477; in Holy Roman Empire, 196–97, 199, 210, 216–17, 241–44, 260–63, 360, 381, 516; Index of, 389; internal reforms in, 214–17, 249, 254, 359–60, 363, 375–77, 388–90, 403; Investiture Conflict, 215–17, 240, 301; literature, 119–20, 179, 183–84, 233; medieval, 149–55, 163, 179–87, 190, 208, 213–25, 237, 243–45, 249, 253, 262–63, 277, 374–75, 378, 489; mendicant orders, 248–50; missionaries, 153, 173, 180, 181, 312, 338, 339, 341, 389, 442; monaster-

ies, 149–53, 155, 190, 214, 219–20, 280, 373, 379; in New World, 400–01, 402–03; organization and administration, 149, 151, 181–82, 219, 243, 249, 279; parish system, 181–82, 213; and Protestant Reformation, 363, 377–82, 388–90, 413; revival of, 549, 551–52; schism with Greek Church, 180, 218, 300–01, 308, 313, 596; and social reform, 652; Thirty Years' War, 429–33. *See also* Christianity; crusades; papacy; theology; individual countries
Romance of the Rose, 266
Roman Empire, early, 23, 50, 79–101; arts, 94–95; bureaucracy, 80, 84, 87, 100; Christianity in, 85, 88, 89–91, 95, 96, 100; cities, 97, 99–100; corruption in, 87, 94; economy, 98, 100; expansion, 51, 54, 64, 65, 77, 81, 84, 86–87; "five good emperors," 86–87; Flavian emperors, 86; frontiers of, 80–81, 86–87, 99–100; at its height, 85–98; Jews in, 88–89; Julio-Claudian emperors, 84–85; literature, 95–96; military of, 80, 84, 85, 86, 98–101; principate of Augustus, 77, 79–84; provinces under, 79–80, 82, 84, 85–86, 87–94, 97, 98–100, 106; Senate of, 79–80, 81–82, 84, 85, 86, 98; society, 79, 81, 92–94, 97, 100, 106; succession problem, 83–84, 86, 98; third-century weaknesses of, 98–100; "year of the four emperors," 85. *See also* Roman era
Roman Empire, late, 103–20; barbarian attacks on, 109–18, 119, 133; bureaucracy, 103, 104, 109, 110–11; Christianity in, 103, 104–09, 111–12, 114, 149; cities, 110, 112, 117, 159; divided authority in, 103, 108, 115; divinity of emperor, 103–04; economy, 104, 110–11; frontiers of, 103, 108, 109, 112, 114–15; military of, 103, 104, 105, 107, 108, 109–10, 113–15, 117, 118; provinces under, 109, 110–11, 114; reforms in, 103–04; reign of Constantine, 107–09; reign of Diocletian, 101, 103–07; religion in, 104–07; society, 106, 110, 117–18; succession problem, 103, 107; of West, 109, 110, 112–18, 143, 159, 160–62, 165. *See also* Roman era
Roman era: agriculture, 57, 67–68, 93, 110, 111; aristocracy, 58–61, 67–69, 85; arts, 65, 66, 67, 94, 118–20, 162, 355; citizenship, 69, 84, 88, 98; city-states, 61, 65, 80, 87–88; colonies, 59, 61, 69, 71, 75, 82; commerce and industry, 93, 99, 108, 111, 117; drama, 66–67, 95; early history, 57–58; equestrians of, 67, 69–70, 72, 81, 84, 87, 92; Greek influence in, 54, 65–67, 83, 87–88, 90, 145; historians, 66, 82, 94–95, 96, 233; language, 83, 88; Latin culture, 87–88, 143–45, 352–53, 482, 492, 552; law, 60, 67, 69, 94, 96–97, 117, 145, 164–65, 224–25, 236; literature, 65, 66, 82–83, 94–95, 96, 118, 145, 179, 183–84, 224, 350; oratory, 72, 96; patriotism, 82, 104, 106, 115, 159, 161; philosophers, 82, 86, 95, 96, 145; public spectacles, 82, 92; scholars, 145–46, 247–48; science, 83, 95–96; slavery, 58, 64, 65, 66, 67–68, 71, 91, 92–93

Vienna, 317, 370, 432, 463–64, 516, 562, 563–64, 566, 660, 728, 747; Conference (1961), 813; Peace of (1864), 607
Vietnam, 328, 829–30. *See also* North Vietnam; South Vietnam
Vietnam War, 799, 805, 806, 814
Vigilius, Pope, 164
Vijayanagar kingdom (India), 325
Viking I, 816
vikings, 188–91, 209, 211, 310
Villafranca agreement, 603
villages: medieval, 206; Stone Age, 4–6
Villon, François, 292
Vilna, 716
Virgil, 83, 265; *Aeneid,* 146
Virginia, 437, 441, 442
Virginia Company, 442
Visconti, Gian Galeazzo, 347–48
Vishnu, 128, 131–32, 322
Visigoths, 113, 143, 154, 155, 159, 175, 183; in Gaul, 143, 145, 154; sacked Rome, 115; in Spain, 115, 116, 143, 154, 155, 161–62, 175. *See also* Goths
Vitry, Jacques de: quoted, 249
Vivaldi, Antonio, 481
Vladivostok, 638, 684
Voltaire, 353, 463, 485–92 *passim,* 503, 506, 512, 514, 525; *Candide,* 492; *History of Civilization,* 486; *Philosophical Letters on the English,* 485; quoted, 486
Vondel, Joost van den, 414
Vorster, Balthazar J., 838

W

Wafd party (Egypt), 736
Wakefield, Edward Gibbon: *Letter from Sidney,* 633
Wake Island, 782
Waldeck-Rousseau Law (1884), 652
Waldensians, 244–45
Wales, 116, 143, 152; conquered by England, 267
Walesa, Lech, 810
Wallace, William, 267
Wallachia, 556, 595–98
Wallenstein, Albrecht von, 431, 432
Walpole, Sir Robert, 501–02
Wang An-shih, 333, 335
Wang Yang-ming, 338
warfare: in ancient Middle East, 13, 53; beginnings of treaties, 16; cavalry, 192; and Darwinism, 667; dread of nuclear, 832; in eighteenth century, 454; feudal, 195, 213–14; guerrilla, 541; limited, 497–98; medieval, 192, 284, 289; nationalism as cause of, 553, 555, 563, 568, 590, 693; *philosophes* on, 489. *See also* weapons
Warner, Philip: quoted, 598
War of 1812, 539
War of the Austrian Succession, 506, 507–09
War of the League of Aubsburg, 453
War of the Spanish Succession, 453–54
Warsaw: Grand Duchy of, 539; Pact (1955), 812
Wars of the Roses, 285 and n, 368
Washington, George, 520
Washington Naval Conference (1921, 1922), 729, 737, 738

Watergate affair, 805
Waterloo, battle of, 542
Watt, James, 501, 573
Watts, Isaac, 490
weapons: bayonet, 452; Chinese, 294, 335; industry, 435; medieval, 282, 294–95, 335; and metallurgy, 363; Second World War, 773. *See also* atomic weapons
Webb, Sidney and Beatrice, 650
Webster-Ashburton Treaty (1846), 625
Weihaiwei, 639
Weimar Republic, 726, 800
Weitling, Wilhelm: *Guarantee of Harmony and Freedom,* 586
Weld, Theodore Dwight: quoted, 625
Wellington, Arthur Wellesley, Duke of, 541, 542
Wells, H. G., 650
Wesley, Charles, 490
Wesley, John, 490
Wessex, 188, 190–91, 201
West Germany, 790, 802; economy, 788, 800; foreign affairs, 799, 800–02, 812, 814; government, 788, 800–02; as nuclear power, 816; terrorism in, 801
West Indies, 440–41, 448, 500, 506, 508, 511
Westphalia, 539; battle at, 511; Peace of (1643–48), 432–33, 434, 462
Weyden, Rogier van der, 293
Whigs, 454, 457–59, 497, 502, 519, 558–59
Whitehead, Alfred North, 473; quoted, 474
Whitman, Walt, 631; quoted, 632
Whitney, Eli, 573
Wiclif, John, 279–80, 361
Wilkes, John, 519
William, Count of Poitou and Duke of Aquitaine: quoted, 233
William I, German Emperor, 605, 609–10, 611
William II, German Emperor, 657, 679, 682, 687, 688, 689, 692, 700, 703, 709, 712
William (Rufus), King of England, 213
William III, King of England, 434, 453–54, 458–60
William I, King of the Netherlands, 557
William I (the Silent), Prince of Orange, 406
William III, Prince of Orange. *See* William III, King of England
William the Conqueror, 202, 204, 210–11, 267; as William I, King of England, 211–13, 235–36
Williams, Ralph Vaughan, 743
"Will of the People," 662
Wilson, Harold, 798
Wilson, Woodrow, 704, 708, 709, 710–11, 716, 728
Winged Victory of Samothrace, 52
witchcraft: European, 412–14; medieval delusion in, 280, 413
Witt, Jan de, 434
Witte, Count Sergei, 663
Wittenberg, University of, 377–79
Wolfe, Thomas: *Look Homeward, Angel,* 742
Wolsey, Thomas, 368
women: in ancient Greece, 35, 41; in Arabia, 168; and First World War, 703, 704,

725; in India, 131, 320, 325; and Industrial Revolution, 578, 583; liberation movement, 845; and medieval Catholicism, 249; rights of, 621, 647, 725; suffrage movement, 580; in Victorian England, 580, 647
Women's Social and Political Union, 647
working class. *See* labor
World Economic Conference: of 1927, 720; of 1933, 731
World's Fair, London, 576
Worms, 378; Concordat of (1122), 217
Wrangel, Pëtr Nikolaevich, 748
Wren, Christopher, 456
Wright, Frank Lloyd, 743
writing: in ancient Crete, 12–13; Arabic, 168; Chinese, 132–33, cuneiform, 10, 17; hieroglyphics, 10, 17; ideograms, 132; Indian, 17; medieval reform in, 183; in Mesopotamia, 7; pictograms, 7, 10, 132; Roman, 183–84. *See also* alphabets
Wundt, Wilhelm, 740
Wu-tsung, 332

X

Xerxes, King of Persia, 38

Y

Yalta Conference (1945), 784–87, 787
Yangtze River Valley, 140, 329
Yarmuk River, battle of, 173
Yellow River Valley, 4, 6, 14, 328
Yemen, 831, 835
Yom Kippur War (1973), 833
York, House of, 285, 368
Young, Owen D. 720
Young Plan, 721
youth: revolt of, 847
Ypres, 207
Yüan Shih-k'ai, 640, 737
Yugoslavia, 709, 711, 712, 716, 717, 755, 759; post-Second World War, 787, 789, 810; Second World War, 775
Yugoslavs, 708

Z

Zacharias, Pope, 179–80
Zaire, 815, 837
Zama, battle of, 64
Zangi, 306
Zara, 307
Zealots, 89
Zeno, Roman Emperor, 116–17
Zenta, battle of, 463
Zeus, 35–36
Zhas Ziyang, 826
Zia ul-Haq, Mohammed, 824
Zimbabwe, 838
Zimbabwe African National Union (ZANU), 839
Zimmermann Telegram, 705
Zinc Development Association, 841
Zinoviev, Grigori, 714, 749, 752
Zionist Organization, 735
Zola, Émile, 670
Zollverein, 576
Zoroastrianism, 24, 105, 331
Zurich, 382
Zwingli, Ulrich, 382

B 4
C 5
D 6
E 7
F 8
G 9
H 0
I 1
J 2